OLIVER STONE'S FILM-FLAM

THE DEMAGOGUE OF DEALEY PLAZA

FRED LITWIN

CONTENTS

ALSO BY FRED LITWIN

Conservative Confidential

I Was a Teenage JFK Conspiracy Freak

On the Trail of Delusion—Jim Garrison: The Great Accuser

First North American edition published in 2022 by NorthernBlues Books,
a subsidiary of NorthernBlues Music, Inc.

Cover design by Kathleen Lynch

Edited by Michael Totten

Manufactured in the United States on acid-free paper.

First North American Edition

Litwin, Fred

Oliver Stone's Film-Flam: The Demagogue of Dealey Plaza

ISBN: 978-0-9948630-6-5

Dedicated to the memory of Admiral George Burkley, a baselessly accused loyal American who served his country honorably

"Too often we enjoy the comfort of opinion without the discomfort of thought."
—John F. Kennedy

ABOUT THE AUTHOR

Fred in Clarksdale, Mississippi

Oliver Stone's Film-Flam: The Demagogue of Dealey Plaza is Fred Litwin's fourth book. In 2020, he published *On the Trail of Delusion—Jim Garrison: The Great Accuser,* which chronicled Garrison's persecution of Clay Shaw. In 2018, he published *I Was a Teenage JFK Conspiracy Freak,* detailing his journey from believing in a JFK conspiracy at eighteen to slowly moving to believe that Lee Harvey Oswald was the lone assassin. In 2015, he released *Conservative Confidential* about his move from left-wing anti-nuclear activist to Conservative Party campaigner.

Fred.Litwin@gmail.com

© *Chuck Asay, December 29, 1991, Colorado Springs* Gazette Telegraph

INTRODUCTION

In the spring of 2020, as I was finishing my book *On the Trail of Delusion —Jim Garrison: The Great Accuser*, I heard that filmmaker Oliver Stone and conspiracy theorist James DiEugenio were teaming up to make a documentary series about the JFK assassination. I included in my conclusion what Stone told the press in October of 2019, that "This documentary film represents an important bookend to my 1991 film. It ties up many loose threads, and hopefully repudiates much of the ignorance around the case and the movie."

Stone was completely wrong. Not only did *JFK: Destiny Betrayed* not "tie up many loose threads," it mostly ignored former New Orleans District Attorney Jim Garrison and his sham prosecution of Clay Shaw. The heroic protagonist of *JFK* is named only once in the entire four-part series. And far from repudiating ignorance, *JFK: Destiny Betrayed* spews out additional nonsense, nonsense that is easily debunkable.

Before we get to how bad the film is about the JFK assassination, let's see what Stone and DiEugenio are like in general and on other political matters.

I published my book in September 2020, and Alecia Long, a distinguished professor of history at Louisiana State University, published her book *Cruising for Conspirators: How a New Orleans DA Prosecuted the Kennedy Assassination as a Sex Crime* in September 2021. Not surprisingly, James DiEugenio thought the timing was conspiratorial. On the Education Forum, he wrote that Long "is the soul sister of Fred Litwin. They both thought that Oliver's upcoming documentary would be about my book on New Orleans. It is not. He only used the title for the long version. So, her and Fred both came out with these hatchet pieces in advance."

Of course, both Alecia and I wrote our books well before anyone knew that Oliver Stone would once again go down the rabbit hole.

My initial belief that the series would be based on DiEugenio's 2012 book, *Destiny Betrayed,* was wrong. In fact, it was based upon his 2018 book, *The JFK Assassination,* which argued that much of the physical evidence in the JFK assassination had been either planted or is suspect in some manner.

DiEugenio believes that JFK was assassinated by forces that wanted a change in American foreign policy—in other words, to thwart Kennedy's supposed plans to withdraw from Vietnam and thereby usher in a new era of peace and detente. According to Stone and DiEugenio, the United States since the assassination has been on a militaristic trajectory that can only be rectified by revealing the truth about the JFK conspiracy and its cover-up.

Right from the start, *JFK: Destiny Betrayed* was in trouble. Netflix turned the series down, and it was clear that their fact-checkers had some issues. *Paris Match* asked Oliver Stone why it had been rejected, and he answered that "The country has become very conservative." But Stone revealed more in an interview with filmmaker Spike Lee:

Lee: Netflix said no?

Stone: Yeah. Today I just got the word that *National Geographic* said no.

Lee: What was the reason they said no?

Stone: They said they did their fact check. Yeah. Where are you going to find this information except in this film? If they do a fact check, according to conventional sources, of course, it'll come out like this is not true. How can you go and prove that it's true? It's very, it's very tough. You have to have some imagination here.

With Netflix out of the picture, it was necessary for Stone's distributor to go to Cannes to market the film. Even then, it was only able to get Showtime to stream the two-hour version. The only streaming service to pick up the four-hour version was in the UK and Australia.

Without a streaming partner, the distributor of *JFK: Destiny Betrayed* had to just put it up for sale on a variety of digital platforms like iTunes and Google Play. And with no one to help with marketing, Oliver Stone was on his own.

When *JFK: Destiny Betrayed* wasn't ignored by the mainstream media, it was panned.

Tim Weiner wrote in *Rolling Stone* that "We have a moral obligation to call bullshit when we see it. Especially when public figures promote lies for profit. Stone's JFK films are fantasies. Conspiracy theories are not facts. They're a kind of collective psychosis. And they're driving our country down the road to hell."

Historian Max Boot was similarly dismissive in the *Washington Post*:

> What the hell happened to Oliver Stone? When I was growing up in the 1980s, he was one of the most respected directors in Hollywood, producing hits such as "Platoon," "Wall Street" and "Born on the Fourth of July." But in more recent decades, he has become a dollar-store Leni Riefenstahl, churning out sickening tributes to Fidel Castro, Hugo Chávez and Vladimir Putin.

But Stone knew where to turn for publicity, and that was to people whom he can always count on: the Russians. And RT (formerly Russia Today) was only too willing to help promote a film that showcases American foibles around the world. His writing partner James DiEugenio was busy being interviewed on outlets like Izvestia.

One particularly embarrassing appearance on RT was Stone's interview with Abby Martin, a 9/11 Truther. She had previously appeared in a 2008 video of a 9/11 Truth Movement protest in which she said the attacks were an "inside job." James Kirchick wrote a revealing profile of Martin in *Tablet* magazine in 2014 in which he noted that "she regularly gives air to outrageous conspiracy theories, including the notion that water fluoridation is a pernicious government plot to poison unsuspecting American citizens ... She has also accused Israel of using 'Hitler's methods ... to maintain a Jewish majority.'"

Stone told her that the Zapruder film might have been edited:

> **Abby Martin:** The Zapruder film had to play a role in ...
>
> **Oliver Stone**: What?

Abby Martin: The Zapruder film really contradicted what they said…

Oliver Stone: Yeah, and that too had been concealed from the public for a long time until 1975 when it was on the Geraldo Rivera show. Garrison got it out for the trial which was amazing by the way. That was against all plans. They really, uh, and who knows what they cut out of the film? I don't know, but basically, there was enough in the film for us to claim in our movie that his head went back … to the left; you don't have to be a genius to figure that out, the shot came from the front, the kill shot.

In an interview with Trey Elling, Stone came up with an old conspiracy story:

Trey Elling: Who are doctors Kemp Clark and Doctor Malcolm Perry and why is their story one that not more people know about? Especially the press conference that they held shortly after the President's death.

Oliver Stone: All that information's available because they said right away the first thing they do is try to save his life. There was a wound in his throat, possibly it was a bullet but probably, possibly it was a flechette. We don't know.

A flechette? Conspiracy theorist Robert Cutler proposed this ridiculous theory in the 1970s:

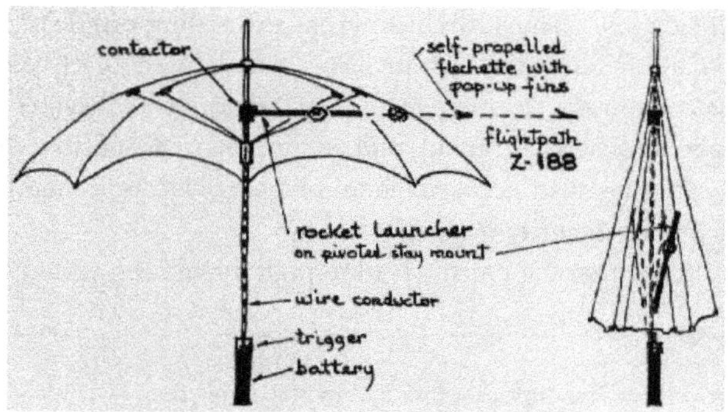

An illustration from the June 1978 issue of Gallery *magazine.*

The Zapruder film shows a man holding an open umbrella as the motorcade passes by. Cutler believed that this man fired a flechette to paralyze Kennedy, thus making him an easy target. The umbrella man, Louis Witt, was found by the HSCA. He was just trying to heckle JFK by using the umbrella as a symbol of appeasement.

As Stone did more and more interviews, he gradually learned his new lines. This was even acknowledged by James DiEugenio on Twitter:

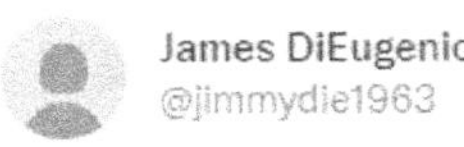

Good interview by Oliver. He has gotten much better since the first time around. He is quite good on what Kennedy was trying to do with detente with Cuba and Moscow. Bobby Kennedy knew about this and sent the letter about it from Walton to the Kremlin.

And so, once his dalliances with the Russians had run their course, Oliver Stone had to turn to alternative media. Here is DiEugenio on the Education Forum:

> Oliver had to do all of these interviews with alternative outlets. Because he knew the MSM was not going to acknowledge the film at all, or if they did it would be in a disdainful way e.g., Max Boot, and Tim Weiner.

While DiEugenio claims that Stone "knew" he would not be acknowledged in the mainstream media, Stone believed something totally different. He told Abby Martin:

> I can't believe we haven't gotten one review from a major media, publication, of this film. One review. Editorials, but no reviews. Not one movie critic. Not one television critic. The assassination community has done tremendous amount of work. Nobody reports it. These are facts. Not made-up bullshit.

And then there was Ukraine.

Oliver Stone made a pro-Putin documentary, *Ukraine on Fire*, in 2017, arguing that the event that led Ukrainian President Victor Yanukovych to leave for Russia was a coup d'état led by the United States. In fact, protests started when he refused to sign an EU trade agreement, and ultimately the Ukrainian parliament voted in a new government.

Political historian James Kirchick called Stone's documentary a "dictator suckup" and wrote:

> It is astoundingly patronizing for Stone to lecture Ukrainians—thousands of whom have fought and died defending their dismembered country from an all-out invasion by their much more powerful neighbor—about what they do and do not know about Viktor Yanukovych, Russia and the potential for a new Cold War.

In December 2021, Stone scoffed at the idea that Putin would invade Ukraine. In a fawning interview conducted by the American pop controversialists Matt Taibbi and Katie Halper, Stone said: "Ukraine is so rabid, the leaders in Ukraine are so nuts. And they need to get re-elected, so they'll do just about anything. Lie, steal, cheat, and say that Russia is going to invade Ukraine. What a joke! Russia could, if it invaded Ukraine, it could take what it wanted in a day or two. I mean it's not an issue for them."

After Putin invaded Ukraine in February, Stone said Putin had no choice because he was provoked. He told Robert Scheer, former editor of *Ramparts* magazine: "The United States and its allies in NATO have been provoking Russia for, since two years now—actually three years over the Ukraine, more. I mean, they started this in 2014. But they have been using Ukraine as bait, as a temperature-taker of that region. And now we've reached this place where they have threatened the Russians so much that they had to react, because I don't think Putin could have stayed in office if he had not reacted."

In an interview in May 2022 with Lex Fridman, a Russian-American podcast host, Stone suggested Putin may have invaded Russia because he's been so isolated owing to COVID-19. "Some people would argue that the isolation from normal activity … It was very hard—perhaps he lost touch with, contact with, people." In that same interview Stone suggested that the United States was preparing a "false-flag" operation involving "a low-yield nuclear explosion of unknown origin, somewhere in the Donbas region, killing thousands of people … It would be a very dramatic solution to sealing this war off as a major victory for the United States."

In April 2022, at the Barcelona Film Festival, Stone described Putin as a "rational, calm, thoughtful man," and he called the U.S. "a Doberman, a methodical killer animal with lots of money, too much money."

Well, what about Moscow's savage conduct in Syria, where the civil defense White Helmets first-responder organization has documented Russia's bombing campaign, in alliance with Bashar Assad's barrel bombers, targeting and destroying hundreds of hospitals and medical clinics? Stone claims Putin has been a "stabilizing force" in Syria.

He told Fridman that the White Helmets are "corrupted" and that their evidence of Assad's chemical weapons is merely part of an American plot to "demonize Assad and the Russians." United Nations investigations of the attacks have been tampered with, and the culprit is the United States, Stone said. "So, the United States is willing to use chemical in Syria freely."

When it was announced in April 2022 that Oliver Stone would be the guest of honor at the Quebec City Film Festival, conspiracy theorist Sandy Larsen was worried:

Sandy Larsen Posted April 21 ···

Members

While this does indeed seem to be great news, I worry that Stone's interviews with Putin will be brought up in the Q&A session. Which will destroy Stone's credibility in the minds of most people IMO.

And while there was much slobbering in the press, there was also some pushback. For instance, two Ukrainians wrote an article for the Quebec City daily *Le Soleil*:

> We can't help but note that Mr. Stone continued to praise Russia after his first public "soul-searching" message, while spreading lies about the "fake corpses of Bucha" and other nonsense, which only serve to poison people's hearts and minds. What else could one really expect from a man whose son until the day of the invasion hosted a show on an international TV channel owned by the Kremlin and who believes in the conspiracy theories of QAnon? What else could we really expect from a man who asked the Russian president in 2019 to become his

> daughter's godfather, according to the official transcript of the interview posted online by the Kremlin?

I wrote an article about Oliver Stone for my friend Terry Glavin's Substack newsletter, and a lot of it was used by *La Presse* in Montreal:

> In 2016, Oliver Stone also collaborated on Ukraine on Fire, a propaganda film popular in Russia, according to which the CIA orchestrated the Ukrainian revolution of 2014 …
>
> Knowing all this, how can anyone believe the veracity of the "documentary" on the assassination of John F. Kennedy that the 75-year-old director came to present in Quebec City?

And that's the money quote. How can anybody trust Oliver Stone on the JFK assassination when he gets international affairs so wrong? And why would anybody respect the judgment of a multimillionaire who fetes dictators and grovels at their feet?

Let's look at some of his talking heads unmuzzled, i.e., without having been edited for the film, where they come across badly enough but less wacko than in their native habitats.

For instance, Lisa Pease appears in *JFK: Destiny Betrayed* as an expert on Indonesia. She is the author of a book that argues that assassin Sirhan Sirhan fired blanks at Robert Kennedy in 1968. This was her response to the May 2022 mass shooting in Uvalde, Texas:

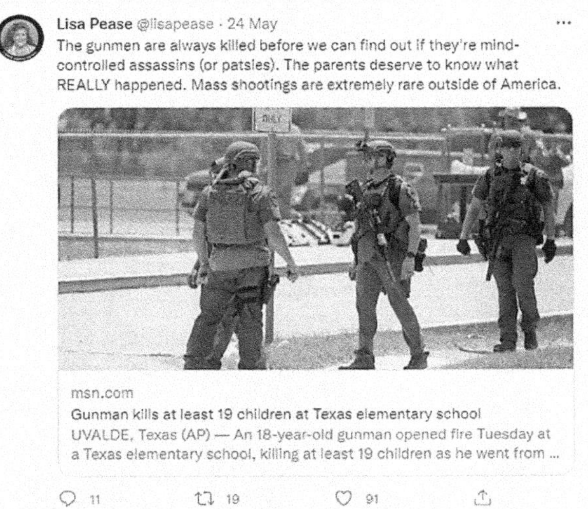

Lisa Pease @lisapease · 24 May
The gunmen are always killed before we can find out if they're mind-controlled assassins (or patsies). The parents deserve to know what REALLY happened. Mass shootings are extremely rare outside of America.
msn.com
Gunman kills at least 19 children at Texas elementary school
UVALDE, Texas (AP) — An 18-year-old gunman opened fire Tuesday at a Texas elementary school, killing at least 19 children as he went from ...
11
19
91

Another expert that Stone relies upon is Robert F. Kennedy, Jr., who claims in *JFK: Destiny Betrayed* that his father's death "has never been investigated properly." Since 2005, RFK, Jr. has promoted a connection between vaccines and autism, and he has since become the leading anti-vaxxer of our time. His latest book, *The Real Anthony Fauci: Bill Gates, Big Pharma, and the Global War on Democracy and Public Health,* was a massive bestseller in the United States.

In his book, he wrote that "The pervasive CIA involvement in the global vaccine putsch should give us pause." And then there is this:

> After twenty years of modeling exercises, the CIA—working with medical technocrats like Anthony Fauci and billionaire Internet tycoons—had pulled off the ultimate coup d'état: some 250 years after America's historic revolt against entrenched oligarchy and authoritarian rule, the American experiment with self-government was over. The oligarchy was restored, and these gentlemen and their spymasters had equipped the rising technocracy with new tools of control unimaginable to King George or to any other tyrant in history.

Even his wife Cheryl Hines was taken aback when he publicly compared the experience of anti-vaxxers to victims of the Holocaust: "Even in Hitler's Germany, you could cross the Alps into Switzerland, you could hide in an attic like Anne Frank did." Robert F. Kennedy Jr. was forced to apologize.

Meanwhile, his crusade against Bill Gates continues unabated:

Robert F. Kennedy Jr @RobertKennedyJr · Feb 4, 2021
READ + SHARE my latest on #TheDefender as I dive deep on #BillGates quietly becoming the largest owner of farmland in the U.S. and the irresistible pull #Gates has to exert monopoly control over global food supplies.
childrenshealthdefense.org
Bill Gates and Neo-Feudalism: A Closer Look at Farmer Bill
Bill Gates has quietly made himself the largest owner of farmland in the United States. For a man obsessed with monopoly control, the ...

Another talking head in Stone's documentary is Dr. Donald Miller, who accuses JFK's personal physician Dr. George Burkley of being involved in a cover-up. Miller also has a variety of wacky views. For instance, here is his chart about conspirators in the JFK assassination:

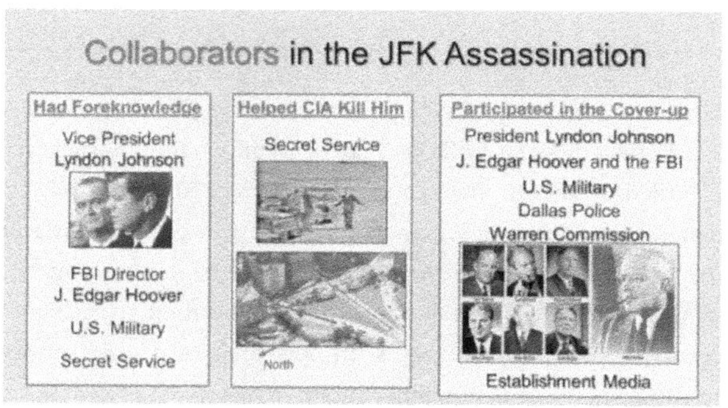

Gee, who wasn't involved?

Dr. Miller writes extensively for LewRockwell.com, where he has posted articles about the dangers of fluoride and vaccines, argued that HIV might not be the cause of AIDs, and said that people shouldn't get flu shots. He even believes that JFK, Jr. was killed by a bomb rather than in a plane crash

Another major contributor to *JFK: Destiny Betrayed* is Douglas Horne, a former analyst for the Assassination Records Review Board (ARRB). He is featured in *JFK: Destiny Betrayed* in several segments. But you won't hear his belief that the Zapruder film was altered. Nor will you hear him opine that the reason for the modification was to cover up the fact that the presidential limousine stopped on Elm Street and that the driver, William Greer, then fired at JFK with his revolver.

Even *JFK: Destiny Betrayed* has its red lines. But as you will see, that leaves more than enough room for all sorts of conspiracy nonsense.

A NOTE ABOUT MY TRANSCRIPTS

Oliver Stone made two versions of the same documentary. *JFK Revisited: Through the Looking Glass* is the two-hour presentation. *JFK: Destiny Betrayed* is a four-part, four-hour presentation. In this book, I am relying on *JFK: Destiny Betrayed* to discuss his documentary.

Virtually everything in *JFK Revisited* is in *JFK: Destiny Betrayed*. The two exceptions are the Oliver Stone line "Conspiracy theories are now conspiracy facts" and the Jefferson Morley claims about Oswald and the handbills he handed out on the streets of New Orleans. See the chapter "Did the ARRB Prove a Conspiracy in the JFK Assassination?" for more details on the first example and Chapter 43 for the second.

THE ENABLING OF OLIVER STONE

In March 1969, the *New York Times* called Jim Garrison's prosecution of Clay Shaw for conspiring to kill JFK "one of the most disgraceful chapters in the history of American jurisprudence." The only evidence Garrison had was the false memory of a man who had been injected with sodium pentothal and then hypnotized on three occasions.

Not only were the best years of Clay Shaw's life stolen, but he was outed to the world as a homosexual, and one with a predilection for S&M. With a large part of his savings depleted, he was forced to come out of retirement and go back to work. Shaw sued Garrison for $5 million in damages, but the case floundered when he died of cancer in 1974.

One would have hoped that would have been the end of Jim Garrison. In 1988, he wrote a self-serving memoir, *On the Trail of the Assassins*, that once again defamed Clay Shaw. Rosemary James, a former journalist for the New Orleans *States-Item*, said the book was a "well-written, fast-moving, exciting piece of cold war spy genre fiction."

Unfortunately, Oliver Stone believed it was a work of nonfiction. He felt it "read like a Dashiell Hammett whodunit" and that Garrison was "somewhat like a Jimmy Stewart character in an old Capra movie." He read the book three times and purchased the movie rights for $250,000.

Not surprisingly, gay groups were incensed at Stone's film. David Ehrenstein, a writer for *The Advocate*, said that "Oliver Stone's *JFK* is the most homophobic film ever to come out of Hollywood." How could it not be? After all, Jim Garrison exploited homosexuality all throughout his nonexistent case. For a brief but crucial period, Garrison thought that Kennedy had been killed by a homosexual conspiracy.

JFK effectively destroyed Oliver Stone's career. In his zeal to portray the United States as a malignant player on the world stage, he has since produced a variety of hagiographic documentaries on dictators like Hugo Chavez, Fidel Castro, Vladimir Putin, and most recently Nursultan Nazarbayev. He sees NATO and Ukraine as being threatening to Russia. He even blamed the United States for tensions regarding Taiwan.

JFK: Destiny Betrayed shows that Stone is susceptible to conspiratorial thinking unimaginable to JFK researchers from the 1960s. By giving screenwriter James DiEugenio free rein over the course of four hours, Oliver Stone has redefined gullibility. A tiny amount of due diligence would have told Stone that DiEugenio's analysis of the evidence is not just wrong but easily debunkable.

A central DiEugenio premise is that had Lee Harvey Oswald stood trial, he would have been acquitted. He believes that most of the incriminating evidence, because of anomalies in the chain of possession, would have been thrown out of court. The problem with this unfalsifiable theory is that DiEugenio wants to extend this to historical truth.

The murder of Lee Harvey Oswald meant that there was not going to be a trial. The Warren Report noted that "under our system there is no provision for a posthumous trial." In any trial, it is the defendant who guides the defense, both in strategy and tactics, and with no defendant, one cannot be sure how a trial would have proceeded.

Even if Oswald had been tried, there still would have been a need for some sort of investigation. The purpose of a trial is just to determine if a defendant is guilty. That necessitates very restrictive rules of evidence, and thus only a narrow part of the whole story is uncovered. Questions about Jack Ruby, the murder of Officer Tippit, the attempted shooting of General Walker, and a variety of other important areas would still have had to be answered.

Richard Mosk, who served as a staff member of the Warren Commission, noted that:

> The Commission did not utilize an adversary system. Although lawyers persist in extolling the virtues of the adversary system, I doubt whether truth would have emerged from a Commission that presided over a bitter proceeding in which evidence would have been

> constructed and dissected towards partisan ends, and reconstructed in distorted summations.

Mosk felt that "such a method might have resulted in the chaos that sometimes accompanies Congressional Committee hearings."

There are several important differences between a trial and an investigation. The Warren Commission, for example, decided to take testimony from witnesses in private. It is important to note that these hearings weren't secret; transcripts were published two months after the Warren Report. In a trial, witnesses would have to testify publicly in open court. Mosk noted that many "witnesses, who at first seemed to be hesitant and nervous, seemed to gain confidence in the quiet atmosphere of a private hearing."

The Warren Commission also allowed hearsay. They were interested "in any rumors which might provide leads to a conspiracy." Testifying in public might have cast undue suspicion on innocent people.

Alfredda Scobey, a lawyer on the staff of the Warren Commission, wrote that "the fact is inescapable that the report, although crammed with facts that would not be admissible on the trial of a criminal case, sets out the whole picture in a perspective a criminal trial could never achieve."

For instance, Marina Oswald would not have been allowed to testify at his trial. She would not have been able to confirm Oswald's ownership of his blue and white jackets. She would not have been allowed to discuss Oswald's admission of shooting at General Walker or his ownership of the Mannlicher-Carcano rifle, and she would not have been allowed to admit that she took the photographs of Oswald in their backyard.

> More important, she alone identified the rifle as the one which he owned, and testified that she had seen him practice with it, that it had been moved from New Orleans to Dallas in Ruth Paine's station wagon and that it had been stored in a green and brown blanket in the Paine garage.

Scobey believes that other pieces of evidence also might not be admissible at trial. The search in Ruth Paine's garage might have been unconstitutional because it's possible that Ruth Paine and Marina Oswald did not give informed consent. She also wonders whether the Tippit murder itself could have been brought up at trial.

James DiEugenio completely misunderstands what Scobey wrote:

> I have always felt that the saga of [Senator Richard] Russell was an underrated and ignored story. I mean, his assistant, Scobey—who he brought up from Atlanta—later wrote an article which said that Oswald would not have been convicted in a real court of law.

Scobey did not say that at all. She wrote:

> If we assume that our defense counsel was very, very lucky, he would be able, if Oswald stood trial, either to exclude or impeach the testimony of a large number of key persons whose accounts add so much to the strength of the report. This is not to say that what would be left, granting the unlikely event of success in all these endeavors, would leave room for a reasonable doubt of Oswald's guilt, but the surprising fact is that the conviction in such an event would depend to an amazing degree on documentary evidence and its interpretation by experts.

To her, an important part of determining truth was the "documentary evidence and its interpretation by experts." She writes that "the Warren Report, conceived as a criminal investigation carried to its utmost limits, illustrates the importance of utilizing the laboratory and the expert as sources of the most cogent evidence in criminal proceedings."

And so, DiEugenio is right that a lot of evidence against Oswald might not have been admissible in a court of law. But his perspective is diametrically opposed to that of Scobey. He doesn't care if Marina Oswald could testify or not, he has no interest in whether the Tippit murder or the attempt on Walker's life could be brought up at trial, and he really doesn't care if the search of Ruth Paine's garage was constitutional.

DiEugenio believes that supposed anomalies in the chain of possession of much of the underlying evidence (Oswald's rifle, the bullet found at Parkland Hospital, etc.) renders them not just inadmissible in a court of law but also renders them inadmissible in an investigation. He has no interest in getting Oswald off on a technicality; he wants the judgment of history to use courtroom standards to declare Oswald innocent of killing JFK.

A good example of how James DiEugenio wants evidence to be discarded is CE 399, the bullet found on Governor Connally's stretcher at Parkland Hospital. There was a time when JFK researchers would argue about its so-called pristine condition. Because it is now clear that its state is entirely consistent with the wounds it caused, conspiracy theorists have to take a new tack.

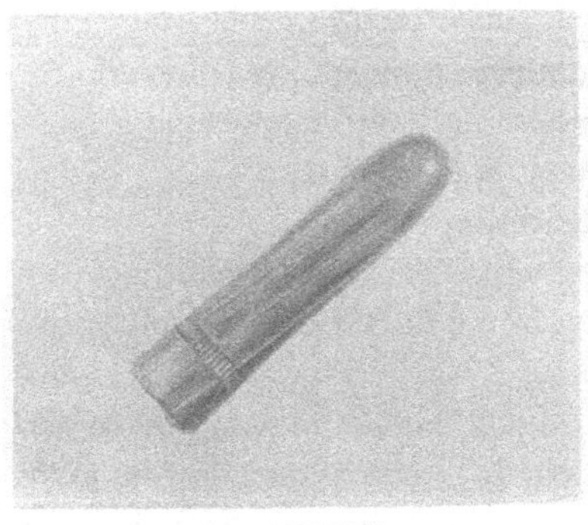

COMMISSION EXHIBIT 399

CE 399 traversed JFK's upper back and went on to hit Connally. It was not pristine. It was flattened on one side, and lead extruded from the core. The trajectory of CE 399 is shown in Chapter 21.

James DiEugenio would have you believe that issues with its chain of possession can only mean that somewhere between Dallas and Washington, the conspirators changed the bullet. But Kenneth Rahn noted that "the window of opportunity [to plant items] came well before anyone knew what kind of fragments to plant and where." How would conspirators know the nature of the wounds of Connally and Kennedy? How would they know what kinds of fragments or bullets to plant? What if they planted an extra bullet?

The Mannlicher-Carcano rifle was found at about 1:00 p.m. on November 22. It was kept by the Dallas police until about 11:45 p.m., at which time it was released to the FBI. We know with certainty that CE 399 was fired by Oswald's Mannlicher-Carcano rifle. If the conspirators planted it at Parkland, they would have had to fire the bullet well before the assassination.

Perhaps the conspirators switched out the bullet in Washington. But

CE 399 was in the possession of the FBI on the evening of November 22, well before they took possession of the rifle. Does DiEugenio believe the Dallas police fired the rifle and sent the bullet to Washington?

Since DiEugenio believes that multiple gunmen wounded and killed JFK, the conspirators must have expected that a lot of fragments would have been recovered. How could they know that CE 399 would fit into any scenario of what had happened?

But that's just one example. DiEugenio and Stone would have you believe the following:

- JFK's brain was substituted.
- Oswald's Mannlicher-Carcano was planted.
- Autopsy photographs have disappeared.
- Backyard photographs were faked.
- An extra bullet disappeared.
- The hole in the windshield was covered up.
- JFK's doctor, Admiral Burkley, was involved in the cover-up.

Who could organize all this? Who would have decided what evidence was needed and when? How many people were involved in this massive cover-up? On any of these details, DiEugenio and hence Stone are silent, as they must be. Because there is not a shred of evidence to support any of this.

And so, when you ask DiEugenio about how this supposed conspiracy unfolded, he won't answer. He said on the Education Forum that "In the talk I will give in San Francisco this weekend, I will explain that one of the things I told Oliver [Stone] was that I did not think we should advance a theory as to how the crime was actually committed. Because that had been the graveyard of others."

But every now and then, DiEugenio lets you have a peek at his conspiracy. On the Education Forum, he opened up about General Curtis LeMay: (emphasis added)

> In my opinion, **LeMay was a part of the pre planned cover up**. I believe the cover up was planned with the conspiracy.

JFK: Destiny Betrayed is an intellectual monstrosity. Oliver Stone was hoodwinked by a conspiracy theorist who is more than willing to reject any piece of physical (or other) evidence that does not fit his case. If the major pieces of physical evidence are fraudulent, then there is little possibility that any theory might turn out to be verifiable. However weak, evidence could at least refute theories, but Mr. DiEugenio would like to destroy the entire empirical edifice of the JFK assassination.

Oliver Stone wasn't just hoodwinked. He has willingly brought DiEugenio's cockamamie theories to the mainstream. DiEugenio has unfortunately enabled Stone to continue his JFK fantasy, now based on a tendentious factual analysis supported by seemingly serious footnotes.

And what makes this all even more ridiculous is that many of the talking heads in the film provide anecdotes that are hearsay and that certainly would have been excluded from a trial:

- Warren Commission member and later President Gerald Ford supposedly told French President Valéry Giscard d'Estaing that there was a conspiracy.
- Secret Service agent Elmer Moore told Jim Gochenaur that he pressured Dr. Malcolm Perry to say that Kennedy's throat wound was an entrance wound.
- Dr. Donald Miller said that Dr. Perry told him that Kennedy's throat wound was one of entrance.
- Dr. George Burkley supposedly admitted to two researchers that more than one gunman fired at Kennedy.
- Robert Knudsen allegedly told his wife and son that an autopsy photograph had been altered.

Some of this information should not be flatly excluded from consideration from the judgment of history but should certainly be treated with some skepticism. I don't believe Gerald Ford told d'Estaing any such thing (see Chapter 34), and as you will see, James Gochenaur is not a credible witness (see Chapter 8).

The film briefly mentions that Clay Shaw was indicted by Jim Garrison for conspiracy to kill JFK. It's a bit rich that while the film bemoans the fact that Oswald did not receive a trial, it does not even mention that Clay Shaw had one and that he was acquitted. And his acquittal was not based on a technicality like chain of possession but because the jury quickly recognized that the case for his participation in a conspiracy was not convincing.

Oliver Stone suffers from a poverty of imagination. Yes, he can imagine a massive conspiracy and cover-up. But he cannot imagine any sort of non-conspiratorial explanation for any of the suspicious allegations in his film.

Now on to the debunking of *JFK: Destiny Betrayed*. Hold on, it's going to be a bumpy ride.

THE WARREN COMMISSION

JFK: Destiny Betrayed tries to make the case that the Warren Commission was fraudulent and that its conclusions were preordained. In addition, the film alleges that former Director of the CIA Allen Dulles was placed on the Commission to cover up the conspiracy.

CHAPTER 1
DID THE CIA LOBBY TO HAVE ALLEN DULLES PUT ON THE WARREN COMMISSION?

(EPISODE 1, 11:49)

JFK: Destiny Betrayed misleads viewers on how Allen Dulles was selected to serve on the Warren Commission.

Here is an excerpt from the transcript:

Oliver Stone: In regard to the Warren Commission, who do you think was the most puzzling appointment to this Commission?

David Talbot: Allen Dulles's appointment to the Warren Commission, I think, is one of the great frauds of American history.

[Archive Clip] **Eric Sevareid**: Have you ever committed any acts of violence in your life?

[Archive Clip] **Allen Dulles**: No.

David Talbot: Lyndon Johnson went around telling people that Bobby Kennedy, of all people, lobbied to have Dulles put on the Commission.

[Archive Clip] **Allen Dulles**: I don't think that even if you had ten more Commissions, that you'd never get away from the idea that maybe there was a plot. We just didn't find any traces of it.

David Talbot: What really happened with Allen Dulles was the CIA lobbied to have him put on the Commission, because they needed to

> have one of their own on the Commission, to make sure that certain doors remain closed.

The segment of the Eric Sevareid interview with Allen Dulles is taken out of context. Here is an excerpt from a transcript:

> **Eric Sevareid**: Mr. Dulles, the Russian writer and propagandist Ehrenburg once wrote that if the master spy Mr. Dulles ever got to heaven by anybody's absent-mindedness you would mine the clouds and begin to slaughter the angels.
>
> **Allen Dulles**: 'Shoot the stars and slaughter the angels.'
>
> **Eric Sevareid**: Have you ever committed any act of violence in your life?
>
> **Allen Dulles**: No.

It really wasn't a serious question.

Talbot claims that the CIA lobbied to have Dulles put on the Commission. I went to his book, *The Devil's Chessboard,* to determine the source of this statement. He included a picture of Earl Warren handing Lyndon Johnson a copy of the Warren Report with the notation that "Dulles lobbied aggressively" as opposed to the CIA. He further notes:

> The Dulles camp itself made no bones about the fact that the Old Man aggressively lobbied to get appointed to the commission. Dick Helms later told historian Michael Kurtz that he "personally persuaded" Johnson to appoint Dulles. According to Kurtz, Dulles and Helms "wanted to make sure no agency secrets came out during the investigations ... And, of course, if Dulles was on the commission, that would ensure the agency would be safe. Johnson felt the same way—he didn't want the investigation to dig up anything strange."

Talbot's source of the allegation that Helms "personally persuaded" Johnson comes from Michael Kurtz's book *The JFK Assassination Debates*. The footnote says that it comes from an interview with Richard Helms.

The second statement, that Helms "wanted to make sure no secrets came out…" is from an interview Talbot conducted with Michael Kurtz.

However, Pat Speer, one of the more credible conspiracy theorists, has questioned Kurtz's credibility:

> The point is that Kurtz has made a series of claims in his JFK-related books and articles that are erratic and smell to high heaven, and that his sources for these claims are erratic and often involve interviews with people that were already dead. Well, geez Louise, it follows from this that Kurtz's wilder claims, particularly his claims of talking to people few ever talked to in which they told him things they never told anyone else, should be thoroughly disregarded.

Talbot's claim that Dulles lobbied to be put on the Warren Commission comes from Joseph Trento's book *The Secret History of the CIA*:

> According to William Corson, the former spymaster "lobbied hard for the job." Once appointed, Dulles wasted no time installing himself as the intelligence expert on the Warren Commission.

But just who was William Corson? He was a former Marine Corps officer who eventually became *Penthouse* magazine's Washington correspondent. He collaborated closely with Trento, and they even cowrote a book together. Corson told Trento a lot of stories that are too fantastic to be believed. For instance, he said that Allen Dulles recruited him to check out Jack Ruby in 1964 and that Lyndon Johnson, right after the assassination, sent him to Dallas to investigate.

I can find no corroborating evidence for either of those claims. Corson was also the source for Victor Marchetti's 1978 story that the CIA was planning to admit that E. Howard Hunt was in Dallas in November 1963. He claimed that there was a memo from 1966 that said the CIA would have to explain Hunt's presence in Dallas. There was no such memo.

So, the allegations in Talbot's book all stem from interviews with Michael Kurtz and William Corson.

Talbot then writes:

> Among those urging Johnson to give Dulles the Warren Commission job were establishment allies like Secretary of State Dean Rusk, former president of the Rockefeller Foundation. These same voices were raised on behalf of McCloy.

Talbot's source is Peter Grose's book *Gentleman Spy: The Life of Allen Dulles*:

> At 4 P.M. that day [November 29th] Johnson got through on the telephone to Richard B. Russell, Democrat of Georgia and a respected dean of the Senate. He said he would "try to get Allen Dulles" to serve on an investigating commission. Russell concurred, "Dulles is a good man." Secretary Rusk had also commended Allen: "Dulles, on this kind of issue, I think would not be partisan. I think that would be good." Then the President put the call in to Allen.

Sounds to me like Johnson was asking Russell and Rusk what they thought as opposed to them "urging Johnson to give Dulles the Warren Commission job."

Lyndon Johnson spoke to Secretary of State Dean Rusk on November 29, 1963:

> **Johnson**: I'm trying to appoint this presidential commission and make a statement right now. And I want to tell you about this Commission—you already told him—the Chief Justice, John McCloy, Allen Dulles, Senator Russell, Senator Cooper, Congressman Boggs and Congressman Ford.
>
> **Rusk**: So, absolutely fresh plan.
>
> **Johnson**: Now, his worry is I got more Republicans than Democrats. Chief Justice is not regarded, McCloy I don't guess is regarded as a red-hot partisan, is he?
>
> **Rusk**: Oh, he's not a partisan. The Chief Justice is certainly never ...
>
> **Johnson**: What about Dulles?
>
> **Rusk**: Dulles on this kind of an issue would not be partisan. I think that would be good.
>
> **Johnson**: Ok, my friend.

Johnson tells Rusk who will serve on the Commission and wonders if there were too many Republicans. When Rusk said, "I think that would be good," he was referring to the entire commission.

That is the extent of the evidence to support the allegation that Dulles, or the CIA, lobbied to have him put on the Warren Commission.

As Talbot mentioned in that short clip from *JFK: Destiny Betrayed*, Lyndon Johnson wrote in his memoirs, *The Vantage Point*, that Attorney General Robert Kennedy asked him to put Dulles on the Commission:

> As for the makeup of the rest of the commission, I appointed the two men Bobby Kennedy asked me to put on it—Allen Dulles and John McCloy—immediately.

Of course, it is easy to say. Is there any documentation to support what Johnson is saying?

Here is a memo from top aide Walter Jenkins to President Johnson:

November 29, 1963

MEMORANDUM:

TO: The President

FROM: Walter

Abe has talked with Katzenbach and Katzenbach has talked with the Attorney General. They recommend a seven man commission - two Senators, two Congressmen, the Chief Justice, Allen Dulles, and a retired Military Man (General or Admiral.) Katzenbach is preparing a description of how the Commission would function. Abe needs quickly the following answers:

(1) Is the composition of the Commission outlined above satisfactory?

(2) Could you talk to Eastland and the appropriate Member on the House side (Celler), Boggs, or whoever - and tell them what you are doing.

(3) Is it agreeable for Abe and Katzenbach to talk to the Chief Justice and feel him out?

WJ:MS

RECEIVED
APR 20 1965
CENTRAL FILES

Orig not sent to Files

There was a second page with a list of possible members:

The Chief Justice

The Honorable John J. McCloy

The Honorable Allen W. Dulles

Representative Hale Boggs

Senator Richard Russell

Senator John Sherman Cooper

Congressman Gerald Ford

5 Republican
2 Dems

The HSCA mentioned this memo:

(11) On November 29, 1963, Walter Jenkins wrote a memorandum to President Johnson, which stated:

> Abe [Fortas] has talked with Katzenbach and Katzenbach has talked with the Attorney General. They recommend a seven man commission—two Senators, two Congressmen, the Chief Justice, Allen Dulles, and a retired military man (general or admiral). Katzenbach is preparing a description of how the Commission would function * * *.(*10*)

(12) This memorandum also included a list of possible members of the Commission and asked Johnson if they were satisfactory. This list was in fact apparently satisfactory since all of the people noted were appointed to the Commission.

The foremost biographer of Lyndon Johnson, Robert Caro, discussed this in his book *The Passage of Power*:

> The purpose of the commission was to reassure the country, so he [Lyndon Johnson] felt its members must be public figures whose very presence on it would be reassuring, "men," in his phrase, "known to be beyond pressure and above suspicion." When, in response to his request, Robert Kennedy suggested two names—former CIA director Allen Dulles and a longtime adviser to Presidents, John J. McCloy, both of them Republicans—Johnson made them two of the seven, along with three respected Capitol Hill figures.

Caro's source was Johnson's autobiography and an Oral History of LBJ:

> I called every man on that Commission. Senator Russell said "You mean I have to serve on that commission with Warren?
>
> I said, "Yes, and don't tell me you're less patriotic than Earl Warren because I don't believe that—and he feels more strongly about this than you do."
>
> Everybody Bobby wanted to have me appoint, I appointed to that commission.

There is another piece of evidence supporting the view that Robert Kennedy suggested Dulles and McCloy. Johnson discussed this in a conversation with Abe Fortas on December 17, 1966:

No, but I would just say that you hear from [Bennett] Cerf or some of 'em stories, that you['re] involved, that he [Katzenbach] came over to talk to you ... and that there's some rumor that we didn't want a national commission, that you came in [and] urged it ... we urged it. We went to the top to get the chief justice [to] do it, and we even asked the attorney general to name people he wanted. [And] he recommended people like Allen Dulles and John McCloy.

Talbot is half right here:

> What really happened with Allen Dulles was the CIA lobbied to have him put on the Commission because they needed to have one of their own on the Commission, to make sure that certain doors remain closed.

I believe that the reason Robert Kennedy wanted Dulles on the Commission was to ensure "that certain doors remain closed." Kennedy did not want the assassination attempts against Castro to come out because he and his brother were deeply involved.

And that is an area that *JFK: Destiny Betrayed* just can't visit.

And did Bobby Kennedy hate Allen Dulles? In 1964 President Johnson and Robert Kennedy spoke to Allen Dulles about sending him to Mississippi in 1964. Here is a short excerpt from a transcript:

> **Lyndon Johnson**: I know you are. Now let the attorney general tell you what he thinks about it, and I'll be back on in a minute.

[Robert Kennedy takes the telephone]

Robert Kennedy: Allen?

Allen Dulles: Bob?

Robert Kennedy: How are you?

Allen Dulles: [I'm] very well.

Robert Kennedy: Good.

[There is a brief discussion of Senator Edward Kennedy's injuries from a plane accident.]

Robert Kennedy: I think this could be awfully important. You know the situation is extremely explosive in Mississippi.

Allen Dulles: Oh, I know it is.

Robert Kennedy: And there's very little contact—and [it] has been] that way] for the last few years—between the authorities down there and the federal authorities. And the fact that the [Mississippi] governor said that this was a possibility that he'd accept, and have some impartial person go down there and look at the situation, I think could, you know, be a big help and give us some breathing space. And also, somebody with your reputation around the country and around the world, I think, could perform a real service.

JFK: Destiny Betrayed misleads viewers into believing that Allen Dulles was appointed to the Warren Commission against the wishes of Robert Kennedy. Nothing could be further from the truth.

CHAPTER 2
WERE THE CONCLUSIONS OF THE WARREN COMMISSION PREORDAINED?

(EPISODE 2, 53:30)

JFK: Destiny Betrayed misleads viewers about a memo written by Nicholas Katzenbach about investigating JFK's assassination.

Here is an excerpt from a transcript:

> **Narrator (Whoopi Goldberg)**: J. Edgar Hoover wrote a memo to the newly sworn-in President Johnson that evening, saying "The thing I am concerned about is having something issued so we can convince the public that Oswald is the real assassin." The day before, he had told Johnson that the case, "as it stands now, isn't strong enough to be able to get a conviction." The next day, Deputy Attorney General Nicholas Katzenbach wrote a memo to the White House saying, "The public must be satisfied that Oswald did not have confederates who are still at large, and that evidence was such that he would have been convicted at trial. We need something to head off public speculation or Congressional hearings of the wrong sort." With those two memos, the FBI became the main investigatory arm in the JFK case. There was never any serious discussion that independent investigators were needed. The idea in Washington now became to contain the crime to Oswald, therefore, cutting off any connections to a wider Russia-Cuba communist conspiracy, which could provoke the threat of atomic war.

Here is an excerpt from a transcript of a phone call between J. Edgar Hoover and Lyndon Johnson about the state of the evidence. This phone call took place at 10:00 a.m. on November 23, which was very early in the investigative process. Hoover notes that the "evidence that they have at the present time is not very strong." But importantly, there is a new development:

> **Hoover**: I just wanted to let you know of a development which I think is very important in connection with this case. This man in Dallas. We, of course, charged him with the murder of the President. The evidence that they have at the present time is not very strong. We have just discovered the place where the gun was purchased and the shipment of the gun from Chicago to Dallas, to a post office box in Dallas, to a man —no, to a woman by the name of A. Heidel [sic]. It was purchased in March of this year. That gun is now in our possession here in Washington, we had it flown up last night, and our laboratory here is making an examination of it.

The FBI had just tracked down the purchase and shipment of Oswald's Mannlicher-Carcano rifle, and Hoover realized that that was important. I doubt James DiEugenio would have been impressed had Hoover said at that time that the evidence *was* strong enough for a conviction.

Note that the memo also contains some incorrect information. On page 3, Hoover notes, "I think that the bullets were fired from the fifth floor and the three shells were found on the fifth floor. But he apparently went upstairs to the sixth floor to have fired the gun and throw the gun away and then went out." As Howard Willens, staff member of the Warren Commission, noted in his book *History Will Prove Us Right*, "As I would later learn, Hoover's version of facts and reports of conversations were often unreliable."

The next day Hoover called Walter Jenkins:

> The thing I am concerned about, and so is Mr. Katzenbach, is having something issued so we can convince the public that Oswald is the real assassin. Mr. Katzenbach thinks that the President might appoint a

> Presidential Commission of three outstanding citizens to make a determination. I countered with a suggestion that we make an investigative report to the Attorney General with pictures, laboratory work, etc. Then the Attorney General can make the report to the President and the President can decide whether to make it public. I felt this was better because there are several aspects which would complicate our foreign relations. For instance, Oswald made a phone call to the Cuban Embassy in Mexico City which we intercepted. It was only about a visa, however. He also wrote a letter to the Soviet Embassy here in Washington, which we intercepted, read, and resealed. This letter referred to the fact that the FBI had questioned his activities on the Fair Play to Cuba Committee and also asked about the extension of his wife's visa. That letter from Oswald was addressed to the man in the Soviet Embassy who is in charge of assassinations and similar activities on the part of the Soviet government. To have that drawn into a public hearing would muddy the waters internationally. To use all that would reveal our failure to carry out international courtesy laws. And since this has nothing to do with proof that Oswald committed the murder, I made the suggestion to Mr. Katzenbach that instead of a Presidential Commission, we do it with a Justice Department report based on an FBI report.

Note that *JFK: Destiny Betrayed* claims this was a memo from Hoover when it was really a Hoover phone call to Walter Jenkins. One mistake in the phone call: the Oswald letter was not directed to Kostikov, the KGB man responsible for assassinations.

By this time, Hoover had a fuller appreciation of the case against Oswald. Vincent Bugliosi notes:

> Conspiracy theorists have maintained for years that this statement by Hoover ["The thing I am concerned about is having something issued so we can convince the public that Oswald is the real assassin."] means Hoover was trying to set Oswald up. It wouldn't enter their minds that another interpretation of these words was that Hoover (like virtually everyone else in law enforcement at the time) was convinced that Oswald was guilty, and Hoover wanted to help make sure a vulnerable and severely traumatized American public, susceptible to rumors and speculation, also became convinced of this reality.

Here is the Katzenbach memo:

November 25, 1963

MEMORANDUM FOR MR. MOYERS

It is important that all of the facts surrounding President Kennedy's Assassination be made public in a way which will satisfy people in the United States and abroad that all the facts have been told and that a statement to this effect be made now.

1. The public must be satisfied that Oswald was the assassin; that he did not have confederates who are still at large; and that the evidence was such that he would have been convicted at trial.

2. Speculation about Oswald's motivation ought to be cut off, and we should have some basis for rebutting thought that this was a Communist conspiracy or (as the Iron Curtain press is saying) a right-wing conspiracy to blame it on the Communists. Unfortunately the facts on Oswald seem about too pat--too obvious (Marxist, Cuba, Russian wife, etc.). The Dallas police have put out statements on the Communist conspiracy theory, and it was they who were in charge when he was shot and thus silenced.

3. The matter has been handled thus far with neither dignity nor conviction. Facts have been mixed with rumour and speculation. We can scarcely let the world see us totally in the image of the Dallas police when our President is murdered.

I think this objective may be satisfied by making public as soon as possible a complete and thorough FBI report on Oswald and the assassination. This may run into the difficulty of pointing to inconsistencies between this report and statements by Dallas police officials. But the reputation of the Bureau is such that it may do the whole job.

The only other step would be the appointment of a Presidential Commission of unimpeachable personnel to review and examine the evidence and announce its conclusions. This has both advantages and disadvantages. It think it can await publication of the FBI report and public reaction to it here and abroad.

I think, however, that a statement that all the facts will be made public property in an orderly and responsible way should be made now. We need something to head off public speculation or Congressional hearings of the wrong sort.

Nicholas deB. Katzenbach
Deputy Attorney General

Of course, *JFK: Destiny Betrayed* does not mention this part of the memo:

> It is important that all of the facts surrounding President Kennedy's Assassination be made public in a way which will satisfy people in the United States and abroad that all the facts have been told and a statement to this effect be made now.

Katzenbach wanted to ensure that "all the facts have been told." He also says:

> I think, however, that a statement that all the facts will be made public property in an orderly and responsible way should be made now.

Katzenbach indeed worried about Congressional hearings, but that reflected a feeling that undue partisanship could be counterproductive. He does add:

> The only other step would be the appointment of a Presidential Commission of unimpeachable personnel to review and examine the evidence and announce its conclusions.

Katzenbach testified in 1978 before the House Select Committee on Assassinations and was asked about the urgency of getting a report out:

Mr. Cornwell: Why in your mind was there such an urgency to make the preliminary findings of the FBI that there was no conspiracy available to the public? The memos and the letter are all dated within days of the assassination.

Mr. Katzenbach: I think because the speculation that there was conspiracy of various kinds was fairly rampant, at that time particularly in the foreign press. I was reacting to that, and I think reacting to repeated calls from people in the State Department who wanted something of that kind in an effort to quash the beliefs of some people abroad that the silence in the face of those rumors was not to be taken as substantiating it in some way.

That is, in the face of a lot of rumors about conspiracy, a total silence on the subject from the government neither confirming nor denying tended to feed those rumors. I would have liked a statement of the kind I said that nothing we uncovered so far leads us to believe that there is a conspiracy, but investigation is continuing, everything will be put out on the table.

Indeed, I still think today it would have been a good idea to have done it. We might have gotten a better report.

After Katzenbach's memo was submitted, a memo was then written to Alan Belmont, the number three man at the FBI:

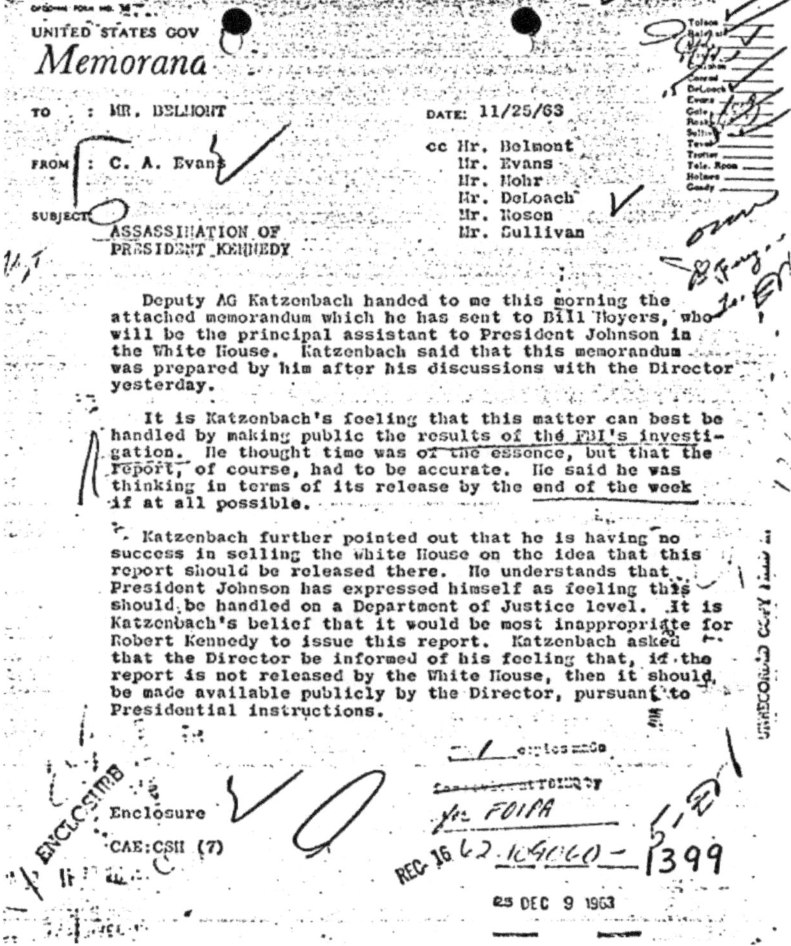
UNITED STATES GOV
Memorana

TO : MR. BELMONT DATE: 11/25/63

FROM : C. A. Evans

cc Mr. Belmont
Mr. Evans
Mr. Mohr
Mr. DeLoach
Mr. Rosen
Mr. Sullivan

SUBJECT: ASSASSINATION OF PRESIDENT KENNEDY

Deputy AG Katzenbach handed to me this morning the attached memorandum which he has sent to Bill Moyers, who will be the principal assistant to President Johnson in the White House. Katzenbach said that this memorandum was prepared by him after his discussions with the Director yesterday.

It is Katzenbach's feeling that this matter can best be handled by making public the results of the FBI's investigation. He thought time was of the essence, but that the report, of course, had to be accurate. He said he was thinking in terms of its release by the end of the week if at all possible.

Katzenbach further pointed out that he is having no success in selling the white House on the idea that this report should be released there. He understands that President Johnson has expressed himself as feeling this should be handled on a Department of Justice level. It is Katzenbach's belief that it would be most inappropriate for Robert Kennedy to issue this report. Katzenbach asked that the Director be informed of his feeling that, if the report is not released by the White House, then it should be made available publicly by the Director, pursuant to Presidential instructions.

Enclosure
CAE:CSH (7)

ENCLOSURE

REC-16 62-109060-1399

25 DEC 9 1963

The memo noted:

> It is Katzenbach's feeling that this matter can best be handled by making public the results of the FBI's investigation. He thought time was of the essence, but that the report, of course, had to be accurate.

Researcher John McAdams commented on the nature of Katzenbach's memo:

> So just how is the Katzenbach memo sinister? If one begins with the assumption that there was a conspiracy, that the evidence of conspiracy was obvious on the Monday after the Friday assassination, and that Katzenbach knew (or somehow suspected) a conspiracy was afoot, then the memo is certainly nefarious. But you have to begin with that assumption. If Katzenbach believed that Oswald was the lone assassin —as the Dallas Police Department said and as the FBI believed and told Katzenbach as of November 24—it's entirely different. And if you believe that rumors and speculation can be harmful—for example, they could fan a war with Russia by implying Communist involvement or hurt the international reputation of the United States if right-wingers could pull off the murder of a president—then a public-spirited person would advocate doing exactly what Katzenbach did. Today such action is called transparency.

Katzenbach was asked during his HSCA deposition about the FBI being the investigative arm of the Warren Commission:

> **Mr. Cornwell**: Would you tell us what your views are today, using all the hindsight that is now available to you about the adequacy of the mechanisms that were ultimately chosen?
>
> **Mr. Katzenbach**: I think the mechanisms were first-rate. They did not work entirely. If I were doing it again, I would do exactly the same thing. I think you have two inherent facts that you have to live with. One was that there is no investigative agency in the world that compares with the Federal Bureau of Investigation then and I suppose it is probably true today. The notion that you could create a separate investigative agency to investigate something of that kind that would do the job better than the FBI I would have rejected then, and I would reject now.

Katzenbach's intention was to ensure that the Warren Commission had the ability to properly evaluate the material it received from the various agencies:

> **Mr. Katzenbach**: Perhaps I could put it differently and say in terms of the capacity of the FBI, they are extremely good. When it comes to the synthesis of the information it seems to me at that point my own experience was that it was worth having other people review it and ask for, as we often did in civil rights matters and quite often in criminal matters, further investigation of various leads that had been rejected as being unproductive. That is what I asked the Warren Commission to do.

It didn't take Lyndon Johnson long to realize that he had to head off a Texas state inquiry and a Congressional inquiry, and by Executive Order 1130 he created a presidential commission:

IMMEDIATE RELEASE NOVEMBER 30, 1963

Office of the White House Press Secretary

- -

THE WHITE HOUSE

EXECUTIVE ORDER
NO.11130
- - - -

APPOINTING A COMMISSION TO REPORT UPON THE ASSASSINATION OF PRESIDENT JOHN F. KENNEDY

Pursuant to the authority vested in me as President of the United States, I hereby appoint a Commission to ascertain, evaluate and report upon the facts relating to the assassination of the late President John F. Kennedy and the subsequent violent death of the man charged with the assassination. The Commission shall consist of --

The Chief Justice of the United States, Chairman;

Senator Richard B. Russell;

Senator John Sherman Cooper;

Congressman Hale Boggs;

Congressman Gerald R. Ford;

The Honorable Allen W. Dulles;

The Honorable John J. McCloy.

The purposes of the Commission are to examine the evidence developed by the Federal Bureau of Investigation and any additional evidence that may hereafter come to light or be uncovered by federal or state authorities; to make such further investigation as the Commission finds desirable; to evaluate all the facts and circumstances surrounding such assassination, including the subsequent violent death of the man charged with the assassination, and to report to me its findings and conclusions.

The Commission is empowered to prescribe its own procedures and to employ such assistants as it deems necessary.

Necessary expenses of the Commission may be paid from the "Emergency Fund for the President".

All Executive departments and agencies are directed to furnish the Commission with such facilities, services and cooperation as it may request from time to time.

LYNDON B. JOHNSON

Howard Willens noted that "The executive order empowered the commission to prescribe its own procedures and employ such personnel as it deemed necessary."

JFK: Destiny Betrayed leaves out many important points. The objective of Nicholas Katzenbach wasn't to "contain the crime to Oswald" but to contain undue rumors and speculation. He worked for Robert Kennedy, and he wanted the truth to come out.

THE CIA

JFK: Destiny Betrayed tries to demonstrate that President Kennedy was angry with the CIA. The documentary also tries to show that the CIA was out of control and was involved in foreign plots.

"The C.I.A. did it. Pass it along."

Credit: Alan Dunn / The New Yorker Collection / The Cartoon Bank / December 11, 1965

CHAPTER 3
DID JFK THREATEN TO SHATTER THE CIA INTO A THOUSAND PIECES?

(EPISODE 1, 23:05)

JFK: Destiny Betrayed greatly misleads its viewers on JFK's attitudes toward the CIA.

Here is an excerpt from a transcript:

> **David Talbot**: Jack Kennedy did stand firm. He did not send in the military; he did not make it into an even bigger global crisis than it already was. Kennedy, after the Bay of Pigs debacle, is just furious. He knows he's been lied to, deceived by his senior military and intelligence advisors. He announces that the Agency is going to be downsized, and he vows, famously, he tells friends, he's going to shatter the CIA into a thousand pieces and scatter it to the wind.

Did President Kennedy actually say that he was going to shatter the CIA into a thousand pieces and scatter it to the wind?

The answer is perhaps. There are no contemporaneous sources for the quote. All we have is a *New York Times* article from April 25, 1966, "C.I.A.: Maker of Policy, or Tool," by a team of correspondents including Tom Wicker, John Finney, Max Frankel, and E. W. Kenworthy. The article noted:

> And President Kennedy, as the enormity of the Bay of Pigs disaster came home to him, said to one of the highest officials of his Administration that he wanted "to splinter the C.I.A. in a thousand pieces and scatter it to the winds."

Rather than saying that Kennedy said this to friends, it would be more accurate to say that the *New York Times* claimed in 1966 that Kennedy had said this to a (high-ranking, unnamed) subordinate. There is a difference.

The phrase has an interesting history:

> The phrase "splinter into a thousand pieces and scatter it to the winds" actually dates back to at least the early 19th century and has decidedly religious origins. You can find versions of the phrase in Methodist sermons from 1819, in letters from clergy of the 1840s, and in fiction of the early 20th century.

Is the quote reliable? A bit of humor:

> All we do know is that this could be another game of Telephone, not unlike the way we see quotes morph on the internet today. And as Abraham Lincoln once told his secretary Fakesy Kennedy, quotes from a third party after you're dead aren't the most reliable sources.

The same *New York Times* article also said:

> The critics shrug aside the fact that President Kennedy, after the most rigorous inquiry into the agency's affairs, methods and problems after the Bay of Pigs, did not "splinter" it after all, and did not recommend Congressional supervision.

Arthur Schlesinger, in his book *A Thousand Days: John F. Kennedy in the White House,* was measured in his evaluation of the leadership of the CIA:

> None of this is to suggest that the CIA constituted, in the title of a popular exposé, an "invisible government" or that its influence was always, or often, reactionary and sinister. In my experience its leadership was politically enlightened and sophisticated. Not seldom CIA representatives took a more liberal line in White House meetings than their counterparts from State.

In fact, John and Robert Kennedy chewed out Richard Bissell, CIA deputy director for plans, for inaction on Cuba. Here is an excerpt from the Church Committee Interim Report:

> According to the Assistant to the head of Task Force W, sometime early in the fall of 1961, Bissell was "chewed out in the Cabinet Room of the White House by both the President and the Attorney General for, as he put it, sitting on his ass and not doing anything about getting rid of Castro and the Castro regime.
>
> The Assistant said Bissell told him about the meeting and directed him to come up with some plans. Bissell did not recall the White House meeting described by the Assistant, but agreed that he had been, in essence, told to "get off your ass about Cuba."

During this segment in *JFK: Destiny Betrayed,* a graph appears on screen alleging that there was a 20 percent budget cut to the CIA. James DiEugenio's book of the annotated film transcript claims that the source for this comes from David Talbot's book *The Devil's Chessboard: Allen Dulles, the CIA, and the Rise of America's Secret Government*:

> In August, months after the failed venture, when longtime veteran Ralph McGehee returned from Vietnam to agency headquarters, he, too, found the CIA in turmoil. Rumors spread that Kennedy was going to exact his revenge by slashing the CIA workforce through a massive "reduction in force," code-named the "701 program" by the agency.

McGehee wrote in his book *Deadly Deceits: My 25 Years in the CIA* that "it seemed that the RIF program was aimed more at the CIA than other agencies of government, possibly as a result of the Bay of Pigs misfire, and President Kennedy's anger at it." He added that "about one of every five was fired."

There is ambiguity in McGehee's paragraph, and Talbot conveniently leaves out his qualifier that the force reduction was "possibly" because of the Bay of Pigs.

The CIA was not the only department that lost personnel:

Deterrent to Good Men

Getting good men to accept governmental posts is a problem which besets every level of government activity from the nation's capitol to the humblest municipal building. And the problem is growing worse.

Some of the public-minded citizens who came running to Washington early this year in response to the New Frontier's call for good men for government may wish they had stayed home.

Prospects of a $7 billion budget deficit have prompted President Kennedy to issue hold-down orders to various government agencies. Cries and alarums about payroll cuts are echoing through Washington.

The most spectacular uproar emanates from the State Department. Secretary Rusk is cutting 500 jobs from his Washington work force of 7,200, a statistic which translated into human terms means that one out of fourteen employes will be out of a job by Christmas.

Civil service procedures generally protect the jobs of the older bureaucrats the new administration would most like to be rid of. State Department bureau heads are said to be wondering how to break the bad news to young men who have abandoned jobs elsewhere and bought homes in Washington in response to the New Frontier's summons to duty.

Anonymous letters and phone calls to Washington correspondents obviously originating within the department, blame the personnel cutbacks on unwise spending and budget practices by Kennedy's new team.

But department officials say the reduction in force is made necessary by Congress which appropriated $7.2 million short of the department's request for salaries and expenses in the current fiscal year.

In any event, the reduction in force at the State Department amply demonstrates one of the reasons why Republican and Democratic administrations alike in recent years have found it difficult to recruit talented men for government.

Scranton Tribune, November 14, 1961

The fact is that the 701 program was originally proposed by the Director of Personnel of the CIA in November of 1959. A study that accompanied the proposal said that the "Clandestine Service Career Service would not be able to maintain a proper level of operational activity unless steps were taken to provide for the recruitment annually of a substantial number of capable young officers and for their advancement at a reasonable pace." The goal of the program was to professionalize the Clandestine Service, and it did not affect the entire CIA. The program was officially adopted on February 10, 1961, which was before the Bay of Pigs. In fact, surplus personnel were designated before John McCone became director of the CIA.

In the Clandestine Service, a total of 153 people were identified as being surplus. Fifty-eight were retained, twelve retired, fourteen resigned, and sixty-nine were terminated, with most actions occurring during 1962 and 1963. Tim Weiner described what happened in his book *Legacy of Ashes: The History of the CIA*:

> McCone started firing hundreds of clandestine service officer—aiming first to purge the "accident-prone," the "wife-beaters," and the "alcohol-addicted," noted his deputy director, General Marshall S. Carter.

Of course, this all "seemed" to McGehee to be because of the Bay of Pigs. That view was not uncommon in the CIA. The Report of the Task Force on Personnel Management in CIA noted that:

> A part of the unrest that is currently prevalent in the Agency has been occasioned by the episodes of the U-2 and the Cuban invasion, and more directly by the 701 exercise. The first two events have been widely discussed in the press with uninformed speculation to the effect that this probably meant the CIA would be broken up and that many functions would be transferred to other agencies.

The only other source for a 20 percent budget cut comes from Arthur Schlesinger's book:

> "The Agency itself suffered from doubt and gloom after Cuba, and it was feared that drastic measures would cause total demoralization. Instead, Kennedy moved quietly to cut the CIA budget in 1962 and again in 1963, aiming at a 20 per cent reduction by 1966."

Because of the secrecy of the CIA's budget, we can't be sure just how much JFK cut the CIA budget. It certainly appears that the 20 percent number was a goal.

The budget for the CIA in 1963 was $550 million. I am not sure if the budget decreased in 1963 from 1962.

The CIA budget appears to have also declined in the early years of the Johnson administration:

CIA Cost Reduction Program

❶ Program Description

Cost reduction and management improvement in the Central Intelligence Agency is a dynamic and ongoing process. Elimination of lesser priority activities, absorption of new tasks, and continuous streamlining of management procedures are built into the formal program review mechanisms of the Agency. Over the past four years the program has fostered sizeable year-end savings and has permitted reduced appropriation requests to the Congress.

Fiscal Year	Appropriation
1963	$550 million
1964	517 million
1965	525 million
1966	505 million *

In 1965 the program resulted in record savings. This allowed the Agency to absorb over $8 million of the skyrocketing costs in Southeast Asia, $1 million of unprogramed costs to meet the Dominican Republic crisis, and $3 million of Federal pay increases. The cost reduction concept also permitted a wide range of reprograming to meet critical intelligence needs throughout the year. Beyond this, we anticipate over $5 million can be returned to reserve for contingency from the FY 1965 appropriation.

The Agency's cost reduction program is also directly responsive to the guidelines set forth in Bureau of the Budget Circular A-44. It provides: 1) a regularized and timely system to report cost reduction plans and goals; 2) a validation procedure to guard against double counting and inappropriate submissions; and 3) a progress reporting system to ensure an orderly march toward pre-established goals. The program has the full and energetic support of all echelons of the CIA management team.

* Supplemented by $40 million for Southeast Asia escalation

As can be seen, there was less than a 10 percent reduction in the CIA's budget from fiscal year 1963 to 1966. A large reason for the decrease was because JFK transferred some functions to the Department of Defense.

PENTAGON TO GET SOME C.I.A. DUTIES

Plan Reflects Kennedy Aim to Centralize Control of All Types of Warfare

By JAMES RESTON
Special to The New York Times.

WASHINGTON, April 28—The Department of Defense will soon be asked to take over new responsibilities in the fields of subversive warfare and civil defense, responsible sources said tonight.

New York Times, April 29, 1961

National Security Action Memorandum 57, dated June 28, 1961, moved some paramilitary operations to the Pentagon:

~~SECRET~~

RESPONSIBILITY FOR PARAMILITARY OPERATIONS

1. For the purpose of this study, a paramilitary operation is considered to be one which by its tactics and its requirements in military-type personnel, equipment and training approximates a conventional military operation. It may be undertaken in support of an existing government friendly to the U.S. or in support of a rebel group seeking to overthrow a government hostile to us. The U.S. may render assistance to such operations overtly, covertly or by a combination of both methods. In size these operations may vary from the infiltration of a squad of guerrillas to a military operation such as the Cuban invasion. The small operations will often fall completely within the normal capability of one agency; the large ones may affect State, Defense, CIA, USIA and possibly other departments and agencies.

2. In order to conduct paramilitary operations with maximum effectiveness and flexibility within the context of the Cold War, it is recommended that current directives and procedures be modified to effect the following:

a. Any proposed paramilitary operation in the concept stage will be presented to the Strategic Resources Group for initial consideration and for approval as necessary by the President. Thereafter, the SRG will assign primary responsibility for planning, for interdepartment coordination and for execution to the Task Force, department or individual best qualified to carry forward the operation to success, and will indicate supporting responsibilities. Under this principle, the Department of Defense will normally receive responsibility for overt paramilitary operations. Where such an operation is to be wholly covert or disavowable, it may be assigned to CIA, provided that it is within the normal capabilities of the agency. Any large paramilitary operation wholly or partly covert which requires significant numbers of militarily trained personnel, amounts of military equipment which exceed normal CIA-controlled stocks and/or military experience of a kind and level peculiar to the Armed Services is properly the primary responsibility of the Department of Defense with the CIA in a supporting role.

~~SECRET~~

When John McCone became the new director of the CIA in October 1961, Kennedy sent a memo outlining some changes:

2. Internal Organization of the
Central Intelligence Agency

The new Director of Central Intelligence should undertake at once organizational studies which would result in a strengthening of the Central Intelligence Agency. He should consider the question of the proper alignments within the organization and the proper staffing. Particular attention should be given to the budget and the number of personnel employed within the Agency. It is possible that benefit would result from relocating clandestine activities and covert operations to points outside of Washington in an effort to achieve deeper cover for such activities. More emphasis must be given to acquiring "hard" intelligence essential to the national security. In this connection, attention must be directed toward the expansion of those advanced scientific and technical projects which are proving to be so valuable in the procuring of "hard" intelligence.

Kennedy wanted to relocate some clandestine activities "to points outside of Washington in an effort to achieve deeper cover for such activities." Clearly, Kennedy still wanted clandestine activities; he just wanted to hide them better.

Kennedy was also not that interested in oversight:

5. Congressional Investigation of
Intelligence Activities

From time to time, efforts are made in Congress to institute investigations of intelligence activities or establish a joint congressional committee on foreign intelligence. Such efforts must be stoutly and intelligently resisted for they could seriously hamper the efficient and effective operation of our intelligence activities.

According to historian Tim Weiner, John and Robert Kennedy had a keen interest in covert action:

In his wrath after the Bay of Pigs, John Kennedy first wanted to destroy the CIA. Then he took the agency's clandestine service out of its death

> spiral by handing the controls to his brother. It was one of the least wise decisions of his presidency. Robert F. Kennedy, thirty-five years old, famously ruthless, fascinated with secrecy, took command of the most sensitive covert operations of the United States. The two men unleashed covert action with an unprecedented intensity. Ike had undertaken 170 major CIA covert operations in eight years. The Kennedys launched 163 major covert operations in less than three.

Kennedy revamped covert action. He set up the Special Group, or the 303 Committee, to oversee the Clandestine Service with McGeorge Bundy as its chairman:

> The members were McCone, the chairman of the Joint Chiefs, and senior deputies from Defense and State. But until very late in the Kennedy administration it was left to the CIA's covert operators to decide whether to consult with the Special Group. There were more than a few operations that McCone [director of the CIA after Dulles] and the Special Group knew little or nothing about.
>
> In November 1961, in the greatest secrecy, John and Bobby Kennedy created a new planning cell for covert action, the Special Group (Augmented). It was RFK's outfit, and it had one mission: eliminating Castro.

The Kennedys were serious about getting rid of Castro, and they started Operation Mongoose:

> The Kennedys did not want to hear that [the CIA had limited intelligence on Cuba]. They wanted swift, silent sabotage to overthrow Castro. "Let's get the hell on with it," the attorney general barked. "The President wants some action, right now." Helms saluted smartly and got the hell on with it. He created a new freestanding task force to report to Ed Lansdale and Robert Kennedy. He assembled a team from all over the world, creating the CIA's largest peacetime intelligence operation to date, with some six hundred CIA officers in and around Miami, almost five thousand CIA contractors, and the third largest navy in the Caribbean, including submarines, patrol boats, coast guard

> cutters, seaplanes, and Guantanamo Bay for a base. Some "nutty schemes" against Fidel were proposed by the Pentagon and the White House, Helms said. These included blowing up an American ship in Guantanamo Harbor and faking a terrorist attack against an American airliner to justify a new invasion.

A memo from October 1962 highlighted the need for sabotage:

4 October 1962

MEMORANDUM FOR RECORD

SUBJECT: Minutes of Meeting of the Special Group (Augmented) on Operation MONGOOSE, 4 October 1962

PRESENT: The Attorney General; Mr. Johnson; Mr. Gilpatric, General Taylor, General Lansdale; Mr. McCone and General Carter; Mr. Wilson

1. The Attorney General opened the meeting by saying that higher authority is concerned about progress on the MONGOOSE program and feels that more priority should be given to trying to mount sabotage operations. The Attorney General said that he wondered if a new look is not required at this time in view of the meager results, especially in the sabotage field. He urged that "massive activity" be mounted within the entire MONGOOSE framework. There was a good deal of discussion about this, and General Lansdale said that another attempt will be made against the major target which has been the object of three unsuccessful missions, and that approximately six new ones are in the planning stage.

John and Robert Kennedy had an extremely active interest in clandestine operations. Their irritation at the CIA did not lead them to "scatter" it to the wind. They just reorganized the way these operations were run and managed. *JFK: Destiny Betrayed* misleads viewers by making it appear that Kennedy wanted to end covert activities like the Bay of Pigs when, in fact, he wanted more.

CHAPTER 4

DID THE CIA SUPPORT A 1961 COUP ATTEMPT IN FRANCE?

Four ex-generals responsible for the failed revolt in Algiers. From left to right: Andre Zeller, Edmond Jouhoud, Raoul Salan, and Maurice Challe. Credit: Bettmann, April 24, 1961.

(EPISODE 1, 23:05)

JFK: Destiny Betrayed greatly misleads its viewers on supposed CIA support of an April 1961 coup attempt against French President Charles de Gaulle.

Here is an excerpt from a transcript:

David Talbot: It wasn't just the Bay of Pigs that angered President Kennedy, when it came to the CIA. In that same month, in April of 1961, he was also being lied to about a coup in France. A military coup that was aimed at overthrowing President Charles de Gaulle, one of our strongest allies.

Narrator (Donald Sutherland): Allen Dulles, who had a long history of antagonism with de Gaulle, falsely reported to Kennedy that the vast majority of the French military was staunchly opposed to de Gaulle's support of Algerian self-determination. What he didn't tell him was that, as far back as 1959, the CIA had discussed his overthrow. This coup attempt, orchestrated by four French generals, was quickly put down, and several news reports pointed to Allen Dulles's hand in supporting the episode.

The evidence for the allegations in *JFK: Destiny Betrayed* comes from David Talbot's book *The Devil's Chessboard: Allen Dulles, The CIA and the Rise of America's Secret Government.*

Here is an overview of what happened.

The general's putsch took place in late April 1961. Maurice Challe (former commander in chief in French Algeria), Edmond Jouhaud (former inspector general of the French Air Force), André Zeller (former chief of staff of the French Army), and Raoul Salan (former commander in chief in French Algeria) were all part of the plot. They were opposed to Algerian independence.

Parachutists took control of major points in Algiers on April 22. An announcement was made that the army had taken control of Algeria. A state of emergency was declared, and de Gaulle went on television on April 23 to rally the country. The people stood behind de Gaulle, and the insurgency quickly failed.

JFK: Destiny Betrayed alleges that "several news reports pointed to Allen Dulles's hand in supporting the episode."

Is there any truth to this?

The documentary shows on screen an article, "Pentagon to Get Some C.I.A. Duties," from the *New York Times* of April 29, 1961, written by James Reston. The paragraph on the screen reads as follows:

> Second, the disappointing performance of the Central Intelligence Agency, which masterminded the rebel attack on Cuba last week, the U-2 spy plane incident a year ago, and which was involved in an embarrassing liaison with anti-Gaullist officers who staged last week's insurrection in Algeria.

But Oliver Stone doesn't dare quote the following from the same *New York Times* article:

> Also, in the last few days the President has looked into angry reports from Paris that the C.I.A. was in touch with insurrectionists who tried to overthrow the de Gaulle Government of France.
>
> These reports apparently go back to the fact that C.I.A. agents have recently been in touch with the anti-Gaullist generals in Algiers and that C.I.A. officials gave a luncheon for Jacques Soustelle, a leader of the anti-de Gaulle movement, when M. Soustelle was last in Washington.

Richard Bissell, director of the CIA's Operations section, met with Soustelle on December 7, 1960, about five months before the coup attempt. The luncheon was given by the French intelligence chief in Washington, and Bissell and Soustelle were his guests. Given that the CIA's work is in intelligence and that Soustelle had a major position in Algeria, there was nothing amiss with the lunch.

The real question is about the "angry reports from Paris." This was indeed true. There were angry reports from Paris. But what was the source of these reports, and were they true?

It is important to understand that the relationship between de Gaulle and the United States was difficult. De Gaulle was a staunch nationalist who wanted to chart a course independent of the United States, and he took umbrage at the slightest hint of American interference in French internal affairs.

Talbot writes that "De Gaulle quickly concluded that Challe must be acting with the support of U.S. intelligence, and Elysée officials began spreading this word to the press." Talbot's source is the London *Observer* of May 2, 1961, and Vincent Jauvert's book *L'Amérique Contre De Gaulle: Histoire secrète 1961–1969.*

Let's start with the London *Observer* article. I had trouble finding the *Observer* article in question because the newspaper was only published on Sundays, and so there was no edition for May 2, 1961. However, the edition for April 30, 1961, does have a few articles about the coup attempt. The front page article, "Conspiracy 'leaders' still at large," says this:

> One reaction, at least in President de Gaulle's own entourage and perhaps inspired by him, is to blame the Americans. Repeated American denials that any American—military or civilian—encouraged General Challe's rebellion have not succeeded in preventing official French spokesmen from telling journalists there must have been some unofficial American backing.

Talbot would never report what the same article said near the end:

> There is no evidence that General Challe received active encouragement from American secret agents. But he seems to have hoped for some help from this direction.

What about Jauvert? What does his book say about de Gaulle? Here is a translation of an excerpt:

> What did de Gaulle really think of this secret service affair? Back from Paris, where he probed the Elysée, Jean-Claude Winckler, adviser at the French embassy in Washington, dines with Pentagon number two, William Bundy, and tells him about his discoveries. Bundy brings them back to the White House. "Pierre Guillaumat [minister without portfolio] told Winckler that de Gaulle really believed that a few US government officials had encouraged Challe. De Gaulle did not have in mind any action by people from the CIA, but a series of conversations - of which he was told - between General Challe and American officers linked to SHAPE [Supreme Headquarters Allied Powers Europe]." What would they be talking about? "In January, Challe reportedly told

> these officers that De Gaulle's policy vis-à-vis NATO was totally bad, that an independent Algeria opened the way to chaos and communism and that a government of pro-American generals would lead to France's acceptance of greater NATO integration and other American desires. The American officers would have nodded." That's all. In any case, this is the official version of De Gaulle's discontent.

So, de Gaulle did not "have in mind any action by people from the CIA" but just a nod from American officers.

Even Talbot realized that the rumors had spread from the French Foreign Ministry:

> De Gaulle's foreign ministry was the source of some of the most provocative charges in the press, including the allegation that CIA agents sought funding for the Challe coup from multinational corporations, such as Belgian mining companies operating in the Congo. Ministry officials also alleged that Americans with ties to extremist groups had surfaced in Paris during the coup drama, including one identified as a "political counselor for the Luce [media] group," who was heard to say, "An operation is being prepared in Algiers to put a stop to communism, and we will not fail as we did in Cuba."

Talbot's source for this is Jauvert's book, but he doesn't tell readers the full story. Jauvert writes that the rumor of CIA support came from the French Ministry of Foreign Affairs. The director of information wrote to the foreign affairs minister about the allegations. At the end of his paragraph on the rumors, Jauvert writes, "Rumors, unconfirmed information, but no proof."

And *JFK: Destiny Betrayed* doesn't mention this quote from Jauvert's book:

> Confidentially, "a French official from Agency A [code for Direction de la Surveillance du Territoire (DST; English: Directorate of Territorial Surveillance, part of the French National Police]" gives the US Army counter-intelligence service some details on the alleged American support for Challe. They would be people "linked to the CIA and

> certain American soldiers belonging to the NATO structures. All would be opposed to the policy of the Kennedy administration in Africa and more particularly North Africa." The proof? None.

Of course, the rumors emanating from the Foreign Ministry were greatly amplified by the communist press. The communist-controlled Rome daily *Il Paese* (the morning edition of *Paese Sera*) ran a story about the CIA that traveled throughout the communist world and then back to the mainstream press. Here is a paragraph from Christopher Andrew's and Vasili Mitrokhin's book *The KGB and the World: The Mitrokhin Archive II*:

> In April 1961 the KGB succeeded in planting on the pro-Soviet daily Paese Sera a story suggesting that the CIA was involved in the failed putsch mounted by four French generals to disrupt de Gaulle's attempt to negotiate a peace with the FLN which would lead to Algerian independence. Among other media taken in by the story was the leading French newspaper Le Monde, which began an editorial on the putsch: "It now seems established that some American agents more or less encouraged [General Maurice] Challe.

Richard Helms testified before Congress in June 1961 about the KGB operation:

> One of the devices used by the Communists is the documentary fraud. Of these there are several kinds, and I propose to present examples of each: The false news article, the forgery, the fabricated intelligence report, the distortion of a genuine document, and the false or true account attributed to a nonexistent organization.

The story started in *Paese Sera* and then went to *Pravda* and was then sent out in a TASS dispatch. Then the communist daily in Paris, *L'Humanité*, printed the story. The story then appeared in a non-communist newspaper in Paris with a story by an anti-American journalist, Genevieve Tabouis. Her article cited a nonexistent letter alleged to have been written by British Prime Minister Macmillan to President Kennedy. She then published an article titled "The Strategy of Allen Dulles," in which she wrote "The fact that the effort of Challe was encouraged, if not supported, by the most Atlantic of American services, is from now on a secret everyone knows." TASS then quoted from her article but did not inform readers about the questionable nature of the rumors.

James DiEugenio, in his book based on the *JFK: Destiny Betrayed* screenplay, listed the sources for the allegations about the CIA in the film:

- *Paris-Jour*
- Jauvert's book *L'Amérique Contre De Gaulle*
- London *Observer*, May 2, 1961
- Andrew Tully's book *CIA: The Inside Story*
- *The Nation*, May 20, 1961
- *Washington Post*, April 30, 1961
- *New York Times*, April 29, 1961

Interestingly, DiEugenio lists the May 2, 1961, date for the London *Observer*. He just took the sources from Talbot's book and did not check them. As noted earlier, the *Observer* article actually appeared on April 30, 1961.

Do DiEugenio's sources back up the story? We've already covered the *Observer*, the Jauvert book, and the *New York Times*. What about the other sources?

1. Andrew Tully's book, *CIA: The Inside Story*

I am not sure if James DiEugenio has read Tully's book. Here is an excerpt:

> Paul Ghali of the Chicago Daily News got into the act, too. He reported that "a determined campaign of anti-Americanism" had been started "within Army circles here in the French capital. These circles made it known that they had 'irrefutable' documents proving that CIA agents in Paris and Algiers promised General Challe full U.S. support if the coup succeeded. Simultaneously, the Polish Ambassador in Paris, Stanislaw Gajewski, volunteered the same information with even more precision to colleagues and social acquaintances."
>
> Certainly, the Soviet propaganda machine was having a field day.

> But now the gossip was taken up by respected and responsible French newspapers which could not, by any stretch of the imagination, be including in the normally anti-American fringe of French opinion. The story was considered important enough to be the subject of the lead editorial in Le Monde, the most respected and influential newspaper in France.

Pierre Salinger went to Paris on May 2 to make arrangements for Kennedy's upcoming trip to visit de Gaulle. Salinger met with Pierre Baraduc, chief of the press section of the Foreign Office:

> "Why are you putting out this story?" Salinger asked Baraduc, his voice sharp with irritation.
>
> "I'm not putting it out," Baraduc replied. "It seems to have sprung from nowhere. But you have to admit the story sounds logical. It seems to me that President Kennedy should investigate and see if it is true."
>
> "What do you want him to investigate?" Salinger asked. "No charge has been made, no evidence has been submitted. There's nothing to investigate. It looks to me as if somebody is trying to place the President at a disadvantage for his meeting with President de Gaulle."

The next day there was a scene at a luncheon with James Gavin, the American ambassador to France. A reporter asked him about the rumors, and Baraduc, the French press chief of the Foreign Ministry, asked the reporter to leave. Gavin just answered that he was not concerned about the rumor.

He then met with Maurice Couve de Murville, foreign minister of France:

> **Salinger**: Monsieur de Mourville [sic], do you have any evidence at all that the United States Central Intelligence Agency was involved in the revolt of the French generals in Algeria?
>
> **De Mourville**: No, we have no evidence.
>
> **Salinger**: Then I suggest you stop peddling the story.

De Murville then testified before the Foreign Affairs Committee of the Chamber of Deputies, where he told them that there was no evidence of CIA complicity.

2. *The Nation*, May 20, 1961

The Nation's article, "The CIA in Algeria," took its information from an article in the left-wing French newspaper *L'Express* by journalist Claude Krief. He claimed that:

> Both in Paris and Washington the facts are now known, though they will never be publicized.
>
> In private, the highest French personalities make no secret of it. What they say is this: The CIA played a direct part in the Algiers coup, and certainly weighed heavily on the decision by ex-general Challe to start his putsch …"

Krief also mentions the Washington lunch meeting with Soustelle but then goes further:

> The next episode related by Krief is a meeting in Madrid on April 12 between "various foreign agents, including members of the CIA and the Algiers conspirators, who disclosed their plans to the CIA men."

Jauvert reported on these rumors in his book. They came from an article in the newspaper *Afrique-Action* written by their American correspondent. The meeting in Madrid was allegedly attended by a French general, two French colonels, and agents from the United States, Spain, and Germany. No evidence has ever surfaced that such a meeting took place.

3. The *Washington Post*, April 30, 1961

The *Washington Post* ran an article on April 30, 1961, entitled "Challe Felt He Had Vow of U.S. Aid" by Waverley Root. The opening few paragraphs are illuminating:

> When former Gen. Maurice Challe agreed to assume command of the Generals' revolt in Algeria, it was in part because he was convinced that he had unqualified American support.
>
> In fact, an informant qualified to interpret Challe's motives told this writer, he believed that he had received assurances from President Kennedy himself of eventual support.
>
> "Who gave them?" This correspondent asked.
>
> "They came from the Pentagon," was the answer.
>
> "I thought everybody was blaming the CIA?"
>
> "The Pentagon, the CIA—it's all the same thing."
>
> From other sources, it appears that France is shifting to the opinion that the supposed inspiration for Challe came not from American intelligence services but from the U.S. Army.

The article then goes on to discuss NATO and the fact that Challe commanded the Europe-Center Sector. He might have gotten some inspiration for his coup from military personnel and diplomats at NATO.

The only other source mentioned by DiEugenio is *Paris-Jour,* which published pieces by Genevieve Tabouis, who was just repeating rumors of the day.

Waverley Root of the *Washington Post* commented on her in the April 30 article:

> Only columnist Genevieve Tabouis—The Pythoness, as she is called here—continued to belabor CIA chief Allen Dulles, by heading an article, "The Strategy of Allen Dulles." But she also seemed confused about who does what when she writes:
>
> 'The fact that the effort of Challe was encouraged, if not supported, by the most Atlantic of American services, is from now on a secret everyone knows.'
>
> This cryptic description must mean NATO, where Challe until early this year commanded the Europe-Center Sector, and not the Dulles-headed CIA.

To sum up, none of the sources cited by James DiEugenio provide any evidence that the CIA supported or encouraged the coup attempt against de Gaulle. The rumors about the CIA started from the Foreign Ministry and were then played up by the communist press.

A key question is why the Foreign Ministry spread such rumors.

Irwin Wall, in his book *France, the United States, and the Algerian War,* writes:

> Joseph Alsop wrote that Challe believed he could get U.S. support by playing the anti-communist card, given de Gaulle's hostility to NATO. Another reason was thus handed de Gaulle for blaming the Americans: the generals' revolt was the consequence of the American refusal to accept French plans for the reform of NATO.

Another possible answer comes from Thomas Powers's book *The Man Who Kept the Secrets: Richard Helms and the CIA*:

> In late 1961, for example, the CIA arranged for Frantz Fanon, author of The Wretched of the Earth and a theoretician for the FLN [National Liberation Front], to be flown to Washington for treatment of terminal cancer. After Fanon's death on December 6, a CIA officer named Oliver Iselin accompanied Fanon's body back to Tunis, where the FLN carried it across the border into Algeria for burial. Iselin, accompanied by another CIA officer who flew to Tunis from Geneva, according to a State Department source, was present at the funeral. This sort of thing angered de Gaulle.

Might this have been the reason why de Gaulle or others started the rumors against the CIA? Powers' source was Peter Geismer's book *Fanon.* Fanon had leukemia, and his treatment in Moscow had not gone well. He was desperate to go to the United States and get some first-rate care. Geismer writes that "it was the C.I.A., working within the [U.S.] Foreign Service, that negotiated Fanon's transportation to the United States."

The coup attempt was in April 1961, and I wondered if the CIA contacts with Fanon started before the coup. If they did, then perhaps that is what angered de Gaulle. Thomas Meaney, author of "Frantz Fanon and the CIA Man," provides some important answers:

> During the height of the war between the FLN and France, Iselin continued to develop contacts within the FLN. By 1960, he had two reliable informants. "One turned out to be, when Algeria became independent, very high-level. The second one I recruited was medium-level, and after a while, when he went back, he decided to pursue a business career, which lost his access. While he was an agent being paid and everything, he provided us with an unbelievable amount of material from the FLN, really. All the files of the whole Tangiers setup." Iselin also made regular trips across the border into Algeria to get information from the ALN [Algerian Liberation Army]. "Obviously I hoped the French didn't know about [it]. I felt very strongly, being American, what we went through here in this country, I was entirely for independence as the rightful thing to do. I was morally into this completely."
>
> French authorities in Algeria were aware of the CIA's interest in national liberation movements across North Africa, where the agency worked through the American Federation of Labor to infiltrate trade unions in Morocco, Tunisia, and Algeria, building on its earlier support for anti-communist trade unions on the French mainland. The CIA first became interested in Fanon sometime in the late 1950s.

Iselin came back to the United States at the end of 1960 and was contacted by M'hamed Yazid, an FLN representative in New York, to discuss Fanon's health. Joseph Alsop wrote in his syndicated column in February 1969 that Fanon asked the local CIA representative for help in February 1961.

It is quite possible that de Gaulle knew about these CIA contacts with the FLN. And this might indeed be the reason why the CIA was blamed for the coup attempt in April 1961.

Irwin Wall agrees with Thomas Powers but offers yet another possible explanation:

> Redha Malek in his book, *L'Algerie a Evian*, claimed that the rumors arose because two American military attaches were seen using the studios of Radio France, which was under the control of the insurgents in Algiers, to transmit their dispatches; the Quai was alleged to have protested, but then to have withdrawn the protest with apologies.

And last but not least, *U.S. News and World Report* had a simple explanation:

> *[There was] a search for scapegoats, particularly for non-French scapegoats. It was against this background that officials of the French government, including Cabinet Ministers and other high officials, privately encouraged the idea that U.S. generals were to blame for supporting the conspirators.*

Whatever the reason, Kennedy was certainly not happy about the rumors regarding the CIA. Wall notes:

> Kennedy was so irritated at continued French charges of CIA complicity with the insurrection that he considered calling off his June 1961 trip to Paris.

To summarize, in a desperate bid to score points against the CIA, *JFK: Destiny Betrayed* reported speculation and rumors about purported CIA involvement in the coup attempt. Instead of offering a measured, realistic approach to what happened, it gives viewers a quick cartoon, devoid of any nuance, and without any intent to educate viewers.

CHAPTER 5
DID JFK SAY THAT HE WAS NOT IN CONTROL OF THE CIA?

(EPISODE 1, 24:59)

JFK: Destiny Betrayed misleads viewers into believing that JFK told de Gaulle that he was not in full control of the CIA.

Here is an excerpt from a transcript:

> **David Talbot**: JFK assures the French ambassador, "I had nothing to do with this [the coup attempt against de Gaulle]. I stand in full support of President de Gaulle," but he says something very, very alarming. He tells the French ambassador, President Kennedy [does], that I am not in full control, though, of my entire government. I'm not in control of the CIA. And I can't speak for what's happening there. That's a stunning admission for a U.S. President to make.

James DiEugenio writes that the source for this allegation comes from Talbot's book *The Devil's Chessboard: Allen Dulles, The CIA, and the Rise of America's Secret Government,* where he writes:

> JFK took pains to assure Paris that he strongly supported de Gaulle's presidency, phoning Hervé Alphand, the French ambassador in Wash-

> ington, to directly communicate these assurances. But, according to Alphand, Kennedy's disavowal of official U.S. involvement in the coup came with a disturbing addendum—the American president could not vouch for his own intelligence agency. Kennedy told Alphand that "the CIA is such a vast and poorly controlled machine that the most unlikely maneuvers might be true."

Talbot's source is Vincent Jauvert's book *L'Amérique Contre De Gaulle.* Dean Rusk, the secretary of state, told the French ambassador in Washington, Hervé Alphand, on April 30 that their investigations into supposed contacts between the rebel generals and Americans "have shed no light." Rusk also told Alphand that "if they [contacts between Americans and the rebel generals] had actually occurred, they would have been contrary to the interests and policies of the United States."

Jauvert writes:

> Alphand wrote the Foreign Minister that, according to Kennedy, "the CIA is a machine so vast and so poorly understood that the most improbable maneuvers can be true. The most improbable maneuvers…"

Jauvert finds Rusk's words "if they had actually occurred" to signify something important. "In other words, the very young Kennedy administration is not very sure of the CIA, that it does not control well." [In French: "S'ils s'étaient effectivement produits", dit Rusk à Alphand … Autrement dit, la toute jeune administration Kennedy n'est pas très sûre de la CIA, qu'elle ne contrôle pas bien.]

So, is Talbot quoting Kennedy, or is he just quoting Jauvert?

We can't even be sure of Kennedy's actual quote. All we know is what Alphand wrote to the French foreign minister. And that is very different from what is alleged in *JFK: Destiny Betrayed*. Kennedy did not tell Alphand that he is not in control of his government. He did not tell Alphand that he is not in control of the CIA. All we have is an admission that the CIA is very big, and you never know when someone somewhere may have said something.

Some of this comes from the intentions of the French to differentiate JFK from the CIA:

> As Paris officials knew, the new American president already had something of a prickly relationship with de Gaulle, but he had strong feelings for France—and they made sure to absolve JFK of personal responsibility for the coup in their leaks to the press. French press accounts referred to the CIA as a "reactionary state-within-a-state" that operated outside of Kennedy's control.

And this sort of talk hit the *New York Times* on May 2, 1961:

> The rumors, which include at least one written report circulating here, repeated speculations in the French press, a dispatch from Washington to the Tunisian weekly Afrique-Action and widespread speculation in Left-wing circles, boil down to this:
>
> President Kennedy is said to have reacted as he did because he had learned of encouragement to the mutineers by the Central Intelligence Agency, which is said to have become a reactionary state-within-a-state in the United States.

Once again, *JFK: Destiny Betrayed* removes all nuance and misleads viewers with a false quote from JFK.

CHAPTER 6
WAS THE CIA INVOLVED IN A 1967 PLOT AGAINST DE GAULLE?

(EPISODE 1, 25:24)

JFK: Destiny Betrayed misleads viewers by alleging that the CIA was involved in a plot against the life of French President Charles de Gaulle. Here is an excerpt from a transcript:

Narrator (Donald Sutherland): Beyond a coup, in fact, there were at least six attempts to assassinate de Gaulle by the OAS, and others that continued even after he agreed to grant Algeria its independence.

A short clip from the film *The Day of the Jackal:* shooting at a car, no voiceover.

Narrator (Donald Sutherland): In one of these plots, there is evidence that French dissidents and the CIA conspired to poison de Gaulle.

But the CIA had absolutely nothing to do with the 1962 plot against de Gaulle in the fact-based but fictional film *The Day of the Jackal*. Right after the clip, the film quickly transitions to the June 12, 1975, edition of the *Chicago Tribune*:

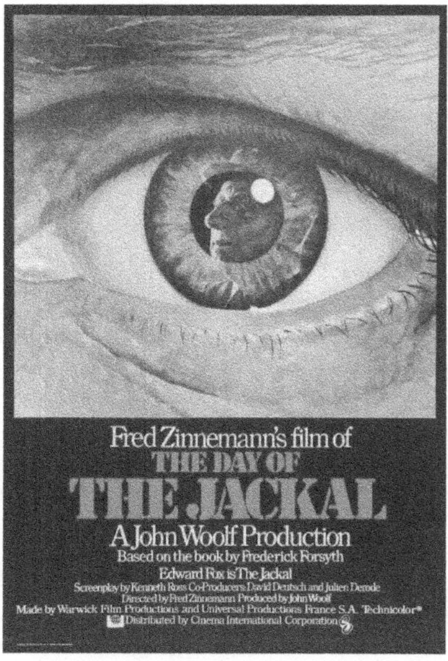

Fred Zinnemann's film of
THE DAY OF
THE JACKAL
A John Woolf Production
Based on the book by Frederick Forsyth
Edward Fox is The Jackal
Screenplay by Kenneth Ross Co-Producers David Deutsch and Julien Derode
Directed by Fred Zinnemann Produced by John Woolf
Made by Warwick Film Productions and Universal Productions France S.A. Technicolor®
Distributed by Cinema International Corporation

(Original Caption) The four ex-generals responsible for the abortive revolt in Algiers walk from the government house. They are (from left to right) Andre Zeller, Edmond Jouhoud, Raoul Salan, and Maurice Challe. Credit: Bettmann, April 24, 1961.

Chicago Tribune

THE WORLD'S GREATEST NEWSPAPER

Final Edition

Sunday June 15, 1975

50¢

Bare CIA role in plot to murder DeGaulle

The alarmist headline belies the text in the body of the article:

> In the outline presented to the congressional leaders, there is no hint of what the CIA's actual role might have been had the plot reached fruition. Also, there is no indication whether the CIA was to have arranged the assassination, provided the [poison] ring, or merely given its unofficial sanction to the killing thru financial or other support.

There are very few specifics, and there is no indication that the CIA initiated or did anything in this supposed plot.

Here is William Colby's submission to the Rockefeller Commission about the supposed poison pen attack:

> Charles DeGaulle
>
> On 25 May 1967, a French citizen, who had had contact with the Agency since 1955 and was recruited in Africa in 1958, signaled his case officer by means of an accommodation telephone in Germany for an emergency meeting. He was met the same night in Rome by his case officer. The French citizen had long been distressed with DeGaulle's foreign policy in Africa and offered to take advantage of his invitation to a reception for DeGaulle on 30 May 1967 in Italy to shake DeGaulle's hand, wearing a poison ring if we cared to provide one for the purpose. The case officer immediately treated the proposal not only as not meriting serious consideration but also stating that he did not engage in such activities. In a dispatch dated 8 June 1967, Headquarters replied that the case officer's "response to [the] proposal related in [the cable] and his handling of the situation was correct and fitting."

This never turned into a CIA embarrassment because nothing happened. The producers of *JFK: Destiny Betrayed* thought the *Chicago Tribune* headline could serve their purposes without informing their audience that the proposal to poison de Gaulle was rejected.

A NOTE ON HUMAN MEMORY

An important factor that is quite often unexplored in the JFK assassination literature is human memory. Witnesses remember all sorts of things, and quite often their memories clash with one another. Estimates of size, length, and timeframes can vary dramatically. And so, it is vitally important to consider the frailties of human memory when evaluating evidence.

This was all brought home to me several years ago when I was visiting my sister in Boston. She had bought front-row tickets for Andrew and me to a murder mystery play. Right before our eyes, we saw the supposed perpetrator walk into a building, we heard shots being fired, and we saw him run from the building. A police detective then came on the set and started asking the audience questions about what had happened. What was the perpetrator wearing? What was he carrying? How many shots were fired?

I was amazed that despite this all playing out right in front of me just seconds earlier, I couldn't answer all his questions. Furthermore, the answers from the audience were all over the map. It was a vivid illustration of how memory works or how it doesn't work.

In the JFK assassination, even the witnesses who testified before the Warren Commission often were called several months after the fact. They were subject to no shortage of news stories about what had happened, and no doubt that affected some witnesses. Witnesses before the HSCA were testifying over a decade after the assassination.

JFK: Destiny Betrayed relies upon many witness statements before the ARRB, some thirty years after JFK was killed. That is a lot of time. Elizabeth Loftus, an expert on memory, noted that:

> Individuals are particularly susceptible to having their memories modified when the passage of time allows the original memory to fade. In its weakened condition, memory, like a disease-ridden body, becomes especially vulnerable to repeated assaults.

And as we know, many witnesses read a variety of JFK assassination books and were exposed to a variety of conspiracy theories. Can we be certain that did not affect their memories?

An internal ARRB staff report on medical records said that their "single largest problem is the passage of time and the fallibility of memory."

This concern was reflected in their final report:

> Memories fade over time. A very important figure in the chain-of-custody on the autopsy materials, and the living person who perhaps more than any other would have been able to resolve some of the lingering questions related to the disposition of the original autopsy materials, is Robert Bouck of the Secret Service. At the time he was interviewed he was quite elderly and little able to remember the important details. Similarly, the records show that Carl Belcher, formerly of the Department of Justice, played an important role in preparing the inventory of autopsy records. He was, however, unable to identify or illuminate the records that, on their face, appear to have been written by him.
>
> Finally, a significant problem that is well known to trial lawyers, judges, and psychologists, is the unreliability of eyewitness testimony. Witnesses frequently, and inaccurately, believe that they have a vivid recollection of events. Psychologists and scholars have long-since demonstrated the serious unreliability of peoples' recollections of what they hear and see. One illustration of this was an interview statement made by one of the treating physicians at Parkland. He explained that he was in Trauma Room Number 1 with the President. He recounted how he observed the First Lady wearing a white dress. Of course, she was wearing a pink suit, a fact known to most Americans. The inaccuracy of his recollection probably says little about the quality of the doctor's memory, but it is revealing of how the memory works and how cautious one must be when attempting to evaluate eyewitness testimony.
>
> The deposition transcripts and other medical evidence that were released by the Review Board should be evaluated cautiously by the public. Often the witnesses contradict not only each other, but sometimes themselves. For events that transpired almost 35 years ago, all persons are likely to have failures of memory. It would be more prudent to weigh all of the evidence, with due concern for human error, rather than take single statements as "proof" for one theory or another.

Jeremy Gunn, executive director and general counsel of the ARRB, gave a speech at Stanford University in 1998. Here is what he had to say about memory:

> The last thing I wanted to mention, just in terms of how we understand the evidence and how we deal with what we have is what I call is the profound unreliability of eyewitness testimony. You just cannot believe it. And I can tell you something else that is even worse than eyewitness testimony and that is 35-year-old eyewitness testimony.
>
> I have taken the depositions of several people who were involved in phases of the Kennedy assassination, all the doctors who performed the autopsy of President Kennedy and people who witnessed various things and they are profoundly unreliable.
>
> There were two FBI agents who were present at the autopsy. They basically, I will exaggerate this, they were with each other all night long and they came out and they wrote a report about what they had seen. I took the depositions of these two people, 35 years later. Their stories just were not the same story. Neither one of their stories moved in any direction to prove that anyone had done anything bad or good with … [break in the tape] didn't witness it, their testimonies are different. So, you are going to come up with two different sorts of stories.
>
> There is one doctor, this will be the conclusion of the eyewitness testimony, there is one doctor who was one of the treating physicians of President Kennedy at Parkland Hospital whom I interviewed. And I asked him some questions and he said he remembered that day, very, very vividly He remembered being in the treating room with President Kennedy in Parkland Memorial Hospital. He remembered seeing Jackie Kennedy walk in. He had never seen her before and what a stunning moment that was for him and how traumatic it was. There was the President who had just died. There's his widow who was there with him. "That just burned in my memory," he said. "I remember Jackie being there in a white suit."
>
> And I thought absolutely everyone in the United States knows that Jackie Kennedy was wearing a pink suit. This is the only guy in the United States who thinks that she was wearing a white suit. There are people who were never present at the autopsy, were never present at Bethesda, never saw Dallas … everyone knows Jackie was wearing a pink suit. Here you have one of the treating physicians who remembers

> Jackie wearing a white suit. I assume he wasn't lying to me. I assume he wasn't trying to trick me, and I assume he didn't have a second suit theory.
>
> None of this was true. But here he has this memory. And he described some other things about the treatment of President Kennedy. Let's suppose that I think he's wrong on what he says about something that happened in the treatment room. What can I say? "This guy is so wrong he doesn't even remember what kind of suit Jackie Kennedy was wearing!" You can dismiss his testimony, just dismiss it.
>
> Or suppose that I think what he says happened at the treating room is what I think happened too. His memory of the suit, that's not relevant. What is relevant is his professional skill as a doctor. He's not into fashion, he's into being into medicine, so I can trust what he is saying here.
>
> And that's one of the problems that you have with the Kennedy assassination. You have all this wealth of information and people pick and choose, and then they refute, they argue against one person, they can use an inconsistency that they have made, and you end up having all this confusion.

At one point in Gunn's speech, he mentions Saundra Spencer and her allegations about the autopsy photographs (see Chapter 18). He then said something interesting:

> One of the things that is crazy about the JFK assassination is that people come up and say all kinds of nutty things. The number of people who claim to be former CIA officers who were present in Dallas on November 22nd … you could fill a stadium with them. And what do you do when somebody says, "I was a CIA officer, or somebody told me that they were a CIA officer, and they were instructed to go to Dallas on Nov. 22nd." You know, that's possible. How do we find that out? And so, we have chased down a lot of leads by that. By, we go to the CIA, we go through the filing system, we go through the record system, and try to identify people. One thing that you end up believing, if nothing else, is that people are not reliable about what they say about what they have done in the past and what they saw and observed. In some cases, because they are just outright con people, not

> con men, but con people and something they don't know or sometimes there is just a little bit of exaggeration of the story.

An interesting juxtaposition to be sure.

As you read through the sections on the medical evidence, you will notice that the issues of memory, which are so prevalent in this case, are never mentioned in *JFK: Destiny Betrayed*.

THE MEDICAL EVIDENCE

JFK: Destiny Betrayed tries to impugn the authenticity of JFK's autopsy X-rays and photographs. The film doesn't come right out and say that the autopsy materials have been altered. It simply implies that there are other autopsy X-rays and photographs that have not seen the light of day. In addition, it relies upon the recollections of the doctors at Parkland Hospital to refute the much better evidence from the autopsy.

CHAPTER 7
WAS JFK'S THROAT WOUND ONE OF ENTRANCE?

(EPISODE 2, 4:01)

JFK: Destiny Betrayed alleges that the wound in JFK's throat was one of entrance. The preponderance of evidence indicates that it was an exit wound. In fact, every forensic pathologist who has examined the autopsy X-rays and photographs believes a bullet exited from Kennedy's throat.

Here is an excerpt from a transcript:

Narrator (Whoopi Goldberg): After Air Force One left Dallas for Washington, two of the key doctors who had tried to save Kennedy's life at Parkland Hospital held a press conference. They were Dr. Malcolm Perry and Dr. Kemp Clark.

Oliver Stone: What were the two major points of evidence that were revealed by Kemp Clark and Malcolm Perry at the press conference?

Dr. Gary Aguilar: Dr. Perry performed the tracheotomy to help Kennedy breathe and at a press conference, right after the failed resuscitation efforts in Dallas, he was asked, well where was the bullet? And he says, well the bullet looked like it was coming at him. He had an entrance wound in the throat.

The film presents a short screenshot from the transcript of the press conference held at Parkland Hospital at 2:16 p.m. in Dallas:

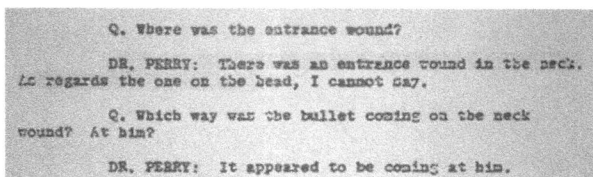

Q. Where was the entrance wound?

DR. PERRY: There was an entrance wound in the neck. As regards the one on the head, I cannot say.

Q. Which way was the bullet coming on the neck wound? At him?

DR. PERRY: It appeared to be coming at him.

Dr. Perry was so uncertain about the wounds that he suggested that the massive head wound might have been related to the bullet entering JFK's throat:

QUESTION: Can't we clear this up just a little more? In your estimation, was there one or two wounds? Just give us something.

DR. MALCOLM PERRY: I don't know. From the injury, it is conceivable that it could have been caused by one wound, but there could have been two just as well if the second bullet struck the head in addition to striking the neck, and I cannot tell you that due to the nature of the wound. There is no way for me to tell.

QUESTION: Doctor, describe the entrance wound. You think from the front in the throat?

DR. MALCOLM PERRY: The wound appeared to be an entrance wound in the front of the throat; yes, that is correct. The exit wound, I don't know. It could have been the head or there could have been a second wound of the head. There was no time to determine this at the particular instant.

I don't think there is any doubt that when Dr. Perry saw the throat wound that he believed it was one of entrance. But he wasn't performing an autopsy; he was frantically trying to save the life of President Kennedy. He only saw the wound for a few seconds—it certainly wouldn't be the first time that an attending physician's initial viewpoint would ultimately be contradicted by the autopsy.

A clear indication that throat wound was one of exit is the fact that the FBI reported that shirt fibers were pointed outward on the front of the shirt:

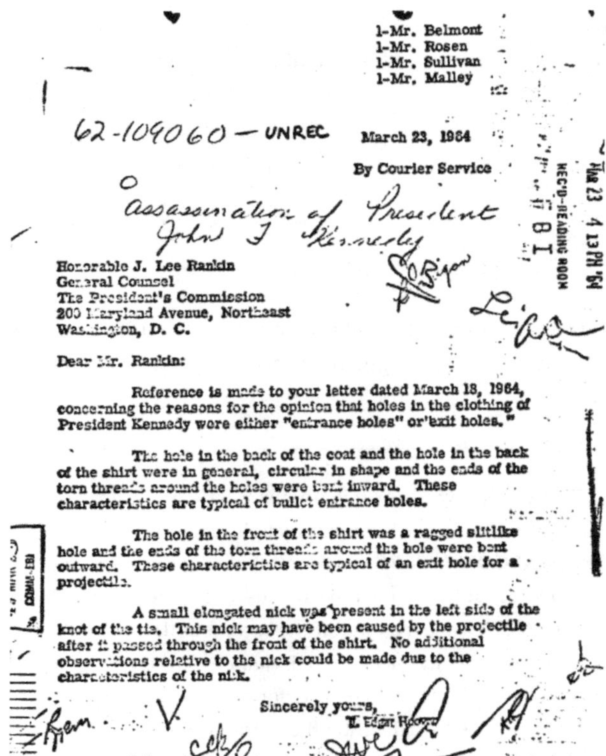

1-Mr. Belmont
1-Mr. Rosen
1-Mr. Sullivan
1-Mr. Malley

62-109060 — UNREC

March 23, 1964

By Courier Service

Assassination of President John F. Kennedy

Honorable J. Lee Rankin
General Counsel
The President's Commission
200 Maryland Avenue, Northeast
Washington, D. C.

Dear Mr. Rankin:

Reference is made to your letter dated March 18, 1964, concerning the reasons for the opinion that holes in the clothing of President Kennedy were either "entrance holes" or "exit holes."

The hole in the back of the coat and the hole in the back of the shirt were in general, circular in shape and the ends of the torn threads around the holes were bent inward. These characteristics are typical of bullet entrance holes.

The hole in the front of the shirt was a ragged slitlike hole and the ends of the torn threads around the hole were bent outward. These characteristics are typical of an exit hole for a projectile.

A small elongated nick was present in the left side of the knot of the tie. This nick may have been caused by the projectile after it passed through the front of the shirt. No additional observations relative to the nick could be made due to the characteristics of the nick.

Sincerely yours,
J. Edgar Hoover

Dr. Cyril Wecht, a renowned forensic pathologist and long-time critic of the Warren Report, reviewed the autopsy X-rays and photographs in 1972. Here is an illustration from Dr. Wecht's article on the medical evidence:

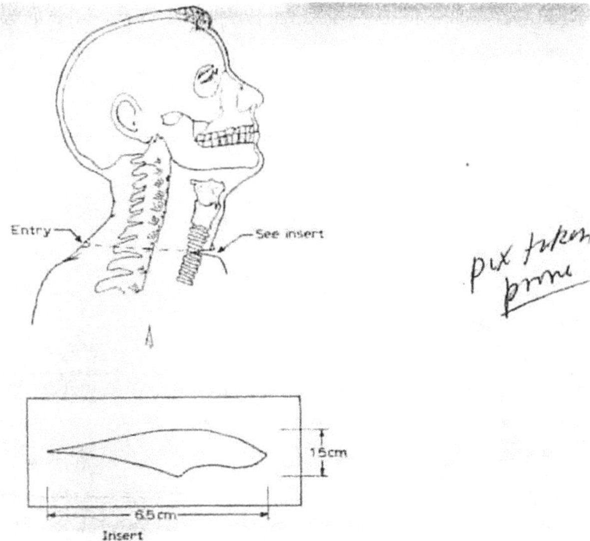

Fig. 6. Schematic representation of the locations of the wounds in the President's back and throat. The presumed entry wound is about 6 cm below the lowest crease in the back of the neck. The tracheotomy incision (see insert) is at about the level of the third and fourth tracheal rings (the thyroid gland is not shown in the sketch). The indicated pathway of the bullet is downward (about 3 cm over a distance of 15 cm), yielding an angle of 11 or 12 degrees, whereas the Warren Commission, without actual measurement of the wound itself, postulated a flight angle of about 18 degrees (after correcting for a 3-degree slope of the street).

In 2021, Dr. Wecht published *The JFK Assassination Dissected*, and he still believes the throat wound was one of exit.

> I explained how the bullet that hit Kennedy and missed Connally likely continued onward to crack the limo's windshield, leaving a dent on the chrome.

Dr. Malcolm Perry was interviewed by the HSCA in 1978:

> **Dr. Perry**: And I asked for a tracheotomy tray. And Betty Henscliff, one of the nurses had already prepared it, and I dropped my coat in the corner and put on some gloves and started to prepare to do a tracheotomy to get the airway. At that time, I noted a wound in the anterior aspect of the neck in the lower third, which was roughly round, exuding very slowly dark blood, partially obscuring its edges. The wound was somewhere probably 4 to 6 millimeters in diameter. I

did not, however, wipe the blood off and inspect the wound, but gave it a cursory glance while I was putting my gloves on and preparing the trach tray.

He said that he "gave it [the throat wound] a cursory glance." Perry was specifically asked about the throat wound:

Q: Could you give us a characterization of the edges of the anterior neck wound?

Dr. Perry: I previously pointed out that they were neither ragged nor clean cut and I supposed that's a misnomer because actually I didn't inspect it that well. What I meant to infer by that initial description was the fact that I couldn't see a clean punched wound. It was roughly round, the edges were bruised and a little blurred, because as I mentioned there was several big drops of old blood and some of it coagulated of course, on and about the wound. I didn't really inspect the margins carefully. I think the terms I used before was neither ragged nor clean-cut, and that may not have been appropriate. I probably should have said, I couldn't see them that well, might have been a better answer.

And as to the origin of the bullet?

Q: Do you have an opinion based on those two points that you described as to the origin of the missile that caused the damage?

Dr. Perry: No, I don't. The reason is that I didn't clearly identify either an entrance or an exit wound, and in the press conference I indicated that the neck wound appeared like an entrance wound. And I based this mainly on its size and the fact that exit wounds in general tend to be somewhat ragged and somewhat different from entrance wounds. Now this doesn't pertain, of course, in bullets that are deformable or bullets that are tumbling. And many bullets, especially fired from handguns and this sort of thing, tend to tumble, and as a result, they may make keyhole injuries and various things. But in general, full-jacketed bullets made pretty small entrance holes, and so, I don't really know. I thought it looked like an entrance wound because

> it was small, but I didn't look for any others, and so that was just a guess.

Perry says, "full-jacketed bullets [which is what Oswald used] make pretty small entrance holes."

The HSCA Forensic Pathology Panel concluded it was an exit wound:

> The panel believes that Parkland doctors mistakenly identified the defect in the neck as an entrance wound because of its small size, which is characteristic of an entrance wound but occurs not uncommonly in exit wounds caused by high velocity missiles that have passed through soft tissue. It is also possible that this exit wound may have been small because the tissues through which the missile exited were supported by clothing, inhibiting the normally extensive distortion or tearing often characteristic of an exit wound. In addition, the Parkland doctors had not looked at the President's back and did not realize there was another perforation.

In August of 1998, Dr. Perry met with the ARRB:

> **Dr. Perry**: As I testified, I made only a cursory examination of the head, and the only person that made the really detailed examination, as far as I know, is Dr. Clark. And I didn't—like Dr. Jones. I didn't look at it. I was in some kind of hurry.
>
> The neck wound—very few people saw that. I didn't even wipe the blood off on the right side, so I estimated it at five millimeters or so of exuding blood and I cut right through it, as Dr. Jones knows, so nobody else saw it after that. It was small, I didn't examine it. I could see that he had one. I mentioned the avulsive wound to the head and what appeared to be some brain tissue and that was during the course of resuscitation, but I didn't examine it.

He reiterated his initial impressions:

Mr. Gunn: Talk briefly about the neck wound, if we could. Dr. Perry, do you think that you were the one who probably had the best view of the neck wound?

Dr. Perry: I'm the one that stuck my foot in my mouth, but actually it looked like an entrance wound and the bullet appeared to be coming at him and I based that mainly on the fact that it was a small wound to the neck and without any other information.

I prefaced those comments at the press conference both before and after by saying that neither Dr. Clark nor I knew how many bullets there were or where they came from. Unfortunately, my comment said it's an entrance wound, and that was taken out of context of the others, but I did say that small wound.

As I mentioned earlier, however, I didn't take any measurements. I didn't wipe the blood off. I just went through it, and it was the thing to do at the time; had no concept about legal things. We did what we were trained to do.

Dr. Ronald Jones told the ARRB that after his testimony to the Warren Commission, Arlen Specter, assistant counsel responsible for determining the facts of the assassination, followed him out into the hall to tell him that they were convinced the shot came from behind. Jones said that Specter asked him not to say anything about the wound. He told the ARRB, "I don't know whether you construe that as pressure or not, but certainly I was surprised that he said don't say about—anything about that to anyone." And so, they asked Dr. Perry if he had been pressured:

Dr. Perry: Apropos, that you asked Dr. Jones, I had exactly the opposite experience. I was advised by almost everybody I talked to, Secret Service, FBI, and the Warren Commission counsel to tell the truth as best I knew it in its entirety and to hold nothing back on every occasion, and that occurred on a number of occasions that they asked me to be sure that it was everything as best I knew it no matter what. So, I can say at least for me they seemed to make every effort to get at—

Mr. Gunn: Uh-huh

Dr. Perry: —the truth.

Dr. Peters: I certainly agree with that.

There is a reason why we have autopsies. A study published in the *Journal of the American Medical Association* concluded that:

> The study, which looked at single, perforating (exiting) gunshot wounds and multiple gunshot wounds, found that trauma specialists made errors in 52% of the cases, either in differentiating the entrance and exit wound, or in determining the number of bullets that struck the victim.

JFK: Destiny Betrayed does not tell the entire truth about the wound in Kennedy's throat. The preponderance of evidence indicates that it was an exit wound.

CHAPTER 8
WAS DR. PERRY PRESSURED TO CHANGE HIS OPINION?

(EPISODE 2, 8:38)

JFK: Destiny Betrayed uses James Gochenaur, a former student at the University of Washington in Seattle, to support the allegation that Dr. Perry was pressured to change his views on the throat wound of President Kennedy.

Gochenaur was not a direct witness to anything, but he did have conversations with ex-Secret Service agent Elmer Moore and ex-FBI agent Carver Gayton.

There are some good reasons to question Gochenaur's credibility. Here is an excerpt from a transcript:

Dr. Donald Miller: One of the main reasons he [Dr. Perry] changed his testimony and publicly agreed it was an exit wound is, a Secret Service agent put the pressure on him, and that person was Elmer Moore. He apparently was also in charge of getting the doctors at Parkland, in addition to Dr. Perry, to change their testimony and agree that there was no big hole in the back of Kennedy's head and that the bullet wound in the neck was an exit wound. In 1970, Elmer Moore was the head of the Secret Service office in Seattle and a graduate student named Jim Gochenaur became friends with him and he admitted to Gochenaur that he regretted putting pressure on Dr. Perry.

James Gochenaur: So, I asked him directly, I said, "Mr. Moore, did you pressure Dr. Perry?" He stopped for a minute, and he says "Well, I was ordered to do that." He expanded on it, and he said that Inspector [Thomas] Kelley had ordered him to talk with Perry and convince him that it could be either an exit or an entry wound. Not an entry wound. And I thought it was pretty interesting that he would admit to something that's pretty close to a felony.

Interestingly, Gochenaur claims that Moore did not pressure Perry to say that it was an exit wound but rather to say that it could be either. But in a 1977 phone interview with the HSCA, Gochenaur said that Moore told him he had "badgered" Perry into "making a flat statement that there was no entry wound in the neck."

Elmer Moore did talk to the Dallas doctors. It's not clear if he pressured Perry at all or if he just informed him of the autopsy conclusions. Is Gochenaur the right witness to back up the allegation?

In the early 1970s, Gochenaur corresponded with conspiracy theorist Harold Weisberg. Here is an excerpt from his letter on May 10, 1971:

Malcom Perry interview

A. No date on notes:
(Moore said it was the 28th
or 29th of NOV.)

B. Moore brought with him
Humes report.

C. Moore told me several times
he did not "twist Perry's arm",
which leads me to believe he
might have.

D. Perry said he did not see
a back wound.

e. Perry did not observe a
hole near the top. front of
right ear.

Courtesy of The Weisberg Collection. Hood College, Frederick, MD, USA. URL: http://jfk.hood.edu/

Point C is interesting:

> Moore told me several times he did not "twist Perry's arm," which leads me to believe he might have.

So, in *JFK: Destiny Betrayed,* we get Gochenaur's interpretation of what Moore said rather than what he actually said. Got it?

CHAPTER 9
IS DR. CHARLES CRENSHAW A CREDIBLE WITNESS?

Charles Crenshaw (Photo by Yann Gamblin/Paris Match via Getty Images)

(EPISODE 2, 9:59)

JFK: Destiny Betrayed features Dr. Charles Crenshaw to bolster its claim that President Kennedy was shot from the front. Viewers are not informed of Dr. Crenshaw's credibility problems.

Here is an excerpt from a transcript:

> **Narrator (Whoopi Goldberg)**: Charles Crenshaw, a third-year resident, was in the emergency room at Parkland that day. He, too, later said in public that he felt the wounds in Kennedy originated from the front.
>
> [Archive Clip] **Dr. Charles Crenshaw**: From here, right through …
>
> **Dr. Gary Aguilar**: Charles Crenshaw wrote a book, *Conspiracy of Silence,* in the wake of the film *JFK,* saying, look, I was at Parkland Hospital. I saw Kennedy and was involved in the treatment. And Kennedy's wounds were not consistent with a shot from above and behind because he had a defect involving the right rear of his head.
>
> [Archive Clip] **Dr. Charles Crenshaw**: I looked at the wound again. I wanted to know and remember this the rest of my life. And the rest of my life, I will always know he was shot from the front.

In 1992, Dr. Crenshaw released his book *JFK: Conspiracy of Silence,* which he coauthored with Jens Hansen and long-time assassination researcher Gary Shaw. He claimed that there was a blowout in the back of Kennedy's head consistent with a shot from the front, that Kennedy had an entrance wound in his neck, that Parkland doctors were afraid to speak out, that he had spoken to Lyndon Johnson while Oswald was being operated on, and that Kennedy's wounds had been altered.

The cover promised "headline-making new revelations" from Dr. Crenshaw, that is, a first-person account, which most of it is.

Crenshaw feared the Secret Service:

> I relived the tactics of intimidation practiced by the Secret Service agents. The "men in suits," as we referred to them, struck fear into Parkland's personnel as the agents went about providing more protection and concern for a dead President than they had shown for a living President. I followed the heavily armed agents as their entourage surrounding the casket escorted President Kennedy's body out of Parkland Hospital, their arrogance almost palpable; Jacqueline Kennedy walked alongside, her hand resting on the coffin.

Dr. Crenshaw explained what he meant by a "conspiracy of silence":

> Every doctor who was in Trauma Room 1 had his own reasons for not publicly refuting the "official line."
>
> I believe there was a common denominator in our silence—a fearful proposition that to come forward with what we believed to be the medical truth would be asking for trouble. Although we never admitted it to one another, we realized that the inertia of the established story was so powerful, so thoroughly presented, so adamantly accepted, that it would bury anyone who stood in its path. ... I was as afraid of the men in suits as I was of the men who had assassinated the President. Whatever was happening was larger than any of us. I reasoned that anyone who would go so far as to eliminate the President of the United States would surely not hesitate to kill a doctor.

Researcher John McAdams said that this "is almost breathtaking in its absurdity."

> Crenshaw published a book in 1992 claiming he was breaking a "conspiracy of silence." Yet the other Parkland doctors had been talking their heads off for nearly 30 years by this time. Many have talked to conspiracy authors like Groden, Lifton and Livingstone. Their statements can be seen in books like *Six Seconds in Dallas, High Treason, High Treason II,* and *Best Evidence*. They can be seen in videos such as *The Men Who Killed Kennedy*, Bob Groden's *The Case for Conspiracy*, and NOVA's Who Shot JFK? Most have given statements that—if they have been quoted accurately—imply a conspiracy. The conspiracy writers (including Gary Aguilar) know this, because the have been quoting these doctors extensively!

Crenshaw believed that the cover-up efforts included "even death":

> Efforts to suppress and distort the truth about the assassination on the part of government officials and agents, as well as certain representatives of the media, have been well documented in previous works on the subject. That these efforts included threats, intimidation, falsification and destruction of evidence, and even death, have played no small

> role in my silence of the past twenty-eight years. I am fifty-nine years old. My medical career is over, and I no longer fear the "men in suits" nor the criticism of my peers.

Really?

Crenshaw and his coauthors even got basic details wrong:

> With sickening clarity, I recall a full-page editorial purchased by an extremist group that viciously attacked the integrity of President Kennedy by claiming he was a Communist. The President was posed in a frontal and side mug shot atop the message, "This man is wanted for treasonous activities against the United States." The article further claimed President Kennedy was "... turning the sovereignty of the U.S. over to the communist controlled United Nations." I didn't consider him a conservative Democrat, not in the southern style, anyway, but he was a long way from being a Communist.

Crenshaw recalls the editorial with "sickening clarity." The only problem is that he is describing a handbill and not the ad that was placed in the *Dallas Morning News*.

His book also contained many ridiculous conspiracy factoids, speculations that are repeated so often that they're taken as fact. For instance, Crenshaw buys into the Rose Cherami story:

> Rose Cheramie was killed on September 4, 1965, one of more than fifty individuals associated with the investigation of the Kennedy assassination who died within three years of that event. Her death, like her allegations concerning two men planning to kill the President, is shrouded in mystery.

This beggars belief. "More than fifty" mysterious deaths? This was investigated by the House Select Committee on Assassinations, and it could not find even one. As for Rose Cherami, her story was nonsense. She was a drug addict who suffered a "traumatic head wound" after being hit by a car in rural Texas.

Crenshaw also believes Julia Mercer's story that Jack Ruby was the driver of a truck that dropped off Lee Harvey Oswald, with a rifle, at about 11 a.m. the morning of the assassination:

> On Sunday, the day following her identification, she viewed the television coverage of the Oswald shooting. She immediately identified Ruby as the driver of the truck and Oswald as the man with the rifle—the same men she had previously selected from the FBI photographs.

This story is demonstrably false. Jack Ruby was in the offices of the *Dallas Morning News* and was seen by several people.

Crenshaw claimed that 75 percent of witnesses said the shots came from the grassy knoll:

> In all, 277 of the more than 700 witnesses to the shooting have been identified; 107 of these 277 have given their statements as to the origin of the shots that killed the President. Seventy-five percent, or 77 of the 107, reported at least one shot came from the President's right front—the area of the wooden fence. Though the Warren Commission stated emphatically that all of the shots were fired from the Depository building to the President's right rear, the majority of witnesses refute this conclusion.

The HSCA tally is very different—only 20 out of 171 witnesses said there was a shot from the grassy knoll. In addition, they found only 4 witnesses that "mentioned dual locations."

When discussing the single bullet theory, Crenshaw makes a bizarre statement:

> This implausible theory was presented to the American people as fact and portrayed Lee Harvey Oswald as the lone, unaided killer of the President. In doing so, the Warren Commission had to ignore the missile's broken chain of evidence, utilize an illusionary bullet trajectory, and approve obvious wound fabrication or alteration of the President's body.

"Obvious wound fabrication or alteration of the President's body"?

Dr. Crenshaw had this to say about Kennedy's head wound in his book:

> I was standing at about the President's waist, making a quick inspection of his general appearance. His face was unmarked and exquisite. His eyes were open and divergent. They were still and devoid of life. I immediately became pessimistic.
>
> Then I noticed that the entire right hemisphere of his brain was missing, beginning at this hairline and extending all the way behind his right ear. Pieces of skull that hadn't been blown away were hanging by blood-matted hair. Based upon my experience with trauma to the head from gunshots, I knew that only a high-velocity bullet from a rifle could dissect a cranium that way. Part of his brain, the cerebellum, was dangling from the back of his head by a single strand of tissue, looking like a piece of dark gray, blood-soaked sponge that would easily fit into a palm of a hand.

Crenshaw then went on the ABC show *20/20* to discuss his theories. He pointed to his temple to show where JFK's head wound started:

Dr. Marion Jenkins told Dennis Breo that he doubted Crenshaw got a great look at the head wound:

> I was standing at the head of the table in at the position the anesthesiologist most often assumes closest to the President's head. My presence there and the president's great shock of hair and the location of the head wound were such that it was not visible to those standing down each side of the gurney where they are carrying out their resuscitative maneuvers.

Dr. Perry had this to say about Crenshaw:

> When I first heard about Crenshaw's claims, I was considering a lawsuit, but after I saw Charles on TV one day all my anger melted. It was so pathetic to see him on TV saying this bogus stuff to reach out for his day in the sun that I ended up feeling sorry for him. Crenshaw says that the rest of us are part of a conspiracy of silence and that he withheld his information for 29 years because of fear his career would be ruined. Well, if he really felt he had valuable information and kept it secret all those years, I find that despicable.

Dr. Crenshaw wrote that he entered Trauma Room 1 with Dr. Robert McClelland and that he saw Kennedy's throat wound:

> Blood was still seeping from the wound onto the gurney, dripping into the kick bucket on the floor. Seeing that, I became even more pessimistic. I also identified a small opening about the diameter of a pencil at the midline of his throat to be an entry bullet hole. There was no doubt in my mind about that wound. I had seen dozens of them in the emergency room. At that point, I knew that he had been shot at least twice.

The only problem is that Dr. McClelland said that when he arrived, Dr. Perry had already made the tracheostomy incision.

> **Mr. Specter**: What did you observe, if anything, as to the status of the neck wound when you first arrived?
>
> **Mr. McClelland**: The neck wound, when I first arrived, was at this time converted into a tracheotomy incision. The skin incision had been made by Dr. Perry, and he told me—although I did not see that—that he had made the incision through a very small, perhaps less than one quarter inch in diameter wound in the neck.

When Gary Shaw showed Dr. Crenshaw a picture of Kennedy's throat wound, he said this:

> One picture showed President Kennedy's neck at the point where the bullet had entered, the spot where Dr. Malcolm Perry had performed the tracheotomy at Parkland to help the President breathe. The opening was larger and jagged—significantly different from the way it had looked to me in Dallas. There was no doubt in my mind—someone had tampered with the body, or the photographs.

The Dallas doctors took great exception to this:

> Well, the physician who did that work at Parkland—Dr. Perry—and three physicians who observed the tracheostomy—Drs. Baxter, Carrico and Jenkins—all say that the autopsy photos of the throat wound are "very compatible" with what they saw in Parkland Trauma Room 1. Dr. Baxter says, "I was right there and the tracheostomy I observed and the autopsy photos look the same—very compatible." Dr. Carrico says, "I've seen the autopsy photos and they are very compatible to the actual tracheostomy," Dr. Jenkins adds, "They're the same." Dr. Perry concludes, "Of course, tissues sag and stretch after death, but any suggestion that this wound was intentionally enlarged is wrong."

Researcher Pat Speer noticed that when Dr. Crenshaw was interviewed by the ARRB, his description of JFK's head wounds was not consistent:

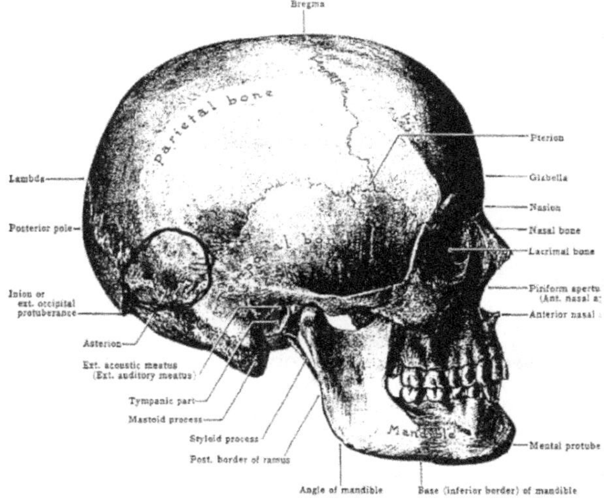

7-6 SKULL, FROM THE SIDE (NORMA LATERALIS)

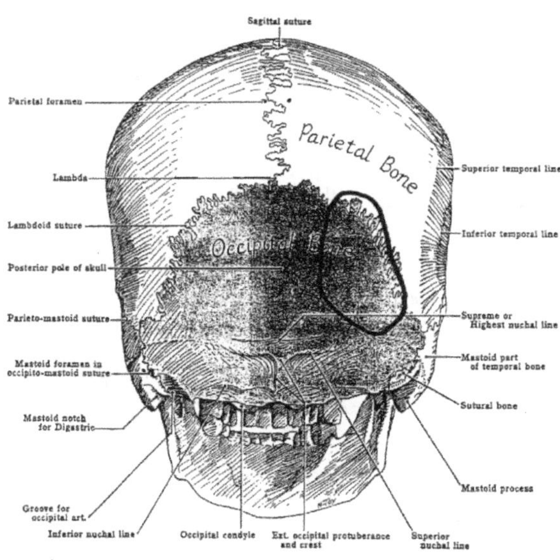

More telling, when asked to mark the wound location on a lateral drawing of the skull, Crenshaw placed the wound on the occipital and

> parietal bone, an inch or so lower, and perhaps as much as two inches forward, from the location he'd marked on the drawing from behind.

Researcher David Perry noted the strange timing of Crenshaw's belief in a conspiracy:

THE STRANGE CASE OF DOCTOR CRENSHAW

After re-reading *"JFK: Conspiracy Of Silence"* I have determined three dates are important with regard to Doctor Crenshaw's story. They are November 22, 1963 the date he treated John F. Kennedy, November 24, 1963 the date Jack Ruby shot Lee Oswald and <u>November 17, 1990</u>, the date the doctor decided his part in the "conspiracy of silence" should end.(Page 9)

Unfortunately, reviewing the book in light of those dates presents major problems. The most glaring being that Doctor Crenshaw does not remember when he decided there was a conspiracy. The result is that his motivation for coming forward is thrown into question.

Page 152 - On November 22, 1963 he states, "But if I tell them (CBS television) the medical truth, that President Kennedy was shot from the front, they have more than one gunman, they have a conspiracy." This would lead you to believe that Crenshaw knew Oswald did not act alone shortly after the doctor found Oswald was apprehended and was named as the lone assassin.

This statement looses all credibility based upon additional quotes.

Page 111 - "It wasn't until years later, when I saw autopsy pictures of John Kennedy taken at the Bethesda Naval Hospital, that I realized there was something rotten in America in 1963."

Page 154 - ". . . and when I recently saw the official autopsy pictures. I knew something had been askew."

Page 11 - Crenshaw looks at the autopsy photos again and responds, "No, these aren't the same wounds I saw at Parkland. From these pictures it appears someone performed some surgery on the head."

Crenshaw claims he saw the photographs for the first time at The JFK Assassination Information Center after November 17, 1990. He was shown those photographs by J. Gary Shaw.

If the reader becomes confused by the doctors apparent incongruity as to when he finally decided there was a plot, you need only dig a little more. It may be the doctor is on a subliminal guilt trip over his failure to act in an honest and sincere manner.

Page 203 - "From the silence of the people involved came a great miscarriage of justice . . . At best, they may be considered cowards . . . at worst, coconspirators or accessories after the fact." This statement was made after November 17, 1990.

Courtesy of The Weisberg Collection. Hood College, Frederick, MD, USA. URL: http://jfk.hood.edu/

Perry also researched one of the bigger stories to come out of Crenshaw's book: his assertion that he talked to Lyndon Johnson while Lee Harvey Oswald was being operated on after being shot on November 24, 1963. Johnson supposedly told Crenshaw to get a deathbed confession from Oswald.

The only problem with this claim is that none of the White House records show any calls from LBJ to Parkland Hospital. Perry retrieved all the phone logs and his calendar of events:

THE WHITE HOUSE
WASHINGTON

TELEPHONE MEMORANDUM

The President Nov 24, 1963

TIME	NAME	ANSWER
	Fe, Res	
10:50	Mrs. Anna Rosenberg	
	apt 249 NYC 3550451	
12:45	Secy Rusk out	"
2:30	Gov. Brown out	
	483-6400 901	
	Sen Mansfield out	
	Fe 81124 out	
2:40	Sen Humphrey out	By Ca
4:40	Gov Brown out	"
	483-6400 Rm 901	
4:55	Cong Brooks X4565 out	"
5:15	Mrs. Bundy	"
5:50	Whitney Young, out	"
6:10	[illegible] NYC	[illegible]
	[illegible]	
6:18	Whitney Young out	"
	New Rochelle	
8:25	Sen. McCarthy out	"
	at sen. Humphrey's res.	
	6543302	

U. S. GOVERNMENT PRINTING OFFICE

Crenshaw claims that he told Dr. Thomas Shires about the call immediately after he got off the phone. But no other doctor has mentioned this phone call.

There also are no contemporaneous documents to support the allegation. All the doctors wrote reports on what happened, and no one wrote about a phone call with Johnson.

Perry interviewed C. Jack Price, who was the Parkland Hospital administrator in 1963. Price told Perry that the Johnson phone call did not occur:

> As an administrator, the switchboard operators reported to Price. Because of the number of Federal officials on scene, Price felt it impossible for a switchboard operator to get a call from the President of the United States and not notify anyone. He also thought it inconceivable that a call would be forwarded to Crenshaw, who Price called a "junior resident" without Crenshaw reporting it.

Conspiracy theorist Harrison Livingstone claimed that originally Crenshaw had written that Johnson wanted Oswald killed. Gus Russo sent an email to John McAdams saying that this story is true:

> One night at the Stoneleigh [Hotel], [Oliver] Stone was having a slew of top-secret meetings in his suite with people like Ricky White, whom Stone paid $80,000 for his fraudulent story, and the positively goofy Beverly Oliver. That night, Stone ushered Gary Shaw, [Robert] Groden and Crenshaw into his room; I was not invited, but I pressed Shaw (Crenshaw's and Oliver's advisor) for info in the lobby. He was the first to tell me that LBJ ordered Oswald killed. Later, Crenshaw came down, and we happened to be in the Stoneleigh men's room at the same time, standing at adjacent urinals. It was there that he told me that Johnson had ordered the Parkland staff to "kill the son-of-a-bitch." It was decided to "drown Oswald in his own blood," i.e., transfuse him until his lungs collapsed. (E-mail to the author dated August 25, 2003)

I sent this to Gus Russo, and he confirmed the story to me.

Viewers of *JFK: Destiny Betrayed* will learn none of this and will not be told that Dr. Crenshaw has significant credibility issues.

CHAPTER 10
WAS THERE A BIG DEFECT IN THE BACK OF JFK'S HEAD?

(EPISODE 2, 11:48)

JFK: Destiny Betrayed misleads viewers on the opinions of Parkland Hospital doctors and Bethesda witnesses regarding JFK's head wound.

Here is an excerpt from a transcript:

> **Dr. Gary Aguilar**: The Warren Commission heard testimony from a number of witnesses, including Parkland doctors by the way, and including a Secret Service agent, Clint Hill, that the right rear quadrant of the head was missing.
>
> **Narrator (Whoopi Goldberg)**: Hill was the only Secret Service agent to run to the presidential limousine during the shooting. He later said there was blood and brain tissue hurling back over the trunk of the car. And as he approached the president, he saw a large wound in the rear of the skull, which he could see through with no brain there.
>
> …
>
> **Douglas Horne:** Both [Frank] Sibert and [James] O'Neill [two FBI agents present at the autopsy] were shown the photographs of the back of JFK's head, the autopsy photographs that are the most controversial. And they both said that they didn't see anything like that at the autopsy. O'Neill had said "it looks like it's been doctored. I don't mean the photo's been doctored, it looks like the head has been put

back together by embalmers and then photographed." That is what he said under oath. Sibert did not remember drawing a diagram of the wound for the House committee, so he drew a new one for the Review Board. and it's one of our most important wound diagrams. And it shows what can only be an exit defect in the right rear of the skull.

[Archive Clip] **Sibert**: There was a piece about the size of a 3x5 card that was missing.

Narrator (Whoopi Goldberg): In 1979, the House Select Committee Report stated that 26 people present at the autopsy in Bethesda all disagreed with the Parkland doctors' descriptions of Kennedy's head wound.

Oliver Stone: When you went through the declassified affidavits that the House Select Committee prepared, what did you find about the alleged differences between the Parkland and Bethesda witnesses on this issue?

Dr. David Mantik: Not only were we allowed to see their statements, but we were allowed to see the sketches where they had drawn the big hole on the back of the head. And this was totally opposite of what the House Select Committee had told us.

Dr. Gary Aguilar: When the Assassination Records Review Board came along, out comes those witness statements, out come the diagrams, and lo and behold, it turns out that the witnesses at the autopsy all agreed with the doctors at Dallas that the defect involved the rear of the head. And the summary statement basically misrepresented that truth. They basically lied about what was there.

The problem with this segment in *JFK: Destiny Betrayed* is that we are dealing with human beings and their imperfect memories. The Parkland doctors saw this mass of matted hair and blood for a very short period. As you can expect, their recollections are all over the map, and there is no unanimity of opinion.

The same goes for other witnesses like Secret Service agents, technicians at the autopsy, and other observers at Bethesda. Over time, their recollections change, and you can imagine that thirty-year-old memories tend to be erratic:

> Since there are often different elements to the testimony of any witness, the odds are pretty good that most witnesses will be wrong about something. Thus, even if you select random witnesses or the best witnesses, you can get a majority that support some wrong conclusions if you pick and choose among the elements of their testimony.

Dr. Aguilar claims that Clint Hill "saw a large wound in the rear of the skull which he could see through with no brain there." Here is an excerpt from his statement from November 30, 1963:

> As I lay over the top of the back seat I noticed a portion of the President's head on the right rear side was missing and he was bleeding profusely. Part of his brain was gone. I saw a part of his skull with hair on it lying in the seat. The time of the shooting was approximately 12:30 p.m., Dallas time. I looked forward to the jump seats and noticed Governor Connally's chest was covered with blood and he was slumped to his left and partially covered up by his wife. I had not realized until this point that the Governor had been shot.

Given the fact that Hill was rather busy trying to help Jackie Kennedy back to her seat, it seems clear that Hill didn't have time to do a forensic examination. His description above is hardly at odds with what happened. He also told *National Geographic* that there was "a gaping hole above his right ear about the size of my palm."

Douglas Horne mentions the wound diagram that Sibert drew for the ARRB in 1997:

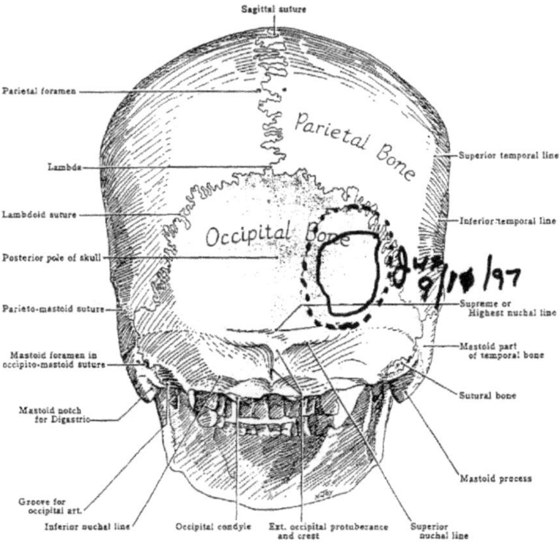

However, Sibert's sketch for the HSCA in 1977 was very different:

Sibert told the HSCA that Kennedy had "a large head wound in the upper back of the head."

And here is the chart that Sibert's partner, Francis O'Neill, drew for the HSCA:

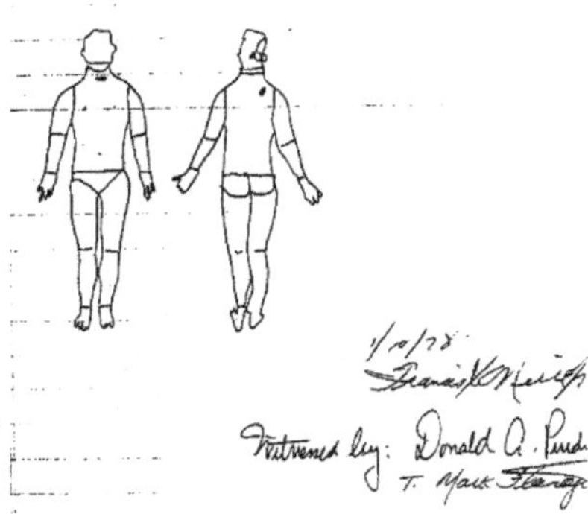

They were partners, and yet their memories differ. This is not out of the ordinary. Witnesses frequently give differing accounts. It is a good illustration of why we needn't rely on nonmedical witnesses for the evaluation of JFK's wounds when the autopsy X-rays and photographs are available for examination.

As for the doctors at Parkland Hospital, it is important to remember that they were trying frantically to resuscitate President Kennedy. It was not their job to examine wounds. A lot of people were in Trauma Room 1, and JFK was in there for less than twenty minutes. Here is an excerpt from testimony before the ARRB by Dr. Peters: (Emphasis added.)

Jeremy Gunn: Now, I am approaching this as a layperson, which may be good or may be bad. I would have imagined myself if I had seen President Kennedy in Trauma Room 1 and this part of the skull—the part that's within Line 1 of Dr. Boswell—if this were missing, I would imagine it would be noticeable to me as a layperson that there is severe damage to the skull. Is—would that be a misperception on my part?

Dr. Peters: Depends on which angle you approached him.

Dr. McClelland: From the front you might not—

Dr. Peters: right.

Dr. McClelland: —think that.

Dr. Peters: That's right.

Jeremy Gunn: So, none of you made observations that would—or maybe the question is: Did any of you see any appearance of damage by looking just at the scalp and just at the hair that would suggest that that much of the skull was missing, or were you even in the position to be able to—

Dr. Jones: Well, I think you could see the top part of the head reasonably well. He had a very thick bushy head of hair—

Dr. Peters: Yeah.

Dr. Jones: —and ***it was difficult to see down through the hair.***

Dr. Baxter: All—

Dr. Jones: I didn't see any indentation of the skull or anything like half of the top of the head was missing.

Dr. Baxter: All matted with blood. ***Unless you were up there and directly examining it, I don't think anybody could make a statement from what I saw. I mean it was just one mass of blood and hair.***

Dr. Peters: I was amazed when I saw the first X-ray of the skull—the lateral skull of the extent of the fragmentation of the skull. I did not appreciate that I think because ***a lot of it was covered by scalp at the time we worked on him. We were doing a resuscitation, not a forensic autopsy.***

Dr. Aguilar, who is an ophthalmologist and not a forensic pathologist, has written about the various Parkland and Bethesda witnesses. John McAdams noted that Aguilar is "massively selective in the testimony he uses and quite tendentious in how he interprets it."

Here are some examples:

Jerrol Custer: He was an X-ray technician who told David Lifton that "he exposed, and returned to the morgue, X-rays showing that the rear of the President's head was blown off." Yet, here is his drawing for the ARRB of the head wound:

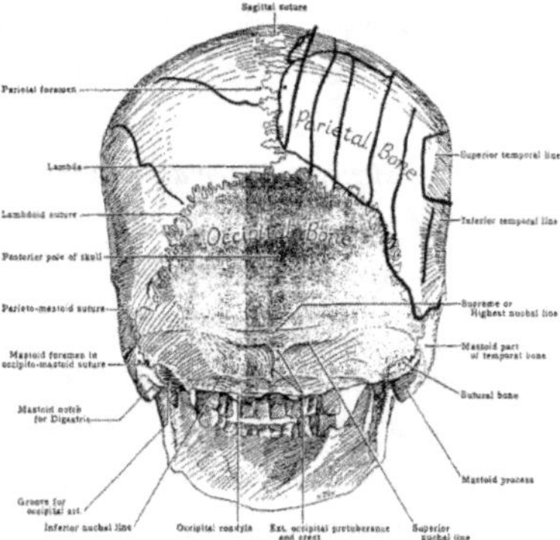

The wound is on the right side of Kennedy's head and excludes occipital bone.

Richard Lipsey: He was an aide to General Wehle and was present at the autopsy. Aguilar claims Lipsey corroborates the back of head wound witnesses, but it is not clear why. Lipsey told the HSCA that one bullet entered the back of the head and exited resulting in part of the face and head being blown away." Here is his diagram:

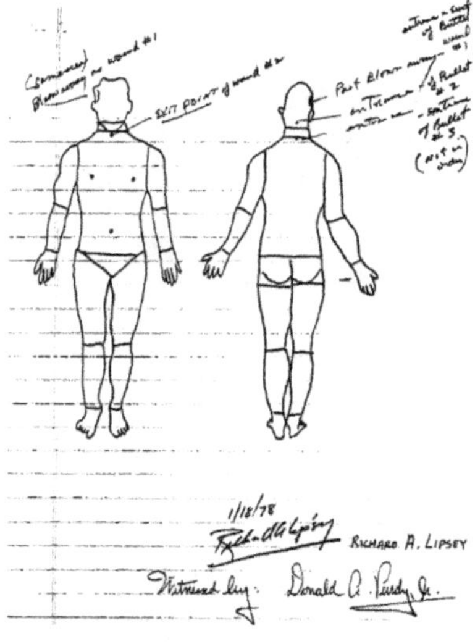

His positioning of the head wounds is quite consistent with the autopsy.

Chester Boyers: He was the chief petty officer in charge of Bethesda's Pathology department. An HSCA staff record of a phone call reported that "In regard to the wounds Boyers recalls an entrance wound in the rear of the head to the right of the external occipital protuberance which exited along the top, right side of the head towards the rear [sic] and just above the right eyebrow." Once again, this sounds quite consistent with the autopsy X-rays and photographs.

John Stringer: He was the autopsy photographer, and here is what Stringer told the ARRB:

Q: Can you tell us what President Kennedy's head looked like when it was first unwrapped?

A: It was covered with matted blood. There was a fist-sized hole in the right side of his head above the ear.

Q: How far did the hole extend?

A: It was the size of your fist, and it was entirely within the hair area. There was a sort of flap of skin there, and some of the underlying bone was gone.

Edward Reed: He was an X-ray technician at Bethesda, and here is what he told the ARRB:

Q: Did you have an opportunity at the beginning to see the back of President Kennedy's head?

A: Yes.

Q: Did you see any wounds on the back of his head?

A: No.

Q: Was the scalp intact, as far as you could observe, on the back of his head?

A: Yes.

General Philip Wehle: He was commanding officer of the military district of Washington, D.C. This is a very strange witness for Aguilar. He quotes Wehle saying he "noticed a slight bruise over the right temple of the President but did not see any significant damage to any other part of the head. He noted that the wound was in the back of the head so he would not see it because the President was lying face up." So, he didn't really see anything. According to the HSCA: "he did not see any damage to the top of the head, but said the President had a lot of hair which could have hidden that."

The key issue here is memory. Pat Speer, hardly a lone-nutter, recognizes the important research of Elizabeth Loftus on memory:

> But who am I to blather on? Here is Loftus' own summary of her findings, as published in her memoir, Witness for the Defense (1991): "As new bits and pieces of information are added into long-term memory, the old memories are removed, replaced, crumpled up, or shoved into corners. Memories don't just fade ... they also grow. What fades is the initial perception, the actual experience of the events. But every time we recall an event, we must reconstruct the memory, and with each recollection the memory may be changed—colored by succeeding events, other people's recollections or suggestions ...Truth and reality, when seen through the filter of our memories, are not objective facts but subjective, interpretive realities."
>
> As a result, I'm forced to reject the primacy of the Parkland witnesses. Their statements have been erratic from the get-go, and have only grown more erratic over time. Those holding them up as a "smoking gun" in the JFK case both misrepresent the location of the wound described by the bulk of these witnesses, and the consistency of these witnesses as a whole. There's just no "there" there.

JFK: Destiny Betrayed unfortunately never acknowledges the issue of human memory.

CHAPTER 11

DID THE HARPER FRAGMENT COME FROM THE BACK OF JFK'S HEAD?

The Harper fragment.

(EPISODE 2, 14:48)

A medical student, William Harper, found a bone fragment in Dealey Plaza on November 23, 1963. Here is an excerpt from an FBI report:

WILLIAM ALLEN HARPER, a student at Texas Christian University, Fort Worth, Texas, but who lives in Dallas at 2378 East Ledbetter Street, advised he was taking photographs during the afternoon of November 23, 1963, at approximately 5:30 P.M., in the area just south of the spot where President KENNEDY was assassinated, and had found a piece of bone. He stated the piece of bone was located approximately 25 feet south of the spot where President KENNEDY was shot.

Harper took the fragment to his uncle, Dr. Jack C. Harper, who then took it to Dr. A. B. Cairns, who was a pathologist. It does appear that his analysis was just cursory:

Dr. CAIRNS advised that he and Dr. HARPER examined the bone at Methodist Hospital of Dallas. Dr. CAIRNS stated the bone specimen looked like it came from the occipital region of the skull. He said he performed no tests on this piece of bone and evaluated it purely from its gross appearance.

JFK: Destiny Betrayed, misleads viewers into thinking the Harper fragment was occipital bone that came from the back of Kennedy's head.

Here is an excerpt from a transcript:

Narrator (Whoopi Goldberg): To make this even worse, if one looks at the official back of the head photo, there appears to be nothing missing, but there likely was something. This was a piece of bone that did not arrive in Washington until after the autopsy was over. And if it came from the back of Kennedy's skull, it created even more problems for that picture.

Dr. David Mantik: The Harper fragment was a piece of fresh skull bone that was found in Dealey Plaza, not on the day of the assassination, but later by Billy Harper.

[Archive Clip] **William Harper**: And, uh, reached down, and picked it up, and at that time, knew that I had something that most likely was significant.

Dr. Gary Aguilar: It was found in a position where the FBI said that was to the left and rear of where Jack Kennedy was when he was assassinated. It was then taken in by this medical student in to his professors and they looked at it and they said it looked like it was occipital bone, which is back here.

Narrator (Whoopi Goldberg): It measured approximately three by two inches, and therefore would have fit neatly in the rear skull wound visualized by Dr. McClelland. This bone was given to the FBI on the

25th, after the autopsy report had been written by Dr. Humes. The FBI gave it to Kennedy's physician, Admiral Burkley, at which point it disappears. All we have today are the pictures taken of it in Dallas. This bit of evidence raises the question: If the rear of the skull in the official autopsy was mostly filled in with bone fragments found in the limousine where does the Harper fragment fit?

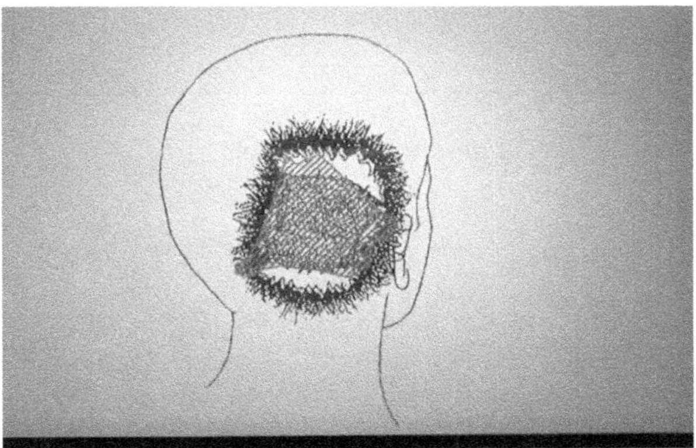

Screen shot from JFK: Destiny Betrayed *showing the Harper fragment fitting in to the supposed gaping head wound.*

So, was the Harper fragment part of Kennedy's occipital bone?

Here is an excerpt from a discussion by members of the HSCA forensic pathology panel while they were interviewing Humes and Boswell:

Dr. Petty: Dr. Angel, we have two photographs here representing what appears to be a skull fragment which was recovered by one Harper at Dealey Plaza some little time after the assassination took place. We would like very much to have your expertise in identifying where this particular fragment of skull might have arisen, that is, what part of the head bone it came from?

Dr. Angel: Well, it's clearly parietal bone, side left or right is not so easy. You can see one, two, or three markings for meningeal vessels on the inner surface.

Dr. Angel reiterated this in a report to the HSCA:

> The Harper fragment photographs show it as a roughly trapezoidal piece, 7 x 5.5 cm in size, coming mainly from the upper middle third of the right parietal bone. Near its short upper edge vascular foramins on the inside and a faint irregular line on the outside indicate sagittal suture. Its postero-inferior pointed angle appears to fit the crack in the posterior section of the right parietal and its slightly wavy lower border can fit the upper edge of the loose lower section of the right parietal. Its upper short border, on the left of the midline near vertex, may meet the left margins of the gap.

Here is his diagram of the Harper fragment:

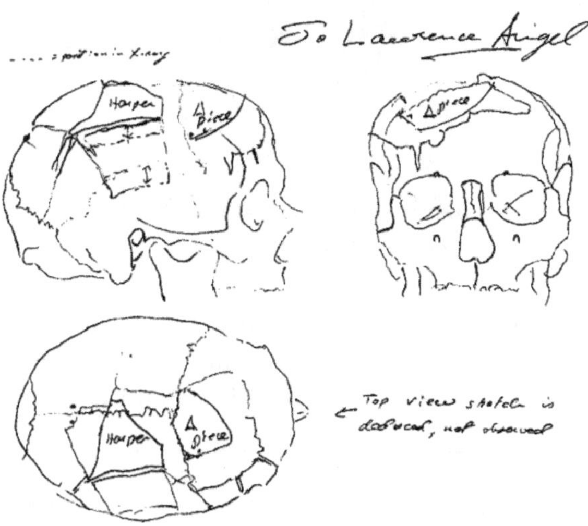

The House Select Committee on Assassinations concluded that the Harper fragment is not occipital bone:

> (324) Paper cutouts were prepared to approximate the shape and size of the bone fragments demonstrated in X-rays Nos. 4, 5, and 6 and the photograph of the "Harper bone fragment." The panel attempted to locate the correct position of these fragments and then, using the paper cutouts, to place these bone fragments on a human skull for the purposes of reconstruction. The largest of the X-ray fragments—that on

> which outer beveling and tiny metal fragments are evident—completes a portion of the exit perforation, with the suture line fitting into the coronal suture; the Harper bone fragment completes the circular perforation in the suture line immediately superior to the temporal bone. No other exit or entrance perforation is identified.

The phrase "immediately superior to the temporal bone" indicates that the Harper fragment is parietal bone.

So, where was the Harper fragment found?

Dr. Aguilar said that the Harper fragment "was found in a position that the FBI said was to the left and rear of where Jack Kennedy was when he was assassinated." There is no support for this statement in the original record. Dr. Aguilar was just applying his interpretation to the FBI language above, that Harper said the fragment was found twenty-five feet south of the spot where President Kennedy had been shot. But Harper was just guessing; he wasn't in Dealey Plaza on the 22nd and couldn't have known the exact location of the limousine at the time of the head shot.

Researcher Howard Roffman wrote Harper a letter in 1969 asking about the location of the fragment. Harper wrote back with a map showing where he found it:

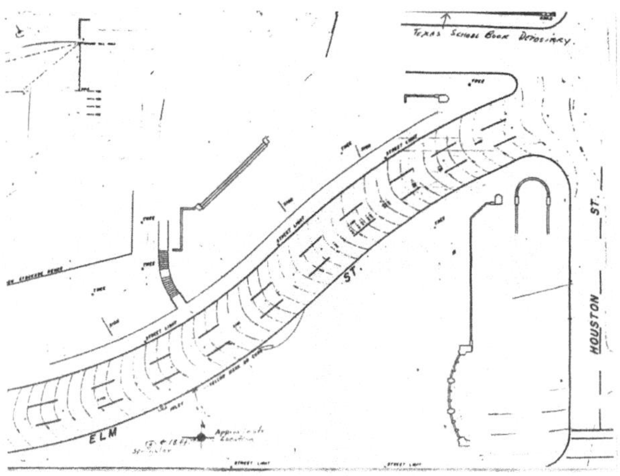

To put this into perspective, researcher Louis Girdler took this map and highlighted the location of the limousine at frame Z-313:

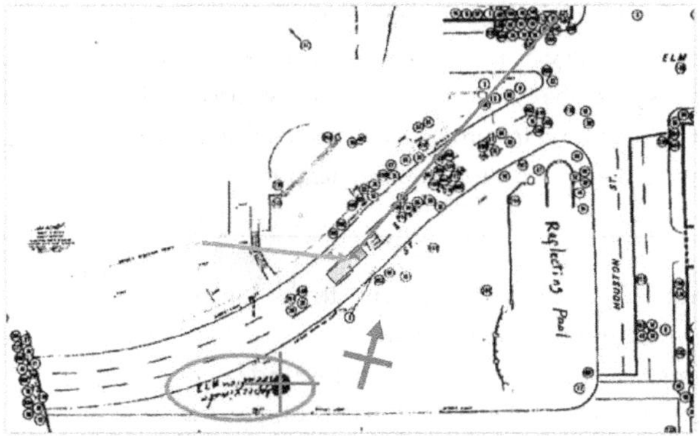

You can see both a trajectory of a shot from the grassy knoll (line on the left) and a shot from the Texas School Book Depository (line on the right):

> Only the most doctrinaire conspiracist would claim that an alleged grassy knoll shot could drive the Harper fragment where it was found.

An analysis of the Zapruder film by Itek Corporation also supports a shot fired from behind the limousine as the source of the forward movement of the Harper fragment:

> There is no question that the explosion from the bullet impact radiates matter in all directions. The fine matter can be seen surrounding the President's head.* However, the major direction of this matter is just forward of the President's head. The major, or large particles which are actually measurable on the film, and have contiguous boundaries which hold together during flight, all radiate in a forward direction.

By the way, in James DiEugenio's book of the annotated script, he notes that "in the film Aguilar says it [the Harper fragment] was found to the rear of JFK, but there is a debate about this so we corrected it in the transcript." And so, the words "to the left and rear" now read "to the left."

JFK: Destiny Betrayed misleads viewers on the Harper fragment. It was parietal bone, and the actual location of the fragment is consistent with a shot fired from behind the limousine.

CHAPTER 12
DID DR. BURKLEY COVER UP THE MEDICAL EVIDENCE?

(EPISODE 3, 1:33)

JFK: Destiny Betrayed makes several outrageous allegations about Admiral George Burkley, JFK's personal physician. The film alleges that Dr. Burkley told conspiracy theorists that more than one gunman killed JFK, that he withheld medical information about JFK's death from the various investigations, and that he engaged in a cover-up to protect his family. The truth is much more mundane.

Here is an excerpt from a transcript:

Narrator (Whoopi Goldberg): The one physician present at both Parkland Hospital and the Bethesda morgue was George Burkley, Kennedy's personal doctor. Like Knudsen, he was a Navy officer and as a rear admiral two ranks above him. Burkley signed the autopsy descriptive sheet with the bullet in the back at the level of T3. He also signed Kennedy's death certificate, which also placed that wound in the back. That death certificate is not in the Warren Commission volumes and the descriptive sheet in the Commission volumes does not have Burkley's signature. Arlen Specter did not depose George Burkley, but Burkley went further than that:

[Clip from Parkland Hospital press conference] **Malcolm Kilduff**:

[pointing to his right temple] Dr. Burkley told me that it was a simple matter, Tom, of a bullet right through the head.

Narrator (Whoopi Goldberg): Doctor Burkley did an interview with the JFK Library in 1967, and was asked this question:

[Archive Clip] **McHugh**: Do you agree with the Warren Report on the number of bullets that entered the President's body?

[Archive Clip] **Burkley**: I would not care to be quoted on that.

Narrator (Whoopi Goldberg): In 1977, through his lawyer, he wrote a letter to Richard Sprague, Chief Counsel of the House Select Committee on Assassinations. He said he had information indicating that "others besides Oswald must have participated" in the assassination. He was willing to talk about it at this time. Sprague, who made clear his intention to fully investigate the CIA's involvement, was forced out two weeks later. Dr. Burkley submitted a written statement to the House Select Committee but there is no official record of him being deposed as a witness.

Douglas Horne: In 1982, he told JFK researcher Henry Hurt "I know there was more than one gunman." And when Henry Hurt tried to recontact Burkley for more details, Burkley cut him off at the knees, "I don't want to talk about it anymore." The very next year, Burkley talked to Michael Kurtz, another JFK researcher, told him that he knew there was a conspiracy to kill the President and that he recalled an exit wound in the back of President Kennedy's head. Now that's a very significant statement, that the only doctor we know of who was present at both Parkland, for treatment, and at Bethesda, during the autopsy, told Michael Kurtz in 1983 that Kennedy had an exit wound in the back of his head. When Kurtz tried to recontact Burkley, Burkley cut *him* off at the knees, "I don't want to talk about this anymore." Dr. Burkley was deceased by the time the Review Board was impaneled. So then [ARRB General Counsel] Jeremy [Gunn] decided, well, we can ask the executor of his estate, his daughter, to sign a waiver so that we could go to the law firm, that Mr. Illig used to work for, since he was deceased also, and see if there were any records in the files of Mr. Illig that would have revealed what it was he wanted to tell the HSCA, in detail. And she said she would do that. And then Jeremy called her on the phone, she had completely changed her mind and adamantly refused to sign it and terminated the phone call.

Dr. Donald Miller: When I was a teenager, Dr. Burkley and his family, four children, and my father and our family of four children, shared a duplex, lived together at the Newport Naval Hospital. He had

> a son George, who was my age, sixteen, and we became buddies. I looked him up again in 2012, and I asked him about what his dad had told him and his siblings about his role in the Kennedy case. That the only thing that he would say was that he couldn't understand why the Warren Commission never asked him to testify. Dr. Burkley knew perfectly well why he wasn't asked to testify before the Warren Commission. The reason he didn't say anything to his children, he didn't want them to know that he was intimately involved in the cover-up. Dr. Burkley's death certificate makes the single-bullet theory bogus. The way the Warren Commission dealt with it was, they didn't publish it, the death certificate.
>
> **Oliver Stone**: If the ARRB had been a criminal investigation, would you have granted Burkley immunity for his testimony?
>
> **Douglas Horne**: We should have redeposed Humes and Boswell, after giving them immunity, and if Burkley had still been around, he would have been another candidate, because he was at the center of the photographic coverup. [referring to JFK autopsy photographs] By the way, George Burkley was a rear admiral; he was promoted to vice admiral by Lyndon Johnson; so, he promoted Burkley to the highest possible rank; kept him on as military physician, and the last person to walk out of the White House with Lyndon Johnson the day he left office was George Burkley.

The allegations regarding Dr Burkley are so numerous that first-generation researcher Paul Hoch and I posted a six-part series about him on my website. Here is a summary:

1. Admiral George Burkley and Conspiracy Theorists

JFK: Destiny Betrayed says that Burkley "told JFK researcher Henry Hurt that 'I know there was more than one gunman.'"

That is not what Hurt wrote:

> In 1982 Dr. Burkley told the author in a telephone conversation that he believed that President Kennedy's assassination was the result of a conspiracy.

Believing in a conspiracy about the JFK assassination is not the same thing as believing there were multiple gunmen.

The ARRB also made a similar error:

> In the late 1970s, at the time of the HSCA's investigation, Dr. Burkley, through his attorney, suggested to the HSCA that he might have some additional information about the autopsy.

As you can see, Richard Sprague wrote a memo about the phone call he received from Dr. Burkley's lawyer, William Illig. At no point was there any mention of the JFK autopsy:

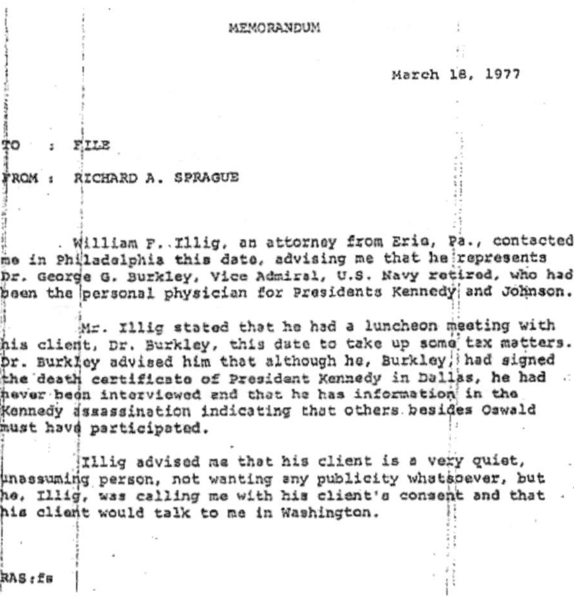

MEMORANDUM

March 18, 1977

TO : FILE

FROM : RICHARD A. SPRAGUE

William F. Illig, an attorney from Erie, Pa., contacted me in Philadelphia this date, advising me that he represents Dr. George G. Burkley, Vice Admiral, U.S. Navy retired, who had been the personal physician for Presidents Kennedy and Johnson.

Mr. Illig stated that he had a luncheon meeting with his client, Dr. Burkley, this date to take up some tax matters. Dr. Burkley advised him that although he, Burkley, had signed the death certificate of President Kennedy in Dallas, he had never been interviewed and that he has information in the Kennedy assassination indicating that others besides Oswald must have participated.

Illig advised me that his client is a very quiet, unassuming person, not wanting any publicity whatsoever, but he, Illig, was calling me with his client's consent and that his client would talk to me in Washington.

RAS:fs

JFK: Destiny Betrayed also claims that Burkley told Michael Kurtz "in 1983 that Kennedy had an exit wound in the back of his head."

As I indicated in Chapter 1, the use of Michael Kurtz as a reliable source is problematic. Researcher Pat Speer questions whether he even interviewed Dr. Burkley:

> If Kurtz had actually interviewed rarely-interviewed doctors such as Canada, Burkley, Humes, and Fisher he would almost certainly have mentioned them before mentioning his interview with a more commonly-interviewed subject as Shaw. That only makes sense.

Paul Hoch noted in his systematic 1993 speech on the evaluation of evidence in the JFK assassination:

> On interviewing witnesses: I don't have any experience worth mentioning, so I'll make just one point: Watch out for principals who have become buffs and are basing conclusions on information outside their areas of direct knowledge or expertise. If John Rosselli, for example, knew there was a shot from the knoll, it might not have been from inside knowledge, but because some of his friends, like many others, heard Mark Lane's stump speech.

In 1986, Paul Hoch corresponded with a relative of Dr. Burkley. The belief in conspiracy was not based on the medical evidence. Here is an excerpt from Paul's newsletter *Echoes of Conspiracy* on May 31, 1987:

> In search of more medical evidence:
>
> One of my unacknowledged letters to the JD last year directed their attention to Adm. George Burkley's comments to Henry Hurt, to the effect that he should be included among the majority of Americans who think there was a conspiracy. (See 8 EOC 1.2 for a discussion.)
>
> Dr. Burkley's comments to Hurt may well not have been based on what he knew about the medical evidence, according to information recently provided to me. William Manchester, who interviewed Dr. Burkley five times from April 1964 through July 1966, told me that at that time Dr. Burkley said he did not believe in a conspiracy theory, and was emphatic on that point.
>
> Also, Dr. Burkley recently told a relative of his that he did think that Oswald must have been part of a conspiracy, because the way he and his family lived and traveled was indicative of financial support. (This suspicion has been voiced by many people over the years, and the Warren Commission attempted to rebut in in Appendix XIV of the Report.) This relative also asked Dr. Burkley about Lifton's book when it was published; Dr. Burkley did not provide any clarification of the issues involved, nor did he indicate that he agreed with any of Lifton's analysis.

I spoke to that relative of Dr. Burkley. He said that Dr. Burkley was very circumspect and would not say much about the assassination to anybody. Many neighbors tried to question Burkley, but he wouldn't say a thing. At one point, Dr. Burkley gave him a copy of David Lifton's book *Best Evidence*. It was all puzzling, and the relative asked Burkley why he had given him the book. Burkley said there was a picture in the book of

Lyndon Johnson being sworn in on Air Force One and that in most versions of that picture, Burkley was cropped out. But not in *Best Evidence*.

I went and checked my copy of *Best Evidence*, and sure enough, there is a picture with Dr. Burkley in it:

the plane leave for Washington immediately. Those visible include General Clifton (at extreme left), Merriman Smith (in corner, to left of Presidential seal), Secret Service Agent Jerry Kivett (back of head to seal), Dr. Burkley (in profile, holding glasses), Bill Moyers (behind Burkley), Liz Carpenter, and Kennedy aide Dave Powers, barely visible at the extreme right.

(Photographs by Cecil Stoughton, White House photographer)

You can also see Dr. Burkley's reticence to talk about the assassination in this article from the *Indiana Gazette* on April 11, 1970:

From The White House To Blairsville R. D.

Burkleys Turn To Rural Living After Serving Three Presidents

Dr. Burkley does not care to discuss the shooting or autopsy. "It's all been said or printed before. Regardless of what anyone has said about the shooting or the autopsy that followed, I was there. I saw, and do not care to add credence to anything anyone else may claim."

That reticence also came through in David Lifton's book *Best Evidence*:

I said nothing to Greer about it, but the night before, I had talked with Burkley. It was one of the most frustrating conversations I had. Burkley was a stone wall.

I had no sooner identified myself, and said that I was attending a class at the UCLA Law School on the Warren Commission, than Burkley cut in: "Well, I'm sorry. I'm not answering any questions. It's all in the Warren Commission, and you get your information from there."

Viewers of *JFK: Destiny Betrayed* will learn none of this. Instead, the reckless propaganda film turns Dr. Burkley, an admirable man, into a villain. Not only are words put into his mouth, but he's accused of being part of the supposed cover-up. This is completely irresponsible, and Oliver Stone, James DiEugenio, Douglas Horne, and Dr. Donald Miller should be ashamed. This rush to judgment without basic knowledge of the facts is unbecoming.

This all could have been avoided had they heeded the advice that Paul Hoch gave in his 1993 speech on how to evaluate evidence:

> It seemed very significant that Dr. George Burkley said he thought there was a conspiracy, but the most I could find out was that he thought Oswald had more money than could be accounted for. One of the Dallas doctors, as I recall, thinks the head snap and simple physics constitute irrefutable proof of a shot from the front. They don't.

I hope at some point that the producers and writers of *JFK: Destiny Betrayed* will apologize to the Burkley family. But I wouldn't hold my breath.

2. Dr. Burkley and the JFK Investigations

JFK: Destiny Betrayed makes it appear that the Warren Commission never received any information from Dr. Burkley:

> **Narrator (Whoopi Goldberg):** The one physician present at both Parkland Hospital and the Bethesda morgue was George Burkley, Kennedy's personal doctor. Arlen Specter did not depose George Burkley …

Warren Commission Exhibit 1126 is a nine-page report from Burkley of his activities related to the assassination.

JFK: Destiny Betrayed also makes it appear that Admiral Burkley never spoke to the HSCA:

> **Narrator (Whoopi Goldberg)**: He was willing to talk about it at this time. Sprague, who made clear his intention to fully investigate the CIA's involvement, was forced out two weeks later. Dr. Burkley submitted a written statement to the House Select Committee but there is no official record of him being deposed as a witness.

Admiral Burkley was interviewed by the HSCA in August 1977.

While Burkley was reticent to talk about bullets in his oral history interview, he did offer this:

> Dr. Burkley said the doctors didn't section the brain and that if it had been done, it might be possible to prove whether or not there were two bullets. Dr. Burkley thinks there was one but concedes the possibility of there having been two.

Dr. Burkley might well have decided that his oral history interview was not the time or place to talk about his thoughts on sectioning Kennedy's brain. After all, Dr. Burkley's specialty was "internal medicine and cardiology." He was not a forensic pathologist, and he understood the need for an autopsy.

Dr. Burkley also signed an affidavit for the HSCA after a second interview.

So Burkley was interviewed and submitted a signed affidavit. If this language is not what a deposed witness would sign, it's a distinction without a difference:

> I understand that this affidavit may be introduced and received into evidence by the Select Committee on Assassinations of the United States House of Representatives, and may lead them to make various findings of fact, and the statutes applicable to Congressional investigations, including but not limited to those concerning false statements, obstruction, or misleading, would subject me to criminal penalties for not telling the whole and complete truth in this affidavit.

I am not surprised that *JFK: Destiny Betrayed* did not include this quote:

> I saw President Kennedy's wounds at Parkland Hospital and during the autopsy at the Bethesda Naval Hospital. There was no difference in the nature of the wounds I saw at Parkland Hospital and those I observed at the autopsy at Bethesda Naval Hospital.

The House Select Committee on Assassinations interviewed Burkley, and he also gave them a statement. If he had wanted to share a belief that "others besides Oswald may have participated," he had plenty of opportunities to do so.

3. Was Admiral Burkley Involved in a Cover-Up?

Dr. Donald Miller makes the extraordinary claim that "the reason [Dr. Burkley] didn't say anything was that he was intimately involved in the cover-up."

However, Dr. Burkley had already answered a question during his JFK Library interview about the cause of death:

> **McHUGH**: I see. Do your conclusions differ at all with the Warren Report of the circumstances or cause of death?
>
> **BURKLEY**: My conclusion in regard to the cause of death was the bullet wound which involved the skull. The discussion as to whether a previous bullet also enters into it, but as far as the cause of death the immediate cause was unquestionably the bullet which shattered the brain and the calvarium.

Notice that he didn't say "bullets."

I've already discussed why Burkley might not have wanted to elaborate on bullets and wounds in his JFK Library interview. Dr. Miller claims that Dr. Burkley did not answer because he was "intimately involved in the cover-up." What is the evidence for this?

In his article on Lew Rockwell's website, Miller writes that he was friends with one of Dr. Burkley's sons:

> My teenage buddy George W. Burkley (both of us are now age 72) writes, "Dad never voiced much of an opinion about a conspiracy but frequently questioned why the Warren Commission never asked him to testify. Dad was [a] very close hold when it came to his professional life."

That doesn't provide any evidence that Admiral Burkley was involved in a cover-up.

Miller's charge comes from his discussion of JFK's death certificate and the back wound.

Here is the death certificate that Burkley signed:

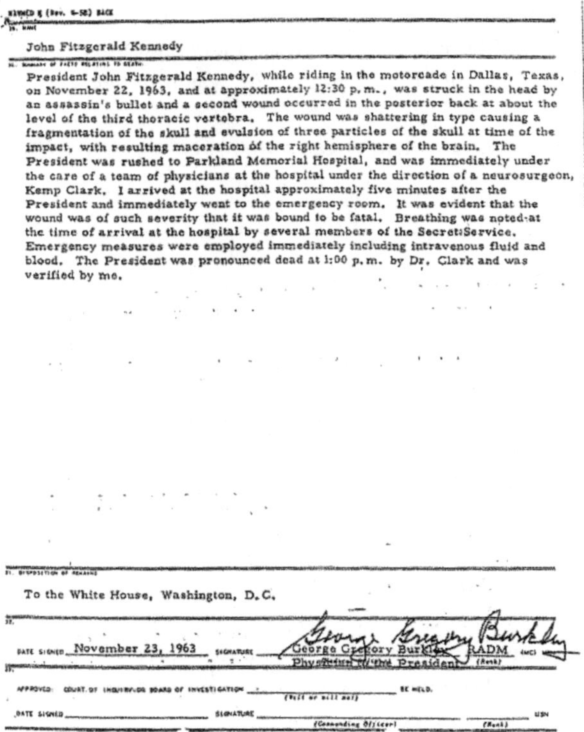

John Fitzgerald Kennedy

President John Fitzgerald Kennedy, while riding in the motorcade in Dallas, Texas, on November 22, 1963, and at approximately 12:30 p.m., was struck in the head by an assassin's bullet and a second wound occurred in the posterior back at about the level of the third thoracic vertebra. The wound was shattering in type causing a fragmentation of the skull and evulsion of three particles of the skull at time of the impact, with resulting maceration of the right hemisphere of the brain. The President was rushed to Parkland Memorial Hospital, and was immediately under the care of a team of physicians at the hospital under the direction of a neurosurgeon, Kemp Clark. I arrived at the hospital approximately five minutes after the President and immediately went to the emergency room. It was evident that the wound was of such severity that it was bound to be fatal. Breathing was noted at the time of arrival at the hospital by several members of the Secret Service. Emergency measures were employed immediately including intravenous fluid and blood. The President was pronounced dead at 1:00 p.m. by Dr. Clark and was verified by me.

To the White House, Washington, D.C.

DATE SIGNED November 23, 1963 SIGNATURE George Gregory Burkley RADM (MC) Physician to the President (Rank)

APPROVED: COURT OF INQUIRY/OR BOARD OF INVESTIGATION ______ (Will or will not) BE HELD.

DATE SIGNED ______ SIGNATURE ______ (Commanding Officer) ______ (Rank) USN

Dr. Burkley describes the wound in JFK's back as being at the "level of the third thoracic vertebra." Dr. Miller goes on to note that:

A second pathologist (of three performing it), Lt. Cmdr. J. Thornton Boswell, made a diagram of the wounds and scars he observed on the body. It places the bullet wound in the back at the same level, T-3, like the death certificate. Dr. Burkley signs the diagram (on the lower left side) and above his signature writes, "Verified."

Here is that diagram:

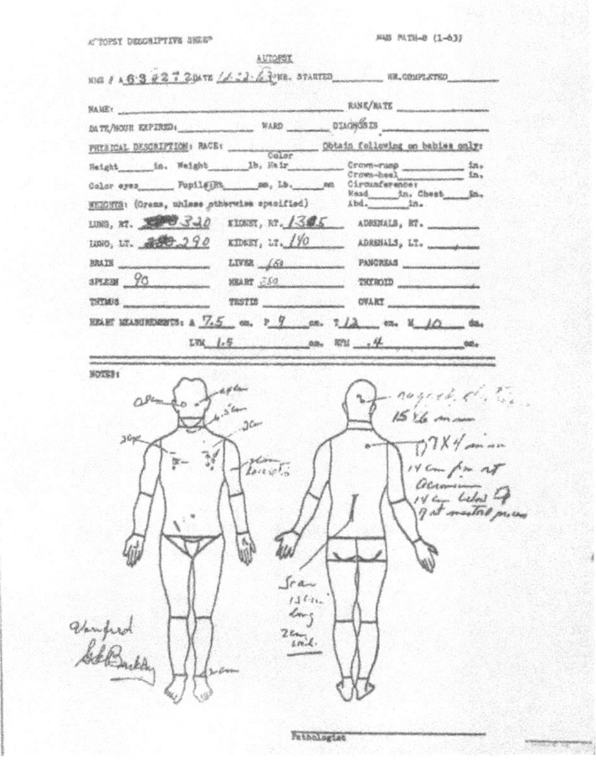
AUTOPSY DESCRIPTIVE SHEET NMS PATH-8 (1-63)

AUTOPSY

NMS # A63-272 DATE 11-22-63 HR. STARTED ______ HR. COMPLETED ______

NAME: ______ RANK/RATE ______

DATE/HOUR EXPIRED: ______ WARD ______ DIAGNOSIS ______

PHYSICAL DESCRIPTION: RACE: ______ Obtain following on babies only:

Height ______ in. Weight ______ lb. Color Hair ______ Crown-rump ______ in. Crown-heel ______ in.

Color eyes ______ Pupils Rt. ______ mm, Lt. ______ mm Circumference: Head ______ in. Chest ______ in. Abd. ______ in.

WEIGHTS: (Grams, unless otherwise specified)

LUNG, RT. 320 KIDNEY, RT. 13[illegible]5 ADRENALS, RT. ______

LUNG, LT. 290 KIDNEY, LT. 140 ADRENALS, LT. ______

BRAIN ______ LIVER 150 PANCREAS ______

SPLEEN 90 HEART 350 THYROID ______

THYMUS ______ TESTIS ______ OVARY ______

HEART MEASUREMENTS: A 7.5 cm. P 9 cm. T 12 cm. M 10 cm.

LVM 1.5 cm. RVM .4 cm.

NOTES:

15 x 6 mm

7 X 4 mm

14 cm from rt acromion

14 cm below tip of rt mastoid process

Verified
GG Burkley

Pathologist

You can see Burkley's signature under "Verified" in the lower left. However, as Dr. Miller should know, the description of the wound on the right indicates its true location: "14 cm from rt acromion" (the bony tip of the outer edge of your shoulder blade) and "14 cm below tip of rt mastoid process" (a conical prominence of the temporal bone behind the ear, to which neck muscles are attached).

This was all explained in an article in the *Baltimore Sun* back on November 25, 1966. The worksheet was shown with a caption that read:

> Dr. J. Thornton Boswell said yesterday President Kennedy's neck wound should have been indicated where the X is, and not, as he did during the autopsy, where the dot on the back is. Notations on the drawing are correct and precise, he said, indicating neck wound.

Here is an excerpt from the second page of that article:

an area just below the shoulder line that, to a physician, is still the neck region.

More disturbingly, it recounts the incident during which the exit wound was undiscovered and leaves, unchanged, a statement in which Dr. Humes concluded the bullet had worked itself out of the same hole it had entered.

Story Left Unchanged

Dr. Boswell said that, at the time, he paid no attention to the presence of the FBI agents but that he can only conclude that they either did not understand what later took place, or else left before the lung contusions were discovered.

Dr. Boswell said that he first saw the photographs taken at the autopsy when they were turned over to the National Archives on November 1.

He said that they show clearly exactly where the bullet entry was. The pictures are absolutely identifiable by inventory numbers, by the recollection of the pathologists, and by the inclusion in several pictures, of the face of the President.

On the autopsy sketch drawn by Dr. Boswell are computations to locate the neck wound by measurement.

Dr. Boswell used, as places of reference, the right acronmion process—the highest point on the shoulder bone that can be felt near the joint of the shoulder and collar bone — and the mastoid prominence—the base of the bone just behind the ear.

He said these were standard reference points used in such cases.

He placed the wound at the intersection of 14 inch arcs described from these reference points.

He said yesterday that he thought he had used a vertebra as a third reference point, but that this did not appear in the autopsy report or in the sketch.

The sketch itself would normally have been thrown away, he said, in any case but this one.

"We didn't anticipate this would have become as important as it did," he said.

Holes In Shirt

He called it a "scratch sheet" that would have been replaced, in other cases, with a photograph to supply the pictorial element.

Dr. Boswell also offered an explanation of another controversial point.

The shirt and jacket worn by the President on November 22, 1963, have holes in the back at approximately the place indicated in his autopsy diagram.

Dr. Boswell said this was only coincidental.

He said that the President, according to movie films, had his arm raised, waving at the crowds, when he was shot. This movement would have raised his coat and shirt resulting in bullet holes lower in the clothing than were indicated by the wound.

The clothing had been removed from the President's body in Dallas, he said, before it was flown to Bethesda for the autopsy.

And the JFK autopsy report confirms the location of the back wound as described in the worksheet:

Situated on the upper right posterior thorax just above the upper border of the scapula there is a 7 x 4 millimeter oval wound. This wound is measured to be 14 cm. from the tip of the right acromion process and 14 cm. below the tip of the right mastoid process.

Is Dr. Burkley guilty of a cover-up or of just making a mistake on the death certificate?

Why is this so important to Dr. Miller and the producers of *JFK: Destiny Betrayed*? Because they want to use Burkley to help prove that the single-bullet theory is impossible. Dr. Miller wrote:

> Dr. Burkley's observations are equally damaging to the lone gunman scenario. He filled out and signed President Kennedy's Death Certificate (see here). It describes a bullet wound in Kennedy's back adjacent to the third thoracic vertebra (T-3). This is 5 inches below the neck. Dr. Burkley places the wound in the back far too low for the bullet to have exited through the throat at neck-tie level. The death certificate, alone, renders the single bullet theory ballistically and anatomically impossible.

Miller went on to level an accusation against the Warren Commission:

> The way it dealt with Dr. Boswell's autopsy diagram demonstrates the chicanery the Warren Commission practiced in its investigation of the assassination. The Commission published Boswell's diagram as Commission Exhibit 397, but Admiral Burkley's signature validating it is gone! It has been erased. The bullet hole's location as placed on CE 397 disproves the single bullet theory, the lynchpin of the Commission's case against Oswald. But like with Dr. Perry, when Dr. Boswell came before the Commission, he also had a change of mind and testified that he had drawn the bullet hole in the back too low, saying now that it was actually considerably higher than shown on the diagram, high enough for the bullet to have come out and left an exit wound in the neck. With his signature not there, the Commission would not need to question Admiral Burkley about it.

Miller ignores the notation on the autopsy worksheet and also ignores the autopsy report itself. So, the Warren Commission published a copy of the autopsy worksheet without Burkley's signature. Is this what Miller considers a cover-up?

Dr. Miller went off the deep end with further charges against Admiral Burkley:

> Dr. Burkley did, however, sign an Affidavit for the HSCA, which states that the casket was constantly observed and not opened or disturbed in its trip to the National Naval Medical Center autopsy laboratory in Bethesda, Maryland. It reads:
>
> "I traveled from Andrew's [sic] Air Force Base in the ambulance with the President's body to the Bethesda Naval Hospital and accompanied the [bronze Dallas] coffin to the autopsy laboratory and saw the body removed from the coffin and placed on the autopsy table."
>
> Admiral Burkley lied. The bronze Dallas casket was opened and was empty when it arrived at the autopsy lab.

This firmly puts Miller into the David Lifton–Douglas Horne camp.

Why was Burkley so reticent to tell his children the truth about the JFK assassination? Miller claimed that Burkley's son had said that his father "frequently questioned why the Warren Commission never asked him to testify." Miller seemingly knows the answer:

> His father knew very well why the Warren Commission never called him to testify. Admiral Burkley knew first-hand that the single bullet theory was bogus. He chose not to tell his children the true facts of the JFK assassination or his involvement in the cover-up. Perhaps to protect them?

So, Dr. Burkley engaged in a cover-up to protect his children?

Where does this all come from? Dr. Miller writes:

> Doug Horne nails it in his book Inside the Assassination Records Review Board:
>
> "[Admiral Burkley's behavior] can only be understood as that of a man who was filled with deep and profound guilt about the massive coverup he participated in—indeed, which he appears to have engineered—a man who wanted to confess his role and unburden himself on some occasions, and who would then abruptly change his mind on other occasions, when he considered the effect this would have had on his reputation and his family's peace-of-mind. His behavior from the time of the assassination up until his death was that of a deeply conflicted man, ridden with guilt and shame, who wanted to confess his involvement in the cover-up for the moral absolution it would have provided to him but who at the same time, was afraid to do so for practical reasons involving his reputation and his family. History will not absolve him, either for his role in the cover-up, or for his failure to come clean when he had a chance to do so with the HSCA, which could have granted him immunity if he had decided to expose the cover-up."

This is insanely reckless and comes from one of the major experts in *JFK: Destiny Betrayed*.

Miller even goes further:

> To ensure his silence President Johnson made Dr. Burkley his personal physician and promoted him from the rank of Rear Admiral to Vice Admiral.

Is Dr. Miller a credible commentator?

One of the books that Dr. Miller recommends on the JFK assassination is John Armstrong's *Harvey and Lee: How the CIA Framed Oswald,* which posits that there were two Oswalds:

> Armstrong has done more field investigation on Oswald than anyone. One seasoned JFK assassination researcher states, "Of all the homerun hitters in this league, John Armstrong is the 'Babe Ruth.'"

And so, Miller buys into the two-Oswalds theory:

> The CIA sent the fluent Russian-speaking Harvey to Russia posing as a disaffected southern-borne [sic] American. When it was later decided to use them in the Kennedy assassination the American-born Oswald helped the agency set up his Russian-speaking double as the patsy for it. The only problem with this was that Oswald kept being seen in two places at once—like when he (Lee) was in the Marines in Japan, from October 1957 to May 1958, while he (Harvey) was working at the Pfisterer Dental Lab in New Orleans. Right after the shooting eyewitnesses saw Oswald (Harvey) on a bus, while Dallas Deputy Sheriff observed him (Lee) getting into a Dodge Rambler on Elm Street in Dealey Plaza.

Again, Carl Sagan's adage comes to mind: Extraordinary claims require extraordinary evidence.

Miller even believes that saying Oswald is innocent is considered a thoughtcrime:

> Unfortunately, we now live in a country where to say that Oswald is innocent is tantamount to committing a "thoughtcrime". Americans increasingly practice what Orwell terms "crimestop," the faculty of stopping short at the threshold of any dangerous thought. But given the facts of the matter, believing the Oswald-did-it-alone official truth is like saying 2 + 2 = 5.

But wait, there's more!

According to Dr. Miller, even John F. Kennedy, Jr. was killed by a conspiracy:

> A small bomb placed on the aircraft that exploded in mid-air may have caused the plane to dive into the ocean.

Dr. Millers writes extensively for LewRockwell.com, and some of his articles speak for themselves:

- Vaccines are Dangerous
- Fluoride is Poison
- Questioning HIV / AIDS
- Don't Get a Flu Shot!
- HIV is Harmless
- Robert F. Kennedy, Jr., Tackles the Covid Coup

By the way, in that last article, Dr. Miller claims that "RFK Jr. shows conclusively that ivermectin has a far better safety record than Dr. Fauci's two chosen COVID remedies, [intravenous] remdesivir (which hospital nurses have dubbed 'Run-death-is-near') and COVID vaccines."

Can ivermectin perhaps cure conspiracy fever?

I reached out to Richard Burkley, one of Dr. Burkley's sons, and he sent me this message:

> I don't think my father ever actually got himself registered to vote. Being in the military he had to move a lot and he was not particularly concerned about politics. I believe that he was inclined to be more of a Republican supporter that a Democratic fan, at least in his earlier years. I do remember him making some pretty negative comments about Franklin Roosevelt. That all changed when he became President Kennedy's physician. He was a great admirer of Kennedy and absolutely told me in 1962 or 1963 that he was going to get himself properly registered so he could vote for Kennedy in the next election. Long after the assassination I pressed him a little on the rumored issue of Kennedy having been a bit of a womanizer and he dismissed the issue as either untrue or unimportant. He was a big fan of Kennedy. He also said that when Kennedy was killed, he was probably as healthy or more healthy than he had ever been in his life.

I am sure the Burkley family is bewildered by these reckless accusations.

The cavalier attitude of conspiracy theorists allows them to ignore the real-life consequences of their baseless charges.

Clay Shaw's life was ruined by Jim Garrison, and he was slandered by Oliver Stone. Larry Crafard, who briefly worked for Jack Ruby, had his marriage broken up because of the nonsense in conspiracy books. Kerry Thornley, who served in the Marines with Oswald, became hyper-paranoid and went off the deep end. Ruth Paine, who allowed Marina Oswald to room with her, has faced ridiculous insinuations that she was connected with the CIA. Carlos Bringuier, an anti-Castro Cuban in New Orleans, sent his wife and children to Argentina to spare them the pain of seeing him arrested by Jim Garrison. His wife then suffered a miscarriage. Roger Craig, a deputy sheriff in Dallas, went down the conspiracy rabbit hole and committed suicide.

As Joseph Welch asked of Joseph McCarthy, "Have you no sense of decency?"

And yet, as bad as all this is, James DiEugenio is determined to go even further. Back in 2017, a conspiracy website carried an article by John Titus in which he claimed that something was stolen from Dr. Burkley related to the JFK assassination while he was traveling to Denver:

> We will probably never know exactly what evidence about conspiracy was stolen from Dr. Burkley. But here's an interesting note; the family member I spoke with told me that every year until Burkley's death he was paid a visit by government agents, presumably Secret Service. Apparently, they wanted to keep a grip on Burkley, the man who could possibly bring down the entire assassination cover-up.

I can't speak for the veracity of this report. Richard Burkley told me that he knows of no government agents [Secret Service or otherwise] visiting the house. He believes the accusation is "absurd." Dr. Burkley moved in and lived with Richard Burkley for five years, and there were no such visits during that time.

Even if true, it is quite possible that Dr. Burkley made friends with a variety of people while he was working in the White House. Perhaps they had an annual get-together. Is it really necessary to make this all sound nefarious?

This line of reasoning was picked up by James DiEugenio:

James DiEugenio Posted January 28 (edited)

Members

9.3k
Gender:Male

And I don' t think he is the only one Micah.

The Illig switcheroo is a real puzzler. Just recall, Burkley was dead at that time and I think Illig was also.

Third point, I have a quiet contact with the Burkley family. He told me the Secret Service would visit the guy each year for an interview. This went on until he passed. Hmm.

In my opinion, and this is why we posed the question to Horne, if Burkley had been alive, and if the ARRB was a criminal inquiry, Jeremy and Doug should have granted him immunity.

Edited January 28 by James DiEugenio

James DiEugenio referenced Titus's article on his website. So, perhaps Titus gave DiEugenio his contact within the Burkley family. Except now, the story becomes much more definite, no more mere presumption about the agents being from the Secret Service.

> I have a quiet contact with the Burkley family. He told me the Secret Service would visit the guy each year for an interview. This went on until he passed. Hmm.

And so now Dr. George Burkley is the go-to guy for almost any part of the cover-up. The 'extra bullet' story gave DiEugenio another opportunity to bring up Burkley: (see Chapter 32)

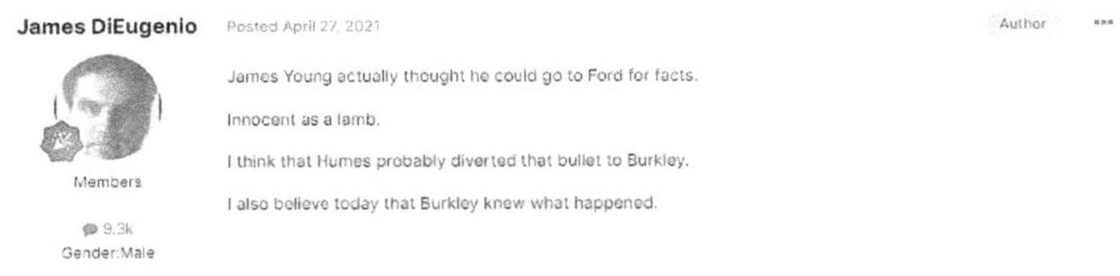

James DiEugenio
Posted April 27, 2021
Author
Members
9.3k
Gender:Male
James Young actually thought he could go to Ford for facts.
Innocent as a lamb.
I think that Humes probably diverted that bullet to Burkley.
I also believe today that Burkley knew what happened.

And Dr. Burkley is now at the center of the supposed cover-up.

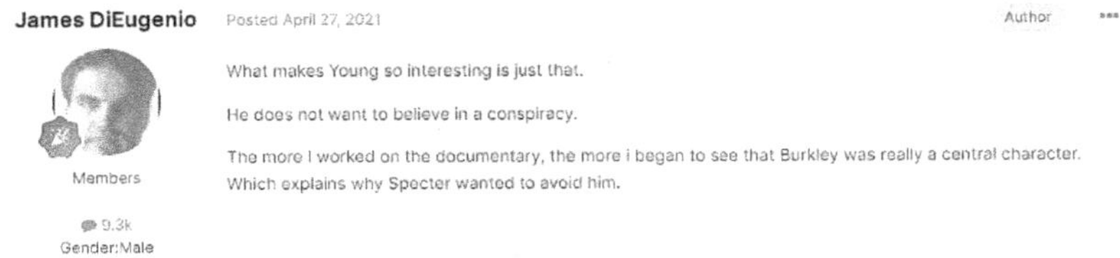

James DiEugenio
Posted April 27, 2021
Author
Members
9.3k
Gender:Male
What makes Young so interesting is just that.
He does not want to believe in a conspiracy.
The more I worked on the documentary, the more i began to see that Burkley was really a central character.
Which explains why Specter wanted to avoid him.

After I reached out to the Burkley family, I was put in contact with a true American hero, Bill Baxley.

In 1963, four members of the KKK blew up a church in Birmingham, Alabama, killing four girls and injuring several others. No one was charged. In 1971, while attorney general of Alabama, Baxley decided to reopen the 16th Street Baptist Church bombing investigation. In 1976, he received an obscene threatening letter of protest from white supremacist Edward R. Fields.

Here is Mr. Baxley's famous reply:

THE ATTORNEY GENERAL STATE OF ALABAMA
MONTGOMERY, ALABAMA 36130

WILLIAM J. BAXLEY
ATTORNEY GENERAL

GEORGE L. BECK
DEPUTY ATTORNEY GENERAL

E. RAY ACTON
EXECUTIVE ASSISTANT

WALTER G. TURNER
CHIEF ASSISTANT ATTORNEY GENERAL

LUCY H. RICHARDS
CONFIDENTIAL ASSISTANT

JACK D. SHOWS
CHIEF INVESTIGATOR

February 20, 1976

"Dr." Edward R. Fields
National States Rights Party
P. O. Box 1211
Marietta, Georgia 30061

Dear "Dr." Fields:

My response to your letter of February 19, 1976, is - kiss my ass.

Sincerely,

BILL BAXLEY
Attorney General

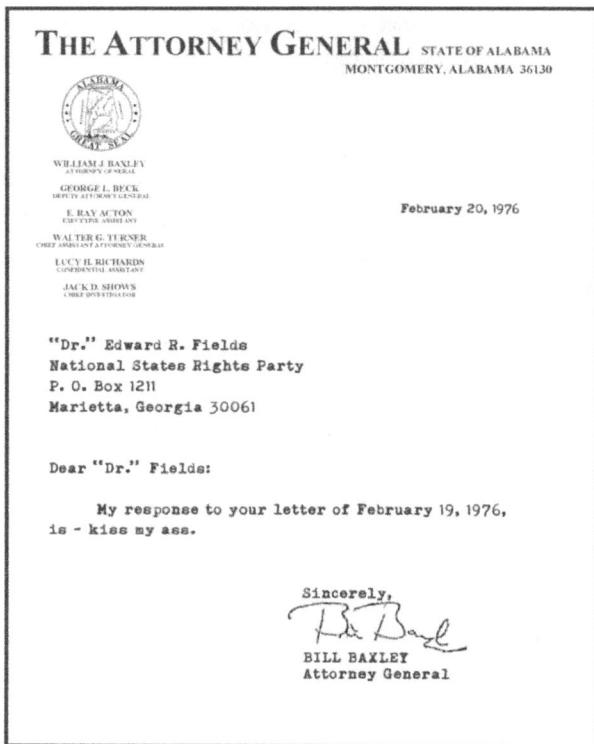

Bill Baxley eventually convicted three people for the bombing.

Bill Baxley was incensed over the way *JFK: Destiny Betrayed* treated Dr. George Burkley and his family, and he sent me this letter:

Dear Fred,

Thank you so much for all you are doing in an effort to correct a slander of a good, honorable man who has been deceased for over 30 years. Dr. George Burkley was a career Naval officer who rose to the rank of vice admiral. He served as the White House physician to three of our presidents, Eisenhower, Kennedy, and Johnson.

One of Admiral Burkley's four children, Dick, is married to my wife's sister Jo Ann. They will have been married for 57 years this October and have raised five wonderful children. By the time I became acquainted with the family in the late 1980s, Dr. Burkley was no longer in good health as his memory had been fading for quite a few years. Throughout his life, he was totally non-political. His admiration and respect for JFK as a person was well-known to everybody who knew him. What Oliver Stone has recently been implying about Dr. Burkley is below disgraceful. Stone is defaming the memory of a loyal American who nobly and honorably served his country for his entire adult life.

I have been aware of Stone's falsehoods and reckless accusations in other matters for a long time. The mere mention or thought of Oliver Stone is akin to describing the south end of a northbound mule. I do not believe anybody in America has caused more harm to as many people as has Oliver Stone. He is well aware that he is spreading and, indeed, marketing falsehoods that damage totally innocent people. He feels that he has the right to invent made up plots and present them as truth as well as falsely attributing words and actions to other human beings, both living and dead.

Stone is so fortunate to live in a country like the USA, where freedom of speech is so basic that he can get away with such outrageous and harmful conduct. Yet, he seems to hate his country and his actions appear geared to undermining competence and respect for our government and its leaders.

Sincerely,
Bill Baxley

That question about decency? We all know the answer.

CHAPTER 13
WAS THE WOUND IN THE BACK OF JFK'S HEAD ONE OF EXIT?

(EPISODE 3, 6:22)

JFK: Destiny Betrayed alleges that the wound in the back of Kennedy's head was one of exit. Audrey Bell is one such witness, and viewers will not learn that there are reasons to question her credibility.

Here is an excerpt from a transcript:

[Assassination Records Review Board Medical Interview 3/20/97]

Interviewer: Using the most precise medical terminology that you can use.

Audrey Bell: Ok, let's see, it was on the right rear, and he shifted the head a little bit, to the left. Lifted up the, kind of matted area, the flap. And you could see the ... hole, and there was ... brain, and spinal fluid ... dripping down out of it. Then I noticed it was dripping down into a bucket.

Audrey Bell was the operating room supervisor at Parkland Hospital, and here is her short summary of Kennedy's wounds from her ARRB interview:

-She did not see the throat wound herself;

-Although only in Trauma Room One for 3-5 minutes, she did see the head wound. After asking Dr. Perry "where is the wound," she said he turned the President's head slightly to the President's anatomical left, so that she could see a right rear posterior head wound, which she described as occipital in both her oral remarks, and in her drawings;

-She said she could see brain and spinal fluid coming out of the wound, but could not tell what type of brain tissue it was;

-She said it was her recollection that the right side of the President's head, and the top of his head, were intact, which is why she had to ask Dr. Perry where the wound was in the first place.

If Audrey Bell was in Trauma Room 1, it was for a very short period, just a few minutes. It is hard to believe that in the middle of the doctors' frantic attempt to save Kennedy's life that she asked Dr. Perry, "Where is the wound?" It is even harder to believe that he interrupted whatever he was doing to move Kennedy's head to show her.

JFK: Destiny Betrayed edited what she said in her ARRB interview. Here is an excerpt from a transcript of the interview:

Douglas Horne: Okay. Thank you. Would you describe for me, using the most precise medical terminology that you can use, the president's head wound, the location?

Audrey Bell: Okay. Let's see, it was on the right rear. I think it's called the parietal area.

Clearly, the producers did not want mention of the "parietal area" in the film. It clashed with their viewpoint that the back of Kennedy's head was blasted out.

Horne resumed by asking Bell where she was standing:

Douglas Horne: Okay. We're back on the record. Before I ask you to describe the president's head wound, would you tell me where you were standing when you observed, in relation to the cart?

Audrey Bell: Oh, I was at the head of the table.

She was supposedly very close. Here is another description of the head wound:

Audrey Bell: They were also setting up to do a tracheostomy. Dr. Perry was going to do that. And when I took a first look, I could recognize the president, but I didn't see an injury because there was no injury around his face. I asked, I said, "Well, where's the injury?" And Dr. Perry was standing there, and he reached up on the president's head and just pulled up a little bit, turned his head to the left a little and there was a gaping hole and that's where the brain and the fluids were dripping out. And I don't know, it could have been three or four inches that I saw.

Douglas Horne: In diameter?

Audrey Bell: In diameter, yeah. And some of the - they were wanting to start an IV on the right arm. And I remember getting my scissors or getting a pair of scissors and cutting the president's shirt up the seam.

Three or four inches in diameter?

Audrey Bell's diagram does not look like a three–four-inch diameter hole:

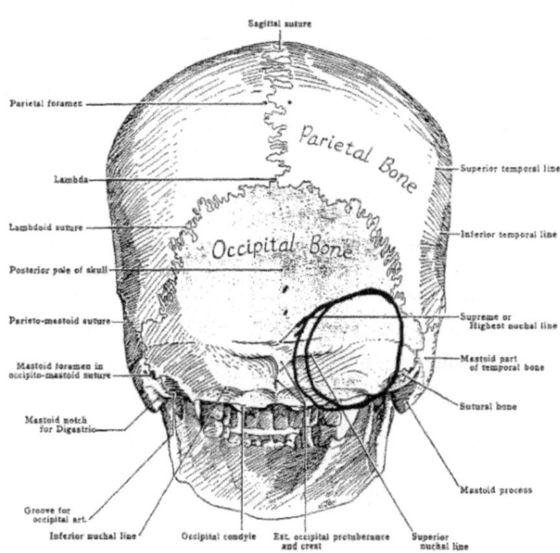

Bell marked up another diagram for the ARRB but admitted that her location was "very unscientific."

> **Douglas Horne**: Okay. If you feel comfortable with Bell exhibit four, I would ask you to represent what part of the brain that would've corresponded to. If you feel comfortable marking that drawing.
>
> **Audrey Bell**: Well, I'd say it would have to come down into this lower section, but I'm not, it would probably be somewhere like that. But I would say that's very unscientific.

Researcher Pat Speer is not convinced that Bell was even there:

> Her claim Dr. Perry showed her the back of Kennedy's head—when no one else remembered Dr. Perry showing the wound to anyone, or her even being in the room—is as smelly as smelly can get … At the head of the gurney (on the far side of the room) stand Drs. Jenkins and McClelland. Along the sides of the gurney stand Drs. Perry, Baxter, Jones, Peters, Salyers, etc. There is no way a nurse would push past these men, go to the head of the gurney, and ask to be shown the head wound. No way … I don't believe Bell's story, and I'm embarrassed for you if you do.

Dr. Ron Jones provided an oral history to the Sixth Floor Museum:

> I hung up the phone and turned around and noticed a table. This was a fairly large cafeteria. And just a few feet away behind me sat Dr. M. T. Jenkins, who … [was] better known as "Pepper" Jenkins, and he was head of the department of anesthesia, and Miss Audrey Bell, who was the operating room supervisor at Parkland. And so, people were beginning to look at me at that time from … employees in the cafeteria, knowing that something must be going on. I went over to that table, and I said, "You aren't going to believe this, but the president's been shot and they're bringing him to the emergency room." And Dr. Jenkins said, "Well, I'll get an anesthesia machine from the operating room and

> bring it right down." And Miss Bell said, "I'll get an operating room ready."

It certainly makes sense that the operating room supervisor would get an operating room ready. Did she have time to do that and then get to Trauma Room 1?

Furthermore, Dr. Jenkins told Dennis Breo that he doubted "any of the Parkland physicians even had a good look at the President's head." He noted:

> I was standing at the head of the table in at the position the anesthesiologist most often assumes closest to the President's head. My presence there and the president's great shock of hair and the location of the head wound were such that it was not visible to those standing down each side of the gurney where they were carrying out their resuscitative maneuvers.

Why the producers of *JFK: Destiny Betrayed* present witnesses with limited credibility is beyond comprehension.

CHAPTER 14
WAS CEREBELLUM EXTRUDING FROM JFK'S HEAD WOUND?

(EPISODE 3, 6:52)

JFK: Destiny Betrayed claims that JFK had an exit wound in the back of his head because Parkland Hospital doctors supposedly saw cerebellum at the rear of his skull.

Here is an excerpt from a transcript:

Narrator (Whoopi Goldberg): In addition to this large avulsion of wound [sic; should be avulsive wound] in the rear of the skull, seven personnel at Parkland Hospital saw cerebellum at the bottom of the skull.

Dr. Cyril Wecht: The brain consists of two large cerebral hemispheres, and then lower down, posteriorly, are two hemispheres, the cerebellum. They differ in coloration; they differ in the topographical markings.

Oliver Stone: So, seven doctors at Parkland Hospital claimed to have seen cerebellum?

Dr. Michael Chesser: In 1963, it was one of the top trauma centers in the country, and it is still one the top trauma centers. Dr. Robert McClelland saw a clump of the cerebellum, a large clump, fall out of the skull on to the emergency room bed.

[Archive clip] **Dr. McClelland**: In my mind, as sure as you can ever be about any observation, there was cerebellum extruded out to the gurney while I was standing there looking at it.

Dr. Michael Chesser: Then we have Dr. Kemp Clark. He went into detail with the Warren Commission about the result of all this loss of cerebellar tissue, if President Kennedy had survived the wound. So, there was no doubt that there was loss of cerebellar tissue.

Narrator (Whoopi Goldberg): This reliable eyewitness testimony indicates that the wound in Kennedy's rear skull extended quite low. And also, there was severe damage to that sector of the brain. Yet in the autopsy report, written at Bethesda by James Humes, there is no mention of the cerebellum, and he did not testify about it to the Warren Commission.

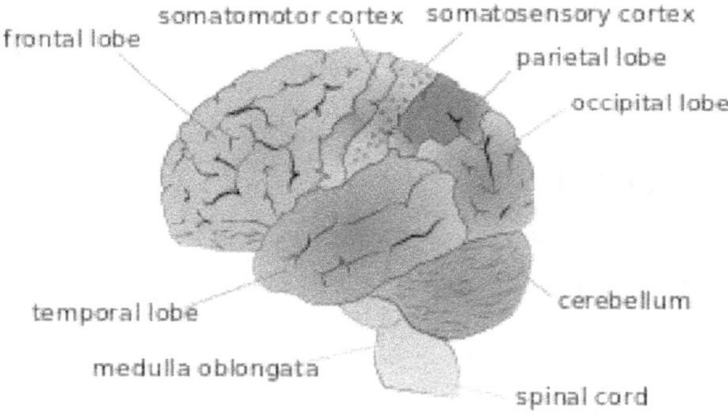

Dr. Cyril Wecht: So, these guys, good old Texan, respected doctors, and they've seen hundreds and thousands of brains, especially the neurosurgeon, saw cerebellum having been damaged, significantly displaced, in the occipital area. The doctors who did the autopsy—read the autopsy report from Humes and Boswell. The cerebellum is intact. Who do you believe? Do you believe these Texas doctors? Or do you believe the two career naval pathologists working under military control? Who do you believe as to whether or not the cerebellum was damaged?

There are two major reasons why *JFK: Destiny Betrayed* makes this claim. First, it is important to show that there was a massive blowout in the back of Kennedy's head, which would suggest a large exit wound.

Second, the autopsy photographs of the brain show the cerebellum intact. So, this claim is further proof that either the brain was substituted or that the photographs have been altered.

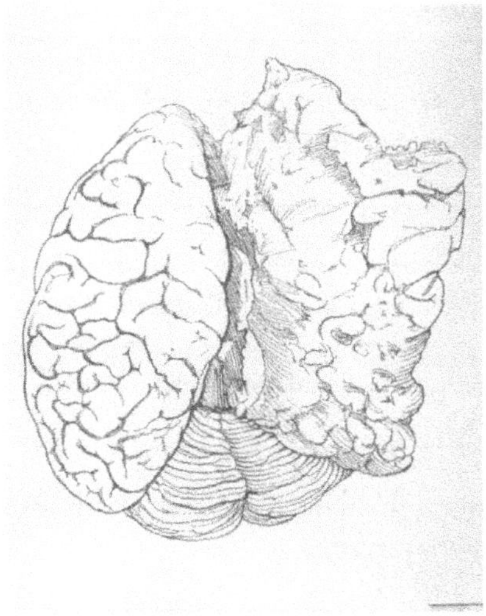

This is a drawing of a photograph of JFK's brain that shows the cerebellum to be nearly intact.

One of the doctors who saw cerebellum was Dr. Charles Carrico:

> **Dr. Carrico**: The second wound that I saw was a large gaping wound, located in the right occipitoparietal area. I would estimate to be about 5 to 7 cm. in size, more or less circular, with avulsions of the calvarium and scalp tissue. As I stated before, I believe there was shredded macerated cerebral and cerebellar tissues both in the wounds and on the fragments of the skull attached to the dura.

Vincent Bugliosi asked Dr. Carrico in October 2000 if the Parkland doctors were "confused about the cerebellum being damaged." Carrico replied:

> Oh, absolutely. Looking at the shredded pieces of brain on the gurney, it looked like some of it had the characteristics of cerebellum, which

> kind of has a wavy surface. But because these brain pieces were shredded, this could easily have led to confusion as to whether it was all cerebrum—which has broader bands across the surface—or some cerebellum.

Another doctor who saw cerebellum was Dr. Marion Jenkins. Here is his account from November 22, 1963:

> There was a great laceration on the right side of the head (temporal and occipital), causing a great defect in the skull plate so that there was herniation and laceration of great areas of the brain, even to the extent that the cerebellum had protruded from the wound.

In 1988, Dr. Jenkins went to the National Archives to view the JFK autopsy X-rays and photographs:

> I did say cerebellum in my first official report. And the cerebellum ordinarily is in a posterior part. And here I know very well that the wound was more anterior than that, but there was a portion of the brain that looked like it had a stalk, and is convoluted to look like what I thought was cerebellum.

Gerald Posner talked to Dr. Jenkins in 1992, who told him:

> The description of the cerebellum was my fault. When I read my report over, I realized there could not be any cerebellum. The autopsy photo, with the rear of the head intact and a protrusion in the parietal region, is the way I remember it. I never did say occipital.

Another Parkland doctor who saw cerebellum was Dr. Malcolm Perry:

> And I looked at the head wound briefly by leaning over the table and noticed that the parietal occipital head wound was largely evulsive and there was visible brain tissue in the macard [sic] and some cerebellum seen and I didn't inspect it further. I just glanced at it and I went on outside and later was summoned up to the operating room to help in the care of Governor Connally.

Gerald Posner also talked to Dr. Perry in 1992:

> I did not really look at it that closely. But like everyone else, I saw it back there. It was in the occipital/parietal area. The occipital and parietal bone join each other, so we are only talking about a centimeter or so in difference. And you must remember the President had a lot of hair, and it was bloody and matted, and it was difficult to tell where the wound started or finished. I did not see any cerebellum.

The doctors at Parkland Hospital were frantically trying to save the life of President Kennedy. They were extremely busy, and no one had the time to examine his wounds in detail. Dr. Michael Baden explained this to Gerald Posner:

> Parkland was not concerned with whether the bullet was going from front to back or vice versa, they were only treating the symptoms, not the wounds. Some of them could be good surgeons but lousy pathologists. A third of the time, an autopsy shows something was missed by the treating doctors at the hospital. In unnatural deaths, it is common for the treating physicians to mix up stab wounds and gun shots, and they are wrong about half the time about exit or entrance. The Parkland doctors did not clean Kennedy off—there is just no way they could have hazarded a real guess about that wound, since it was covered with blood and tissue. If they say they saw cerebellum, they are just wrong because the cerebellum was perfect.

Dr. Paul Peters examined the autopsy X-rays and photographs in 1988:

> I said that I thought perhaps part of the cerebellum was missing, and that shows how even a trained observer can make an error in moment of urgency.

Two doctors still maintain that they saw cerebellar tissue at Parkland, Dr. Robert McClelland and Dr. Charles Crenshaw.

The other Parkland doctors disagreed with Dr. McClelland. Here is what Dr. Marion Jenkins told Gerald Posner:

> Bob is an excellent surgeon. He knows anatomy. I hate to say Bob is mistaken, but that is clearly not right. In 1988, when I went to the National Archives, the photos showed the President's brain was crenelated from the trauma, and it resembled cerebellum, but it was not cerebellar tissue. I think it has thrown off a lot of people that saw it. I guess a last point is that Bob and Groden [co-author of High Treason] are such good friends. I believed it has changed his attitude.

As for Dr. Crenshaw, you can read more about him in Chapter 9.

The fatal shot hit Kennedy just above the occipital protuberance. It just missed the cerebellum and slightly pushed it on its way through Kennedy's head. There was a deflection of the bullet by the skull.

Researcher Pat Speer explains:

> But there's another factor to be considered. And that factor is the curvature of the skull. According to Spitz and Fisher's Medicolegal Investigation of Death, "if the bullet strikes the head at a shallow angle or in an area of significant curvature, at least some deflection of the bullet's trajectory may be expected." According to Aarabi and Levy's Missile Wounds to the Head and Neck, "if a bullet is fired at an angle or hits a curved portion of the skull, deflection will usually result." According to Brogdon's Forensic Radiology: "The natural curvature of the ribs and the skull can cause bullets to change trajectory significantly."

Speer then quotes from scientist Larry Sturdivan:

At the time of the final shot, he was leaning forward and to his left. Figure 54 shows a drawing of the President at frame 312 with an entry trajectory from the sixth-floor window of the Depository and an exit trajectory that leads to the known impact points on and just above the windshield. This curvature shown in this drawing is about the amount of curvature to be expected in the trajectory of a badly deformed or broken bullet. Because the amount and direction of the curvature is unpredictable, the only way to reconstruct the path of the bullet in a drawing such as this is to use independent facts to establish the approach and exit trajectories. Without this independent information, the only thing we know for sure is that the approach and exit trajectories cannot lie on a single straight line.

Here is how Sturdivan sees the trajectory:

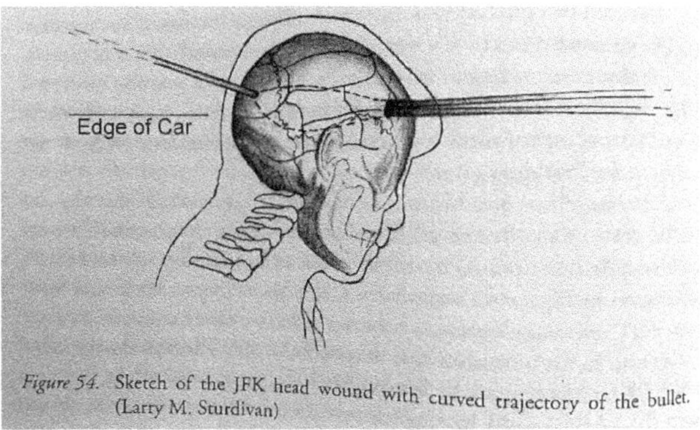

Figure 54. Sketch of the JFK head wound with curved trajectory of the bullet. (Larry M. Sturdivan)

Diagram courtesy of Larry Sturdivan

JFK: Destiny Betrayed doesn't tell viewers the whole story. The Dallas doctors were busy trying to save JFK's life. They were mistaken about seeing cerebellar tissue and over the years have recognized their error.

CHAPTER 15
IS THERE A PROBLEM WITH THE WEIGHT OF JFK'S BRAIN?

(EPISODE 3, 10:08)

JFK: Destiny Betrayed tries to make the weight of JFK's brain an item of controversy. This is in furtherance of its attempt to prove that another brain was substituted for JFK's.

Here is an excerpt from a transcript:

Dr. Gary Aguilar: And when you look at the autopsy photographs of the brain, which I've seen the originals of, you can just see that the brain is disrupted but very little of the tissue is missing, then we looked at the autopsy report of the brain, what they called the supplemental brain examination, the brain in evidence that's weighed there weighs 1,500 grams.

Dr. Michael Chesser: 1,500 grams is above average weight of an adult male brain. There was one report of eight thousand autopsies and the average weight of an adult male brain was 1,336 grams. So, they're saying that President Kennedy's brain was well above the average weight.

Dr. Gary Aguilar: Where did all that brain tissue disappear to, that flies around Dealey Plaza, that Jackie has in her hand, that everybody's picking off of their clothing?

Douglas Horne: An FBI agent, Frank O'Neill told the Review Board that over half of the mass of the brain was missing. He saw the brain removed at the autopsy. A lot of the mass missing was in the back. That's what mortician Tom Robinson said.

Dr. Michael Chesser: So, it's impossible for the actual weight of President Kennedy's brain to be 1,500 grams. This is just one more reason that this cannot be President Kennedy's brain in the photographs we have stored at the Archives.

Here is an excerpt from Vincent Bugliosi's book *Reclaiming History: The Assassination of President John F. Kennedy*:

The answer is that the president's brain did not lose much brain matter. "Contrary to the myth," Dr. Michael Baden told me, people who have said that the president lost a good part of his brain "are absolutely wrong." Baden says he saw the photographs taken of the president's brain at the time of the autopsy, and under his direction the HSCA's medical illustrator, Ida Dox, drew a diagram of the brain viewed from the top. As Baden said in his testimony before the HSCA, the diagram "represents extensive damage and injury to the right top of the brain" (1 HSCA 304). ("It's an exact depiction," he told me.) Note the words "damage and injury" as opposed to saying a large part of the brain was "missing." And, indeed, the autopsy report says nothing about any significant part of the brain being missing, merely saying, "The right cerebral hemisphere is found to be markedly disrupted." (CE 391, 16 H 987)

And as for the weight of JFK's brain:

"Basically, the president's whole brain was still there," Baden said. "The right hemisphere was severely damaged and torn, but less than an ounce or two of his brain was actually missing from the cranial cavity. If you squash a tomato, some would look at it and loosely say that most of the tomato was missing, but actually it's still all there, only it's mashed. That's the only explanation I can give you for how some people have said that a big part of the brain was missing. But they are wrong." However, since Baden conceded that the president had indeed lost at least an ounce or two of his brain (there are 28 grams to an ounce), I asked him how he explained that the president's brain, which weighed 1,500 grams (CE 391, 16 H 987), ended up weighing as much as it did, more than the average brain of around 1,400 grams? Was it simply that he had a larger brain? "When the brain is injured," Baden said, "this causes edema fluids to leak out of the blood vessels into the surrounding brain tissue, causing the brain to be swollen and increasing its weight. The increased weight to the president's brain is from the swelling." (Telephone interview of Dr. Michael Baden by author on March 29, 2002)

JFK's brain was weighed after it was fixed in formalin:

SUPPLEMENTARY REPORT OF AUTOPSY NUMBER A63-272
PRESIDENT JOHN F. KENNEDY

12/6/63

PATHOLOGICAL EXAMINATION REPORT No. A63-272 Page 1

GROSS DESCRIPTION OF BRAIN: Following formalin fixation the brain weighs 1500 gms. The right cerebral hemisphere is found to be markedly disrupted. There is a longitudinal laceration of the right hemisphere which is para-sagittal in position approximately 2.5 cm. to the right of the of the midline which extends from the tip of the occipital lobe posteriorly to the tip of the frontal lobe anteriorly. The base of the laceration is situated approximately 4.5 cm. below the vertex in the white matter. There is considerable loss of cortical substance above the base of the laceration, particularly in the parietal lobe. The margins of this laceration are at all points jagged and irregular, with additional lacerations extending in varying directions and for varying distances from the main laceration. In addition, there is a laceration of the corpus callosum extending from the genu to the tail. Exposed in this latter laceration are the interiors of the right lateral and third ventricles.

Here is a table on brain weights from the book *Current Methods of Autopsy Practice* by Jurgen Ludwig:

BRAIN: ADULTS*

	Brain weight (g)			
	Men		*Women*	
Age (yr)	Mean	Range	Mean	Range
17–19	1,340	1,170–1,527	1,242	1,120–1,420
20–29	1,396	1,158–1,620	1,234	1,057–1,565
30–39	1,365	1,075–1,685	1,233	1,038–1,440
40–49	1,366	1,069–1,605	1,240	995–1,543
50–59	1,375	1,113–1,665	1,200	820–1,447
60–69	1,323	1,018–1,610	1,178	920–1,372
70–85	1,279	1,039–1,485	1,121	832–1,370

* Data from Sunderman FW, Boerner F: Normal Values in Clinical Medicine. Philadelphia, W. B. Saunders Company, 1949.

The weight of the brain is approximately 1.4% of the body weight.[8] Various effects of fixation with formalin solution have been reported.[7] On fixation by penetration there is a mean weight increase of 8.8% (range, 3.3 to 19.2%).[21] On fixation by perfusion with 1,000 ml of 10% formalin solution there is a mean weight increase of 5.7% (range, 0.7 to 31.8%).[14] On fixation by perfusion with 2,000 ml of 10% formalin solution the mean weight increase is 8.8% (range, 1.0 to 26.3%).[14]

You can see the range of weights for men's brains as well as the increase in weight due to fixation in formalin.

Here is another source, *The Human Brain in Figures and Tables*:

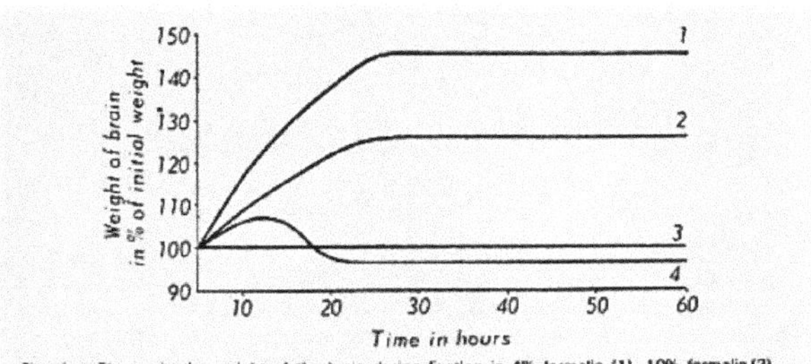

Fig. 1. Change in the weight of the brain during fixation in 4% formalin (1), 10% formalin (2), Bouin's fluid (3), and formalin with alcohol (4) (Stéphan, 1960).

Dr. Humes used a formalin concentration of 10 percent.

> **Q**: What did you do with the brain when it was removed from the cranium?
>
> **Humes**: Placed it in formalin. The blood vessels were somewhat disrupted. Normally we would inject the brain with formalin through the basal artery or some place. But some of these arteries were disrupted, and I can't recall—don't ask me exactly where the disruptions were. But the brain was damaged, and it didn't lend itself well to infusing it like we normally do. So, we placed it in a very generous quantity of 10 percent formalin, in a, you know, specimen container.

According to the chart above, a 10-percent formalin solution would likely lead to a 20–30 percent increase in brain weight.

By the way, Guy Banister's (see Chapter 44) brain weighted 1,540 grams:

William Guy Bannister 2.

KIDNEYS: The left kidney weighs 180 grams and the right kidney weighs 250 grams. The capsules strip with ease, revealing a relatively smooth but quite congested surface. On cut section the corticomedullary markings are distinct and abundant cortex is present. No abnormalities to the pelves, great vessels or ureters are noted. The bladder shows no abnormalities. It contains a small amount of cloudy, yellowish urine.

CENTRAL NERVOUS SYSTEM: The scalp is reflected in the usual manner and there is no hemorrhage or other abnormalities noted. The calvarium is removed. The brain in situ shows no abnormalities. The brain weighs 1540 grams. The Circle of Willis shows moderately severe atherosclerotic plaqueing without obstruction. The external surface of the brain shows no abnormalities. There is no evidence of fracture when the dura is stripped from the base of the skull.

PROVISIONAL ANATOMICAL DIAGNOSIS:
1. Coronary thrombosis, anterior descending branch of left coronary artery.
2. Recent and old myocardial infarction, left ventricle.
3. Hypertrophy of heart.
4. Acute pulmonary edema and congestion, bilateral.

Charles M. Wasson, Jr., M.D., Pathologist
smk

JFK: Destiny Betrayed creates controversy where none would otherwise exist. James DiEugenio's book *The JFK Assassination* examined Vincent Bugliosi's book *Reclaiming History*, which discussed the brain weight issue. And so, while DiEugenio should have been aware of what Bugliosi wrote about JFK's brain, viewers of *JFK: Destiny Betrayed* are not—because he deemed that information not worthy of inclusion.

CHAPTER 16
DID THE CONSPIRATORS SUBSTITUTE JFK'S BRAIN?

(EPISODE 3, 12:16)

JFK: Destiny Betrayed alleges that JFK's brain was substituted at Bethesda. Here is an excerpt from a transcript:

Douglas Horne: The Review Board had a consultant, a renowned forensic pathologist [Dr. Robert Kirschner]. He looked at the brain photographs, and he said, "this is a very well-fixed brain, it's all gray, it's not pink at all, it's been fixed for two or three weeks in formaldehyde. It's been fixed at least two weeks, maybe as long as three weeks." I looked at Jeremy Gunn, and he looked at me, and the hair stood up on the back of my neck. Because I knew that JFK's brain was examined less than three days after he was killed.

Dr. Gary Aguilar: One can only imagine that they wanted the damage to the brain to be consistent with the hypothesis that Oswald had done the shooting. So, if you had a defect going all the way to the back of the head, like so many witnesses testified to it, it might raise questions about whether that huge defect could have been caused by a single shot to the head, as Oswald is supposed to have done.

Dr. Michael Chesser: There are two photographs of the brain at the Archives. I viewed those in 2015. The brain looked to me to be distorted. My first thought was that the brain had been sitting in a jar of

> formaldehyde for a long time. At a teaching hospital, there was no shortage of brains. Autopsies were very frequent. Frequently, the brain was saved for teaching medical students, so it would not have been difficult to find a brain, a replacement for these photographs.

Dr. Kirschner conducted an independent review of JFK's autopsy X-rays and photographs. Here is his conclusion about the brain and its fixing in formaldehyde:

> When asked how well the brain in the brain photograph was fixed, Dr. Kirschner said that it was very well fixed, and initially estimated that it had been fixed two weeks or more, based on its appearance (very firm, and very pale—no pink color at all). After further discussion, he modified his original impression by saying that it may have been fixed between 1–2 weeks only, and that for it to have been fixed less than a week this brain would have to have been placed in an extremely concentrated solution of formaldehyde.

This is not exactly what Douglas Horne says in *JFK Revisited*. Kirschner's longest estimate for the amount of time the brain had been fixed in formaldehyde was "two weeks or more." However, Horne claimed it was "two or three weeks" and "maybe as long as three weeks." Kirschner then amended his estimate to maybe "1–2 weeks" or even less.

Kirschner explains that less than a week was possible with an "extremely concentrated solution of formaldehyde."

So, which is more likely? That the powers that be switched out another brain to fool the pathologists, or that they just used a higher concentration of formaldehyde?

CHAPTER 17
DID JOHN STRINGER TAKE PHOTOGRAPHS OF JFK'S BRAIN?

(EPISODE 3, 15:09)

JFK: Destiny Betrayed claims that autopsy photographer John Stringer said that he did not take the photos of JFK's brain that are in the current inventory.

Here is an excerpt from a transcript:

Oliver Stone: Who was the autopsy photographer?

Douglas Horne: John Stringer. He was a Navy civilian. He was widely respected; he had written a textbook on medical photography for the Navy. So, he was the photographer of record. He photographed the autopsy itself and also photographed the President's brain three days later.

Dr. David Mantik: So, the brain autopsy or autopsies, there were probably two such events, occurred later and were not done on November 22nd. John Stringer reports that he was present at the brain autopsy, which apparently occurred on the Monday after, which would have been November 25th.

Douglas Horne: We were very careful to question Mr. Stringer at the very beginning of his deposition about all the photographs he took and ask him what kind of film he used for black and white. What kind of film he used for color? Jeremy Gunn showed Stringer the color posi-

> tive transparencies of the brain, and Stringer immediately noted, "well, these aren't Kodak. These might be ANSCO," also, he said, "I don't see the name of the manufacturer on there, but these might be ANSCO, he said, but these don't have the right notches in the corner." So, Jeremy Gunn said, "Did you use this film with these notches in it when you shot the brain?" He says, "Not as far as I know." Half of the brain photos are taken of a brain from above. Superior views. Which is what Stringer said he shot of the complete organ. But the other half of the brain photos in the archives are taken of the bottom. They're called basilar views. And he said, "Did you take basilar views?" Stringer said, "No, not as far as I know."

JFK: Destiny Betrayed does not inform viewers that Stringer authenticated the autopsy photographs. He told ARRB interviewers:

> **Q**: Does anything about the appearance of the photos that you saw cause you to question their authenticity?
>
> **Stringer**: No.

The ARRB showed Stringer various autopsy photographs, and he confirmed, every single time, that he took the photographs. Here is the page number in his deposition and the autopsy photographs that he authenticates:

Page Number	Autopsy Photographs
161	29, 30, 31
162	1, 2, 3, 4
164	5, 6, 26, 27, 28
168	7, 8, 9, 10, 32, 33, 34, 35, 36, 37
173	11, 12, 38, 39
188	13, 14, 40, 41
192	15, 16, 42, 43
206	17, 18, 44, 45
216	19, 21, 22, 46, 47, 48, 49 (basilar photographs of the brain)
222	20, 24, 25, 50, 51, 52 (superior photographs of the brain)

However, during his deposition to the ARRB, Stringer had serious memory failures:

Q: In the document marked Exhibit 19, it refers on page 14 to a visit that a Mr. Stringer and Jim Kelly and Colleen Boland took to the National Archives. Does that help refresh your recollection as to whether you ever went to the Archives?

Stringer: It does not. I don't remember it.

Q: As you're sitting here today, does it seem to you to be very unlikely that you went to the Archives; or you just have no recollection, one way or another?

Stringer: I don't think I went. I don't have any recollection of it. And after '77. I was living in Vero Beach. It does say that I was staying with my daughter. Whose name is wrong here. It's R-u-s-k.

Q: Mrs. Rusk, rather than Mrs. Ross?

Stringer: Rusk. I certainly don't remember going to the Archives with these people. I don't know how I would have gotten there.

Here is an excerpt from the document in question, "Search for missing autopsy materials." (The 'myself' in the quote is Andy Purdy of the HSCA.)

MR. STRINGER lives at 23 Dolphin Drive, Vero Beach, Florida 32960. He is currently staying with his daughter, MRS. ROSS, until about Thursday, the 18th.

On the morning of August 15, 1977, MR. STRINGER went with Jim Kelly, Colleen Boland and myself to the National Archives to view the photographs.

More on Stringer's memory:

Mr. Gunn: I'd like to show you a document that has been marked as Exhibit MD 80. Could you take a look at that document and tell me whether you've ever seen that previously?

Stringer: Yes. I, evidently, wrote that; yes.

Mr. Gunn: I'll state for the record that on its face Exhibit MD 80 appears to be a letter, dated September 11th, 1977, from Mr. John T. Stringer, Jr. to Mr. Donald A. Purdy, Jr.

Mr. Gunn: Mr. Stringer, do you have any recollection of having written the letter?

Stringer: I guess, I must have. But that was in 1977. I don't have a copy of it.

Mr. Gunn: As best you can tell, is that your signature -

Stringer: Yes.

Mr. Gunn: - at the bottom of the page?

Stringer: Yes, I would say it is. Yes.

Mr. Gunn: Does the letter help refresh your recollection about any contacts, even through writing, that you may have had with the House Select Committee on Assassinations?

Stringer: Well, evidently, this was from them, but - But I don't even, - I mean, this is bringing back memories, but I don't remember—

Here is that letter that Stringer sent to Purdy:

23 Dolphin Drive
Vero Beach, Florida 32960
11 September, 1977

Mr. Donald A. Purdy, Jr.
Staff Counsel
Select Committee on Assassinations
U. S. House of Representatives
3331 House Office Building, Annex 2
Washington, D. C. 20515

Dear Mr. Purdy:

It is most difficult to attempt to think back and make sense of the copies of the letters that you sent and the copy of the letter enclosed. I faintly recall one of the letters that you sent - the one that I had signed. It is now obvious that black and white film was exposed during the post mortem.

As the film holders were exposed, they were taken by one of the Special Agents in attendance at the post mortem. In my opinion, the copy of the letter enclosed is an accurate version of the film involved.

In regards to the copies of the letters that you enclosed. As I said above, I do faintly remember the one letter that I had signed. I do not recall the facts concerning the corrections, numbers or circumstances surrounding same.

I have not been able to locate a copy of the letter that Dr. Stover required the participants at the post mortem to sign.

Sincerely

John T. Stringer Jr.

In terms of the photographs of the brain, Stringer noted the different type of film:

Q: Okay. And these are not Ektachrome notches, or you're not certain? It's just that they're different.

Stringer: I'm not certain, but they're different. It's—I think it's a different type of film. It could be Ansco film, like this.

Q: Did you ever use Ansco film yourself in conducting medical photography?

Stringer: Not very often.

Q: Did you use Ansco film in the—taking the autopsy—

Stringer: Not as far as I know.

Q: —photographs of President Kennedy?

Stringer: Not as far as I know.

Q: Is there any question in your mind whether you were the photographer of these images that are before you right now.

Stringer: Yes, if it's Ansco film, and if it's a film pack. I have no—I have no recollection of using a film pack.

Not surprisingly, Stringer is just not certain:

Q: Mr. Stringer, if I recall correctly, during the course of the deposition you identified three different factors relating to photography of the brain that would suggest that you would not have an identification number in it; you would not have used a film pack; and that you did not take a basilar view of the brain. Is that correct?

Stringer: I think so, yeah. That is what—Whether I took that, I don't know.

He had trouble remembering what happened at the autopsy:

Q: After the autopsy, did you ever speak to any of the physicians who were present at the autopsy regarding the autopsy?

Stringer: No, I don't think so.

Q: So, for—

Stringer: I can't remember.

And this:

Q: Okay. Could we switch from cameras now and talk a little about film?

Stringer: Mm—hmmm.

Q: You mentioned that you would—it would be typical to take black and white, as well as color film during an autopsy. And that it would typically be the two sheets of black and white that would be used. What kind of black and white film was used around 1963?

Stringer: Panatomic X rings a bell. I don't remember, to tell the truth.

And this:

Q: Do you recall the kind of color film that was used around 1963?

Stringer: Kodachrome, it was. Kodachrome.

Q: Kodachrome or Ektachrome?

Stringer: I think it was Koda—I'm not sure, to tell the truth. I think it was Kodachrome, though.

And this:

Q: Do you remember seeing an image of the entire—or the full length of the body of the President?

Stringer: I don't remember.

Q: Under sub–A on Exhibit 78, it refers to Ektachrome E3 film. Does that help refresh your recollection as the type of film—

Stringer: Yes, it does.

Q: —that was used?

Stringer: Yes.

Q: Earlier, if I recall correctly, you had said that you understood that it was Kodachrome.

Stringer: Yeah.

Q: It was Ektachrome E3.

Stringer: I would say it was Ektachrome, yes.

Here is another example of Stringer's memory trouble:

Q: Okay. Early in the deposition, you made reference to identification tags being used. Do you have a recollection as to whether there were identification tags used at the time of the photography of the brain?

Stringer: No. I don't remember. But there should have been.

Here is an excerpt of his testimony about the brain photographs:

Q: Mr. Stringer, If I remember correctly from earlier in your testimony, you said you had not recalled that there were any basilar photographs of the brain of President Kennedy. Can you identify whether the photographs that are in front of you now are basilar or superior views of a brain?

Stringer: They're basilar.

Q: If I recall correctly, earlier in your testimony, you said that there were identification cards that were used for identification of the brain when photographs were taken. Was that correct?

Stringer: Well, there's a ruler there, but there's no identification on there.

Q: Based upon on these being basilar views of a brain and based upon there being no identification cards, are you able to identify with certainty whether these photographs before you now are photographs of the brain of President Kennedy?

Stringer: No, I couldn't say that they were President Kennedy's. I mean, there's no identification. All I know is, I gave everything to Jim Humes, and he gave them to Admiral Burkley.

Q: Do you have any recollections in 1996 about what the appearance of the brain of President Kennedy looked like at the supplementary examination?

Stringer: No.

Q: Are you able to determine whether the photographs in front of you now are consistent with or not consistent with the brain, as you remember it from 1963?

Stringer: Well, it has to be, if that's Mr. Kennedy.

Q: Well, that's the question.

Stringer: Yeah.

Q: Does the brain in the photograph that you're looking at seem to be more hardened or drier than you recall at the time you conducted this supplementary autopsy?

Stringer: No.

Stringer does not deny that the brain photographs are of President Kennedy. It's just that there is no identification tag, and we have seen that Stringer said that he did not remember if identification tags were used at the time the brain was photographed.

Faced with Stringer's poor memory, one could easily conclude that he just didn't remember using Ansco film. We have already seen him get confused by Kodachrome and Ektachrome.

But to Oliver Stone and James DiEugenio, that is enough for them to reach another conclusion: that a different brain was photographed.

Which is more likely? A different brain or an inability to remember minor details after thirty-two years?

CHAPTER 18
DID A WHITE HOUSE PHOTOGRAPHER TAKE AUTOPSY PHOTOGRAPHS?

(EPISODE 3, 17:08)

JFK: Destiny Betrayed misleads viewers about the JFK autopsy photographs, making it appear that a White House photographer took additional pictures that are not in the record.

Here is an excerpt from a transcript:

Narrator (Whoopi Goldberg): Doesn't this all lead to the question, if Stringer did not take these photographs, then who did?

Narrator (Whoopi Goldberg): Robert Knudsen was one of the most fascinating stories that the Review Board encountered. Knudsen was a Navy photographer who was detailed to the White House in 1958. If you read his obituaries in the *New York Times* and the *Washington Post*, you will see that he is credited with photographing Kennedy's autopsy. Except officially, he was not.

Douglas Horne: Robert Knudsen was not interviewed by the Warren Commission. So, they finally found Robert Knudsen in 1978 and to its credit, the House Select Committee did a deposition. To their discredit, they never published it, they buried it, for fifty years. And it got released in 1993 and I know why they buried it. Because everything he told them about autopsy photography contradicted what they thought they knew in the official record.

Oliver Stone: What did Knudsen tell them?

Douglas Horne: So he says, "Burkley had me develop these black and white negatives on Saturday, November 23rd, and that's when I saw photographs of probes in the body." Well, they didn't like that. They really didn't know whether to believe him or not, because there are no pictures of probes in the body, in the official collection. But he was sure that he developed those negatives and saw them.

Dr. David Mantik: He has never said that he took photographs of the brain, but he implies that he was very busy taking photographs of the body. His wife was interviewed later by the Assassination Records and Review Board. He told her that the photographs had been burned, deliberately by the Secret Service, and that one photograph in particular, presumably the back of the head, had been severely altered. Gloria Knudsen was so disturbed by this after this death in 1989 that she actually contacted some of his colleagues there in the Navy, and they assured her that this was what he had told them, too. In fact, he had told them that he had seen photographs of the back of JFK's head that showed a large wound, low in the back of the head.

Douglas Horne: Stringer's still the autopsy photographer of record. I think they both took pictures, and I personally think that many of John Stringer's pictures never made it into the official collection, and a lot of the ones we are looking at are Robert Knudsen's pictures.

Knudsen told the HSCA that he processed autopsy photographs at the Naval Photographic Center. He said that he did "see the images" but that he did not study them.

Mr. Purdy: You stated earlier at the Naval Photographic Center you had checked the print for quality, but not for detail. Is that true?

Mr. Knudsen: Yes.

Mr. Purdy: Did you have a chance, subsequent to that examination, to look a little more closely at the prints?

Mr. Knudsen: I never saw the pictures after we brought them back.

Knudsen remembered a picture with metal probes going in and out through the wounds in the neck. He was then shown the autopsy photographs and was asked for his opinion:

Mr. Purdy: The witness has looked through photographs 26 to 29 so far.

Mr. Knudsen: These are roughly what I recall seeing, and there is the ruler that I recall on one.

A few minutes later:

Mr. Purdy: A photograph of the back of the President's head. Let me just ask you if that looks like one that you saw, or that matches your recollection. This is the back of the President's head here.

Mr. Knudsen: There again, I did not study it in detail. It seems to me that there was a little more of the piece of skull hanging in one of the photographs. Here, this is it.

Mr. Purdy: Now we are referring to Photograph No. 37F, showing the top of the President's head. So, it is your testimony here today that these photographs are not inconsistent with the ones that you saw?

Mr. Knudsen: No, not at all.

Knudsen had a vague recollection of a photo with metal probes. Purdy probed for more information:

Mr. Purdy: Looking at this photograph, approximately how much lower? Was it at a point that would not be visible in the photograph?

Mr. Knudsen: I am beginning to wonder now. I do not see anything here. But it is in the back of my mind there was a probe through the body.

Knudsen then says it was only a negative and not a print:

Mr. Knudsen: It seems to me that the one I saw with the probe was strictly a negative. I do not remember seeing a print of it. The first day, when we processed the film, we were just checking the negatives. I believe it was black and white. I do not know. I believe it was the negative of the probe.

Mr. Purdy: You think it was black and white, or you think it might have been, or you are just not sure?

Mr. Knudsen: It was a negative. I do not recall ever having seen a print, but it seems to me that there was a negative, in checking the negatives.

Knudsen's memory is not the greatest. Purdy suggests that perhaps he saw an artifact:

Mr. Purdy: It did not look like an artifact of any kind?

Mr. Knudsen: It did not appear that way to me. Like I say, I did not take it down and study it over a view, or anything like that. I just glanced at it. The wall was approximately this color and the negatives were hanging like this (Indicating).

The truth is that Knudsen only glanced at the negatives:

Mr. Knudsen: At this point, I wish I had studied the negatives rather than glance at them. At this point, I am confused why it sticks in my mind so strongly that there was this photograph, yet nobody else recalls it, and it is apparently not in any report. If it is not in any report—I cannot conceive why it would not be in the report. If it were there—it is really bothering me as to why it does stick in my mind so much.

Robert Knudsen did not testify that he had taken any autopsy photographs. He also authenticated the existing autopsy photographs. His only concern was his memory of one negative that showed a probe through JFK's body.

Douglas Horne alleges that the HSCA "buried" Knudsen's deposition. But all unpublished HSCA documents were sealed after the investigation because the House did not pass a bill to declassify its material. Knudsen's deposition is hardly earth-shattering, and I can certainly understand why it was not included in the HSCA volumes of evidence.

In 1996, the ARRB met with Robert Knudsen's wife, Gloria, and then two days later with her and two of her four children.

She told the ARRB that just before the Dallas trip, Knudsen got a metal splinter in his eye and had to recuperate instead of going to Texas. Did that perhaps affect his vision when he was developing the autopsy photographs? In her interview with the ARRB, Mrs. Knudsen wondered whether he would be able to work on the day of the funeral.

Mrs. Knudsen told the ARRB that "her husband had participated in another investigation into the assassination which she thought the public knew nothing about." She thought the invitation was in 1988 and promised to bring "the letter which invited him to appear in this forum," but that letter never turned up.

When the ARRB met with Mrs. Knudsen and her two children, they said that Knudsen not only photographed the autopsy but that he "was the only one to do so." We know this is not true.

Knudsen is not on the list of people who attended the autopsy prepared by FBI agents O'Neill and Sibert.

To my knowledge, no one outside the family said that Knudsen attended the autopsy.

The family remembered that Knudsen talked about metal probes being inserted in Kennedy's body. This is consistent with his deposition except that the family believed he took the photographs.

After Knudsen appeared before the HSCA, his family claimed that he told them that four or five of the photographs "did not represent what he saw or took that night, and that one of the photographs he viewed had been altered." His son Bob claimed that his father "told him that 'hair had been drawn in' on one photo to conceal a missing portion of the top-back of President Kennedy's head."

The problem here is that the HSCA conducted comprehensive tests that authenticated the autopsy X-rays and photographs. In addition, researcher John Canal has shown that the "high" entry point in JFK's head was an artifact of the scalp being stretched upward to show the entry wound.

Knudsen's family also elaborated on his supposed appearance at an inquiry in 1988:

- all 3 family members agreed that Mr. Knudsen appeared before an official government body again sometime in 1988, about 6 months before he died in January 1989. They all had the impression that it was "on Capitol Hill," and that it may have been a Congressional inquiry of some kind. They were unanimous that Mr. Knudsen came away from this experience very disturbed, saying that 4 photographs were "missing," and that one was "badly altered;" Mrs. Gloria Knudsen used the phrase "severely altered" regarding the one altered photograph when recounting her husband's statements afterwards. She further elaborated that the wounds he saw in the photos shown him in 1988 did not represent what he saw or took. He also told them that some of the details in the room in the background of the photos were "wrong." He had recounted that this experience was a waste of time for him because as soon as he would answer a question consistent with what he remembered, he would immediately be challenged and contradicted by people whom he felt already had their minds made up;

But there was no official investigation in 1988. Might they be referring to a conspiracy buff conference held in Pittsburgh to commemorate the twenty-fifth anniversary of the assassination?

Pitt holds review on Kennedy killing

The University of Pittsburgh will hold a three-day symposium this weekend called "The Kennedy Assassination: A Critical Review."

The series of lectures, films and exhibits is sponsored by Dr. Cyril H. Wecht, the first independent medical expert to challenge the findings of the Warren Commission Report into the assassination. Kennedy was shot to death in Dallas on Nov. 22, 1963.

In addition to Wecht, several authors are to speak, including Josiah Thompson, author of Six Seconds in Dallas, one of the first critical books.

Pittsburgh Post-Gazette, *November 18, 1988*

Somehow, assassination researcher Dr. Randy Robertson got into the action. He called Douglas Horne of the ARRB and told him that he should talk to Joe O'Donnell, another White House photographer, who could corroborate the allegations that Knudsen had taken autopsy photographs. O'Donnell had worked for the United States Information Agency in 1963.

He told the ARRB that Knudsen showed him autopsy photos on two occasions. On the first occasion, he saw a photograph that showed a hole in the back of Kennedy's head the size of a grapefruit. Another photo showed a hole in JFK's forehead above the right eye. A few days later, he was shown a photograph that showed no hole in the back of the head. He said he never discussed with Knudsen the discrepancy in the photos.

But was O'Donnell a credible witness? Definitely not.

He also remembered showing the Zapruder film to Jackie Kennedy:

> Mr. O'Donnell further volunteered that he was asked to show Jacqueline Kennedy the Zapruder film in a private screening within a few weeks of the assassination; his recollection of the timing was uncertain. He said that no one was present except Jacqueline Kennedy and him, and that the screening was held at the USIA screening room at the USIA building at 1776 Pennsylvania Avenue.

He then said that he had altered the Zapruder film:

> He said that following her viewing of the head shot sequence in the film, Jacqueline Kennedy told him in a very forceful way, "I don't ever want to see that again," which he said that he interpreted as an order to alter the film so as to remove the offending images of the head shot—namely, a halo of debris around the President's head. He told us he knows it was wrong but that he removed about 10 feet of film from the Zapruder film.

The ARRB noted that "O'Donnell's memory was uneven. He sometimes had trouble remembering the names of Presidents. He also gave a different timing on his viewing of the two different showings of post-mortem photographs (i.e., both events within a month or so of the assassination) from his first interview (in which he said both viewings occurred within a week or so of the assassination)."

Dr. Robertson called Mrs. Knudsen, who became upset when he told her he doubted that Knudsen photographed the autopsy. She then called associates of her husband to see if they could verify that he took pictures at the autopsy:

> Without naming names, or telling me the precise number of her husband's former associates that she called, she said that she spoke last week with some former Navy people who in one case (along with her husband, Robert Knudsen) saw, and in another case helped Robert Knudsen print, photos of President Kennedy's autopsy. She

> said that these former Navy people said they never directly asked Bob Knudsen whether he had been present at the autopsy, and he never volunteered such information either, but that from certain remarks he had made, and by evaluating the quality of the photographs, these people were of the belief that he may well have been present at the autopsy. When I asked her for the names of these former Navy people, she had that she had promised these people last week not to divulge their names, and consequently would not do so under any circumstances. When I made a second attempt later in the conversation to impress upon her the importance of the ARRB's pursuit of photographic leads pertaining to the autopsy, she again politely but very firmly refused to divulge names, and said that her word of honor was the most important principle at stake here.

In addition, one of the Navy people told her that they did recall a photo showing the back of Kennedy's head to be "blown out." She would not say who this was.

Toward the end of her interview, Mrs. Knudsen said that "the first 6 pages of the transcript" of his HSCA deposition "did not sound like her husband." She said he would not have signed a deposition with several spelling mistakes. However, the rest of the transcript did sound like her husband.

A few months later, Jeremy Gunn called Mrs. Knudsen and asked if she had any more leads. She promised to call back, but she never did.

Douglas Horne said in *JFK: Destiny Betrayed* that many of John Stringer's photos did not make it into the collection and that some of the photographs were taken by Robert Knudsen. I see no basis for this conclusion. Stringer told the ARRB that he was the only person to take photographs at the autopsy, and he further said the pictures in the inventory are authentic. Knudsen did not tell the HSCA that he took any photographs.

In his book, *MEDPHOTO: Snapshots of Life in Peace & War with the U.S. Navy*, John Stringer wrote:

> Just recently there has been additional information released from the Assassination Review Board concerning photographs allegedly taken by Bob Knudsen the Official White House Photographer. I knew Bob,

> he was an honorably man and if he said he had photographed the body, I would believe him. He was not present in the morgue while the autopsy was being conducted and I know that he did not take any photographs while the postmortem examination was being conducted.

In its zeal to prove that something is amiss with the autopsy materials, *JFK: Destiny Betrayed* once again ignored the issue of memory.

CHAPTER 19
DID SAUNDRA SPENCER DEVELOP A COMPLETELY DIFFERENT SET OF AUTOPSY PHOTOGRAPHS?

(EPISODE 3, 19:30)

JFK: Destiny Betrayed doubled down on its allegation that there are missing autopsy photographs by discussing the testimony of Saundra Spencer. While she told the ARRB that she developed a different set of photographs than those in the current inventory, it is clear that her memory was questionable. She perhaps saw post-reconstruction photographs of JFK.

Here is an excerpt from a transcript:

Dr. David Mantik: Saundra Spencer worked at the Anacostia facility, a Naval Photographic Center, which was quite separate from the Bethesda lab. And that weekend, she received film from both James Fox in the Secret Service, and from Robert Knudsen.

Douglas Horne: The photographs that Saundra Spencer developed, which never made it into the official record. The only evidence we have of them is her testimony. Saundra Spencer was visibly upset when she looked at the official autopsy photographs. She started to cry.

Oliver Stone: In front of the Review Board.

Douglas Horne: Yes, she started to cry in front of [ARRB General Counsel] Jeremy and I and the person from the Archives. Because, she said, "I developed pictures of him and his family for almost three years, and he never looked like this." And she said, "He did not look this bad

> in the photographs I developed on Sunday." She said, "He looks terrible in these photographs. He's all beat up. There's blood everywhere, that open body cavity." She said, "There were no open body cavities. It was very cleaned up. It was very respectful." And in one of the photographs she developed, there was a brain, an intact brain sitting next to the body, the nude body of the president. Strange, first of all, that it's intact because we know from FBI agent Frank O'Neill that the brain was more than half missing when they removed it from the cranium.

Saundra Spencer worked at the Naval Photographic Center (NPC) at Anacostia from 1960 until six months after the assassination. She was in charge of the White House Photo Lab, which was responsible for color still photography. She claimed that on November 23, 1963, a federal agent went to the lab with film holders that she then developed.

On December 13, 1996, she was interviewed by the ARRB.

She recalled that the autopsy photographs showed no measuring devices, that they had no identification tags, and that there were no instruments. She remembered that the body of Kennedy was "clean" and that there was "no blood and no gore" visible. She also believed the photographs showed "no damage to the right side of President Kennedy's head" and that "the top of the head was not visible in the photos." She also saw a circular wound in the front of Kennedy's neck, "about the size of a person's thumb," and a wound in the back of Kennedy's head, which she said was a "blown-out chunk," about 2 to 2.5 inches wide.

Saundra Spencer was then deposed by the ARRB in June 1997 and said that she remembered a "pristine" body:

> **Q**: Did you have an opportunity to observe the content of the negatives and the print as you were working on them?
>
> **Spencer**: Yes, I did.
>
> **Q**: Can you describe for me what you saw as best you can recollect?
>
> **Spencer**: Briefly, they were very, what I consider pristine for an autopsy. There was no blood or opening cavities, opening or anything of that nature. It was quite reverent in how they handled it.

She also saw a brain next to the body:

Q: So, there was a brain in the photograph beside the body, is that correct?

Spencer: Well, yes, the side of the body, but, you know, it didn't appear that the skull had been cut, peeled back and removed. None of that was shown. So, you know, as you whose brain it was, I cannot say.

Q: But was it on a cloth or in a bucket or how was it—

Spencer: No, it was on the mat on the table.

And perhaps the most important question of the day:

Q: About how much time were able to look at the photographs, did you get a good observation of them, was it fleeting? How would you describe that?

Spencer: It was—they traveled. You placed them on the drum, they would travel around, so after you place it on, probably about 15 seconds or so, they start under the drum and it rotates around, and then they drop off, and you grab them and stack them. So probably just 10 or 15 seconds.

So, Saundra Spencer only had a fleeting look at these photographs. Now does this sound like an autopsy?

Q: Do you remember what the walls looked liked or whether they—

Spencer: No, everything basically concentrated straight on the body. It didn't appear like the normal medical setting, you know. I don't know whether they did it in a separate room or they used special coverings on their tables or what, but I don't remember, you know, hospital stainless-steel gleaming or anything, or people running around in green scrubs or anything. It was just, like I said, it looked like a very reverent laid out arrangement.

A "reverent laid out arrangement."

Spencer was then shown the actual autopsy photographs of JFK:

Q: Ms. Spencer, could you go to the light box and tell me whether you can identify the color transparency of View No. 1 and Image No. 29, as having seen that before.

Spencer: No.

Q: In what respect is Image No. 19 different from what you previously saw?

Spencer: Like I said, there was none of the blood and matted hair.

Q: Can you explain what you mean by that? Are you seeing blood and matted hair on Image 29?

Spencer: On the transparency.

Q: But that was not present, the blood and matted hair was not present—

Spencer: I don't remember.

They asked her to look again at Image 29:

Q: Could you look again at the image of View No. 29? In what respect is the image that you see in 29, in the color print, different from what you observed on the prints that you made at NPC?

Spencer: Like I said, the body was pristine, and this has dried blood on the support, the ear, and the hair.

The body was pristine? Doesn't sound like a photograph from an autopsy.

Spencer was then shown pictures of JFK's head:

Q: Ms. Spencer, have you had an opportunity now to look at the second view corresponding to color Nos. 26, 27, and 28?

Spencer: Yes, I have.

Q: Do those two images correspond to the photographs that you developed at NPC in November of 1963?

Spencer: No.

Q: In what way are they different?

Spencer: There was no—the film that I seen or the prints that we printed did not have the massive head damages that is visible here.

Q: Putting aside the question of the damage of the head, does the remainder of the body, the face, correspond to what you observed?

Spencer: No.

Q: In what way is it different?

Spencer: The face in the photographs that we did, did not have the stress that these photos—on the face that these photos show.

Q: Could you describe a little bit more what you mean by that?

Spencer: The face, the eyes were closed and the face, the mouth was closed, and it was more of a rest position than these show.

She seems to be describing the kind of pictures you would get at a funeral home rather than at an autopsy.

Spencer is shown additional images of Kennedy's head:

Q: Could we next look at View 3, identified as the superior view of the head corresponding to color Nos. 32, 33, 34, 35, 36 and 37. Ms. Spencer, have you had an opportunity to look at the third view?

Spencer: Yes, I have.

Q: Do you those two images, again when you are looking at a positive transparency and a print, do those correspond to the photographs that you developed in November of 1963?

Spencer: No.

Q: In what way are they different?

Spencer: Again, none of the heavy damage that shows in these photographs were visible in the photographs that we did.

Spencer's photographs apparently did not show Kennedy's tracheotomy:

Q: Ms. Spencer, could you look at the wound in the throat of President Kennedy and tell me whether that corresponds to the wound that you observed in the photographs that you developed?

Spencer: No, it does not.

Q: In what way are they different?

Spencer: This is a large, gaping gash type.

Q: That is, in the fifth view, it's a large, gaping gash, is that correct?

Spencer: Uh-huh. In the one what we had seen, it was on the right side, approximately half-inch.

The photographs shown to Saundra Spencer were not the photographs she developed in 1963:

Q: Ms. Spencer, you have now had an opportunity to view all of the colored images, both transparencies and prints, that are in the possession of the National Archives related to the autopsy of President Kennedy. Based upon your knowledge, are there any images of the autopsy of President Kennedy that are not included in those views that we saw?

Spencer: The views that we produced at the Photographic Center are not included.

Q: Ms. Spencer, how certain are you that there were other photographs of President Kennedy's autopsy that are not included in the set that you have just seen?

Spencer: I could personally say that they are not included. The only thing I can determine is that because of the pristine condition of the body and the reverence that the body was shown, that—this is speculation on my part—that perhaps the family had the second set show and developed as possible releases if autopsy pictures were demanded, because at the time, Mrs. Kennedy was attempting to keep all sensationalism out of the funeral and maintain the President's dignity and name.

Spencer then suggests that the photographs she developed were taken after the reconstruction of the body:

Q: Is there any doubt in your mind that the photographs that you saw in November 1963 also were of President Kennedy?

Spencer: No, that was President Kennedy, but between those photographs and the ones we did, there had to be some massive cosmetic things done to the President's body.

Q: Do you have an opinion as to whether the photographs that you

> developed in 1963 were taken before or after the photographs that you observed today?
>
> **Spencer**: I would say probably afterwards.
>
> **Q**: So, you would think that the photographs that you developed were taken after reconstruction of the body?
>
> **Spencer**: Yes.

What to make of all this? Spencer's sequence of events is at odds with the Secret Service record. The autopsy film was developed on November 27, 1963, rather than one or two days after the assassination. James Fox brought the film to the NPC, black-and-white negatives were developed, and "color positives were made from the colored film." All processing was done by Lieutenant Vincent Madonia.

By the time the ARRB talked to Madonia, he remembered very little.

A few days later, additional black-and-white photos were made by James Fox at the White House. He returned to the NPC on December 9, 1963, to make color prints from the internegatives they had made.

He mentions in his HSCA interview that "two women in drying room passed out when [the photos] came through." Was Saundra Spencer perhaps one of the women?

Saundra Spencer made these allegations thirty-three years after the assassination. She only saw the photos for seconds. Might human memory be a factor here? Once again, *JFK: Destiny Betrayed* does not acknowledge the possibility that her memory might be somewhat imperfect.

Vincent Bugliosi raised the possibility that White House photographer Robert Knudsen took some post-reconstruction photographs and that these were the photos that Saundra Spencer developed:

> And since Knudsen's family said he was extremely close to JFK and took his death very hard, it makes sense that he might have wanted to take photos of the president when Kennedy once again approximated the handsome, dynamic leader he once knew, and that could only have been after the embalming process.

I am not saying that is what happened, only that it is a possibility, an innocent explanation that was never explored by the producers of *JFK: Destiny Betrayed*.

CHAPTER 20
ARE THERE ANY MISSING AUTOPSY PHOTOGRAPHS?

(EPISODE 3, 20:59)

JFK: Destiny Betrayed egregiously misquotes John Stringer to help prove there are missing autopsy photographs.

Here is an excerpt from a transcript:

> **Douglas Horne**: On November 1st, 1966, the National Archives and an official from the Department of Justice met with Humes, Boswell, photographer John Stringer, and the radiologist Ebersole. And they looked at the autopsy photographs for the first time and they created a catalog, an inventory simply saying, "this is what this picture describes." During this discussion, the DOJ witness Mr. Belcher, who was an attorney, noted they were discussing missing photographs. Jeremy Gunn, my boss, the General Counsel, did ask why these people signed an inventory which they knew not to be true. And Stringer said, "well, some people do object, but they don't last very long."

John Stringer's statement "some people do object, but they don't last very long" is quoted outrageously out of context. He was talking about offering suggestions to a doctor in charge of an autopsy:

Q: Do you remember identification tags during the time of the original autopsy?

A: There were one or two. The rest of the time, they were done away with.

Q: Why were they done away with?

A: There was no time to put them in to get them set up.

Q: When you're referring, then, to being done away with, are you referring to the exposure on the film that would identify it? Or do you mean to the ruler, or the—

A: Well, the ruler.

Q: Does it really take that much time to put a ruler in the photo?

A: Well, they get it set up and all that. I mean, when they were doing it, they were in a hurry and said, "Let's get it over with."

Q: Did you object to that at all?

A: You don't object to things.

Q: Some people do.

A: Yeah, they do. But they don't last long.

If there were awards for statements taken out of context, this would surely take the gold.

But let's set aside the misquotation and look at the alleged substantive issue: the inventory and other evidence of missing photos.

Here is the last page of the document from 1966 about the inventory of autopsy X-rays and photographs:

- 11 -

(4) One roll of 120 film (processed but showing no recognizable image) which we recall was seized by Secret Service agents from a Navy medical corpsman whose name is not known to us during the autopsy and immediately exposed to the light. This item is numbered as item 4 in Appendix B to the letter dated October 29, 1966 referred to above.

Upon completion of our examination, identification, marking, arrangement and listing of all of these photographic materials as described above, we left these materials with Dr. Rhoads. The X-rays and photographs described and listed above include all the X-rays and photographs taken by us during the autopsy, and we have no reason to believe that any other photographs or X-rays were made during the autopsy.

James J. Humes — Nov 10, 1966
James J. Humes
Captain, M. C., USN
date

J. Thornton Boswell — Nov 10, 1966
J. Thornton Boswell, M. D.
Cdr. MC. USN (Ret.)
date

John H. Ebersole — Nov. 10, 1966.
John H. Ebersole
Captain, M. C., USN
date

John T. Stringer — 10 Nov 1966
John T. Stringer, Photographer
Naval Medical Center
Bethesda, Maryland
date

000151

There may very well have been a discussion of missing photographs. Memory is a tricky thing, and given the number of photographs and the nature of the event—after all, it was an autopsy of a president—it is not surprising that they might have thought a certain photograph had been taken.

Stringer was asked about missing views:

Q: If those numbers for the holders, 11 and 9, were correct, then, your assumption would be that there would have been approximately 40 negative—or 40 films exposed on the night of the autopsy.

A. Yeah.

Q: Give or take one or two, I presume.

A: Yeah. There were some views that we—that were taken that were missing.

Q: Why is it that you say that some of the views that were taken are missing?

A: We went down to see them two years afterwards, and I remember some things inside the body that weren't there.

Stringer was asked specifically about missing photographs:

Q: Did you ever speak to Mr. Riebe about the apparent discrepancy in the number of films that had been exposed on the night of the autopsy?

A: I don't know whether I did or not.

Q: After the conversation with Captain Stover that you discussed earlier, did you ever raise the issue with him again?

A: I don't know, but we raised the issue when we saw the photographs in '66.

Q: What happened in 1966 when you raised the issue?

A: Nothing.

Q: To whom—when you say, "we raised the issue", whom are you referring to?

A: Well, when we were at the Archives—whoever was there.

Q: Did you go with Dr. Humes?

A: Dr. Humes and Boswell.

Q: Were Dr. Humes and Boswell under the impression that there were some photographs missing?

A: We talked about it, yes.

Q: And whom did you talk to about it?

A: We talked when we were there. I said there were some missing—because of that memorandum that it came back that there were some empty holders there. And the fellow that loaded them said there was no way there were any empty holders there.

So, was the empty holder the only reason Stringer felt there were missing photographs?

Dr. Humes remembers two photographs that he did not see in 1966:

Q: Other than that series of photographs, were the remainder of the photographs all taken at the beginning of the autopsy, do you recall?

A: Virtually all of them were, yeah.

Q: Do you remember—

A: There's only basically two that weren't. One was the inside of the occipital region, which we interpreted as the wound of entrance, for obvious reasons, and one that never came—whatever happened to it, I was very disturbed by it. We took one of the interior of the right side of the thorax because there was a contusion of the right upper lobe of the

> lung. So, the missile had passed across the dome of the parietal pleura and contused the right lobe. I wanted to have a picture of that, and I never saw it. It never—whether it was under-exposed or over-exposed or what happened to it, I don't know. And it's three years later when we were looking at it, of course. But we didn't see that photograph. So that was taken later, and the one of the inside of the skull was taken later.

Dr. Humes was asked about missing photographs at his deposition with the ARRB:

> **Q**: As of November 1966, were you of the opinion that there were any photographs of the autopsy that had been taken in addition to those that you were able to see at the Archives?
>
> **A**: The only one I recall specifically in that connection is the one I spoke to you about later, was the interior of the thorax. I thought we had seen all the others. Maybe we hadn't. I don't know. You got to remember; this was three years after the fact. That's part of the problem with all of this, temporal distortion of memory and what have you, accentuated when you get 35 years away.

Dr. Boswell was also asked about missing photographs:

> **Q**: We're about to look at some photographs that show just the brain. Putting those photographs aside, are there any other photographs that you remember having been taken during the time of the autopsy that you don't see here?
>
> **A**: The only one that I have a faint memory of was the anterior of the right thorax. I don't see it and haven't when we tried to find it on previous occasions, because that was very important because it did show the extra-pleural blood clot and was very important to our positioning that wound.

It's unclear if a photograph of the entry wound in the occipital region is indeed missing. Even the orientation of the current photographs confused Dr. Humes, and as you can see above, he admitted that his memory was a problem.

The only photograph that might truly be missing is the photograph of the interior of the chest. Here is what Vincent Bugliosi wrote about this issue:

> The 1966 National Archives inventory lists several "miscellaneous items" among the autopsy photographs, including two unexposed, 4 × 5-inch color transparencies. One had been developed (with no image visible), and the other left undeveloped. The 1966 inventory says that "this film was never exposed and therefore never contained an image but was loaded into a camera as a part of a film pack and was unloaded without being used to depict an image." Five unexposed black-and-white negatives, also listed among the miscellaneous items, met the same fate of being loaded and unloaded without an exposure being made. (ARRB MD 13, p.10) However, the two unexposed color transparencies described under "miscellaneous items" might explain the discrepancies between the early listings and the current inventory, and the issue of "missing" photographs. Adding two film sheets to the current inventory would mean that the eleven film holders were loaded on both sides (two sheets of film per holder), which would square with the autopsy photographer's recollection that all the film holders were fully loaded. (ARRB Transcript of Proceedings, Deposition of John T. Stringer, July 16, 1996, pp.131–132, 137, 144)

Bugliosi notes that a missing photograph wouldn't change anything:

> Although conspiracy theorists would have you believe that the "missing" photograph or photographs (if they once existed) in the Kennedy assassination would change everything we know about the assassination, the fact is, their appearance could only support the photographs already in evidence and corroborate the conclusion that the president was shot from behind. First, Dr. Humes testified what the two missing photographs depicted—the inward beveling of the entrance wound as seen from the inside of the skull (which, unless I'm misreading 7 HSCA 129, has not been lost), which proves it was an entrance wound, and the interior of the chest showing the bruise over the top of the right lung,

which corroborates the track of the bullet through the neck. Second, and perhaps most importantly, the "missing" photographs can't show something different from all the many remaining photographs, which were authenticated by the HSCA in 1978. The suggestion that only two views were singled out for destruction makes no sense considering that the photographs and X-rays that were presumably left behind prove beyond any doubt that the president was shot from above and behind. For instance, with respect to the back (or head) entrance wound, quite apart from the eyewitness testimony of the autopsy surgeons that the wound was an entrance wound, since there are surviving autopsy photos of the exterior of the back wound showing all the characteristics of an entrance wound, including the abrasion collar (7 HSCA 86), how could the missing photograph or photographs possibly change this incontrovertible fact?

JFK: Destiny Betrayed would have you believe that there are many missing autopsy photographs. The fact that there might be one missing photograph does not take away from the fact that the autopsy X-rays and photographs in the current inventory are not only authentic but that they conclusively prove JFK was shot from behind.

CHAPTER 21
DID GERALD FORD CHANGE THE LOCATION OF JFK'S BACK WOUND?

(EPISODE 3, 34:22)

JFK: Destiny Betrayed alleges that the Warren Commission and Gerald Ford raised the position of JFK's back wound in the report and that the HSCA then lowered the wound to support the single-bullet theory.

Here is an excerpt from a transcript:

Narrator (Whoopi Goldberg): And in order to make the facts fit the theory of one bullet doing all this damage, the Warren Commission needed to raise the wound in the back so that it would align with the alleged exit wound in the front of Kennedy's neck. Commissioner Gerald Ford did this simply via the stroke of a pen, changing the description in their report from 'back' to 'back of the neck.'

Dr. Cyril Wecht: As I recall, they said about Gerald Ford that he could not chew gum and walk at the same time. Now, all of a sudden, he becomes a forensic pathologist, and a photographer, and a criminalist, and an expert, and he knows where the bullet hole was, and he moved it up.

Narrator (Whoopi Goldberg): But then in 1979, the House Select Committee moved it lower in the back because they had pictures from the autopsy. It is conceivable that, at the time, the Warren Commission thought no one would ever see the autopsy photos. When the Review

> Board declassified the notations showing what Ford had done, the former commissioner replied that it had nothing to do with a conspiracy theory. He was only trying to be more precise.

I must question whether there was any need for Dr. Cyril Wecht to add that comment about Gerald Ford. It's nasty and not relevant.

The controversy about the face sheet (see Chapter 12 for the diagram) is not new. This was raised by Edward Jay Epstein in his book *Inquest* back in 1966. Dr. Thornton Boswell placed the dot in the back a little too low, but his written description on the diagram was accurate.

I'm not sure why we care about Gerald Ford's editing changes in the introductory section of the Warren Report:

> Seconds later shots were heard in rapid succession. The President's hands moved to his neck and he stiffened in his seat. A bullet had entered ~~his~~ the back of his neck at a point slightly ~~above the shoulder~~ and to the right of the spine. It traveled a downward path, and exited from the front of the neck, causing a nick in the left lower portion of the

The neck wounds are discussed in much more detail in a later section in the Warren Report:

> During the autopsy at Bethesda Naval Hospital another bullet wound was observed near the base of the back of President Kennedy's neck slightly to the right of his spine which provides further enlightenment as to the source of the shots.

Ford's change just added consistency between the introductory section and the later, more detailed section.

Author Jean Davison asked a good question on one of the JFK assassination boards:

> I respectfully ask that you take another look at this issue. My question is still, what evidence is there that Ford made his revision in order to support the SBT?

She added:

> To my knowledge, [nobody] has ever explained how moving the back wound up to THE NECK supports the SBT. Nobody CAN support it, because moving the entry to the neck would destroy the WC's SBT trajectory, not strengthen it.
>
> Again I'll refer you to **CE 903**. Although Specter didn't drill a hole in the stand-in's body and drive the rod through it, had he done so, the entry would be in the upper back, not in the neck. There's a string on the wall above his hand that shows an angle of about 18 degrees—that's the approximate angle measured by a surveyor during the re-enactment and the one the WC used for its SBT. If the rod is moved up to the neck, the bullet will exit well above the exit wound under JFK's Adam's apple. Or take a look at this photo of JFK.
>
> Try drawing a line of c. 18 degrees backward from the knot in JFK's tie. Where does it come out? Upper back, right? The claim that Ford's change "strengthens" the WC's SBT is simply not true. If I haven't made my point by now, I give up.

Commission Exhibit 903

Specter's pointer places the back wound exactly where the autopsy photo has it.

Here is the photo that Jean Davison refers to:

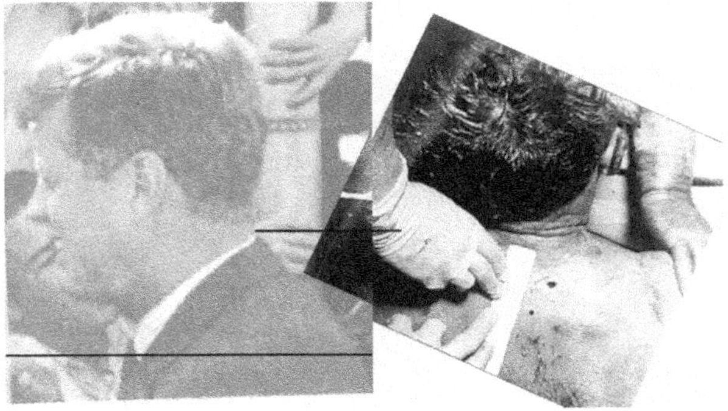

You can see how the single-bullet theory makes sense in the photo below taken by Robert Croft. The bullet fired from the sixth-floor window of the Texas School Book Depository was moving downward at 18 degrees.

Robert Croft photo #3, JFK Exhibit F-135, reproduced with permission of the Croft family

JFK: Destiny Betrayed tries to create a mystery where there is none. It really doesn't matter where Gerald Ford put the entrance wound since we have the autopsy photographs that shows its exact location, which is totally consistent with the single-bullet theory.

CHAPTER 22
DID THE AUTOPSY PATHOLOGISTS HAVE A PRESUPPOSED CONCLUSION?

(EPISODE 3, 56:51)

JFK: Destiny Betrayed alleges that autopsy pathologists were told to fit the wounds to a presupposed conclusion.

Here is an excerpt from a transcript:

> **Dr. Gary Aguilar**: But these three autopsy pathologists, who were not really credentialed to do that kind of an autopsy, were given the body, told 'here's the body, he was shot from behind, he fell forward' which they wrote in their autopsy report, 'figure out how the wounds fit the known circumstances of the shooting.'

Indeed, here are the first two paragraphs from the clinical summary of the autopsy report:

PATHOLOGICAL EXAMINATION REPORT A63-272 Page 2

CLINICAL SUMMARY: According to available information the deceased, President John F. Kennedy, was riding in an open car in a motorcade during an official visit to Dallas, Texas on 22 November 1963. The President was sitting in the right rear seat with Mrs. Kennedy seated on the same seat to his left. Sitting directly in front of the President was Governor John B. Connolly of Texas and directly in front of Mrs. Kennedy sat Mrs. Connolly. The vehicle was moving at a slow rate of speed down an incline into an underpass that leads to a freeway route to the Dallas Trade Mart wherethe President was to deliver an address.

Three shots were heard and the President fell forward bleeding from the head. (Governor Connolly was seriously wounded by the same gunfire.) According to newspaper reports ("Washington Post" November 23, 1963) Bob Jackson, a Dallas "Times Herald"Photographer, said he looked around as he heard the shots and saw a rifle barrel disappearing into a window on an upper floor of the nearby Texas School Book Depository Building.

Where might the information that the "President fell forward" come from? Well, it was all over the wire services:

Johnson was in the car behind Kennedy's when three bullets from a sniper ripped into the open presidential limousine, striking Kennedy in the head and throat and wounding Texas Gov. John Connally.

Blood sprang from the President's face and he fell face forward in the back seat of the car. Mrs. Kennedy, who had been riding with him, tried to lift his head, crying, "Oh, no!"

Half an hour later John F. Kennedy, 46, the first Roman Catholic and youngest man ever elected to the presidency, was dead.

Birmingham News, *November 23, 1963*

Here is a teletype regarding the assassination:

A7WX
WASHINGTON--FIRST ADD JOHNSON--KENNEDY (A5WX) X X X EVER HAD.
ALMOST AS SOON AS HE ARRIVED BACK IN WASHINGTON LAST NIGHT, THE 55-YEAR-OLD TEXAN WITH A REPUTATION AS A TOUGH POLITICAL GENIUS PLUNGED INTO A MEETING OF CONGRESSIONAL LEADERS OF BOTH PARTIES WHERE HE ASKED FOR AND GOT PLEDGES OF SUPPORT IN HIS DAYS OF TRIAL AHEAD.
JOHNSON, WHO FOUGHT A LOSING FIGHT AGAINST KENNEDY FOR THE DEMOCRATIC PRESIDENTIAL NOMINATION IN 1960, AUTOMATICALLY BECAME THE 36TH PRESIDENT OF THE UNITED STATES THE MOMENT THE 46-YEAR-OLD KENNEDY'S LIFE EBBED AWAY IN THE EMERGENCY ROOM OF A DALLAS HOSPITAL.
JOHNSON WAS IN THE CAR BEHIND KENNEDY'S WHEN THE THREE BULLETS FROM A SNIPER RIPPED INTO THE OPEN PRESIDENTIAL LIMOUSINE, STRIKING KENNEDY IN THE HEAD AND THROAT AND WOUNDING TEXAS GOV. JOHN CONNALLY.
BLOOD SPRANG FROM THE PRESIDENT'S FACE AND HE FELL FACE FORWARD IN THE BACK SEAT OF THE CAR. MRS. KENNEDY, WHO HAD BEEN RIDING WITH HIM, TRIED TO LIFE HIS HEAD, CRYING "OH, NO!"
HALF AN HOUR LATER JOHN F. KENNEDY, THE FIRST ROMAN CATHOLIC AND YOUNGEST MAN EVER ELECTED TO THE PRESIDENCY, WAS DEAD.
IT WAS STUNNING, ALMOST UNBELIEVABLE NEWS THAT FLASHED AROUND THE COUNTRY AND TO THE FAR REACHES OF THE WORLD.
EXPRESSIONS OF GRIEF, SORROW, SURPRISE POURED IN FROM FRIENDS AND ANTAGONISTS, ALLIES AND FOES, FROM THE KREMLIN AND FROM THE VATICAN.

Was it so unusual to include some of this information in an autopsy report?

Here is what Dr. Aguilar said in his article "How Five Investigations into JFK's Medical/Autopsy Evidence Got It Wrong": (Emphasis added.)

"Three shots were heard and the President fell forward bleeding from the head," the autopsy report stated. It continued with, "According to newspaper reports ('Washington Post' 11/23/63) (sic) Bob Jackson, a Dallas Times Herald Photographer (sic), said he looked around as he heard the shots and saw a rifle barrel disappearing into a window on an upper floor of the nearby Texas School Book Depository Building."[33] Kennedy's reaction to the fatal shot and the observations of a witness became part of the autopsy evidence that the shots had come from behind. **Using credible background information concerning the scene of a murder in autopsy reports is neither improper nor is it unusual.** However, in this case the information turned out to be as inaccurate as it likely was influential.

Dr. Pierre Finck was asked about this at his deposition by the ARRB: (Emphasis added.)

Q [Jeremy Gunn]: Those are the words that are in the autopsy protocol. Can you tell me why in an autopsy protocol it would be written that a victim fell forward? What relevance does that have to an autopsy protocol?

A: "Fell forward, bleeding from the head." Well, this is part of the clinical summary, the information given, and it's part of the information provided, "fell forward." See, this is not the words of the pathologist. It is information provided to them.

Q: And so, the pathologists **at the time that they wrote the autopsy protocol** were under the impression that President Kennedy had fallen forward after being shot, is that correct?

A: Yes

Dr. Aguilar implies that if the autopsy pathologists knew that JFK's head went "back and to the left" that they would have written a different autopsy report. But would they? They identified the entry and the exit wounds in JFK's head, and they saw the beveling that told them which wound was entry and which wound was exit. The evidence was clear.

Here is a quote from Dr. Humes:

After the brain was removed, we looked more closely at the wound, and noted that the inside of the rear of the skull bone was absolutely intact and beveled and that there could be no question from whence cometh that bullet—from rear to front. When we received the two missing fragments of the President's skull and were able to piece together two thirds of the deficit at the right front of the head, we saw the same pattern on the outer table of the skull—a bullet had traveled from rear to front. Every theorist who says the bullet came from the front has ignored this critical irrefutable diagnostic fact.

And every single forensic pathologist who has examined JFK's autopsy X-rays and photographs has come to the same conclusion: JFK was hit from behind by two shots, one to the head and one to the upper back and neck.

In addition, we also now know that JFK's head actually moves forward between Zapruder frames 312 and 313. Nick Nalli's important review of

Josiah Thompson's book *Last Second in Dallas* clearly demonstrates that the forward motion was not a "blur illusion."

And his important 2018 paper, "Gunshot-wound dynamics model for John F. Kennedy Assassination," examined the subsequent rearward motion of JFK's head:

> It is therefore found that the observed motions [after frame 313] of President Kennedy in the film are physically consistent with a high-speed projectile impact from the rear of the motorcade, these resulting from an instantaneous forward impulse force, followed by delayed rearward recoil and neuromuscular forces.

Dr. Aguilar is a "back-and-to-the-leftist' who believes that the movement of JFK's head outweighs the medical findings from the autopsy. This fantastic claim *from JFK: Destiny Betrayed* is not sustained by the evidence.

PHYSICAL EVIDENCE

JFK: Destiny Betrayed tries to impeach a variety of items of physical evidence in the case. It is the only way it can answer the incriminating evidence from Oswald's gun, the bullet fragments, and the bullet found on a stretcher at Parkland Hospital.

"Then we've agreed that all the evidence isn't in, and that even if all the evidence were in, it still wouldn't be definitive."

Credit: Mischa Richter / The New Yorker Collection / The Cartoon Bank / June 15, 1987

CHAPTER 23
DID LEE HARVEY OSWALD HAVE AN ALIBI?

(EPISODE 1, 49:32)

Before *JFK: Destiny Betrayed* gets into the physical evidence, it claims that three witnesses—Vickie Adams, Sandra Styles, and Dorothy Garner —"provide powerful evidence that Oswald was not on the sixth floor at the time of the shooting."

Here is an excerpt from a transcript:

Barry Ernest: Vicki [Adams] worked on the fourth floor of the Texas School Book Depository. She testified that immediately after the assassination, she ran down the back stairs in an effort to get outside to see what was going on.

Narrator (Whoopi Goldberg): According to the Warren Report, Oswald was seen in the second-floor lunchroom within 90 seconds of the shooting by Dallas police officer Marrion Baker and Oswald's supervisor, Roy Truly, as they went up the stairs to the sixth floor.

[Archive clip] **Marrion Baker**: I turned around and asked him if the man worked for him, and if he knew him. And he said, "Yes, he works for me, and I—I know him."

Narrator (Whoopi Goldberg): For Vicki Adams to have reached the first floor within 60 seconds and not have seen or heard Oswald, or Baker and Truly, on the wooden stairs was in conflict with the

Warren Commission's assumption that Oswald was on those stairs at the time.

Barry Ernest: So, what the Warren Commission did was successfully deceive the public into thinking that Vicki was just another mistaken or confused witness. The whole case based on the Warren Commission is Vicki was wrong because she went down the stairs later than she thought, and she saw two men there who couldn't have been there unless she had come down the stairs later.

Four women—Victoria Adams, Sandra Styles, Elsie Dorman, and Dorothy Garner—watched the motorcade from the fourth floor of the TSBD. After the assassination, Adams and Styles walked down to the first floor and exited the building from the Houston Street dock. They did not see Oswald or anybody else going down the stairs. Adams testified that when she got to the first floor, she saw warehouse workers Bill Shelley and Billy Lovelady. Because of this, the Warren Commission concluded that Adams and Styles had descended well after Oswald had run downstairs:

Shelley and Lovelady, however, have testified that they were watching the parade from the top step of the building entrance when Gloria Calverly, who works in the Depository Building, ran up and said that the President had been shot. Lovelady and Shelley moved out on the street. About this time Shelley saw Truly and Patrolman Baker go into the building. Shelly and Lovelady, at a fast walk or trot, turned west into the railroad yards and then to the west side door of the Depository Building. They reentered the building by the rear door entrance. On entering, Lovelady saw a girl on the first floor who he believes was Victoria Adams. If Miss Adams accurately recalled meeting Shelley and Lovelady when she reached the bottom of the stairs, then her estimate of the time when she descended from the fourth floor is incorrect, and she actually came down the stairs several minutes after Oswald and after Truly and Baker as well.

However, a wrench was thrown into this scenario when researcher Barry Ernest discovered a document in which Dorothy Garner said that "after Miss Adams went downstairs she saw Mr. Truly and the policeman come up." If Garner did see Truly and Baker, then Adams and Styles went down earlier than the Warren Commission believed. Ernest believes that they should have seen Oswald on the stairs.

The problem here is that we don't have exact time intervals. We don't know exactly how long it took Oswald to make his way down the stairs. And since we are talking about seconds, it makes it impossible to claim, with any degree of certainty, that Adams should have seen Oswald. Styles told an interviewer that "he [Oswald] could have been behind us, he could have been ahead of us."

Let's start with the testimony of Vicki Adams.

> **Mr. Belin**: How long do you think it was between the time the shots were fired and the time you left the window to start toward the stairway?
>
> **Miss Adams**: Between 15 and 30 seconds, estimated, approximately.

There is a lot of ambiguity in that statement. But note that it took her fifteen to thirty seconds, at least, just to decide to move from the window.

Sandra Styles said, "I saw people running and others lie down on the ground and realized something was happening. Victoria Adams and I left the office at this time, went down the back stairs, and left the building at the back door."

They lingered at the window for a brief period. They then made their way across the floor, in three-inch high heels, to get to the stairway.

> **Mr. Belin**: How long do you think it was, or do you think it took you to get from the window to the top of the fourth floor stairs?
>
> **Miss Adams**: I don't think I can answer that question accurately, because the time approximation, without a stopwatch, would be difficult.

Remember, human memory is not like a video camera "preserving the details of our memories until we need them." Adams and Styles saw people reacting to the assassination, and so they stayed at that window at least several seconds after the last shot.

In 2002, Barry Ernest asked Adams how long it took her to get from the window to the top of the stairs and then to the first floor. Her answer was revealing: "I am sorry about this, but I have no concept of how long."

Sandra Styles told researcher Sean Murphy that "we did linger at the window a bit trying to sort it out." She added that "I am certain that we went to the public elevator first, but may not have waited long there either." Her overall view: "Logic tells me that it had to take a couple of minutes at least for things to sink in and to make the decision to go."

Jerry Dealey is a researcher in Dallas who knows more about the Texas School Book Depository than almost anybody. He believes that Oswald might not have been heard:

> Sandra and Vicki have since told interviewers that they believed they should have been able to hear anyone else ahead or behind them, as they were noisy wooden stairs. However, they were in a hurry, and wearing 3" heels, so were probably making a great deal of noise themselves. If Oswald was trying to be quiet, I doubt they would have heard him ahead of them, with the noise they were likely making themselves.

He has prepared this estimate of the various witnesses and their movements and has come up with a tentative timeline:

Seconds after last shot	Shooter/Oswald	Styles/Adams (Garner)	Truly and Baker	Others	Recreations
+10	Withdraws weapon, views drive away of limo underpass	"What Happened?"	Baker turns corner, parks motorcycle	Dougherty working Williams, Norman, Jarman watch motorcade away	
+20	Traveling to north TSBD along east wall			Scramble away from east	
+30	Across to west – stash rifle	Decision to go down	Baker's foot on bottom porch step **(per films)**		
+40	Crosses 5th floor (4 seconds stairs – 6 to cross floor)	Walk quickly through office front of 4th	Encounter Eddie Piper in lobby – Truly enters	Head to west window – looking some time after	
+50	Crosses 4th floor – not seen by ladies on 4	Approaches wall in front of warehouse area	Crosses 1st floor to Elevators	Dougherty on 5th floor with west elevator door open	
+60	Crosses 3rd floor – (hears Truly?)	Girls to stairs, while Garner waits at office wall/door	At elevators – hollering up shaft to release	Dougherty getting books does not hear Truly	
+1:10	Emerges 2nd floor into lunchroom vestibule	Crosses 4th floor	Takes stair up to 2nd.		Baker 2 1:15 Oswald 1:17
+1:20	Oswald in lunchroom	Crosses 3rd floor	Baker diverts to lunchroom where he has seen movement – Truly starts up	Dougherty takes west elevator down to take order and investigate sound	Baker 1 1:30
+1:30	Oswald/Baker/Truly in lunchroom	Girls cross 2nd floor – not seeing Truly/Baker/Oswald	Oswald/Baker/Truly in lunchroom	Dougherty and elevator descending	
+1:40	Oswald buys coke	Girls emerge 1st floor – leave building	Baker/Truly continue up to 3rd floor. Crosses		
+1:50	Oswald leaves lunchroom across 2nd floor office space	Dorothy Garner sees Baker and Truly cross 4th floor	Baker/Truly crosses 4th floor	*Mrs. Reid comes across 2nd office area to call husband*	
+2	Oswald down stairs front of building		Baker/Truly emerge 5th floor – head to east (manual) elev	Williams sees Baker/Truly cross 5th to manual elevator	
+2:10	Oswald exits building & gives newsmen phone directions	Jerry Dealey		Williams/Jarman/Norman head back to stairs	

Timeline courtesy of Jerry Dealey

Oswald simply beat Sandra Styles and Victoria Adams down the stairs. Given the ambiguity of the times involved, this scenario makes as much sense as any and certainly as much as Oswald being downstairs when the shots were fired.

Vicki Adams also said something that gives us even more than the usual reasons to question the precision of her testimony:

> **Mr. Belin**: Is there any other information that you have that could be relevant?
>
> **Miss Adams**: There was a man that was standing on the corner of Houston and Elm asking questions there. He was dressed in a suit and a hat, and when I encountered Avery Davis [a fellow worker] going down, we asked who he was, because he was questioning people as if he were a police officer, and we noticed him take a colored boy away on a motorcycle, and this man was asking questions very efficaciously, and we said, "I guess he is maybe a reporter," and later on television, there was a man that looked very similar to him, and he was identified as Ruby. And on questioning some police officer, they said they had witnesses to the fact that he was in the Dallas Morning News at the time. And I don't know whether that is relevant or what.

Of course, this man could not have been Jack Ruby because he was indeed at the *Dallas Morning News* at the time of the assassination.

When Barry Ernest found Vickie Adams in 2002, she was certain she had encountered Jack Ruby:

> "We ran outside and noticed a lot of people running toward the railroad tracks. The railroad yard behind the grassy knoll was quite a distance away. I could not see anything other than people running toward the railroad cars and I tried to run that way, too. But a policeman stopped us. I didn't get very far—maybe 10 or 20 feet from the Depository building. So, we turned back to Houston and to the front of the building.
>
> "It was mass confusion. That was when I noticed Ruby."
>
> How sure was she it was Jack Ruby?
>
> "Supposedly Jack Ruby was a great admirer of President and Mrs. Kennedy," she answered. "What was peculiar was according to his

> testimony he was several blocks away at the newspaper office when the motorcade was passing by on Houston and Elm. But I saw him immediately after the gunshots on the corner of Houston and Elm and just happened to notice him since he was asking questions of people, like he was a reporter. He was rather distinctive in that he had on a suit and hat. I didn't see anyone else acting like that. I mentioned this in my testimony more than once, trying to give as much information as I could about what I saw that day. From what I know nothing ever was said about that."
>
> "But when I met Mark Lane, he showed me a picture of Ruby dressed like I had seen him and where I said he was. He said the Warren Commission had cropped the photo."

Notice the use of the word "immediately." She saw him "immediately after the gunshots." But we know that can't be true. She had to run across the floor and go down the stairs, out the back of the TSBD, and then over to Elm and Houston. It wasn't immediately. This is a good illustration of how memory plays with time.

Did Adams "immediately" go to the stairs after the last shot, as Barry Ernest said in the transcript at the start of this chapter?

And like other witnesses in the case, Vickie Adams got infected with the conspiracy bug. Barry Ernest writes:

> Her husband by now [1975] had become an avid reader of all things assassination. He convinced her that she should remain quiet about her background. Too many people were dying. It would be much safer.

We know that there was a shooter on the sixth floor. Adam and Styles did not see this person either. Barry Ernest says that a supposed assassin "could have come down later, since the sixth floor remained vacant and was not discovered as the sniper's 'man cave' for some 35 minutes after the assassination."

But the TSBD was sealed off by 12:40 p.m. An assassin on the sixth floor not only missed Styles and Adams on the stairs but all the other employees on the first floor. Jerry Dealey notes that "they would also have to thread their way past the many officers and FBI agents which started searching the building about 12:36 PM."

JFK: Destiny Betrayed overreaches when it claims that Adams, Styles, and Garner "provide powerful evidence that Oswald was not on the sixth floor at the time of the shooting." They don't. A more sensible and simpler scenario is that Lee Harvey Oswald just simply beat Adams and Styles down the stairs.

CHAPTER 24
DID MARINA OSWALD TAKE THE BACKYARD PHOTOGRAPHS?

(EPISODE 2, 38:40)

JFK: Destiny Betrayed carefully uses a snippet of a Marina Porter interview to make it sound like she denied taking backyard photographs of Oswald holding a rifle.

The three known backyard photographs of Lee Harvey Oswald

Here is an excerpt from a transcript:

Narrator (Whoopi Goldberg): The Warren Commission was aware of something else that was wrong with their evidence.

[Archive clip] **Tom Brokaw**: All kinds of ballistic tests show that the bullets, in fact, came from that rifle. That was his rifle, you took a picture of him with it. His …

[Archive clip] **Marina Porter**: No. No.

[Archive clip] **Tom Brokaw**: palmprints, and …

[Archive clip] **Marina Porter:** No. No.

[Archive clip] **Tom Brokaw**: fingerprints were all over the School Book Depository.

[Archive clip] **Marina Porter**: You have been misinformed. The ballistics tests did not prove anything at all.

[Archive clip] **Stock Footage Narrator**: This is the weapon that was used. A rather well-worn military rifle.

Narrator (Whoopi Goldberg): Is this really true, or is it a myth that has been allowed to assume the status of accepted fact since few have challenged it?

Oliver Stone: Is the rifle in evidence today the same rifle the Commission said Oswald ordered through the mail?

This short segment in *JFK: Destiny Betrayed* makes it clear that her denials were about the ballistic tests (unclear which tests) and not the photos. But it is placed in the section of the so-called documentary that discusses the legitimacy of the backyard photographs (see the next two chapters).

It doesn't clarify the issue; it misleads.

Oliver Stone is being disingenuous with this clip. He is so desperate to prove that the Mannlicher-Carcano rifle was not Oswald's that he is willing to insert an interview segment that didn't touch upon that issue.

The HSCA showed the backyard photographs to Marina Porter:

Mr. McDonald: Mrs. Porter, do you recognize the photographs placed in front of you?

Mrs. Porter: Yes, I do.

Mr. McDonald: And how do you recognize them?

Mrs. Porter: That is the photograph that I made of Lee on persistent request of taking a picture of him dressed like that with rifle.

The HSCA introduced another picture that had been found:

Mr. McDonald: So, with these to refresh your memory, can you say, can you recall if you took any additional pictures?

Mrs. Porter: No, I cannot remember how many exactly to me it looks like all of them. It looks like Lee.

Mr. McDonald: That is correct.

Mrs. Porter: That is the only thing I can say, but I do not remember how many pictures I was taking.

Mr. McDonald: But since we have three in front of you, we know now that you at least took three; correct?

Mrs. Porter: Yes.

By the way, Marina said Oswald used to practice with his rifle:

Mr. McDonald: Did he ever take it out, outside the apartment, to practice with it, to do anything with it?

Mrs. Porter: Yes, he did.

Mr. McDonald: And what did he do?

Mrs. Porter: He will, like before it gets very dark outside, he would leave apartment dressed with the dark raincoat, even though it was a hot summer night, pretty hot weather anyway, and he would be wearing this, and he would be hiding the rifle underneath his raincoat. He said he is going to target practice or something like that.

Mr. McDonald: This was one occasion you are talking about with the raincoat?

Mrs. Porter: It is several occasions, maybe more than once.

Mr. McDonald: He did the same thing on several occasions, put the raincoat on?

Mrs. Porter: Yes.

Mr. McDonald: And the rifle under the raincoat?

Mrs. Porter: Yes.

Mr. McDonald: And how long would he be gone?

Mrs. Porter: A few hours.

Mr. McDonald: And what did he say as he was going out to do this? Did he have any specific comment? Did he tell you any reason?

> **Mrs. Porter**: Well, he said that it is a practice range somewhere apparently. That is the purpose of him taking the rifle, in order to practice.

The evidence is overwhelming that the Mannlicher-Carcano rifle found in the Texas School Book Depository belonged to Lee Harvey Oswald.

CHAPTER 25
IS THERE AN ISSUE WITH THE STRAP AND SLING MOUNTS ON THE MANNLICHER-CARCANO?

(EPISODE 2, 39:16)

JFK: Destiny Betrayed alleges that there are issues with the strap and sling mounts on Oswald's Mannlicher-Carcano rifle.

Here is an excerpt from a transcript:

Oliver Stone: Is the rifle in evidence today the same rifle the commission said Oswald ordered through the mail?

Brian Edwards: The rifle that Lee Oswald allegedly ordered under an alias of Alex Hidell was obtained through Klein's Sporting Goods store in Chicago as a mail order. Got it out of *American Rifleman* Magazine. He wrote on the coupon he wanted a 36-inch model, Mannlicher-Carcano, 6.5 millimeter, for $19.95. Robert Frazier was one of the examiners, he was a firearms expert for the FBI, and he testified that he did measure it, and the measurement was 40.2 inches in length, from barrel to stock. There's a 4.2-inch difference in the one he ordered, versus what they found in the Book Depository.

Narrator (Whoopi Goldberg): Klein's may have indeed delivered a different Mannlicher-Carcano model to Oswald, but there are other anomalies to this story. The model that Oswald ordered showed these strap attachment points on the bottom of the barrel and stock.

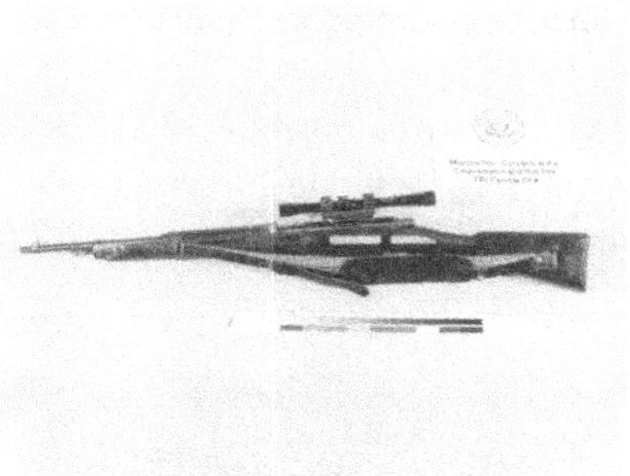

Warren Commission Exhibit 139, Photo 2

Brian Edwards: In the photograph is Lieutenant Carl Day, Dallas Police Department, bringing a rifle out of the Book Depository. One of the straps at the back of the gun is on the left side of the stock, embedded in the stock. That's clearly not the rifle that was ordered, or at least appears in the Klein's Sporting Goods store.

Narrator (Whoopi Goldberg): The straps shown in the so-called backyard photos are at the bottom and not on the side of the stock.

My colleague Steve Roe has debunked this segment of *JFK: Destiny Betrayed*. Oswald saw this ad in *American Rifleman* magazine and ordered the 36-inch model.

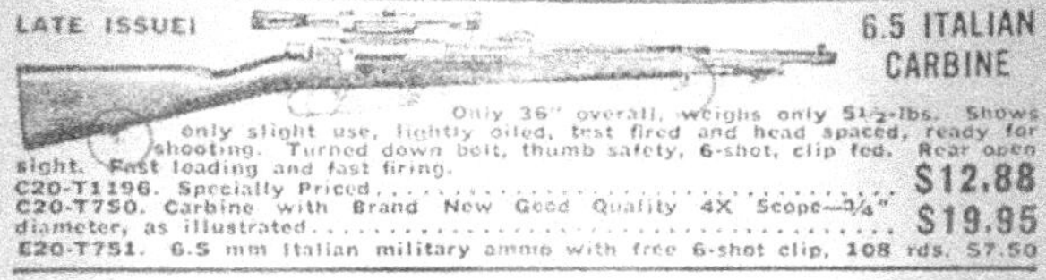

Steve Roe notes:

In the Klein's ad, the model shown was a Carcano Model 91-TS (Moschetto). Those models were 36" in length. Both models fired the same 6.5 x 52mm ammo.

When Oswald ordered his rifle, he did not receive the Model 91-TS, he received the Model M91/38 This is because Klein's ran out of the

Model 91-TS (with bottom sling / strap mounts) and replaced them with M91 / 38s.

In Waldman Exhibit #1, you will see the evidence Once Klein's sold off their Carcano M91-TS (as pictured in the ad), they replaced them with M91 / 38s that were shipped to Klein's in April 1962.

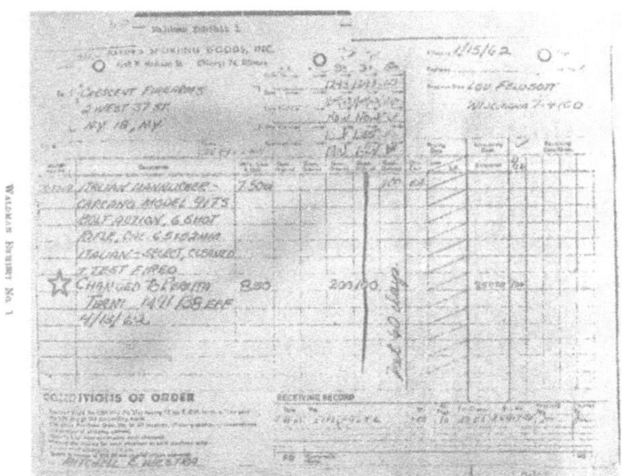
Waldman Exhibit No. 1

Crescent Firearms
2 West 37 St.
N.Y. 18, N.Y.

Lou Feldsott

Italian Manlicher
Carcano Model 91TS
Bolt Action, 6 Shot
Rifle, Cal. 6.5
Italian - Select, Cleaned
& Test Fired

Changed B. Perrin
Term M91/38
4/18/62

Conditions of Order

Waldman Exhibit #1, Warren Commission

Klein's updated the ad in the next issue of *American Rifleman* to reflect the fact that it had run out of the 36-inch models.

Credit: Dave Von Pein JFK Archives

As for the straps, Steve Roe brightened one of the backyard photographs that shows the top sling mounted on the side and not the bottom:

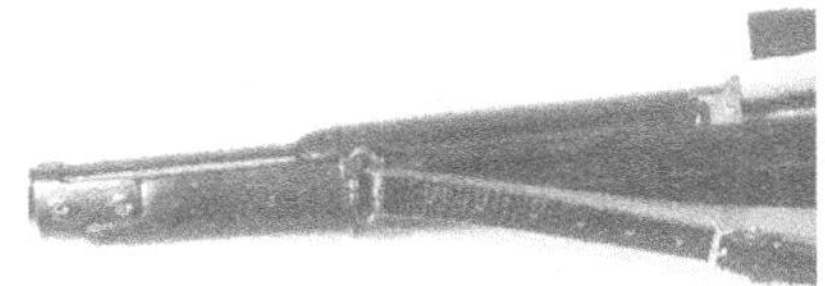

JFK: Destiny Betrayed tries to fool the audience with a complete non-mystery. In addition, the way the documentary formulates the question is problematic, focusing on the rifle that Oswald "ordered" as opposed to the rifle that Oswald "received." The inference is that Oswald did not order the rifle, that the chain of custody is faulty, and that abracadabra, Oswald was innocent. None of the legs of this argument stands on their own, and viewers of *JFK: Destiny Betrayed* aren't told the complete truth about Oswald's Mannlicher-Carcano.

CHAPTER 26
WERE THE BACKYARD PHOTOGRAPHS FAKED?

(EPISODE 2, 40:41)

JFK: Destiny Betrayed once again raises the issue of the legitimacy of the backyard photographs of Lee Harvey Oswald. Over the years there have been several scientific studies that have conclusively found that the photographs are legitimate. *JFK: Destiny Betrayed* seems to make the argument that while the forgery was good enough to fool experts decades later, the conspirators somehow made ridiculously clumsy errors with his rings.

Here is an excerpt from a transcript:

Brian Edwards: Marina Oswald took backyard photographs of Lee Oswald holding a rifle and a pistol on his hip, and in that first photograph, that she took three of, Commission Exhibit 133-A and 133-B, show a ring on the ring finger of the right hand. 133-C the ring appears on the left hand. In fact, the Dallas police showed Lee Oswald one of the pictures, while he was still in custody, and he said, "that's my face but I don't remember ever having had that picture taken of me."

That is not even the correct quote from Lee Harvey Oswald. Here is an excerpt from the testimony of Dallas police officer Guy Rose:

> **Mr. Rose**: In Captain Fritz's office—yes. Well, the occasion was—I got back to the office and I took this small picture of Oswald holding the rifle, and left the rest of them with the Captain and I took one up to the I.D. bureau and had them make me an enlargement of it, and they made an almost 8" by 10" enlargement of this picture and I brought it back to the captain and Oswald was brought in and the captain showed him this picture, and Oswald apparently got pretty upset when he saw the picture and at first he said, "Well, that's just a fake, because somebody has superimposed my face on that picture." Then, the captain said, "Well, is that your face on the picture?" And he said, "I won't even admit that. That is not even my face." I remember that part of it distinctly.

The first photo alterationist was Lee Harvey Oswald—he wouldn't even admit that the face was his.

I don't believe there is a great mystery here. Lee Harvey Oswald wore two rings: his wedding ring, typically on his right hand (Russian style), and his Marine ring. Might he have been wearing two rings?

Here is a close-up of CE 133-A:

There also appears to be a ring or an indication that there had been a ring, on his left hand as well:

Here is 133-C:

The ring on his left hand does look like a Marine ring and not a wedding ring:

On the morning of November 22, 1963, Oswald left his wedding ring in a cup on the dresser at Ruth Paine's house. Here is a picture of Oswald in handcuffs, and you can see his Marine ring on his left hand:

Credit: Bettmann / Contributor

The backyard photographs have been scientifically studied by the HSCA and Professor Hany Farid of Dartmouth College. Farid's 3D study concluded:

> It has long been argued that the photo of Lee Harvey Oswald in his backyard is a fake. Among other purported evidence of photo tampering, it has been argued that Oswald's pose in the photo appears physically implausible. We have described a detailed 3-D stability analysis that refutes this argument. In addition, our 3-D model of Oswald and his surroundings provide further evidence refuting other claims of photo tampering: the lighting and shadows are physically consistent, and the length of the rifle in Oswald's hands is consistent with the length of this type of rifle.

The HSCA noted that it would have been impossible to alter the photographs without being detected:

> In summary, it is possible to make copy photographs that are acceptable as originals. Nevertheless, because such a process poses many technical problems, any one of which if not solved would lead to detection under close examination of the photographs, we do not believe such a procedure was used to produce the three backyard photographs of Oswald.

Oliver Stone is so desperate to prove that the Mannlicher-Carcano rifle is not Oswald's that he included this clunker.

CHAPTER 27
WAS OSWALD'S PALMPRINT ON HIS MANNLICHER-CARCANO RIFLE?

(EPISODE 2, 42:06)

JFK: Destiny Betrayed wants people to believe that Oswald's palmprint was not found on his rifle.

Here is an excerpt from a transcript:

Oliver Stone: Was there a palmprint found on the rifle?

Brian Edwards: The foremost fingerprint expert the FBI had, Sebastian Latona, took that rifle and attempted to lift prints off of the rifle, the stock and/or the barrel. He testified to the Warren Commission that he found no usable prints anywhere on that rifle, on the metal or the stock. But yet, Lieutenant Day in Dallas before the rifle went to Washington, said he found a partial palmprint on the trigger guard on the left side and a partial print underneath the stock on the barrel. But Sebastian Latona said there was no evidence of a lift that had even been attempted.

Oliver Stone: No partials at all?

Brian Edwards: Nothing that he could use in court. There has to be eight points of identification. He found nothing that would match that.

Steve Roe has debunked this allegation on his blog. It is certainly true that Sebastian Latona could not find any "usable prints" on the rifle. Edwards claims that Latona said there was "no evidence of a lift that had even been attempted."

Here is what Latona said to the Warren Commission:

Mr. Eisenberg: Mr. Latona, could you describe to us what a lift is?

Mr. Latona: A lift is merely a piece of adhesive material which is used for purposes of removing a print that has been previously developed on an object, onto the adhesive material. Then the adhesive material is placed on a backing, in this case which happens to be the card. The adhesive material utilized here is similar to scotch tape. There are different types of lifting material. Some of them are known as opaque lifters, which are made of rubber, like a black rubber and white rubber, which has an adhesive material affixed to it, and this material is simply laid on a print which has been previously developed on an object and the full print is merely removed from the object.

Mr. Eisenberg: When you say "the print" is removed, actually the powder—

Mr. Latona: The powder that adhered to the original latent print is picked off of the object.

Mr. Eisenberg: So that the impression actually is removed?

Mr. Latona: That is right.

Latona was asked about the print lifted by the Dallas Police Department:

Mr. Eisenberg: Now, may I say for the record that at a subsequent point we will have the testimony of the police officer of the Dallas police who developed this print, and made the lift; and I believe that the print was taken from underneath the portion of the barrel which is covered by the stock. Now, did you attempt to identify this print which shows on the lift Exhibit 637?

Mr. Latona: Yes; I did.

Mr. Eisenberg: Did you succeed in making identification?

Mr. Latona: On the basis of my comparison, I did effect an identification.

Mr. Eisenberg: And whose print was that, Mr. Latona?

Mr. Latona: The palmprint which appears on the lift was identified by me as the right palmprint of Lee Harvey Oswald.

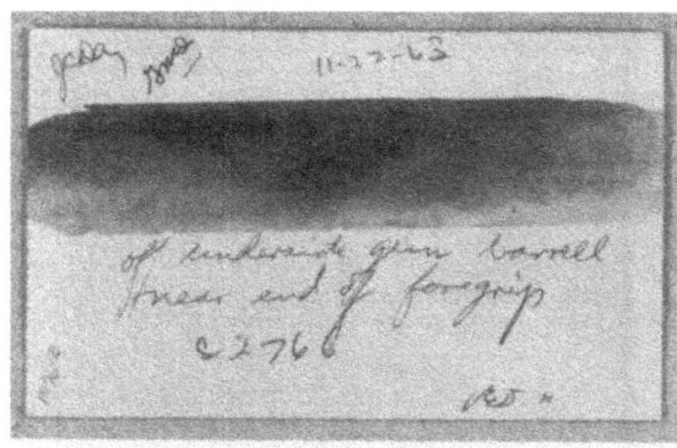

Commission Exhibit 637

Steve Roe notes that "of course there was no evidence of the print being lifted, because the dusting powder on the print is totally lifted off with the cellophane." Oliver Stone would have you believe that there is no evidence the print was even lifted.

CHAPTER 28
WAS THERE A PROBLEM WITH THE CHAIN OF CUSTODY OF CE 399?

(EPISODE 2, 44:36)

JFK: Destiny Betrayed claims there are significant problems with the chain of custody of CE 399. First, the initials of FBI Agent Elmer Todd are supposedly missing from the bullet, and second, it is alleged that there is a discrepancy as to the timing of the receipt of the bullet.

Here is an excerpt from a transcript:

Oliver Stone: Can you walk us through the magic bullet's chain of custody, from the Parkland employees to the Secret Service to the FBI?

Dr. David Mantik: Well, the magic bullet was supposedly found on a stretcher at Parkland Hospital, and it went through several hands before it got to the Secret Service. Richard Johnsen was the first Secret Service agent to handle it, and he carried it back to Washington, DC. When he got back to Washington, DC, he gave it to the chief of the Secret Service, who was James Rowley. And at the White House, James Rowley gave it to Elmer Lee Todd and Todd then took it to the FBI lab and gave it to Robert Frazier. We have interesting information produced by John Hunt, a private citizen who went to the archives on four or five occasions to track down the story about the magic bullet and what he found was truly astounding.

...

Narrator (Whoopi Goldberg): Working with FBI and Warren Commission documents, John Hunt asked the most basic question: Was CE 399, in evidence, the same bullet that was found on the stretcher?

Dr. David Mantik: At 7:30 at night, this is the day of the assassination, November 22nd, 1963, a bullet appears in the record, it's signed for by Robert Frazier, who is the main investigator at the FBI lab. And it's not just one document. There are multiple documents that indicate that Frazier signed for a bullet at 7:30 that night. Now, here's where things get interesting. Elmer Lee Todd received the bullet at the White House from chief of the Secret Service, James Rowley. And Todd documents, very clearly in writing, that he got this bullet at 8:50 PM. How is that possible? How can Robert Frazier receive the bullet in the lab at 7:30 from Elmer Lee Todd when Todd didn't get the bullet until 8:50?

...

Dr. David Mantik: It gets worse, though. Todd initialed that bullet. The one that he got at 8:50, and everyone else who touched the bullet after that initialed it too, including Robert Frazier. I went to the archives to look at this bullet. And specifically, what we want to know is do we see Todd's initials on this bullet? He said he initialed the bullet. It is not there. Todd's initials are not on the magic bullet.

In 2015–2016 the National Archives in association with the National Institute of Standards and Technology (NIST) published high-resolution images of CE 399 and other artifacts from the JFK assassination.

Researcher Steve Roe examined these pictures and easily found the initials of Elmer Todd.

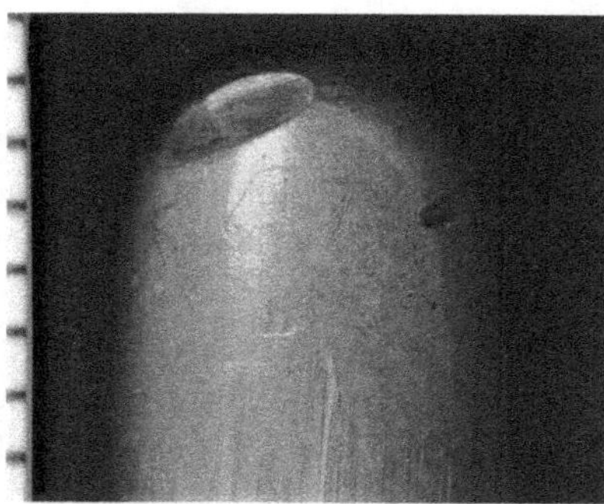

He writes:

> Stone and DiEugenio, who claim to stay abreast of all the latest assassination-related research, should have known about the landmark NARA/NIST effort and could have fact-checked Hunt's and Mantik's claims about missing initials. That they did not bother tells everyone all they need to know about their spurious documentary.

Even without examining the NIST photographs, James DiEugenio should have known that Todd's initials were on CE 399. In 1996, the ARRB sent a staff member, Tammi Long, to the National Archives to look for herself:

> I can personally verify that I have seen the item identified as CE 399 in the National Archives, JFK Collection, at College Park, Maryland. On April 23, 1996, I observed the item labeled CE 399. The bullet looked the same as depicted in the pictures published in the Warren Commission documents. I was able to discern the initials representing the chain of custody of CE 399.

After Steve Roe published his groundbreaking article, Dr. David Mantik admitted that Todd's initials were on CE 399. But James DiEugenio demurred, saying that "three people, probably four, said they were not there, plus we had photographic evidence." Then on Sunday, July 10, 2022, DiEugenio admitted that "This appears to be an error, and I asked my editor if he could include an errata in the book. It was too late." He added that "I have someone going to NARA to check on this in person." Why he has to go to NARA when he just has to download the NIST photographs is beyond me.

JFK: Destiny Betrayed also alleges that there is a timing issue, that Robert Frazier signed for a bullet at 7:30 p.m. when he, in fact, received the bullet at 8:50 p.m.

So, what's going on here?

The allegation about the timing comes from an article by researcher John Hunt, who believed that Frazier received the bullet from Elmer Todd at 7:30 p.m.

As we can see from this evidence envelope, Frazier received it from Todd at 8:50 p.m.

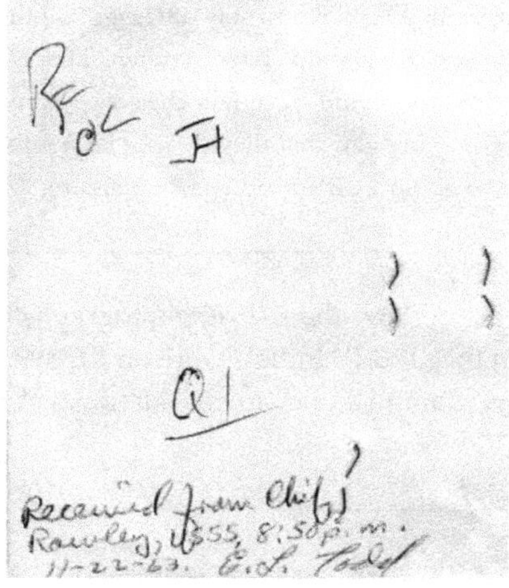

Note the initials of Robert Frazier (RF), Charles Killion (CK), and Cortlandt Cunningham (JH) on this envelope and the staple marks that attached the envelope that contained CE 399 (Q1).

John Hunt believes that this is a critical error and that the following two documents prove that Frazier received the bullet at 7:30.

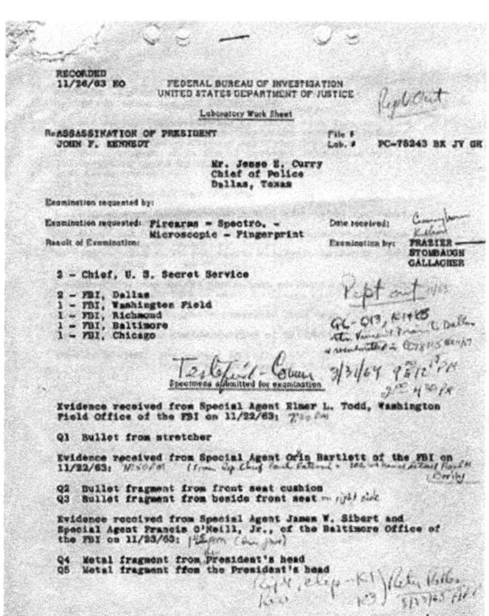

RECORDED
11/26/63 KO

FEDERAL BUREAU OF INVESTIGATION
UNITED STATES DEPARTMENT OF JUSTICE

Laboratory Work Sheet

Re: ASSASSINATION OF PRESIDENT JOHN F. KENNEDY

File #
Lab. # PC-78243 BX JY GK

Mr. Jesse E. Curry
Chief of Police
Dallas, Texas

Examination requested by:

Examination requested: Firearms - Spectro. - Microscopic - Fingerprint

Date received:

Result of Examination:

Examination by: FRAZIER, STOMBAUGH, GALLAGHER

2 - Chief, U. S. Secret Service

2 - FBI, Dallas
1 - FBI, Washington Field
1 - FBI, Richmond
1 - FBI, Baltimore
1 - FBI, Chicago

Testified - Comm 3/31/64

Specimens submitted for examination

Evidence received from Special Agent Elmer L. Todd, Washington Field Office of the FBI on 11/22/63: 7:30 PM

Q1 Bullet from stretcher

Evidence received from Special Agent Orin Bartlett of the FBI on 11/22/63:

Q2 Bullet fragment from front seat cushion
Q3 Bullet fragment from beside front seat

Evidence received from Special Agent James W. Sibert and Special Agent Francis O'Neill, Jr., of the Baltimore Office of the FBI on 11/23/63:

Q4 Metal fragment from President's head
Q5 Metal fragment ffom the President's head

You can see the notation written by Frazier noting the date and time of his testimony before the Warren Commission. "Testified - Comm 3/31/64 (9:00 - 12:15, 2:00 - 4:30)." The copies sent to Curry and others in November did not have handwritten notations.

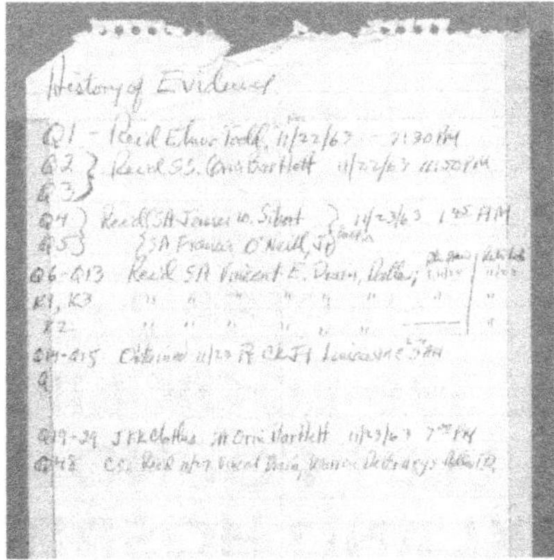

History of Evidence

Q1 - Rec'd Elmer Todd, 11/22/63 - 7:30 PM
Q2 } Rec'd S.S. Orrin Bartlett 11/22/63 11:50 PM
Q3 }
Q4 } Rec'd SA James W. Sibert } 11/23/63 1:45 AM
Q5 } SA Francis O'Neill, Jr. }
Q6-Q13 Rec'd SA Vincent E. Drain, Dallas; [illegible]
K1, K3 " " " " " " "
K2 " " " " " " "
Q14-Q15 Obtained 11/23 Fr. [illegible]
Q
Q19-29 JFK Clothes SA Orrin Bartlett 11/23/63 7:00 PM
Q48 [illegible]

Steve Roe notes that the handwritten notes are simply Frazier's guide for his Warren Commission testimony in March 1964. So why would Frazier write 7:30 p.m. on the first line?

This document might shed some light:

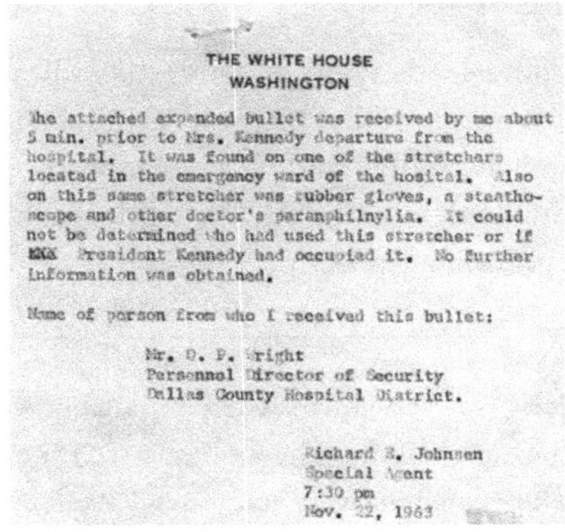

THE WHITE HOUSE
WASHINGTON

The attached expended bullet was received by me about 5 min. prior to Mrs. Kennedy departure from the hospital. It was found on one of the stretchers located in the emergency ward of the hosital. Also on this same stretcher was rubber gloves, a stethoscope and other doctor's paranphilnylia. It could not be determined who had used this stretcher or if XXX President Kennedy had occupied it. No further information was obtained.

Name of person from who I received this bullet:

Mr. O. P. Wright
Personnel Director of Security
Dallas County Hospital District.

Richard E. Johnsen
Special Agent
7:30 pm
Nov. 22, 1963

Frazier received CE 399 in an envelope attached to the Richard Johnson note, which was typed or dictated at 7:30 p.m. There is no suggestion that the bullet was provided by Todd to Frazier at that time. Frazier just made the note on his Warren Commission worksheet. And his testimony did not mention when he received CE 399.

There are no issues with the chain of custody of CE 399.

CHAPTER 29
DID CE 399 LOOK LIKE THE BULLET FOUND AT PARKLAND HOSPITAL?

(EPISODE 2, 47:56)

JFK: Destiny Betrayed misleads viewers about the bullet found at Parkland Hospital, CE 399. It implies that Darrell Tomlinson, the maintenance employee who found the bullet, and O. P. Wright, the man he gave it to, both said that it didn't look like CE 399. The truth is somewhat different.

Here is an excerpt from a transcript:

Dr. Gary Aguilar: I was very interested in finding out what the Review Board would show us about this. So, we began scouring their evidence, and we found out something very interesting. We found out that the Warren Report had, from the FBI, a report saying that the guys that found the bullet later identified that as the bullet they'd seen. The internal record didn't show that at all. The internal record said this bullet didn't look like that bullet at all. But the FBI reported to the Warren Commission that it did, it lied.

Here is the FBI Airtel shown in *JFK: Destiny Betrayed*:

Re: Rifle Bullet, C1 (Item #2 in Commission letter)

For information WFO, neither DARRELL C. TOMLINSON, who found bullet at Parkland Hospital, Dallas, nor O. P. WRIGHT, Personnel Officer, Parkland Hospital, who obtained bullet from TOMLINSON and gave to Special Agent RICHARD E. JOHNSON, Secret Service, at Dallas 11/22/63, can identify

bullet. On 11/22/63, JAMES ROWLEY, Chief, U. S. Secret Service, Washington, D. C., gave this bullet to SA ELMER LEE TODD, of WFO, who, on 11/22/63, took to FBI Laboratory and delivered to SA ROBERT A. FRAZIER. Both TODD and FRAZIER identified bullet by placing initials thereon.

That Airtel was based upon interviews from June 12, 1964, that indicate that Tomlinson and Wright did say that CE 399 looked like the bullet found at Parkland:

Re: LEE HARVEY OSWALD

Rifle Bullet, C1

On June 12, 1964, Darrell C. Tomlinson, Maintenance Employee, Parkland Hospital, Dallas, Texas, was shown Exhibit C1, a rifle slug, by Special Agent Bardwell D. Odum, Federal Bureau of Investigation. Tomlinson stated it appears to be the same one he found on a hospital carriage at Parkland Hospital on November 22, 1963, but he cannot positively identify the bullet as the one he found and showed to Mr. O. P. Wright. At the time he found the bullet, the hospital carriage was located in the Emergency Unit on the ground floor of the hospital.

On June 12, 1964, O. P. Wright, Personnel Officer, Parkland Hospital, Dallas, Texas, advised Special Agent Bardwell D. Odum that Exhibit C1, a rifle slug, shown to him at the time of the interview, looks like the slug found at Parkland Hospital on November 22, 1963, which he gave to Richard Johnsen, Special Agent of the Secret Service. He stated he was not present at the time the bullet was found, but on the afternoon of November 22, 1963, as he entered the Emergency Unit on the ground floor of the hospital, Mr. Tomlinson, an employee, called to him and pointed out a bullet, which was on a hospital carriage at that location. He estimated the time as being within an hour of the time President Kennedy and Governor Connally were brought to the hospital. He advised he could not positively identify C1 as being the same bullet which was found on November 22, 1963.

Tomlinson told the FBI that C1 (CE 399) "appears to be the same" bullet he found at Parkland. O. P. Wright said that C1 (CE 399) "looks like" the bullet found at Parkland.

In 1966, researcher Raymond Marcus spoke to Tomlinson and asked him about CE 399. He told Marcus that the bullet he found was "pretty clean":

Marcus: OK. Now do you recall when you saw that bullet, was there anything about it that struck you, was it, uh, was it, uh, banged up, or was it neat and clean, or do you remember that, was it mangled at all?

Tomlinson: No, it wasn't mangled, it was a pretty clean bullet.

Marcus: Pretty clean shape?

Tomlinson: Yep.

He then told Marcus about the June 1964 meeting when FBI agent Odum questioned him about the bullet:

Marcus: When Shanklin [sic; it was Odum] and Mr. Wright called you in at that time, did they show you the bullet?

Tomlinson: Yes.

Marcus: Did they ask you if it looked like the same one?

Tomlinson: Yes, I believe they did.

Marcus: And as far as you could tell—of course, you weren't making a ballistics test of it—but as far as you could tell, did it look like the same one to you?

Tomlinson: Yes, it appeared to be the same one.

While it is true that Tomlinson and Wright could not "identify" the bullet, they did say that CE 399 "appears to be the same" and "looks like" the bullet found at Parkland. This is not all that surprising since neither marked the bullet with identifying initials. They never said or implied that CE 399 was not the bullet they found.

In April 1977, Tomlinson told *Dallas Morning News* reporter Earl Golz that some federal agents "came to the hospital with the bullet in a box and asked me if it was the one I found. I told him apparently it was, but I had not put a mark on it … If it wasn't the bullet it was exactly like it."

JFK: Destiny Betrayed gives the false impression that CE 399 did not look like the bullet that was found.

CONSPIRACY

JFK: Destiny Betrayed does not tell viewers exactly who killed Kennedy. Instead, it skirts around the issue of conspiracy and presents a variety of supposedly suspicious events. When you examine these events in detail, the conclusions of conspiracy dissipate, and all you are left with are unwarranted suspicions.

"Please, Daddy, just one more conspiracy theory."

Credit: David Sipress / The New Yorker Collection / The Cartoon Bank / February 27, 2017

CHAPTER 30
WAS JACK RUBY SIGNALED IN THE DALLAS POLICE DEPARTMENT BASEMENT?

(EPISODE 2, 52:43)

JFK: Destiny Betrayed alleges that Jack Ruby was signaled by car horns in the basement of the Dallas Police Department.

Here is an excerpt from a transcript:

> **Narrator (Whoopi Goldberg)**: He is about to be transferred to the county jail. The FBI has called the Dallas police on both Saturday and Sunday, warning them of threats to kill the alleged assassin of President Kennedy. The police have decided to proceed with the transfer anyway. As you watch, listen for the two car horns. One as Oswald emerges, and the other the moment before Jack Ruby fires.

If you watch the video of Jack Ruby shooting Lee Harvey Oswald, you can hear two car horn blasts.

The notion that these two car horns were signals to Ruby is ridiculous. It was a busy parking area with hundreds of people that morning, so it's not surprising that cars were honking. Ruby reacts to the sight of Oswald and not the car horn, which sounds like it is quite distant.

In a longer video taken in the Dallas police basement, you can hear car horns at approximately 10:50, 11:25, 11:31, and 12:30 before the two car horn blasts referenced above.

Where did this all come from? This segment is not footnoted in James DiEugenio's book of the annotated script, and so a little research was necessary.

Mark Lane testified before the Garrison grand jury on May 10, 1967:

> Soon as Ruby is down there there was a blast on an automobile horn, which is very visible, just as Oswald is led out from the elevator by the police officials and then there is another blast, and just immediately following that second blast, Ruby is seen charging and firing one shot —Oswald, of course, puts his hands over his abdomen where the bullet was directed, and of course he died at that time. Obviously some questions must be resolved: how did Ruby get in the place; who blew the automobile horns, the only vehicles in the basement were Dallas police vehicles, why were the horns blown? Is this a coincidence—the relationship between the sound of the horns and the activity took place just before?

Here is James DiEugenio's analysis from his book *The JFK Assassination*:

> In 2007, Ray Marcus called me and asked an odd question. He said, "Jim, what version of Oswald's killing have you seen?" I said, "What do you mean, what version?" He said: "The one with one horn, two horns, or no horns?" I said I had seen the one with one horn. Marcus then explained that the original version has two horns but through the years, this version has been edited, and I had seen one of the edited versions. He said, "I'll send it to you. You'll understand why immediately." He was correct about the understanding. The first horn goes off at almost the exact second that Oswald emerges from the office and into the corridor. The second horn goes off about a nanosecond before Ruby plunges forward to shoot Oswald. Once you're aware of it, it is almost eerie to watch. Bugliosi describes the horns. He doesn't describe the timing. Ruby made this all even stranger in 1965. Because he then wrote a note in which he alluded to the horns. In a letter secured by Bill Diehl of the St. Louis Post Dispatch, he talks about being gravely ill and going to a hospital. He closes with, "If you hear a lot of horn-blowing,

> it will be for me, they will want my blood." Now I guess someone like Bugliosi could say he was referring to St. Gabriel. But yet, Ruby was Jewish.

DiEugenio complains that Vincent Bugliosi "describes the horns. He doesn't describe the timing." Bugliosi is quite specific and mentions who was doing the honking:

> Lieutenant Swain steps through the doorway of the jail office and into the bright television floodlights. Captain Fritz is a few feet behind him. Swain walks toward the sedan that will carry Oswald as it continues to roll back into position. The driver, Detective Dhority, hits the car horn again to clear the media away.
>
> Leavelle and Graves hesitate momentarily at the doorway, holding Oswald just inside the jail office. "Is it okay?" Leavelle asks. Detective Wilbur J. Cutchshaw, standing just outside the doorway, answers Leavelle, "Okay, come on out, Jim."
>
> Detectives Leavelle and Graves march out, Oswald firmly between them, but manacled only to Leavelle. For a moment Leavelle and Graves are blinded by their first exposure to the lights, making it impossible for them to observe any movements originating from their left front. But they soon regain their vision and are surprised that nothing is ready. The white sedan that is supposed to be parked about thirteen to fourteen feet just outside the door is still rolling back, struggling to get into position against the tide of reporters who have come around or over the railing they have been ordered to remain behind and are now surging toward Oswald. The driver blasts the horn again as Captain Fritz reaches for the backdoor handle.

The horns are not suspicious.

JFK: Destiny Betrayed uses a rather simplistic argument to mislead viewers into believing that Jack Ruby was signaled that Oswald was coming out.

CHAPTER 31
WHY DID JACK RUBY KILL LEE HARVEY OSWALD?

Jack Ruby (center), with his defense attorney, Melvin M. Belli (right), talking with reporters at a pretrial hearing. (Photo by Donald Uhrbrock/Getty Images, February 1, 1964)

(EPISODE 2, 55:07)

JFK: Destiny Betrayed misleads viewers about Jack Ruby's motivations.

Here is an excerpt from a transcript:

> **Jack Ruby**: The people who had to have so much to gain, and had such an ulterior motive, to put me in [the] position I'm in, will never let the true facts come above board to the world.

Here is the full transcript of that video:

> **Jack Ruby**: The only thing I can say—what is your name, and I'll know how to ...
>
> **Interviewer**: Harry Kennedy.
>
> **Jack Ruby**: Harry Kennedy. Everything pertaining to what's happening has never come to the surface. The world will never know the true facts, of what occurred, my motives. Uh, in other words, I'm the only person in the background that knows the truth pertaining to everything relating to my testimony.
>
> **Interviewer**: Do you think it will ever come out?
>
> **Jack Ruby**: No, because, unfortunately, the people who had to have so much to gain and had such an ulterior motive for putting me in [the] position I'm in, will never let the true facts come above board to the world.
>
> **Interviewer:** Are these people in very high positions, Jack?
>
> **Jack Ruby**: Yes.

This video is an interview with Fort Worth TV station *KTVT* and was shot during a break in court proceedings related to Ruby's appeal on September 9, 1965.

What is clear is that Ruby is talking about his testimony before the Warren Commission. The so-called truth that he is talking about is not some conspiracy but the veracity of his Warren Commission testimony.

Indeed, in another clip of Ruby, shot just before the above video, Ruby is upset that the Warren Commission didn't provide a judgment as to whether he passed or failed his lie detector test:

> **Ruby**: The Warren Report never gave me the true authenticity when I requested a polygraph test, there was a little small article in small type that stated that due to the fact that Mr. Ruby's health, we cannot

> divulge the results of it. Why they held back the answers had to do with the results, whether they are true or false, that's for you to find out ... They never released my results of my polygraph test, that was deleted from the Warren Report. Why was that deleted? I don't know why. I insisted upon the polygraph right from the beginning—as a matter of fact, certain questions I created and originated that they would ask me at the time. They spent nine hours with me at the time and yet a finality, the finality of the results of the test, they stated they refused to divulge the answers that I had given, whether true or false, due to the fact of my mental condition.

This was an important point for Ruby because he wanted to prove to the world that he alone killed Oswald. The only way to truly understand why this was so important to Jack Ruby is to understand the importance of his Jewish identity.

He was born Jacob Rubenstein in 1911 to parents born in Poland. He spoke Yiddish in their kosher home, and he received some Hebrew school training. His parents fought violently with each other, and Rubenstein was placed in a foster home in 1923 and was there for eighteen months. He served in the Air Force in 1943 and was discharged in 1946. When a sergeant called him a "Jew bastard," Rubenstein attacked him.

Rubenstein moved to Dallas in 1947, where his sister Eva Grant lived. He became the manager of her nightclub. That same year Jack and his brothers, Earl and Sam, changed their names to Ruby. Earl said, "It was preferable not to use a Jewish name" for his business.

Ruby had a life-long record of volatile responses to antisemites. On one occasion in 1946, Ruby returned from downtown Chicago with his suit covered in blood. He explained that he had fought with a person who had called him a "a dirty Jew or something like that."

He also participated in street fights against the German American Bund before World War II, and he said that he "cracked a few heads." Ruby told Rabbi Hillel Silverman at his synagogue, Shearith Israel, in Dallas that "he frequently engaged in physical combat with persons making derogatory remarks concerning his Jewish background." Ruby forbade comedians at his club to tell stories directed at Jews or about Jewish practices.

On the morning of November 22, 1963, this advertisement appeared in the *Dallas Morning News*:

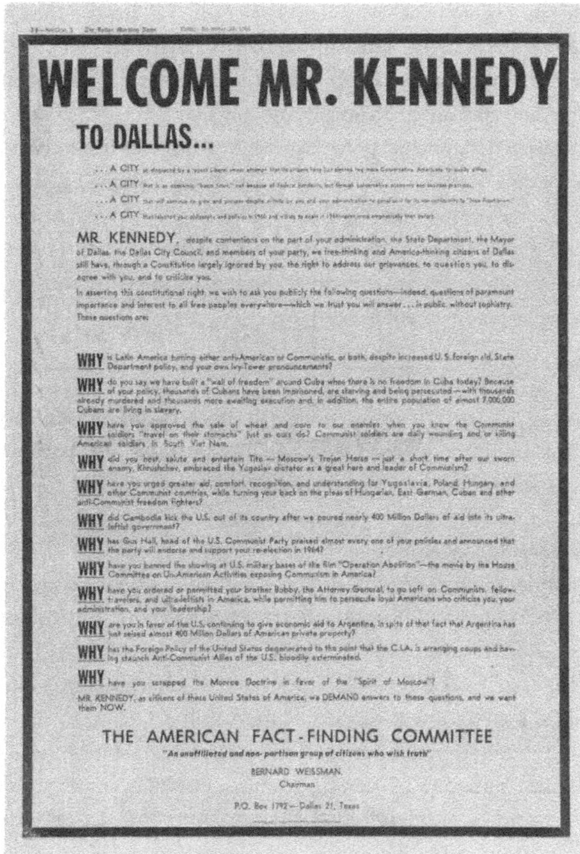

WELCOME MR. KENNEDY

TO DALLAS...

. . . A CITY

. . . A CITY

. . . A CITY

. . . A CITY

MR. KENNEDY, despite contentions on the part of your administration, the State Department, the Mayor of Dallas, the Dallas City Council, and members of your party, we free-thinking and America-thinking citizens of Dallas still have, through a Constitution largely ignored by you, the right to address our grievances, to question you, to disagree with you, and to criticize you.

In asserting this constitutional right, we wish to ask you publicly the following questions—indeed, questions of paramount importance and interest to all free peoples everywhere—which we trust you will answer . . . in public, without sophistry. These questions are:

WHY is Latin America turning either anti-American or Communistic, or both, despite increased U.S. foreign aid, State Department policy, and your own Ivy-Tower pronouncements?

WHY do you say we have built a "wall of freedom" around Cuba when there is no freedom in Cuba today? Because of your policy, thousands of Cubans have been imprisoned, are starving and being persecuted—with thousands already murdered and thousands more awaiting execution and, in addition, the entire population of almost 7,000,000 Cubans are living in slavery.

WHY have you approved the sale of wheat and corn to our enemies when you know the Communist soldiers "travel on their stomachs" just as ours do? Communist soldiers are daily wounding and or killing American soldiers in South Viet Nam.

WHY did you host, salute and entertain Tito — Moscow's Trojan Horse — just a short time after our sworn enemy, Khrushchev, embraced the Yugoslav dictator as a great hero and leader of Communism?

WHY have you urged greater aid, comfort, recognition, and understanding for Yugoslavia, Poland, Hungary, and other Communist countries, while turning your back on the pleas of Hungarian, East German, Cuban and other anti-Communist freedom fighters?

WHY did Cambodia kick the U.S. out of its country after we poured nearly 400 Million Dollars of aid into its ultra-leftist government?

WHY has Gus Hall, head of the U.S. Communist Party praised almost every one of your policies and announced that the party will endorse and support your re-election in 1964?

WHY have you banned the showing at U.S. military bases of the film "Operation Abolition"—the movie by the House Committee on Un-American Activities exposing Communism in America?

WHY have you ordered or permitted your brother Bobby, the Attorney General, to go soft on Communists, fellow-travelers, and ultra-leftists in America, while permitting him to persecute loyal Americans who criticize you, your administration, and your leadership?

WHY are you in favor of the U.S. continuing to give economic aid to Argentina, in spite of that fact that Argentina has just seized almost 400 Million Dollars of American private property?

WHY has the Foreign Policy of the United States degenerated to the point that the C.I.A. is arranging coups and having staunch Anti-Communist Allies of the U.S. bloodily exterminated.

WHY have you scrapped the Monroe Doctrine in favor of the "Spirit of Moscow"?

MR. KENNEDY, as citizens of these United States of America, we DEMAND answers to these questions, and we want them NOW.

THE AMERICAN FACT-FINDING COMMITTEE

"An unaffiliated and non-partisan group of citizens who wish truth"

BERNARD WEISSMAN,
Chairman

P.O. Box 1792—Dallas 21, Texas

The ad was signed by Bernard Weissman, which is a Jewish name. Jack Ruby noticed this and saw that there was a post office box associated with the ad. In addition, there were signs around Dallas calling for the impeachment of Chief Justice Earl Warren.

According to the Warren Report, Jack Ruby was at his sister's apartment that evening:

"Mrs. Grant testified that her brother was still disturbed about the Weissman advertisement when he arrived, showed her the photograph of the Warren sign ... Still curious as to whether or not Weissman was Jewish, Mrs. Grant asked her brother whether he had been able to find the name Bernard Weissman in the Dallas city directory, and Ruby said

> he had not. Their doubts about Weissman's existence having been confirmed, both began to speculate that the Weissman ad and the Warren sign were the work of either 'Commies or the Birchers,' and were designed to discredit the Jews."

At 3:00 a.m. Sunday morning, a highly agitated Jack Ruby awakened his roommate George Senator:

> Ruby and Senator drove to the Carousel Club where they picked up Larry [Crafard, the janitor] with the camera and drove to Hall Street and Expressway where Ruby took three pictures of a poster bearing the words, "Impeach Earl Warren." Senator said that Ruby was quite incensed about this poster and that he could not understand how anyone would have the nerve to put up such a sign and that whoever they were they would have to be "commies" or "birchers." At the same time Ruby was carrying an ad which he had cut from the newspaper in which a number of questions were put to President Kennedy by a Bernard Wiessman [sic]. Senator said that Ruby was also very "hot" about this article commented that Wiessman did not spell his name as a Jew, but if he were a Jew he should be ashamed of himself.

At 4:00 p.m. on November 23, Jack Ruby called his friend Stanley Kaufman, who said that "Jack was particularly impressed with the [black] border [of the Weissman ad] as being a tipoff of some sort—that this man knew the President was going to be assassinated."

Jack Ruby then closed his Carousel Club:

Courtesy of the Granger Historical Picture Archive

On Sunday, November 24, 1963, Jack Ruby shot Oswald. It was an impulsive act. And like other people who commit impulsive acts, Ruby came up with a variety of explanations after the fact:

- He told the police who arrested him, "I hope I killed the SOB and saved a lot of people some trouble."
- He told Assistant District Attorney Bill Alexander, "Well, you guys couldn't do it. Someone had to do it. That son of a bitch killed my President."
- Ruby told his Rabbi that he "did it for the Jewish people." He told Toni Zoppi of the *Dallas Morning News* that "he did it to prove to the world that 'Jews have balls.'"
- He also told a variety of people that he did it so that Mrs. Kennedy wouldn't have to go to a trial.

The assassination of JFK and the killing of Oswald left Ruby totally unhinged. The reaction of the far-right John Birch Society got to him. They always referred to Ruby as Rubenstein to emphasize a Jewish component of a supposed conspiracy to kill JFK. And that made Ruby worry that the Jews might be blamed (however unfairly) for the murder of Kennedy.

Ruby became extremely paranoid. He was examined on April 26, 1964:

> Dr. West had examined Ruby in a private interview room. The prisoner had appeared "Pale, tremulous, agitated and depressed." Previously meticulous about his appearance, he was now "disheveled and unkempt." It was the opinion of Dr. West that "at this time Mr. Ruby is obviously psychotic." On the previous evening, the psychiatrist reported, Ruby had become convinced that "all the Jews in America were being slaughtered." Ruby was certain that he was the cause of the mayhem. "Somehow, through an awful mistake, and the distortions and misunderstandings derived from his murder trial, the President's assassination and its aftermath were now being blamed on him," with the result that he was now also the cause of the massacre of "twenty-five million innocent people." Ruby, according to West, was positive that his brother Sam had been "tortured, mutilated, castrated and burned in the street outside the jail." He had heard his brother's screams and could still hear them at the time of the psychiatrist's visit. When Dr. West attempted to convince him that no such events had taken place, Ruby had become furious.

Jack Ruby testified before the Warren Commission on June 7, 1964. He made an impassioned plea to be taken to Washington:

> **Jack Ruby**: There is only one thing. If you don't take me back to Washington tonight to give me a chance to prove to the President that I am not guilty, then you will see the most tragic thing that will ever happen.

Conspiracy theorists convinced themselves that Ruby wanted to spill the beans about either the conspiracy to kill JFK or his orders to kill Oswald. They ignore parts of his testimony before the Warren Commission where he spelled out exactly why he wanted to go to Washington:

Mr. Ruby: Unfortunately, you don't have, because it is too late. And I wish that our beloved President, Lyndon Johnson, would have delved deeper into the situation, hear me, not to accept just circumstantial facts about my guilt or innocence, and would have questioned to find out the truth about me before he relinquished certain powers to these certain people.

Chief Justice Warren: Well, I am afraid I don't know what power you believe we relinquished to them. I think that it is difficult to understand what you have to say.

Mr. Ruby: I want to say this to you. The Jewish people are being exterminated at this moment. Consequently, a whole new form of government is going to take over our country, and I know I won't live to see you another time.

He then said:

Mr. Ruby: All I know is maybe something can be saved. Because right now, I want to tell you this, I am used as a scapegoat, and there is no greater weapon that you can use to create some falsehood about some of the Jewish faith, especially as the terrible heinous crime such as the killing of President Kennedy. Now maybe something can be saved. It may not be too late, whatever happens, if our President, Lyndon Johnson, knew the truth from me.

The reason he wanted to go to Washington was to tell Lyndon Johnson that the Jews were being blamed for the assassination and that there might be a second Holocaust.

In 1965, Jack Ruby was examined by psychiatrist Werner Tuteur. He told Tuteur about a conspiracy to kill JFK, but when asked for proof, all he did was retrieve the book *Who Killed Kennedy?* by Thomas Buchanan:

His attitude of secrecy and circumstantiality prevailed during all of our meetings. Yet, Ruby was by all means friendly, but not always cooperative. He was the one to do the talking by giving endless orations. Attempts at interrupting him were met with, "Please hear me out, you

> must listen to me." He then proceeded by indicating that he was sane and that his mind was functioning adequately. He promised that after having given such proof, he would make me acquainted with a conspiracy which I was to guard with the utmost secrecy. He had already mentioned this conspiracy in the hall. At the end of the third interview, he insisted he was going to obtain the book "Who Killed Kennedy?" written by the Englishman Thomas Buchanan, from another inmate for me.

Tuteur saw Ruby's paranoia up close:

> There were silences during the interviews, when Ruby would hold his head in his hands and would carefully listen to incidental noises, such as the squeaking of a door or the shuffling of feet by other inmates. He would then look at me, moving his chair somewhat, having a mournful expression, and say "Hoerst Du weinen ...?" (Do you hear crying?). He was convinced Jewish women and children were being slaughtered right there and then. This came to a climax when during the last interview a crew of plumbers began to dismantle a piece of equipment with heavy hammer blows, creating a great noise. Here Ruby found "proof" of his allegation of the manslaughter of Jews on premises.

JFK: Destiny Betrayed uses a short clip of Jack Ruby to try and persuade viewers that he had knowledge of a huge conspiracy. They can only do this by ignoring his experiences with anti-Semitism and how that affected his mental health. Ruby believed that a second Holocaust was coming because some extremists believed that, as a Jew, he was part of a conspiracy. That was why he wanted the Warren Commission to clearly state that he was telling the truth during his polygraph examination.

Viewers of *JFK: Destiny Betrayed* deserve better.

CHAPTER 32
WAS A BULLET FOUND IN JFK'S LIMOUSINE?

(EPISODE 3, 26:05)

JFK: Destiny Betrayed alleges that an extra bullet was found in JFK's limousine the evening of the assassination.

Here is an excerpt from a transcript:

Narrator (Whoopi Goldberg): As it turns out, there was an extra bullet, and it was misshapen. After the assassination, the motorcade raced to Parkland Hospital, where the emergency room doctors tried to save the President's life. After he was pronounced dead, Kennedy's personal physician, George Burkley, got in contact with his assistant, James Young, in the White House and told him to prepare for the autopsy.

Dr. Randolph Robertson: It was James Young who ordered Chiefs Mills and Martinell, their assistants, to go to the White House and retrieve what they knew were skull fragments in the limousine at that time.

Narrator (Whoopi Goldberg): The Presidential limousine, while en route to Washington, was inspected, and a three-inch triangular piece of bone was discovered on the floor near the rear jump seat. During the autopsy, Young sent his two assistants to meet the limo when it arrived at the White House garage.

Dr. Randolph Robertson: And they brought back an additional envelope with the bullet with the bent tip. He described the bullet, brass-colored, about five millimeters in diameter.

Narrator (Whoopi Goldberg): As part of a Naval oral history project, Jan Herman, who had interviewed Dr. Young on this subject, got in touch with Thomas Mills, one of the two men who had gone to the limo to retrieve the skull fragments.

Dr. Randolph Robertson: Jan Herman called up Mills, says "hey do you remember Dr. Young calling you, asking about this bent bullet?" He said, "yeah I remember that, him calling me, and, y'know, he remembered it." He says, "can you shed any light on it?" And he says, "I would rather not talk about that."

Oliver Stone: You know what happened to this bullet?

Dr. Randolph Robertson: It went from Mills and Martinell to Young to Humes, it disappears. That evening, there may have been as little as four people who saw that bullet before it disappeared.

Narrator (Whoopi Goldberg): The reports of this extra bullet substantiate some researchers' claim that there was a fourth shot hitting the limo at Zapruder frame 328.

This started in December of 2000 when James Young wrote to Gerald Ford:

Two of the corpsmen left and returned sometime later with three varying sized pieces of President Kennedy's skull bones. In addition, they brought us back in an envelope a spent misshapen bullet which they had found on the back floor of the "Queen Mary" where they had found the pieces of skull bones. The bullet and pieces of skull were given to Dr. Jim Humes.

Young asked Ford if he could "recall any testimony or comments which would clarify my concerns?"

Ford wrote back to Young and said that he had "no recollection of 'the spent bullet' you refer to."

Young sat down for an oral history project in which he elaborated on what was found:

> The envelope contained three pieces of skull bone, one about three inches in diameter, and another two inches in diameter, and the third one about one to one and a half inches in diameter. It also contained a brass slug about half a centimeter in diameter and distorted.

Sounds like they found a fragment and not a whole bullet. He further added that "maybe it's copper" and that "it was slightly bent on the end. It was not a straight bullet."

So, what happened here?

Warren Commission Document 80 discusses the examination of the limousine:

> In running his hands over the front cushion of the automobile, Deputy Chief Paterni found a metallic fragment in the front seat in the area between the left and right front seats. A second metallic fragment was found by Mills on the floor in front of the right front seat. Both of these fragments were turned over to the FBI for their ballistics examination and are mentioned as Exhibits Q2 and Q3 in the ballistics report made by the FBI addressed to the Chief of Police of Dallas on November 23, 1963.

The FBI analysis found that Q3 "is a portion of the base section of a copper alloy rifle bullet. Q3 weights 21.0 grains and is composed of a section of the jacket from which the lead core is missing."

Here is a picture of Q3, also known as CE 569:

Dr. Gary Aguilar, Dr. Doug DeSalles, and Bill Simpich wrote a paper that debunks the extra bullet theory:

> Dr. Young said the envelope containing three skull fragments "also contained a brass slug about half a centimeter in diameter and distorted." The diameter of CE 569 is, of course, "about half a centimeter in diameter" at exactly 6.5 millimeters. It is made up of only copper jacket material and therefore might easily appear to be "brass." One end of it is obviously "distorted," as in the description Dr. Young provided. Dr. Young used the term "slug" to describe it and it is on this term that Robertson builds his case that a "whole bullet" was found in the limousine.
>
> The Columbia Dictionary of the English Language (2nd Edition Unabridged) lists 17 different meanings for "slug" of which two might conceivably apply to CE 569. Meaning #4 defines "slug" as "a piece of lead or other metal for firing from a gun." Meaning #5 defines "slug" as "any heavy piece of crude metal." Meaning #4 might conceivably apply to a whole projectile while Meaning #5 would more likely apply to a substantial fragment.

Q3 was probably the "bullet" that Young was referring to.

In addition, Mills and Paterni identified fragments Q2 and Q3 (also known as C2 and C3) as the fragments found in the limousine:

C3—On June 2, 1964, Special Agent Orrin H. Bartlett displayed C3, a rifle bullet fragment, to Mr. Paul Paterni, Deputy Chief, United States Secret Service, Washington, D.C. Paterni identified this fragment as the one he recovered from the middle of the front seat of the President's car. This recovery was made on the night of November 22, 1963, after the car was returned to Washington, D.C., from Dallas, Texas. This bullet fragment was turned over to Special Agent Bartlett on November 22, 1963.

Did Dr. Young see the fragment? Did Mills and Martinell bring the fragment to Bethesda? Possibly, but here is an excerpt of testimony from Robert Frazier:

Mr. Specter: Would you state what the chain of possession was from the time of discovery of Exhibit 569 until the time it came into your possession, based on the records of the FBI, please, if you have those records available?

Mr. Frazier: Yes, sir. It was delivered by Secret Service Deputy Chief Paul Paterni, and SAC of the White House detail Floyd M. Boring of the Secret Service again, to Special Agent Orrin Bartlett of the FBI who delivered it to me at 11:50 p.m. on November 22, 1963.

I can understand the bone fragments being delivered to Humes and Boswell. But were the two bullet fragments also sent to Bethesda? It's certainly not part of the chain of possession, and I might add that Young is not listed as being in the autopsy room. He certainly might have been at Bethesda, somewhere in the building, but if an envelope was delivered to Humes, it might not have come from Young.

It is nice to see that one of the experts of *JFK: Destiny Betrayed* (Dr. Gary Aguilar) has debunked another one of its experts (Dr. Randy Robertson). Unfortunately, viewers of the so-called documentary series have no idea that its experts can't even agree with one another. And they certainly deserve to know the full facts about this supposed bullet.

CHAPTER 33
WAS THERE A HOLE IN THE WINDSHIELD OF JFK'S LIMOUSINE?

(EPISODE 3, 27:49)

JFK: Destiny Betrayed misleads viewers by intimating that there was a through-and-through bullet hole in the windshield. The film also misleads by claiming that flares of light are evidence of a shot from the front.

Frame 328 of the Zapruder Film Zapruder Film © 1967 (Renewed 1995) The Sixth Floor Museum at Dealey Plaza

Here is an excerpt from a transcript:

Narrator (Whoopi Goldberg): The reports of this extra bullet substantiate some researchers' claim that there was a fourth shot hitting the limo at Zapruder frame 328.

Dr. Randy Robertson: The bullet itself is important, but what's more important is, when it struck, and where it came from. And previously at 313, when the bullet went forward through JFK's head, a small fragment had cracked the windshield, from the inner surface. Later, the final shot, was at 328 was when it struck. Both times there were flares of reflected light as the glass was deformed from the impacts of, one, of a fragment and two, of the whole bullet. And these two events occurred in 0.9 seconds. So, therefore they couldn't have been shot from the same rifle.

Narrator (Whoopi Goldberg): The Warren Commission's contention is that only three shots were fired, and that one of them had missed its target completely. So how does one account for the extensive damage to the limousine?

Dr. David Mantik: There is a lot of damage in the car. The chrome strip, which went around the windshield, was dented from the inside, which suggests a projectile from the rear. Six witnesses reported a through-and-through hole in the windshield.

Narrator (Whoopi Goldberg): After the Secret Service tried to scrub down the interior at Parkland Hospital, the Presidential limo was then flown to Washington. The interior was completely cleaned up within 36 hours, and the windshield was replaced within 48 to 72 hours. The car was then shipped first to the Ford factory in Michigan, and then to Cincinnati, where it was extensively rebuilt by a car restoration company.

JFK: Destiny Betrayed *shows the first light flare from Zapruder frame 314. Zapruder Film © 1967 (Renewed 1995) The Sixth Floor Museum at Dealey Plaza.*

JFK: Destiny Betrayed *shows the second light flare from Zapruder frame 329. Zapruder Film © 1967 (Renewed 1995) The Sixth Floor Museum at Dealey Plaza.*

First, let's discuss the issue of the flare in frame 314 of the Zapruder Film. Dr. Gary Aguilar, Dr. Doug DeSalles, and Bill Simpich note that the supposed first flare, at Zapruder frame 314, is "restricted to the frame of the vent window, the chrome strip along its leading edge that covers the windshield support, and other chrome objects near it."

You can see the beginning of this flare in frame 309 of the Zapruder film, well before the head shot:

Frame 309 of the Zapruder film. You can see the so-called flare on the right side of the frame. Zapruder Film © 1967 (Renewed 1995) The Sixth Floor Museum at Dealey Plaza

As for the flare in frame 329, Robertson believes that the supposed bullet found in the limousine by Chiefs Mills and Martinell hit the windshield at frame 328:

> A whole bullet directly struck the windshield frame at 328 bending its tip in the process and falling back into the limo where it was later recovered during the initial limo inspection.

Josiah Thompson believes that the flare substantiated his theory of a shot from the rear at frames Z-327–Z-328 but concedes another possibility:

> It is difficult to know what to make of this flare. It endures for only a very short interval. Is it an indisputable sign that the windshield was struck from the rear by a fragment at this time? No. It is possible that the car's angle to the sun changed as it proceeded and this caused the flare.

So, Robertson believes the flare in Frame 329 is the result of a shot from behind hitting the windshield, and Thompson believes the flare is the result (if not a coincidental artifact) of a shot from the rear hitting Kennedy.

I believe the flare is nothing more than a reflection from the sun. Conspiracy theorists are reading way too much into the flares. If you look at frames 325–330 of the Zapruder film, you can see "the progressive movement of the reflected sunlight on the curve of the windshield."

Now on to the supposed through-and-through bullet hole in the windshield.

The presidential limousine arrived in Washington D.C. at 8:00 p.m. It was driven to the White House garage and arrived at 9:00 p.m. At 1:00 a.m., a team of five FBI agents arrived at the garage and examined the limousine.

> Car 100-X arrived at Andrews Air Force Base, Washington, at 8 p.m., November 22. It was driven from Andrews under police escort to the White House garage by SA Kinney, accompanied by SA Charles Taylor of the Washington Field Office. When the car arrived at the garage at 9 p.m., it was turned over to SA Morgan Gies in charge of Secret Service vehicles in the White House garage. The entire car was then covered with a large sheet of plastic by SA Gies and two special agents from the Washington Field Office were assigned to guard the car. These special agents were instructed that no one was to approach the car or touch it until clearance was had from supervisory personnel of the Secret Service. The only access to the car permitted thereafter, until the guards were removed on November 24, was to Deputy Chief Paterni and the party with him and later to the FBI search team, both mentioned below.

At about 10:00 p.m., Chief Mills and Martinell were sent to examine the limousine for bone and bullet fragments. A team of FBI agents then thoroughly examined the car at 1:00 a.m.:

> **Mr. Specter**: Was your examination a thorough examination of all aspects of the interior of the automobile?
>
> **Mr. Frazier**: Yes, sir; for our purpose. However, we did not tear out all of the rugs on the floor, for instance. We examined the rugs carefully for holes, for bullet furroughs, for fragments. We examined the nap of the rug, in the actual nap of the rug, for fragments and bullet holes. We pulled the rug back as far as we could turn it back and even tore the glue or adhesive material loose around the crack at the edges of the rug so we could observe the cracks to see whether they had been enlarged, and we examined all of the upholstery covering, on the back of the front seat, the back of the rear seat, and we examined the front seat in a similar manner, and we found no bullet holes or other bullet impact areas, other than the one on the inside of the windshield and the dent inside the windshield chrome.

Warren Commission Exhibit 350 shows the crack in the windshield. The photo was taken by FBI agent Robert Frazier on November 23:

Warren Commission Exhibit 349 shows a small dent on the chrome strip on top of the windshield:

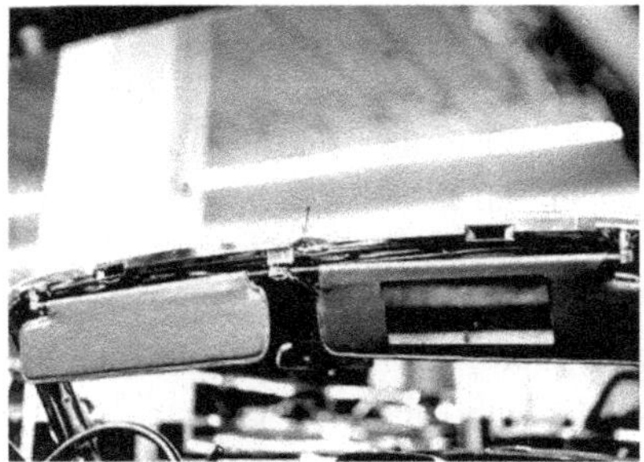

Robert Frazier was asked about the windshield:

Mr. Specter: Did you have occasion then to examine the windshield of the Presidential limousine?

Mr. Frazier: Yes; I did.

Mr. Specter: What did that examination disclose?

Mr. Frazier: On the inside surface of the windshield there was a deposit of lead. This deposit was located when you look at the inside surface of the windshield, 13 ½ inches down from the top, 23 inches from the left-hand side or driver's side of the windshield, and was immediately in front of a small pattern of star-shaped cracks which appeared in the outer layer of the laminated windshield.

Mr. Dulles: What do you mean by the "outer layer of the laminated windshield"?

Mr. Frazier: The windshield is composed of two layers with a very thin layer of plastic in between which bonds them together in the form of safety glass. The inside layer of the glass was not broken, but the outside layer immediately on the outside of the lead residue had a very small pattern of cracks and there was a very minute particle of glass missing from the outside surface.

Mr. Dulles: And the outside surface was the surface away from where the occupants were sitting?

Mr. Frazier: That is correct; yes.

Mr. Dulles: And the inside surface was the surface nearest the occupants?

Mr. Frazier: Yes.

Mr. Specter: What do these characteristics indicate as to which side of the windshield was struck?

Mr. Frazier: It indicates that it could only have been struck on the inside surface. It could not have been struck on the outside surface because of the manner in which the glass broke and further because of the lead residue on the inside surface. The cracks appear in the outer layer of the glass because the glass is bent outward at the time of impact which stretches the outer layer of the glass to the point where these small radial or wagon spoke—wagon wheel spoke-type cracks appear on the outer surface.

Mr. Dulles: So the pressure must have come from the inside and not from the outside against the glass?

Mr. Frazier: Yes, sir; that is correct.

The windshield was removed from the limousine. Here is a memo written by F. Vaughn Ferguson of the Ford Motor Company:

Ford Motor Company

WASHINGTON OFFICE

Intra-Company Communication

December 18, 1963

TO: R.W. Markley, Jr.

FROM: F. Vaughn Ferguson

RE: Changes in White House "Bubbletop"

On November 23rd, the day following the President's assassination, I went to the White House garage in response to a telephone call to my home from the Secret Service. When I arrived about 10:00 a.m., the White House "Bubbletop" was in a stall in the garage with two Secret Service men detailed to guard it. A canvas cover was over the unit. I was permitted only to see the windshield of the car and then only after the guards had received permission from higher ranking Secret Service personnel. Examination of the windshield disclosed no perforation, but substantial cracks radiating a couple of inches from the center of the windshield at a point directly beneath the mirror.

I was at the garage only about one hour that day, but while I was there Morgan Geis contacted the Secret Service and told them to have me make arrangements to replace the windshield.

The following day, when I returned to the garage, the unit was no longer under guard. The Secret Service had cleaned the leather upholstery the day before, but underneath the upholstery buttons dried blood was still in evidence. On my own initiative, I pulled up these upholstery buttons and with a knife removed the caked blood around them. At this time, there was a heavy odor of dried blood still noticeable. There was a large blood spot on the floor covering which the Secret Service had not been able to remove, but I did nothing further about it that day.

In response to my call of November 25, personnel from Arlington Glass came to the White House garage that same day to replace the windshield. The Arlington Glass personnel advised Morgan Geis and me that removal would cause additional damage to the windshield but Geis told them to go ahead and remove it anyway. The Arlington Glass personnel did remove it by putting their feet against the inside of the windshield and pushing it out. In doing so, additional cracks formed (downward to the bottom of the windshield). A Mr. Davis of the Secret Service then took the windshield and put it in the stockroom under lock and key and I have not seen it since.

R.W. Markley, Jr. -2- December 18, 1963

That same day, November 25, I tried to clean the blood spot on the carpet with baking soda with only moderate success. Late that afternoon I called Hess and Eisenhardt who agreed to send new carpeting including masking and binding. It was also that day that Morgan Geis called my attention to a dent in the chrome topping of the windshield at a point just above the rear view mirror and asked why I hadn't fixed it while I was at it. I told him that my experience with chrome had been that in trying to remove a dent of that size lead only to additional marks that further marred the trim. In addition, the dent is not visible when the top is on the unit.

On November 26th, late in the afternoon after I had left, the carpet, masking and binding arrived at the garage from Hess and Eisenhardt. When I got to the garage on the 27th and was told that the carpeting material was in, I contacted Morgan Geis who arranged with the White House upholstery man to receive the metal piece containing the carpet, remove the old carpeting, replace it with the new carpet, and return the piece to me for reinstallation in the "Bubbletop." This upholsterer did not complete the job until late Friday afternoon the 29th.

On the morning of December 2nd, the re-carpeted piece was delivered to me by a Secret Service agent named Davis and I then reinstalled it. Also on the 2nd of December I noticed that the two lap robes had a few blood spots on them but, more than that, were soiled from handling and required cleaning. Two White House chauffeurs were detailed to take the lap robes to Fort Myer for cleaning. These persons remained with the lap robes until they were cleaned and returned the same day.

I think this represents a complete account of changes made in the "Bubbletop" since November 22.

F. V. Ferguson

F. V. Ferguson

Ferguson wrote that "Examination of the windshield disclosed no perforation, but substantial cracks radiating a couple of inches from the center of the windshield at a point directly beneath the mirror."

The windshield was reexamined in March 1964 at FBI headquarters:

> The windshield has been struck by an object at the point at which cracks in the glass join. This point is within an area circled in red on the windshield. The cracks, which radiate from this point, are present only in the outer layer of glass at the confluence of the cracks. In addition, scrapings previously identified as specimen Q15, were obtained from the inside surface of the windshield in the immediate area of the point of impact and these scrapings were previously identified as lead.
>
> When laminated glass is struck, the piece of glass opposite the side of the impact is put into a state of tension which results in cracks in the glass opposite the side of impact. These cracks radiate from the point of impact.
>
> It was therefore concluded that the cracks resulted from the windshield having been struck from the inside; that is, from the rear of the vehicle.

The HSCA firearms panel also examined the windshield, and it concluded that "the presence of fracture lines on the outside is indicative of a foreign object striking the windshield from the inside."

The evidence is clear that there was no through-and-through bullet hole in the presidential limousine. So, what about the six witnesses who said they saw a hole?

Four of the witnesses—Dallas motorcycle policemen Stavis Ellis and H. R. Freeman, reporter Richard Dudman, and medical student Evalea Glanges—all supposedly saw the bullet hole while the limousine was at Parkland.

Stavis Ellis supposedly told researcher Gill Toff in 1971 that "there was a hole in the left front windshield." However, here is what Ellis told author Larry Sneed: (Emphasis added.)

> Some of the jockeys around the car were saying, "Looky here!" What they were looking at was the windshield. To the right of where the driver was, **just above the metal near the bottom of the glass there appeared to be a bullet hole.**
>
> I talked to a Secret Service man about it, and he said, "Aw, that's just a fragment!" It looked like a clean hole in the windshield to me. In fact, one of the motor jockeys, Harry Freeman, put a pencil through it, or said he could.

Of course, that is a different location from the supposed bullet hole.

H. R. Freeman told Toff that he "could of touched it."

Richard Dudman was a reporter for the St. Louis *Post-Dispatch*, and here is an excerpt from an article he wrote for *The New Republic*:

> A few of us noticed the hole in the windshield when the limousine was standing at the emergency entrance after the President had been carried inside. I could not approach close enough to see on which side was the cup-shaped spot that indicates a bullet had pierced the glass from the opposite side.

Note that he didn't get very close to the limousine.

Here is what he wrote in the St. Louis *Post-Dispatch* on December 1, 1963:

Hole in Windshield

Another unexplained circumstance is a small hole in the windshield of the presidential limousine. This correspondent and one other man saw the hole, which resembled a bullet hole, as the automobile stood at the hospital emergency entrance while the President was being treated inside the building.

Here he says, "This correspondent and one other man saw the hole, which resembled a bullet hole."

Robert Branson's column from the December 15, 1963, issue of the *Battle Creek Enquirer* mentions the other reporter:

Another question: Was there a bullet hole in the front windshield of the presidential limousine — and if so, where did it come from? Richard Dudman, respected correspondent of the St. Louis Post-Dispatch, insists that when he inspected the car afterward, he saw what appeared to him to be a small, round hole near the middle of the windshield.

Another reporter who saw the same thing said: "By the time I got to the limousine, I wasn't permitted to approach it closer than about 25 feet. From the rear of the car the windshield damage appeared to be about the size of an orange, a round spiderweb pattern of fractured glass. It was on the upper half of the windshield and just right of the windshield centerline."

The Associated Press carried a similar report, but the correspondent who wrote it said he did not inspect the windshield himself.

The assassination car was put under Secret Service wraps soon after the shooting and flown out of Dallas. This reporter asked the Secret Service this week for permission to inspect it to see if the windshield had been pierced. Permission was denied.

He did not actually "inspect the windshield himself."

Richard Dudman walked back his claim in an article in the November 22, 1988, edition of the *Bangor Daily News*:

> These conspiracy theories required assumptions piled on assumptions. Sometimes I thought I was hearing from every nut in the country. I regretted having written anything that helped feel such fantastic speculation.
>
> Why was a conspiracy so attractive to me at first, as well as to those who spun the elaborate web? Secrecy was in part to blame. It was many months before the authorities would permit close examination of the windshield (showing at last that a bullet probably had nicked the inside, thus indicating a shot from behind the limousine). Access to the autopsy also was long delayed.

Another witness was George Whitaker, a senior manager at Ford Motor Company. He was interviewed in 1993 and said that on November 25 "he discovered the JFK limousine—a unique, one-of-a-kind item that he unequivocally identified—in the Rouge Plant's B building." He then noticed a bullet hole. The only problem is that the car was still in Washington. It was not driven to the Rouge Plant until December 20, 1963.

Evalea Glanges, a medical student in 1963, only told her story about a bullet hole in the windshield in a 1999 episode of the documentary series *The Men Who Killed Kennedy*. She also claimed that she was leaning against the car and pointed out the bullet hole to a friend, upon which a Secret Service agent quickly drove it away. For some reason, she could also tell that the bullet hole was created by a shot from the front and that there were no cracks associated with it. There is no reason to believe Glanges ever got that close to the limousine.

The last witness on Douglas Horne's list is Secret Service agent Charles Taylor, Jr., who wrote a report on November 27, 1963:

> The two blankets on the left and the right rear doors were removed, inspected, and returned to the vehicle. The trunk of the vehicle was opened, and the contents examined, and nothing was removed. A meticulous examination was made of the back seat of the car and the floor rug, and no evidence was found. In addition, of particular note was the small hole just left of center in the windshield from which

> appeared to be bullet fragments were removed. The team of agents also noted that the chrome molding strip above the windshield, inside the car, just right of center, was dented. The FBI agents stated that this dent was made by the bullet fragment which was found imbedded in the front cushion.

Taylor is referring to the defect in the windshield from which metal scrapings were taken.

His allegation was investigated by the Church Committee in 1975. After quoting Taylor's report, this staff report noted:

> Secret Service Agents Davis and Gies were also present for the FBI examination; their respective reports stated that they noticed the damage to the front windshield when the car arrived at the White House garage, that both of them ran their hands over the outside of the windshield and found it to be smooth and unbroken, and that damage to the windshield was entirely to the inside surface.

The Committee staff interviewed Taylor:

> The staff interviewed Secret Service Agent Taylor on December 10, 1975. On that occasion, Taylor was positive that there had been a hole in the windshield. He stated that a pin could definitely be inserted through this hole from one side of the windshield to the other. However, the staff was not convinced that Taylor had actually had the opportunity to examine what he believed to be a hole. With Committee staff present, Taylor recently examined the windshield at the Archives. He stated that the windshield was as he had seen it in 1963; i.e., contrary to his report, there was an internal defect and not a penetration. The staff subsequently prepared an affidavit and forwarded it to the Secret Service for Mr. Taylor's review and signature.

Taylor's affidavit clarified what he saw:

> In my contemporaneous report dated November 27, 1963, on the measures taken to effect security of the Presidential limousine SS-100-X and the follow-up car 679-X, I referred to a "hole" in the windshield from which what appeared to be bullet fragments were removed. However, it was not until December 19, 1975, at the National Archives that I ever examined the windshield—or even got a close look in well-lit conditions.
>
> The windshield I examined at the Archives had several large cracks extending the height and width of the glass. There was also a circle marked in red wax pencil which enclosed a portion of the windshield. This circle contained cracks emanating from a focal point. To the best of my recollection—as aided by contemporaneous FBI photographs of the windshield shown to me by members of the Senate Committee, I have no doubt that the cracks contained in the circle—cracks in the inner layers of the glass only, are the ones I noticed on the trip from Andrews Air Force Base (AAFB) described above. It is clear to me that y use of the word "hole" to describe the flaw in the windshield was incorrect.

By the way, had there been a through-and-through bullet hole in the windshield, it would have looked more like this:

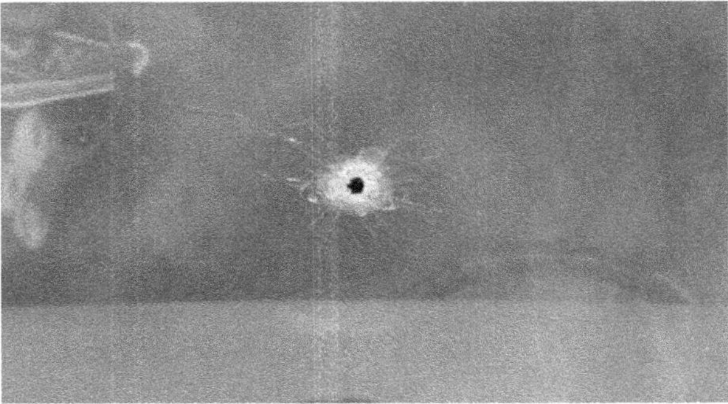

It is relevant that the windshield still exists.

Douglas Horne notes that "the windshield at the National Archives today exhibits long cracks—not a through-and-through bullet hole—and is damaged on the outside." He forgets that there were some cracks added to the windshield during its subsequent handling.

He concluded that the Archives windshield was not the one in the limousine on November 22: "It simply cannot be." Rather, "the windshield evidence was twice switched-out—substituted—by the U.S. government."

Yes, we now have the multiple windshield theory. To Douglas Horne, this is all part and parcel of a series of altered evidence:

> The pattern is the same, and the pattern is one of lying, and intentionally covering up the truth, by destroying some evidence, and substituting altered evidence in its place. All of this substitution of evidence —-tampering with wounds prior to the commencement of the autopsy through clandestine postmortem surgery; the alteration of some of the key autopsy photographs and X-rays (and the destruction of others); and the alteration of the Zapruder film—-was intended to suppress evidence of shots from the front (i.e., proof of conspiracy), so the government could more easily promote its lone assassin cover story.

Why on earth did Oliver Stone leave out the multiple windshield theory and the alteration of the Zapruder film from *JFK: Destiny Betrayed*?

CHAPTER 34
DID GERALD FORD TELL FRENCH PRESIDENT VALÉRY GISCARD D'ESTAING THAT THERE WAS A CONSPIRACY?

(EPISODE 3, 34:45)

JFK: Destiny Betrayed alleges that in 1976 Gerald Ford told French President Valéry Giscard D'Estaing that the JFK assassination was a conspiracy.

Here is an excerpt from a transcript:

Dr. Cyril Wecht: As I recall, they said about Gerald Ford that he could not chew gum and walk at the same time. Now all of a sudden, he becomes a forensic pathologist, and a photographer, and a criminalist, and an expert, and he knows where the bullet hole was, and he moved it up.

Narrator (Whoopi Goldberg): But then in 1979, the House Select Committee moved it lower in the back because they had pictures from the autopsy. It is conceivable that, at the time, the Warren Commission thought no one would ever see the autopsy photos. When the Review Board declassified the notations showing what Ford had done, the former commissioner replied that it had nothing to do with a conspiracy theory. He was only trying to be more precise.

Narrator (Whoopi Goldberg): This is directly contradicted by a conversation Ford had with French President Valéry Giscard d'Estaing. According to d'Estaing, Ford told him the assassination was not the

> work of one person. "It was something set up. We were sure it was set up. But we were not able to discover by whom."

Did Gerald Ford say this? It would be completely out of character and contradicts everything he said publicly for decades.

Giscard supposedly told the story in 2013 when he was eighty-seven years old and thirty-seven years after the incident:

> On this official trip, I am greeted by President Gerald Ford, who was one of the members of the Warren Commission, charged with shedding light on the Kennedy assassination. As we make our way to Mount Vernon, the former home of President George Washington, I ask him if he has formed an opinion on this subject. He answers me: "Yes. We came to the conclusion that this assassination had been prepared. There was a conspiracy. But we weren't able to identify which organization sponsored it."
>
> This opinion, I share it. I was sure of this when, three years after this interview, I broached this issue with a very prominent New Orleans oil contractor with whom I was hunting in Scotland. Naively, I asked him, "Do you know who murdered Kennedy?" He answered bluntly: "Yes. It was not some mad, lone gunman who killed the President of the United States."

Even Jefferson Morley, a journalist who appears in *JFK: Destiny Betrayed*, finds this story hard to believe:

> Perhaps Giscard simply misunderstood what Ford said. As Giscard showed in a 2016 appearance, his command of the language is decent but he is not entirely comfortable speaking English.

It wasn't the only story he told about someone now dead:

> He also once told this *Washington Post* reporter that when Mitterrand was on his death bed, he had admitted to Mr. Giscard: "The only way we could beat you was to destroy you" with fabricated scandal.

This is exactly the sort of story that *JFK: Destiny Betrayed* writer James DiEugenio likes, the single-sourced anecdote about somebody no longer alive. He wrote this story in his review of my book *I Was a Teenage JFK Conspiracy Freak:*

> When asked if Oswald was the actual killer, he [J. Edgar Hoover] replied with, "If I told you what I really know, it would be very dangerous to this country. Our whole political system could be disrupted." (James DiEugenio, *Destiny Betrayed*, Second Edition, p. 246)

The actual source is Anthony Summers' book *Official and Confidential: The Secret Life of J. Edgar Hoover.* Summers quoted Billy Byars, a student who had a conversation with Hoover in the summer of 1964. But did this happen? Was Hoover perhaps thinking the Soviets were involved? Well, we don't know.

DiEugenio also tells a whopper of a story about Clay Shaw. An interior designer, Phil Dyer, met with Shaw in 1972 and said Shaw admitted that he not only knew Oswald fairly well but that Oswald was a double agent. When this supposedly happened, Shaw was in the middle of his damages lawsuit against Jim Garrison. A strange time for a statement that could be used against him. Perhaps Shaw was pulling his leg. Or perhaps this never happened.

DiEugenio is suspicious of just about anything the government does or says, but in this case, he finds no need for any skepticism.

JFK: Destiny Betrayed has no trouble using hearsay when it serves its purposes.

CHAPTER 35
WAS GENERAL CURTIS LEMAY ORDERED TO FLY TO ANDREWS AIR FORCE BASE?

(Original Caption) General Curtis LeMay, USAF, Chief of Staff, U.S. Air Force, smokes his ever-present cigar as he talks to newsmen at a NATO exercise at Camp Voluceau, near Paris. Credit: Bettmann / Contributor/May 28, 1962

(EPISODE 3, 54:07)

JFK: Destiny Betrayed claims that General Curtis LeMay was ordered by General Eugene Zuckert to fly to and land at Andrews Air Force Base from his holiday in Canada and that LeMay then disobeyed orders and landed at National Airport. This would have supposedly put him closer to Bethesda Naval Hospital where JFK's autopsy was performed, which the documentary claims he attended. That is not what happened.

Here is an excerpt from a transcript:

Oliver Stone: Can you tell us about the Air Force One tapes, and General Curtis LeMay?

Douglas Horne: On the new version of the Air Force One tapes, the Clifton tapes, it's revealed that Colonel Dorman, General LeMay's aide, was desperately trying to contact LeMay on the radio.

Excerpt from tape: **Colonel Dorman**: [This is] Colonel Dorman, General LeMay's aide.

Excerpt from tape: **Andrews**: Right.

Excerpt from tape: **Colonel Dorman**: General LeMay is in a C-140.

Excerpt from tape: **Andrews**: Right

Excerpt from tape: **Colonel Dorman**: Last three numbers are "497," He's inbound, His code name is 'Grandson,' and I want to talk to him.

Douglas Horne: A logbook was recovered by the ARRB from the Air Force command post at Andrews. And it was given to us by a civil servant named Chuck Holmes. And this logbook records in-flight conversations between a command post at Andrews and Air Force One as it's flying from Texas back to Washington.

Excerpt from tape: **Command Post**: Air Force One, this is the Air Force Command Post. If possible, request the names of the passengers onboard, please.

Douglas Horne: So, this logbook shows that General LeMay, at the time of the assassination, was in Canada. This is really interesting because his official biographer says he was hunting in Michigan, but we know that's not true. He was in Toronto, for reasons unknown. Without his aide, Colonel Dorman, who went with him everywhere. This logbook reveals that he was ordered by [Air Force] Secretary Zuckert to land at Andrews Air Force Base because all the federal officials were going to meet the President's body at Andrews Air Force Base. A transmission was made from LeMay's plane back to this command post, and it says, General LeMay will not go to Andrews. General LeMay will go to DCA, National Airport. According to this log, his plane lands at 5:15 PM, well before the autopsy starts.

Narrator (Whoopi Goldberg): Very few people in the Pentagon had a worse relationship with Kennedy than Curtis LeMay. During the Missile Crisis he opposed Kennedy's solution of a blockade. When Kennedy left the room after this conference, LeMay openly ridiculed him. LeMay was strongly against the Test Ban Treaty Kennedy was working on and signed in 1963. He wanted to escalate the Vietnam War, with both naval and air power, by carrying the war north. He advocated bombing North Vietnam back to the Stone Age, if need be, and was willing to use atomic weapons if the Chinese intervened.

This is quite the allegation.

Let's start with LeMay's flight back to the United States from Canada. *JFK: Destiny Betrayed* makes it sound suspicious that LeMay flew into National Airport instead of Andrews Air Force Base.

The truth is that General LeMay was never ordered to fly into Andrews Air Force Base.

Here is the sequence of events on November 22, 1963, as provided by researcher Larry Haapanen: (All times are EST.)

1:30 PM JFK is shot in Dallas.

2:20 PM 4197 Set-up to Dept to P/U Gen LeMay at Toronto, Canada (Holmes logbook)

2:46 PM Aircraft 4197 [C-140 jet] departs for Canada, ETA 3:46 PM (Holmes logbook)

2:50 - 3:00 PM Change LeMay P/U from Toronto to Wiarton (Holmes logbook)

3:05 PM Contacted 24197 to change destination to Wiarton (Holmes logbook)

3:47 PM Air Force One departs Love Field for Andrews AFB (Holmes logbook)

4:04 PM LeMay departs Wiarton: "24197 Gen. LeMay dept Wairton [sic] 1604 ETA DCA 1715, Driver & Aide at DCA ETA changed 17:10 Secy Zuckert will meet LeMay at ADW (notified acft)" (Holmes logbook)

~4:15 PM Conversation between Gen. Clifton on AF-1 and SA Jerry Behn in DC.

Behn: WATCHMAN, should the secretary of defense and others be at Andrews on your arrival?

Clifton: No. I am about to—no; negative. I am about to call the White House. President Johnson wants to meet [with] the White House staff; the leadership of Congress; and as many of the cabinet members as possible, at the White House [as] soon as we get there—approximately 1830, 1830 [EST}. Over.

[Apparently, General Clifton makes a call to the White House, not on tapes]

4:30 PM At HQ, Military District of Washington, Major Rutherford informs CG [General Wehle] that Col. Connell, of General Clifton's office at WH, has called to say that he's had a call from General Clifton directing that no DoD personnel meet AF-1 at Andrews, including the Chief of Staff. **(After Action Report, 11/22/63, Military District of Washington, page 36)**

~4:40 PM LeMay is a half hour away from landing. LeMay's aide, Col. Dorman, attempts to place a call to LeMay's plane. Message is not disclosed, but apparently, it needs to get through before LeMay is on the ground, as Dorman says, "But if you can't work him now, it's gonna be too late because he'll be on the ground in a half hour." (Douglas Horne transcript of AF-1 tapes)

5:00 PM "Gen LeMay will land DCA NOT ADW" (Holmes logbook)

5:12 PM LeMay arrives at DCA (National Airport); 48 minutes before AF-1 lands at Andrews

---

The entry at 4:04 p.m. indicates that General LeMay was going to land at National Airport and then be driven to Andrews Air Force Base. There is no evidence that General LeMay was ever ordered to fly to Andrews. The expectation that he and others would meet at Andrews was changed at 4:30 p.m. when General Clifton on Air Force One instructed the military in Washington to have no Department of Defense dignitaries present to greet the plane at Andrews.

Douglas Horne alleges that the entry at 5:00 p.m. about General LeMay landing at National Airport is a change in destination. This is just not true. The previous logbook entry at 4:15 p.m. indicated that his ETA at National Airport was 5:15 p.m. Perhaps the 5:00 p.m. transmission was just a response from his pilot about chatter about other people going to Andrews.

Here is an excerpt from the Military District of Washington After Action Report:

7. At 1630, Major Rutherford informed CG that he had just received a call from Captain Colonel Connell, General Clifton's Office at the White House to the effect that he had received a call from General Clifton, who was aborad the aircraft, directing that no DOD personnel meet the aircraft at Andrews to include the Chief of Staff. He stated that General Wehle had a specific responsibility and that he should make a decision with regards to his presence at Andrews for the arrival of the remains.

This provides the evidence of a call from General Clifton on Air Force One to his own office in Washington stating that there should not be any high-ranking DoD personnel on hand to meet Air Force One at Andrews. That meant that only a small party was on hand to greet Air Force One: General Maxwell Taylor, Secretary of Defense Robert McNamara, and General Philip Wehle.

JFK: Destiny Betrayed ultimately leads viewers to assume that LeMay landed at National to be closer to Bethesda Naval Hospital, the site of JFK's autopsy. In fact, it's only a bit closer to Bethesda. More importantly, National Airport is a substantially shorter drive to the Pentagon than Andrews. One would expect that LeMay would have gone there to confer with the other Chiefs.

Here is an excerpt from the LeMay Oral History at the LBJ Library:

F: Where were you at the time of the assassination?

L: I was in Washington at the time—the Chief of Staff of the Air Force.

F: You were at work on that particular day?

L: No, I was off some place, at the actual time of the assassination, I was called back.

F: Yes, what was the situation that you found when you got back to Washington? Was there a little bit of tenseness or was it pretty well decided that Lee Harvey Oswald was just after one man?

L: Well, there wasn't much of a flap. Everybody was a little concerned that they didn't know what made the attack, the assassination, so they wanted everybody present for duty. That's the reason they were called back.

What was LeMay doing in Canada? He told his biographers that he was hunting in Michigan. Here is his expense report for November 1963:

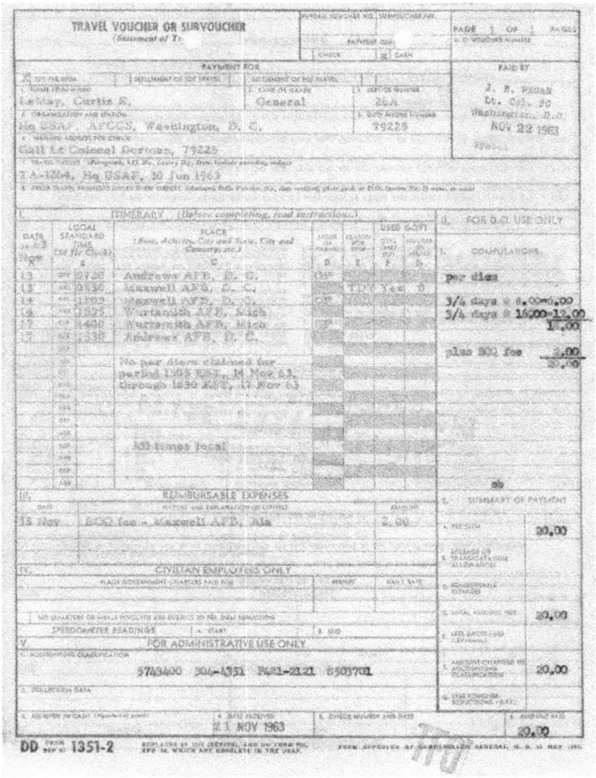
TRAVEL VOUCHER OR SUBVOUCHER

PAGE 1 OF 1 PAGES

CHECK | X CASH

PAYMENT FOR

1. NAME: LeMay, Curtis E.

2. GRADE: General

3. SERVICE NUMBER: 26A

4. ORGANIZATION AND STATION: Hq USAF, AFCCS, Washington, D. C.

5. 79225

6. MAILING ADDRESS FOR CHECK: Call Lt Colonel Dorton, 79225

7. TRAVEL ORDERS: TA-1264, Hq USAF, 10 Jun 1963

PAID BY: J. B. REGAN, Lt. Col. FC, Washington, D.C., NOV 22 1963

I. ITINERARY (Before completing, read instructions.)

DATE	LOCAL STANDARD TIME	PLACE	MODE OF TRAVEL	REASON FOR STOP	USED GOV'T
13	DEP 0728	Andrews AFB, D. C.			
13	ARR 0830	Maxwell AFB, D. C.		TDY	Yes
14	DEP 1355	Maxwell AFB, D. C.			
14	ARR 1525	Wurtsmith AFB, Mich			
17	DEP 1400	Wurtsmith AFB, Mich			
17	ARR 1530	Andrews AFB, D. C.			

No per diem claimed for period 1355 EST, 14 Nov 63, through 1530 EST, 17 Nov 63

All times local

II. FOR D.O. USE ONLY — COMPUTATIONS

per diem
3/4 days @ 8.00=6.00
3/4 days @ 16.00=12.00
18.00
plus BOQ fee 2.00
20.00

III. REIMBURSABLE EXPENSES

DATE	NATURE AND EXPLANATION OF EXPENSE	AMOUNT
13 Nov	BOQ fee - Maxwell AFB, Ala	2.00

IV. CIVILIAN EMPLOYEES ONLY

SPEEDOMETER READINGS

V. FOR ADMINISTRATIVE USE ONLY

1. ACCOUNTING CLASSIFICATION: 5743400 304-4351 P481-2121 8503701

SUMMARY OF PAYMENT

A. PER DIEM	20.00
D. TOTAL AMOUNT DUE	20.00
F. AMOUNT CHARGED TO ACCOUNTING CLASSIFICATION	20.00
AMOUNT PAID	20.00

DATE RECEIVED: 21 NOV 1963

DD FORM 1351-2

You can see that LeMay took leave from November 14–17, 1963. He flew in and out of Wurtsmith Air Force Base, which is only about forty miles from Rose City, Michigan, where he typically went hunting. Larry Haapanen spoke to Air Force Colonel Aaron Burleson in 2001, who told him that LeMay was fishing in Canada on November 22, 1963. And he should know as he served as "the Special Air Mission officer at Air Force Headquarters, a position involving coordination of transportation for the nation's highest-ranking government and military officials."

Note that LeMay's expense report was filed on November 21, 1963. The next expense report that LeMay filed was for December 1963. So, the evidence is pretty clear that LeMay was not away on secret business but was on leave when JFK was assassinated.

Perhaps General LeMay wasn't quite the villain depicted in *JFK: Destiny Betrayed*.

Here is a more nuanced view of LeMay:

> Contrary to popular perception, LeMay never stepped outside the chain of command or even tried to advance his personal views. As he later wrote, "We in SAC were not saber-rattlers. We were not yelling for war and action in order to 'flex the mighty muscles we had built.' No stupidity of that sort. We wanted peace as much as anyone else wanted it." However, he strongly disagreed with the policy that promised the Soviets that the U.S. would never use nuclear weapons first. He believed the entire purpose of having a nuclear arsenal was its threatened use, not its actual use. And by promising not to use it, what was the sense in even having it? Despite this view, however, he stuck to his job. Years after his retirement, he insisted to biographer Thomas Coffey that he never advocated preemptive war with the Soviets, saying, "I never discussed the problem with President Truman or with President Eisenhower. I never discussed it with General Vandenberg when he was Chief of Staff. I stuck to my job at Offutt and in the Command. I never discussed what we were going to do with the force we had or what he should do with it, or anything of that sort. Never discussed it with topside Brass, military or civilian."

According to Carl Kaysen, deputy special assistant to the president for national security affairs, Kennedy thought LeMay was an extremely capable head of the Air Force:

> In fact, just to ramble a bit about this matter, it strikes me that one of the characteristic qualities of Kennedy's mind is that he did hold somewhat opposite points of view in suspension, and he wasn't dogmatic on one thing, and so on. It was a quality which was very attractive, I remember a comment he made about LeMay [Curtis E. LeMay]; that he admired LeMay, that he didn't have LeMay around for policy advice. He didn't think much of the kind of policy advice he was going to get from LeMay, but he had the man around because he knew how to run the Air Force, and if we ever needed an Air Force, you'd want a man like that to run it. And it takes a great capacity to be able to separate these

> two things about the same man, and to be fighting with him about policy and yet talk like that about him. Not only talk like this, but feel like this about him. This was one of his most striking capacities.

However, James DiEugenio believes that General LeMay is at the heart of the conspiracy to assassinate President Kennedy:

James DiEugenio Posted Sunday at 05:23 PM (edited)

In my opinion, LeMay was a part of the pre planned cover up.

I believe the cover up was planned with the conspiracy.

Its difficult to explain why he lied about where he was that day, along with a couple of other things.

Had the writers and producers of *JFK: Destiny Betrayed* done a modicum of research, they would have realized that Douglas Horne's allegations were not supported by the facts. But General LeMay was a compelling villain, and the story fit the narrative of a CIA-military conspiracy against JFK.

CHAPTER 36
DID GENERAL CURTIS LEMAY ATTEND JFK'S AUTOPSY?

(EPISODE 3, 56:29)

JFK: Destiny Betrayed alleges that General Curtis LeMay was at JFK's autopsy.

Here is an excerpt from a transcript:

Douglas Horne: There were a lot of people at the Bethesda morgue. The latest count by all the researchers that I know of is about 33 people. There was a gallery, bleachers. Apparently all three rows were filled with people. Both Dr. Humes has complained after the fact and Tom Robinson, the mortician from Gawler's Funeral Home. They both equated it to a three-ring circus.

Dr. Gary Aguilar: But these three autopsy pathologists who are not really credentialed to do that kind of an autopsy, were given the body, told 'here's the body, he was shot from behind, he fell forward,' which they wrote in their autopsy report, 'figure out how the wounds fit the known circumstances of the shooting.' But what this really speaks to is the fact that the autopsy was not in the control of the surgeons that were charged with doing it, it was in the control of people who were there who were telling them what they could do and what they couldn't do.

Douglas Horne: Paul O'Connor was a Navy Corpsman helping the

> pathologists. He told me in 1999, he told others this in 1992, he's told several people, that Dr. Humes, during the autopsy, complained that somebody was smoking a cigar, 'tell him to put the damn thing out.' So, O'Connor, he went over to the gallery, the three rows of bleachers, and there was General LeMay, sitting in his uniform, with a big fat cigar in his hand, and LeMay looked at him after he asked him to put it out, and promptly blew smoke in his face.
>
> **Douglas Horne**: Did LeMay go to the autopsy to gloat over the death of his nemesis?

So, was General LeMay at JFK's autopsy?

Douglas Horne writes in Volume V of his book series *Inside the Assassination Records Review Board* that a member of the Office of Naval Intelligence, whom he named "Deep Throat," told him LeMay was at the autopsy:

> Deep Throat told me that Curtis LeMay was indeed at President Kennedy's autopsy—to gloat, not to control the coverup—and that he had the arrogance to show up in full uniform. He said that LeMay was essentially there for entertainment, in so many words, to simply enjoy the demise of a political enemy who had greatly frustrated him in life. The witness said his encounter with LeMay was quite contentious, even though LeMay had retired and had been officially put out to pasture by this time.

Horne ultimately dismissed "Deep Throat":

> I later came to distrust the mystery witness, who I decided to refer to as "JFK Deep Throat" and to conclude that he could not possibly be who he said he was. Because Deep Throat turned out not to be who he said he was, everything he told me was, of course, suspect.

In *JFK: Destiny Betrayed,* Horne avoids the details of the story about LeMay's "gloating" and other intentions and reduces it to a question he is posing: "Did LeMay go to the autopsy to gloat over the death of his nemesis?" Horne doesn't tell us that this comes from a very suspect source.

The only support for the allegation that General LeMay was at JFK's autopsy comes from Paul O'Connor, who at the time was a young (twenty-two years old) medical corpsman stationed at Bethesda. As you will see, his story about LeMay keeps changing.

He was interviewed by William Matson Law for his book *In the Eye of History: Disclosures in the JFK Assassination Medical Evidence*:

O'Connor: I remember one general who was sitting in the gallery. It was a teaching morgue, and we had a big gallery. I remember Curtis LeMay sitting there with a big cigar in his hand.

Law: How did you know it was Curtis LeMay?

O'Connor: I knew Curtis LeMay by seeing him before and by the big cigar he smoked all the time.

Law: What was his manner when you saw him?

O'Connor: Nonchalant. Kind of, "well, let's get this show on the road."

Law: You didn't see him nervous, upset?

O'Connor: No. He was just—

Law: Just there in the gallery smoking a cigar.

O'Connor: Right.

O'Connor told a similar story to James DiEugenio:

When this author interviewed the late Paul O'Connor, who was at the autopsy that night, he related an unforgettable story. He said that there were dozens of military brass in the gallery, the likes of which he had never seen. Someone was smoking a cigar. Dr. Humes called him over and said, "Please go tell this man to stop smoking." O'Connor went over, and as he approached him; he saw it was LeMay. Needless to say, he was not going to tell the Air Force Chief to stop anything.

And here is what he told Douglas Horne:

> Former Navy Hospital Corpsman Paul K. O'Connor ... told an anecdote for many years about something he witnessed during the autopsy on President Kennedy at the Bethesda morgue. The anecdote's essentials are that Dr. Humes, smelling cigar smoke in the morgue, loudly ordered whoever was smoking a cigar to 'put the damn thing out,' and told O'Connor to 'see to it,' or words to that effect. According to O'Connor, while Humes had his back turned to the gallery and was busy conducting the autopsy on the President's body, he (O'Connor) went over to the gallery to enforce Humes' dictate, only to run into the Air Force Chief of Staff, Curtis LeMay, who arrogantly blew smoke in O'Connor's face. When O'Connor informed Dr. Humes of the identify of the culprit, so the story goes, Humes turned quite pale, stuck his tail between his legs, and that was the end of the matter. According to O'Connor, when he saw LeMay the General had removed the four-star insignia from his uniform, but O'Connor recognized him, nevertheless.

The story got better from time to time.

- LeMay was there.
- He had a cigar in his hand.
- He was smoking it.
- Humes instructed O'Connor to get it put out, but O'Connor couldn't tell a general what to do.
- O'Connor did instruct LeMay, who then blew smoke in his face.

It won't be long until this story morphs into an exploding cigar!

But wait, there's more!

Researcher Harrison Livingstone held a press conference in May 1992 to discuss the medical evidence and then wrote:

> JAMA [Journal of the American Medical Association], claiming to have interviewed the autopsy doctors, quoted them as ridiculing the idea that generals and admirals were present at the autopsy. In fact, the Assassinations Committee published a list of numerous flag officers present, and some of these men who assisted at the autopsy told the story at my press conference a week after JAMA's that General Curtis LeMay and "the entire Joint Chiefs were there." In fact, that is the most

> reasonable assumption, because enlisted men certainly would not have filled up the large gallery viewing the autopsy.

All of the Joint Chiefs were there?

Paul O'Connor was quoted in the *Dealey Plaza Echo* in November 2004:

> Yes, it was funny. He was smoking a big cigar without his dress blouse on and Humes told me to go tell him to put that damned thing out in 'his' morgue. So, I went up to him, saw who it was and beat a hasty retreat. I told Humes who it was, and he turned white as a sheet. That was the funniest thing that happened that terrible night.

What is most telling about that article is this O'Connor statement:

> Kim, there were a lot of strange things that happened that night—that's why I can recall quite a few things that other people have forgotten—or lied about!

Researcher Bill Kelly has an interesting anecdote:

> I talked to Paul about that, over a beer at the hotel bar in Dallas and then again on the phone at length.
>
> Paul said he remembers a four-star general in the room with a cigar, and one of the doctors telling an aide to have whoever is smoking a cigar removed from the room, but when told who it was negated that order.
>
> Paul was suspicious that it was LeMay but wasn't sure.

He wasn't sure?

In fact, there is absolutely no corroborative evidence that General Curtis LeMay was at JFK's autopsy.

Sibert and O'Neill's FBI report listed the attendees at the autopsy, and General LeMay is not on the list.

In addition, William Matson Law interviewed Francis O'Neill in 2001:

Law: I've been told that there were officers of high rank in the autopsy room that night. Is that true?

O'Neill: There was the commanding officer of the hospital. There was a rear admiral. There was General Godfrey McHugh, who was on the airplane with Kennedy and was his military attaché; he was a one-star general. And there was a Major General Wehle who tried to enter, and I kicked him out and he came back in and told me he was there to get another casket because the other one was broken. There was no one else.

The HSCA also listed the people at the autopsy, and General LeMay was not on their list.

Dr. Humes was asked about this in 1996 during his deposition with the ARRB, and Douglas Horne was present:

Q: Would you have recognized Joint Chiefs of Staff as of 1963?

Dr. Humes: No.

Q: For example, Curtis LeMay, would you have recognized him?

Dr. Humes: Oh, I'd recognize him if he was there, but he was not.

Q: Did you ever hear any speculation about whether any members of the Joint Chiefs of Staff were present at the autopsy?

Dr. Humes: No, never heard, but if they were, it was unknown to me totally. I doubt very seriously that they were. You asked me, would I recognize them? Sure, you know, from newspapers and television, one thing or another. I probably knew them all by sight. But they weren't there.

Dr. Boswell was also asked about the Joint Chiefs of Staff:

Q: Were there any members of the Joint Chiefs of Staff present during the autopsy?

Dr. Boswell: I don't think so.

So, was Paul O'Connor a credible witness?

In his first interview with the HSCA, he said nothing about General LeMay. He also said several unusual things. For instance, he maintained that JFK was in a body bag when the casket arrived:

> O'Connor said that the casket was a pink shipping casket and it arrived approximately eight o'clock. He said the body was in a body bag and the head was wrapped in a sheet. O'Connor said he helped unwrap the sheet. He recalls seeing "... massive head wound ... "and a" ... gaping wound in the neck ... "as well as"... two chest incisions."

But other witnesses said JFK was not in a body bag. Sibert and O'Neill's FBI report says that Kennedy was wrapped in a sheet:

> The President's body was removed from the casket in which it had been transported and was placed on the autopsy table, at which time the complete body was wrapped in a sheet and the head area contained an additional wrapping which was saturated with blood.

Dr. Humes also took exception to the idea of a body bag:

> There was no body bag anywhere near the scene. I cannot imagine how this talk about the President's body being delivered in a body bag got started, but it is absolutely false.

O'Connor also told the HSCA that JFK's brain was gone:

> O'Connor said that he was shocked at what he saw. He said the head had "... nothing left in the cranium but splattered blood mater." O'Connor said he noticed this particularly because it was "... part of my job to remove the brain and fix it."

JFK's brain was removed by the autopsy doctors and was photographed by John Stringer. Vincent Bugliosi spoke to Stringer in September of 2000:

> Dr. Humes took the brain out of the president's head and put it in a jar of formalin. I personally saw this. I don't know how anyone could say that the president had no brain, except for money.

O'Connor's HSCA interview also indicated that he had some difficult moments after the autopsy:

> O'Connor stated that in 1959 he was stationed at Guantanamo, Cuba during the Bay of Pigs invasions. He said he has been "... very distraught regarding the whole autopsy thing." O'Connor believes he was followed at one time, and told us of an alleged incident in Dupont Circle which he never reported. He said the experience of the autopsy took him "... a long time to get over ..." He said he dropped out of school and transferred to Cecilfield and then went to Viet Nam where he was wounded. O'Connor is currently suffering from some back trouble and will have a third operation on his spine very soon.

Of course, the Bay of Pigs invasion took place in 1961.

Might there be some connection between O'Connor's faulty memory and his emotional issues after the autopsy?

And even Paul O'Connor himself understood the issue of memory. When he was interviewed in 1990 by Harrison Livingstone, he said nothing about LeMay. But he did say that JFK was in a body bag when the casket arrived at Bethesda:

> Yeah. We opened it up, unzipped the body bag. Which is another thing everybody is going crazy about, too. The body bag. Seems like I'm the only one who remembers that. They brought him in and opened his body bag. He was nude except for a bed sheet wrapped around his head. Which was totally soaked with blood.

Yes, he is the only one who remembers it that way.

Livingstone tried hard to get O'Connor to recant his belief about the body bag, and here is what O'Connor said:

> You know something, it could, because I thought I remember him being in it and having him zipped in it, but sure—to my mind—it was. But it has been so many years and so much has happened, I kind of doubt my own ability to remember the fine details.

Researcher David Lifton does not believe LeMay was at the autopsy:

> The source for this allegation is Paul K. O'Connor. I first interviewed PKO in Aug 1979. In that original interview, he mentioned nothing about Curtis LeMay being at the autopsy. As I recall, that claim wasn't first made until he became a fixture on the lecture circuit—i.e., was invited to speak at Lancer. Only then did he modify his account to include the assertion that LeMay attended the autopsy. Based on my original telephone interview with O'Connor (Aug 1979), plus my filmed interview with him (a few months later), I would not give any credence to this claim.
>
> One other thing: It is highly unlikely that LeMay attended the autopsy for still another reason: LeMay's presence surely would have been noted in the FBI report written by SA's James Sibert & Francis O'Neill, who kept a list of who attended the autopsy.

In another post, Lifton warned people about some interviews with O'Connor:

> ABOUT THE "Later" Interviews of O'Connor:
>
> I caution anyone reading these posts to tread carefully in evaluating what O'Connor says in these later interviews because, by that time, he was no longer in the mode of genuinely recollecting, for the first time, what resided in his memory; but rather, was repeating—again and again—what he had already said before, and also, and perhaps more important—was reading various books on the assassination.

On this point: I know for a fact—from speaking directly to Paul in 1990-1992—that Harrison Livingstone was calling him up and attempting to talk him out of the fact that the body arrived in a body bag. Another person engaged in that sort of behavior was James Jenkins, who was trying to tell him that there really was a brain, and that he removed it (when Jenkins had said completely different things to me, when I interviewed him in 1979, and then on camera in 1980).

So "beware," is all that I'm saying.

"Beware" is also good advice when it comes to *JFK: Destiny Betrayed.*

CHAPTER 37
WAS LEE HARVEY OSWALD A FAKE DEFECTOR?

(EPISODE 4, 1:37)

JFK: Destiny Betrayed misleads viewers into believing that Otto Otepka uncovered evidence that Oswald was a fake defector. Otepka's whole career was built on finding communist subversion, and his suspicions about the Oswald case were driven by his anti-communism. There is no evidence to support the allegation that Otepka believed Oswald was a fake defector.

Otto Otepka, a U.S. State Department security evaluator, shown here in Washington D.C. on Nov. 1, 1963, is under fire with an investigation that will probably cost him his job. (Associated Press Photo/Henry Burroughs)

Here is an excerpt from a transcript:

[Archive clip] **Richard Schweiker**: This report [Church Committee, Book V on the Performance of the Intelligence Agencies in the JFK Assassination] documents the failures of the U.S. intelligence establishment in their investigation of President Kennedy's assassination, and their coverup to the Warren Commission.

Narrator (Whoopi Goldberg): During the 1975 Church Committee investigation of U.S. intelligence activities, committee member Richard Schweiker, in an interview at the time, remarked about Oswald, that "everywhere you looked with him, there are fingerprints of intelligence." Those fingerprints extended back to 1959 when Oswald defected to the Soviet Union. State Department intelligence officer Otto Otepka had noted the marked increase in the number of Americans defecting to Russia at the time. He also noted that some of them came from the military. He therefore suspected that some of these men were fake defectors. They had been assigned by the CIA to garner intelligence behind the iron curtain. He sent a letter to the CIA, asking which ones were real and which were their agents. Oswald was one of the names on Otepka's list. Otepka's request was forwarded to James Angleton, Chief of Counterintelligence. He instructed that there be no research done on Oswald, but Otepka continued to work on the Oswald case.

Lisa Pease: The only thing of significance was that he was really interested in Lee Harvey Oswald before the assassination. And he actually had a study of these defectors in his safe. Well, things got worse. His office was not only bugged but they planted people in his office to spy on him. They started putting confidential documents in his burn bag and then tried to blame him and say "he's burning confidential documents. The guy's gone, y'know, wacko."

Narrator (Whoopi Goldberg): As a result, he was formally removed from the State Department on November 5, 1963. just seventeen days before the assassination. So, you will not see Otepka's name in the Warren Report and he was not called as a witness before that body. In fact, James Angleton, the man who had access to all the Oswald files at the CIA, coordinated the agency's response to the Warren Commission's requests.

Just who was Otto Otepka? He was the former chief of the State Department's Office of Security (SY) and had been the "leading expert on Communist subversion in the State Department." Otepka's office worked closely with the Senate Internal Security Subcommittee (SISS), which held hearings on the "loss of China" in 1949 and then later on the "loss of Cuba." Part of the job of the Office of Security was to evaluate members of the diplomatic corps for loyalty.

For anybody interested in Otto Otepka, I heartily recommend Eric Paul Roorda's 2007 article in *Diplomatic History*, "McCarthyite in Camelot: The 'Loss' of Cuba, Homophobia, and the Otto Otepka Scandal in the Kennedy State Department."

After the 1954 election, Otepka started a comprehensive review of State Department employees:

> Otepka made up a set of five by eight-inch file cards distilling the damaging "data" on each of 858 employees whose files, Otepka decided, contained some dark mark. "The purpose of the study and the cards," he testified, "was to assure that no person whose record was highly questionable would occupy any critical or policy-influencing position, and also to assure that each case, according to its merits, would be subjected to periodic scrutiny and appropriate reinvestigation."

The Office of Security was so close to the SISS that some considered it "captured." And the SISS played a crucial role in the dismissal of several China hands. Then the SISS turned its attention to Cuba. Its hearings began before the 1960 election and continued after the inauguration.

> The controversy stoked the explosive issue of subversion in the State Department, prompting new Secretary of State Dean Rusk to be more assertive than his predecessors had been in defending the Foreign Service. Rusk realized that the Office of Security had allied with the SISS in the witch hunts that had weakened the State Department. Otepka's domination of security clearances became the first target in Rusk's effort to break the influence of the SISS.

Dean Rusk realized it was time for a change. Otepka's supervisor said he was a man with "a tendency to dwell in the past ... a stickler for detail and a hewer to the letter of the law."

> But Otepka considered himself to be an expert on "communism and its subversive movements in the United States," subscribing to McLeod's dictate that "if one is a security officer, you assume that the enemy has an apparatus in your organization, and you try to root it out." Otepka's activities as an informant for the SISS had troubled even Secretary of State John Foster Dulles in the late 1950s.

Rusk knew that Otepka was yesterday's man. Otepka met with Rusk and Robert Kennedy in December 1960 to discuss the rejection of Walt Rostow's security clearance in 1954 and 1957. Otepka told them he would still not clear Rostow and said that "all new Kennedy appointees would be subject to exhaustive background checks by the Office of Security and the FBI." Two other appointments by Rusk were also rejected by Otepka.

Rusk then eliminated Otepka's position as deputy director of the Office of Security and moved him to the Division of Evaluations. He then had no authority over security clearances. Otepka then testified before the SISS, and over the next five years he offered "approximately 1,750,000 words of testimony." He told them that Rusk's move was politically motivated.

A controversy erupted over Kennedy's appointment of William Wieland, who had previously been director of the Office of Mexican and Caribbean Affairs in the State Department, to help reorganize the Office of Security. Otepka's file on Wieland consisted of eleven volumes, and he objected to Rusk's clearance of Wieland. This all hit the newspapers, and there were insinuations about Wieland:

THURSDAY, OCTOBER 18, 1962 — THE INDIANAPOLIS STAR

DESCRIBED AS HAVING SOFT MINDS

Deviates Called Peril In State Department

By PAUL MARTIN
North American Newspaper Alliance

Washington — The new senate report on State Department security contains a significant discussion on the problem of homosexuals as "security risks" in policy-making positions of sensitive government agencies.

...ends their being discovered in private life.

"You probably have known, as I have, within a community where suddenly the gossip is around that (someone), whoever he is, is a homosexual. Then whatever else he has been doing, he has to leave the community and go somewhere else.

...wants to skate along, take the easy way, go with the tide, not enter into a hard, tough opposition when he sees that his country's welfare is involved.

"The real danger to the U.S. seems to me to come from the fact that these people, when they get into decision-making jobs, do not have the approach to it that

...garding it simply as a sickness?"

McLEOD: "I am somewhat amused by our British brothers in this matter, because while they are publicly — at least some segments of the population are publicly — advocating that these people be recognized as sick and that they not

...of 1955, there was something over 100 a year identified and dismissed in one way or another; I think the thing fell off then statistically.

"I am not aware of what the statistics are since 1957, but it is not a problem that has been solved by any means."

Indianapolis Star, *October 18, 1962*

The hearings moved from Wieland to Otepka himself. The SISS

concluded that the State Department "was seeking to remove 'the last of the breed' left over from the McCarthy era." Otepka testified that the Kennedy administration was abusing the emergency waiver process for hiring. A State Department spokesperson said that Otepka "was out of step with the times. We are not witch hunting any more. We have no security risks, and he knows it."

Otepka met privately with SISS staff to supply them with information:

> Otepka informed the SISS that he had compiled a list of eight hundred current State Department employees whose security files contained "seriously derogatory information." He said he considered liberals in the State Department to be "dissidents" who subverted the efforts of "fair-minded evaluators" like himself.

The State Department suspected that Otepka had given the staff of SISS classified documents and examined his "burn bag" for clues. They found classified seals of documents that Otepka had turned over to the subcommittee. Otepka's phone was tapped, and his office safe was searched.

In May 1963 Rusk transferred Otepka to a new position that did not require the use of security files. By the time Otepka testified before the SISS in August 1963, his name had been removed from the State Department directory. Later that month he was charged with releasing documents to the SISS. Rusk told the SISS that "Otepka worked for the wrong boss."

Otepka did not lose his job, but he was demoted in December 1967. Richard Nixon then appointed him to the Subversive Activities Control Board, but he was never confirmed by the Senate.

Much of the narrative behind the Otto Otepka segment in *JFK: Destiny Betrayed* comes from Henry Hurt's book *Reasonable Doubt*, whose Chapter 9 also has the title "Fingerprints of Intelligence." Another source for this segment is Lisa Pease's article "What Did Otepka Know about Oswald & the CIA?" in the March–April 1977 issue of *Probe Magazine*. In addition, John Newman wrote about Otepka in his book *Oswald and the CIA*.

This all started with an Otepka memo to Richard Gatewood, who worked in the State Department's Office of Intelligence Resources and Coordination (IRC) within its Intelligence and Research Bureau (INR) about defectors to the Soviet Union:

OPTIONAL FORM NO. 10
5010-104
OFFICIAL USE ONL
UNITED STATES GOVERNMENT

Memorandum

TO : IRC - Mr. Richard Gatewood

DATE: October 18, 1960

FROM : SY - Otto F. Otepka

SUBJECT: American Defectors to Soviet Bloc Countries

With reference to our telephone conversations neither the FBI nor SY has maintained any appropriate records in order to readily identify the number of Americans who defected to the Soviet Union, to other Soviet Bloc nations or to Communist China within the past eighteen months. I queried the FBI on this and was informed that that Bureau would look to the Department to obtain such information. At best, I have been able to gather only the following names:

William Martin - NSA employee
Bernon Mitchell - NSA employee
Edward Webster - Tourist
Lee Harvey Oswald - Tourist
Libero Ricciardelli - Tourist
Vladimir Sloboda - U. S. Army
Sgt. Joseph Dutkanicz - U. S. Army

I am certain that reports concerning the defections of all of the above persons have appeared in the press. I am having appropriate files checked to identify the source and account of each defection with the exception of Martin and Mitchell with whose cases you are familiar. This information will be furnished to you as soon as it is obtained.

I suggest that you check out the above names with CIA and also seek any other names which may be known to that agency. I would appreciate being informed if you are successful in having any names added to this list.

THE C.I.A. HAS NO OBJECTION TO THE DECLASSIFICATION OF THIS DOCUMENT.

Hugh Cumming of the Department of State's Intelligence and Research Bureau (INR) then wrote to Richard Bissell of the CIA. He included a list of known defectors and asked if the agency could "verify and possibly expand" the list.

Bissell then replied to Cumming and said that their "files are being searched."

Newman claims that Richard Bissell then asked Robert Bannerman, who was deputy chief of the CIA's Office of Security (OS), to answer the query. He had a close working relationship with Otepka, and he checked with the State Department's Security Office (SY) to see what they had and "told his staff to support Counterintelligence Staff (CI)." Marguerite Stevens was assigned to send information to CI.

The allegation that Angleton "instructed that there be no research done on Oswald" comes from John Newman's book *Oswald and the CIA*: (Emphasis in original.)

> A Stevens memo at the time shows that Bannerman verbally requested Gaynor to assemble information on American defectors. The request, as Gaynor relayed it to Stevens, however, was worded in a peculiar way, as if to dissuade her from doing research on seven people. Bannerman specified that he wanted information on American defectors "**other than** Bernon F. Mitchell and William H. Martin, and five other defectors regarding whom Mr. Otepka of the State Department Security Office already has information" on in his files [emphasis added]. One of the "five other defectors" that Stevens was not supposed to look into was Lee Harvey Oswald.

Here is an excerpt from the memo that Newman references:

CIA HISTORICAL REVIEW PROGRAM
RELEASE IN FULL
1999

31 October 1960

MEMORANDUM FOR: Chief, Security Research S[illegible]

FROM : M. D. Stevens

SUBJECT : American Defectors

Reference is made to a verbal request to you from the DC/OS for information regarding any American citizens who have defected to the USSR, Red China, or other Satellite countries during the past eighteen months—other than Bernon F. MITCHELL and William H. MARTIN, and five other defectors regarding whom Mr. OTEPKA of the State Department Security Office already has information (i.e. Robert Edward WEBSTER, EE-18354; Lee Harvey OSWALD, MS-11164; Libero RICCIARDELLI, MS-8295; Vladimir SLOBODA, MS-10565; and Joseph DUTKANICZ, MS-10724).

The memo says that they don't need to look into Oswald (and others) because they already have information. It is misleading to claim that "no research be done on Oswald."

Bissell then sent a detailed reply to Cumming and included details about various defectors. Here is what he sent on Lee Henry [sic] Oswald:

DECLASSIFIED
By C. I. A.
letter of Jan. 4, 1971
NNL by [illegible] Date 5 MAR 1971

OSWALD, Lee Henry
Defected October 1959

The following information is [illegible]

Born 18 October 1939 in New Orleans, Louisiana, Lee Henry OSWALD joined the United States Marines at the age of seventeen because he did not want to be a "burden" to his mother who was widowed prior to his birth. While in the Marines, OSWALD, a Private First Class, became a radar operator and had fourteen months service in Japan and the Philippines. About a year before his discharge from the Marines OSWALD began to teach himself to read and speak Russian. After receiving an honorable discharge from the Marines on 3 September 1959 OSWALD visited his mother in Waco, Texas for about three days and then departed. A note written to his mother from New Orleans stated that he had booked passage to Europe and that he was doing something he felt he must do. Shortly thereafter he appeared at the United States Embassy in Moscow and renounced his U. S. citizenship, giving as his reason the plight of the American Negro and U. S. "imperialism" abroad. OSWALD acknowledged mail addressed to him at the Hotel Metropole in Moscow in 1959; however, he has failed to do so in 1960. OSWALD is reported to have stated that regardless of any material shortcomings he may find in the USSR, he will never return to the United States.

I can see nothing in any of this documentation about the issue of false defectors. I turned to Henry Hurt's book *Reasonable Doubt,* in which he writes:

> It is known that during the years in question the State Department was engaged in a study of U.S. defectors to the Soviet Union and other Communist countries. One of its aims, according to Otto Otepka, the official in charge of the study, was to determine which "defectors" were genuine and which were U.S. intelligence operatives on espionage missions.

Hurt has three sources. The first is page 324 of William Gill's 1969 book, *The Ordeal of Otto Otepka*. Here is what Gill has to say:

> Some time prior to his exile from the Office of Security Otepka started work on a study of Americans who had defected to the Soviet Union and other Communist countries.

Gill says nothing about determining which defectors were genuine. In fact, Gill notes that what would have made Otepka suspicious about Oswald was not his intelligence connections:

> For example, Otepka almost certainly would have delved very deeply into the curious circumstances surrounding expeditious granting of a visa to enter the Soviet Union from Finland in October 1959. Although the State Department told the Warren Commission that in 1959 it "usually took an American tourist in Helsinki one to two weeks to obtain a visa," Oswald got his within two days after he applied.

Gill claims that Otepka's interest was in whether there was communist infiltration in the State Department, and he was also interested in whether Marina Oswald had KGB connections.

Gill elaborates on what Otepka would have investigated:

> The Otepka study would have traced Lee Harvey Oswald's background to this childhood. It would have determined who influenced him to become a fanatical Marxist. It would have unearthed early evidence of his mental instability. It would, in short, have marked Oswald as a man well worth keeping a wary eye on because all this, and more, was within the scope of the study as Otepka planned it.

That passage is not in Henry Hurt's book.

One of Hurt's other sources is Anthony Summers's book *The Kennedy Conspiracy*:

> Otto Otepka, the controversial former Chief Security Officer of the State Department, said that in 1963 his office engaged in a study of American "defectors," because neither the CIA nor military agencies such as naval intelligence would reveal which were authentic and which were intelligence plants. One of the cases being studied was that of Lee Harvey Oswald.

Summers's source is Bernard Fensterwald's 1977 book, *Assassination of JFK by Coincidence or Conspiracy?*

> Neither the CIA nor the military intelligence people would tell the State Department which of its "defectors" were genuine and which were U.S. agents.

His source for that is an interview with Otto Otepka in the summer of 1971. I have not been able to find that interview, so it is impossible to evaluate exactly what Otepka said. But most of the sources about Otepka's study looking into false defectors derive from that interview.

Jim Hougan, author of the 1978 book *Spooks: The Haunting of America,* also claimed that Otepka's interest was whether defectors were authentic:

> According to Otepka, the study on defectors was initiated by him because neither the CIA nor military intelligence agencies would inform the State Department which defections to the Soviet Union were double agents working for the United States.

Hougan interviewed Otepka in 1977:

> Asked whether Oswald was "one of ours or one of theirs," Otepka recently grouched, "We had not made up our minds when my safe was drilled and we were thrown out of the office."

One of theirs? Otepka's specialty was looking for communist agents. Might he have been interested in whether any of the returning defectors were Soviet agents?

In 1978, Otepka was interviewed by the HSCA, and he told them that "he presently feels that favorable treatment which Oswald received from the U.S. government was peculiar and he is not sure whether Oswald was a genuine political defector."

The first part of that sentence is consistent with his suspicions of communist penetration among State Department diplomats. As for the second part, was Otepka once again wondering if Oswald was a Soviet agent?

What did Otepka really think?

The best source might be Professor Peter Dale Scott:

> I interviewed Otto Otepka at length in 1978; he impressed me as a sincere anti-communist who from his vantage point had rightly concluded that there was far more to the Oswald case than met the eye. He observed, for example, that State Department procedures had been violated when Oswald, a former defector, received a new passport on June 25, 1963, one day after applying for it. (Just two days later, on June 27, Otepka was permanently separated from his office and his defector file.) Otepka also found suspicious Oswald's receipt of a Soviet visa in just two days, when the normal waiting period was one to two weeks.

Scott elaborated in his book *Oswald, Mexico, and Deep Politics*:

> Otepka's frustration in pursuing the Oswald matter, which he shared with me fifteen years ago, are instructive. As a right-winger who shared Angleton's profound mistrust of the Soviet Union, he feared that Oswald's defection had something to do with the KGB. He found it anomalous that Oswald received a visa to enter the Soviet Union from Finland in only two days (rather than the one-to-two weeks it normally took); and also, that the USSR granted Oswald an exit visa a month and a half early. Above all, as a security officer who had spent a lifetime studying State Department procedures, he claimed to know for a certainty that Oswald in 1963 had been granted a passport when he should not have. His efforts to learn why were resisted by his own

superiors at State, which compounded his suspicions of a subversive conspiracy. Otepka was not alone in his suspicions.

There is further evidence to support the view that Otepka was interested in rooting out communist subversion in the State Department. In the early 1970s, researcher Fred Newcomb corresponded with Otepka, who then sent him several documents.

Here is a routing sheet for a file on Lee Harvey Oswald kept in the Office of Security:

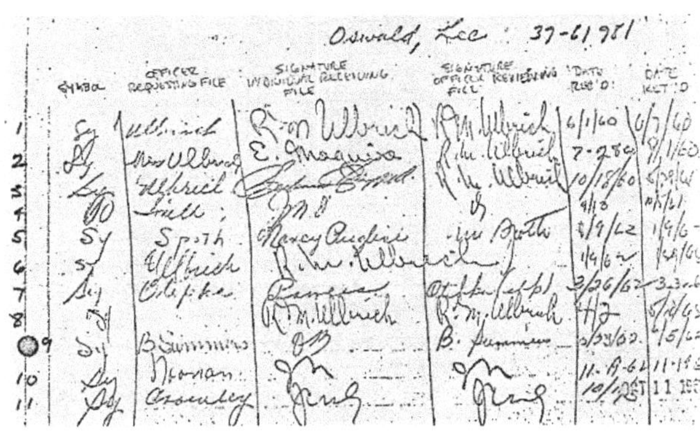

Oswald, Lee 37-61981

SYMBOL	OFFICER REQUESTING FILE	SIGNATURE INDIVIDUAL RECEIVING FILE	SIGNATURE OFFICIAL REVIEWING FILE	DATE REC'D	DATE RET'D

Here is Otepka's letter to Newcomb:

Otepka's answer

Confidential

(1) As requested, I am providing the identity and other data concerning the individuals whose names appear on the "Security File Control Sheet." Since there is i nsufficient space on the extra copy of the sheet furnished, I am recapitulating the requested information below according to the numbers on the control sheet, accompanied by explanatory comment.

The file in question (Lee Oswald, #39-61981) was a file maintained in the Central File Room of the Office of Security. The digits "39" signify that it was an "Intelligence file". The first listing is for p.2:

1. Ruth Ulbrich, Intelligence Analyst, Division of Evaluations, Office of Security.

2. Same as No. 1

3. Same as No. 1

4. Neither the name or initials appearing on this line are legible and no clues to their identity could be found.

5. George Speth, Chief, Passport & Visa Branch, Division of Investigations, Office of Security.

6. Same as No. 1.

7. Otto F. Otepka, Chief, Division of Evaluations, Office of Security.

8. Same as No. 1.

9. Beverly Summers, Clerk, Executive Office, Office of Security (file apparently reviewed by her supervisor, Richard O'Brien, Executive Officer, Office of Security).

10. John Noonan, Chief Records & Services Branch, Executive Office, Office of Security.

11. James D. Crowley, Intelligence Analyst, Office of the Deputy Director for Coordination, Bureau of Intelligence Research.

The single name appearing on page 1 of the control sheet is identical with No. 11, above.

Miss Ulbrich and Mr. Crowley were transferred by internal reorganization during 1962 from the Office of Security to the Bureau of Intelligence Research.

With respect to the names in column three of the control sheet which are not identical with the requestor of the file, they are secretarial personnel in the Office of Security to whom the files were delivered for referral by them to their superiors who requested the file. Their Identities are of no relevance, however the names will be supplied, if desired.

(2) From inquiries,and based on my own knowledge,there is no question that Crowley had authority and legitimate reasons for requesting the SY (Office of Security) file on Oswald, on Nov. 14, 1963. There were active investigations pending on Oswald in connection with his defection and travels and Crowley's branch was the authorized recipient of any reports submi ted by intelligence agencies to the State Dept.

However, see my Memorandum for the Record, prepared in January 1964. The defector files in my possession, as mentioned in that memorandum, were of a special category and were used by me (or under my direction) for the survey that I was conducting. Such files included data that I had culled from various files obtained by me throughout the State Dept.

It is possible that Crowley may have been asked to examine "my" files by management as a part of the gneral inquisition that was being made regarding the files that I had in my possession when I was effectively oused from my position as Chief Evaluator on June 27, 1963.

With respect to the coincidence of the date, Nov. 14, 1963, Crowley's duties included liaison with ONI.

(3) The questions as (a) why Oswald was repatriated and given a loan to return to the United States after he had defected to the Soviet Union and (b) was issued a passport in 1963 for travel to Cuba and the Soviet Union despite a possible "criminal" flag in his ONI file, are not easy to answer.

If the Director of the Passport Office, Frances Knight, had been given full authority in passport matters there would be no compassion and bleeding in the State Department for a Lee Harvey Oswald. At one time Miss Knight stated she would issue a passport to a baboon if she knew that was the policy. State Department passport policy vacillates according to political expediency and the moods of bleeding liberals who occupy strategic positions in management and in the geographical bureaus of the State Department. These characters decide what the policy is as of the moment and frequently overrule a stoong anti Communist like Miss Knight.

I have no information that the privileges extended to Oswald were a part of an internal conspiracy within the State Department because all the pertinent records are now hidden from view, mainly to protect idiots. But the fact is that those who decided all these privileges for Oswald are still in the State Department today and if they had acted intelligently there probably would have been no murders.

(4) INR is the organization symbol for the Bureau of Intelligence Research, Department of State.

(5) SDZ are the initials of Steven D. Zagorski an employee of INR. He is no longer with the State Dept. and I do not know his whereabouts.

Regarding the marginal query pencilled on the Elwood memo of Oct. 25, 1960 to Bissell, the matter of American defectors to Communist nations was often the subject of Congressional inquiries to the White House and it was the practice for White House staff to coordinate a proper reply.

Other comments regarding Oswald that are pencilled on the material sent me, I believe are answered in the separate enclosures sent to FTN.

Note the following paragraph:

I have no information that the privileges extended to Oswald were a part of an internal conspiracy within the State Department because all

> the pertinent records are now hidden from view, mainly to protect idiots. But the fact is that those who decided all these privileges for Oswald are still in the State Department today and if they had acted intelligently there probably would have been no murders.

As you can see, Otepka was concerned with what was going on within the State Department, not with whether Oswald was a false defector. Otepka also sent Newcomb this memo:

MEMORANDUM FOR THE RECORD

I was notified on January 10, 1964 by Mr. Raymond Laugel, Acting Deputy Assistant Secretary for Security, that Mr. Thomas Ehrlich of the Legal Adviser's Office wished to see me together with Mr. Laugel. Mr. Laugel did not indicate to me the topic of the discussion.

On January 13, 1964 Mr. Laugel advised me that he would call on me at my office at 2:00 p.m. that day. He did not state that he would be accompanied by anyone. Mr. Laugel appeared in the company of Mr. Ehrlich. The latter informed me that his office was coordinating the Department's work with the President's Commission on the Assassination of President Kennedy.

According to Mr. Ehrlich Mr. Lee Rankin had advised him that I had information in my files pertaining to Lee Harvey Oswald. Mr. Ehrlich stated he wished to know the nature of the information and whether it was identical or different from that appearing in the central files of the Office of Security which already had been furnished to the President's Commission.

I told Mr. Ehrlich that pursuant to the terms of reference specified to me by the Deputy Under Secretary for Administration in May, 1961, I was authorized to make studies of the pattern of internal subversion and to relate any pertinent cases to the Department's Personnel Security Program. In this connection I obtained from various sources within the Department, including SY files, various information on Americans who defected to the Soviet Union. The file on such defectors was kept in my suite but was available as needed to any evaluator. Included in the defector file was data which I had obtained long prior to November, 1963 concerning Lee Harvey Oswald.

Mr. Laugel informed me on January 14, 1964 that he had found the defector file and had furnished it to Mr. Ehrlich. Mr. Laugel did not specify to me what material was located in that file on Oswald and whether it was of any significance to the President's Commission.

I am deeply concerning about the possibility that the file which I established would not be returned to the Division of Evaluations, but its contents may be dissipated as has been the result previously where I had made other studies for appropriate use in the administration of the Department's Personnel Security Program.

Note that Otepka writes that he "was authorized to make studies of the pattern of internal subversion and to relate any pertinent cases to the Department's Personnel Security Program." Otepka's defector file was found and sent to the Warren Commission. He was not looking for fake defectors.

Otepka confirmed all this in a letter to the reporters working on the 1993 *PBS Frontline* documentary about Lee Harvey Oswald:

> In responding to your first set of questions about my knowledge of records regarding Lee Harvey Oswald. I said that a file was opened in the Office of Security in 1959, when it was reported he defected to the Soviet Union while traveling on a U.S. passport. Prompted by this report, a member of the Bureau of Intelligence Research and I began compiling a list of American defectors to Soviet bloc nations and China with a view to collecting information of possible interest to our respective responsibilities. Owing to my detail to other functions, beginning in 1961, that has been the extent of my official knowledge regarding Oswald. I reported that knowledge to a Department legal officer who interviewed me in 1964 as a representative of the Warren Commission. The list of defectors was later officially released to the public. Thereafter certain writers challenging the Warren Commission report that Oswald was the lone assassin, distorted the list and my limited knowledge, attributing some sinister role to me. Copy-cat writers also sought no verification of the truth.

JFK: Destiny Betrayed completely misses the point about Otto Otepka. He was an ardent anti-communist whose suspicions led him to question the State Department's handling of the Oswald file.

I should add that Mr. Otepka was pretty dismissive of conspiracy theorists. Here is another excerpt from his letter to *PBS Frontline*:

> Any other knowledge I have concerning Oswald's activities, including those relating to your questions to me as to whether Oswald had impersonators, has been derived only from the myriad of published literature generated from investigations of President Kennedy's assassination. I have read much of this material. I understand there are over a thousand titles—books, articles, reports, etc. The mixture of facts, theo-

ries, speculations, errors and prejudices boggles the mind. The number of alleged conspiratorial plots to kill Kennedy seem infinite. Government intelligence agencies, or persons connected with them in various capacities, are frequent targets. Undocumented and poorly documented accusations are like an oil spill; they pollute vast areas of land, water and air; recovery for those covered with the muck, however, innocent, is slow and painful.

CHAPTER 38
WAS LEE HARVEY OSWALD PAID BY THE CIA?

(EPISODE 4, 7:51)

JFK: Destiny Betrayed makes the erroneous claim that Lee Harvey Oswald was not paid for his last quarter of service in the U.S. Marines. Here is an excerpt from a transcript:

Narrator (Whoopi Goldberg): There was another unusual event that took place at the time of Oswald's defection. The source of his income changed.

Douglas Horne: Oswald's last quarter of earnings in the United States, before he defected to the Soviet Union, should have been paid by the United States Marine Corps. And they weren't. Because we asked to see his Marine Corps earnings records that the Marine Corps deposits with the Social Security Administration. They did not pay him any money the last quarter he was in the United States before his defection. Had no income from the Marine Corps, when he should have had.

Narrator (Whoopi Goldberg): Could this all be coincidence? Or was Otto Otepka correct in suspecting Oswald was not a legitimate defector? And is this why Angleton told his secretary to withhold information from Otepka?

This claim is just plain false.

Steve Roe has uncovered evidence that Oswald was paid by the Marine Corps. Here is a page from an FBI report of December 1963:

DL 100-10461
RPG:rmb

On December 13, 1963, Major HENRY MARSHALL, Marine Corps Intelligence, Navy Annex, Washington, D. C., advised that Marine Corps pay records disclose that LEE HARVEY OSWALD's total separation pay, paid on September 11, 1959, amounted to $219.20. This amount included allowance for travel, from El Toro, California to Fort Worth, Texas, unused leave, and final pay.

Oswald upon release from the USMC was paid in cash. See this excerpt from the U.S. Marine Corps record on Oswald: "sett [settled] by cash. Will not reenl [reenlist] RR [Ready Reserves]" below.

11Sep59	Drop rel fr ac du by reason of hard	
	ship xxxxxxxxxtr by SH to Cl III	
	Read/ MCR Asgd MARTC NAS GLEN auth	
	para 10273 MARCORMAN & MCO 1900.2B &	
	CG 3d MAW's End of 31Aug59 23 days UL	
	sett by cash Will not reenl RR	247-59

This excerpt from the USMC pay records published by the Warren Commission in Volume 26 shows that he was paid seven times in the third quarter of 1959: (line 49, box 30)

27 DATE | 28 COLLECTIONS/CHECKAGES | 29 TOTAL TAX WITHHELD | 30 PAYMENTS
FICA (3P$108.00 TAX 2.20
32 AMT OVPD LAST ACCT
33 TOTAL DEBITS
34 CASH/CHECK PAYMENTS
37 DEPOSIT BOOK NO.
DD FORM 113

Commission Exhibit No. 3099—Continued

You can see the withholding of $91.30 for January–September 1959:

DEDUCTIONS

Withholding Tax	Nov-Dec56	$ 8.00
"	Jan-Dec57	66.50
"	Jan-Dec58	58.60
"	Jan-Sep59	91.30
Social Security Tax	Jan-Dec57	22.72
"	Jan-Dec58	20.44
"	Jan-Sep59	22.84
Miscellaneous Clothing Deduction		.46
Summary Court Martial 4/29/58 sentenced to loss of pay $25.00 per month for 2 months		50.00
Summary Court Martial 6/27/58 sentenced to loss of pay $50.00 for 1 month		50.00
Check Sea & Foreign Duty Pay while confined 6/[illegible]/58-8/13/58		12.54
"Queen" allotment Mother August 1959		91.30
Total payments received 1956		111.00
Total payments received 1957		1150.00
Total payments received 1958		1084.00
Total payments received 1959		1107.20
TOTAL DEDUCTIONS		$3946.90

COMMISSION EXHIBIT No. 3099—Continued

Oswald's 1040 tax return for 1959 (no doubt based on the W-2) shows the same amount of withholding:

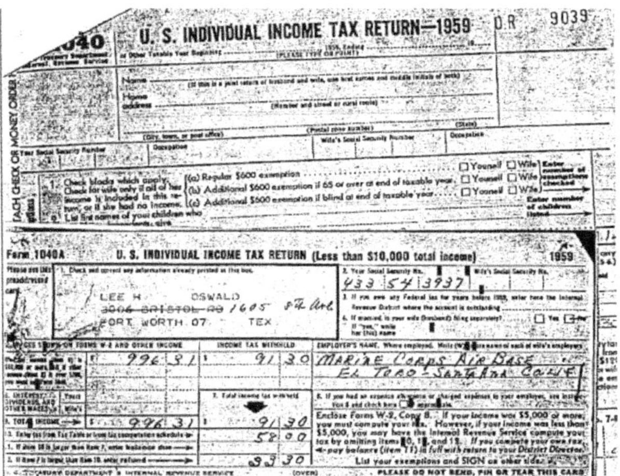

1040 U. S. INDIVIDUAL INCOME TAX RETURN—1959 D.R. 9039

Form 1040A U. S. INDIVIDUAL INCOME TAX RETURN (Less than $10,000 total income) 1959

Your Social Security No. 433 54 3937

LEE H OSWALD
3006 BRISTOL RD 1605 8th Ave
FORT WORTH 07 TEX

Wages	Income tax withheld	Employer's name
996.81	91.30	MARINE CORPS AIR BASE EL TORO - SANTA ANA CALIF

Total income 996.31 — 91.30

Tax 58.00

Refund 33.30

Enclose Forms W-2, Copy B. List your exemptions and SIGN on other side.

PLEASE DO NOT BEND, PIN OR TEAR THIS CARD

His form was indeed filed by Marguerite Oswald:

NOTE FOR SAC, DALLAS:

ReBuairtel 1/6/64 enclosing income tax returns filed by Lee Harvey Oswald for the years 1956, 1958, and 1962.

Enclosed is a Photostat of the 1959 income tax return of Oswald filed by his mother. This return should be reviewed for lead purposes only and the contents thereof should not be included in any investigative report.

And even Douglas Horne admits that the form was signed by Marguerite:

> **-C.D. 90a:** In enclosure (24), it is readily seen that Oswald's mother, Marguerite, signed the signature block on his 1959 1040A tax return on his behalf following his defection to the USSR, and then submitted the return on March 22, 1960. Although at first perusal, the author believed that the printing of the front of the 1040A card was Oswald's, upon further examination it appears to be more consistent with Marguerite's printing. This would be consistent with her signing the card.

This all appears to be consistent with the normal handling of Oswald's third quarter pay.

Douglas Horne wants *JFK: Destiny Betrayed* viewers to believe that he discovered a problem as part of his work with the ARRB. Somehow this discrepancy is supposed to corroborate the allegation that Oswald was on some sort of mission for American intelligence.

The anomaly in the Social Security Administration pay records was first documented in a Warren Commission document. CD 353a is an "Extract of Information" on Oswald from the SSA file. It does say "no earnings reported" for the third quarter of 1959.

1957	All	Mr. Oswald was in the U.S. Marine Corps.
1958	All	Mr. Oswald was in the U.S. Marine Corps.
1959	1st	In Marine Corps
	2d	In Marine Corps
	3d	No earnings reported.
	4th	No earnings reported.
1960	All	No earnings reported.
1961	All	No earnings reported.
1962	1st	No earnings reported

Horne knew about this when he worked at the ARRB:

Anomalies Noted by the Author in the Tax Information Records that are Now Open:

-C.D. 353a: In Attachment A to enclosure 13, the entry "1959, 3d quarter, no earnings reported" cries out for explanation, since Oswald did not separate from active duty service in the U.S. Marine Corps until September 11, 1959. Theoretically, all of his earnings received from the Marine Corps for the period July 1, 1959 through September 11, 1959 should have been reported. The author did not see any documents during his examinations of tax information as an ARRB staff member that provided an explanation for this--*or that anyone else had ever even noticed the discrepancy.*

Horne wrote that it "cries out for explanation." There are three possibilities: an error in the preparation of the Commission Documents, an error by the SSA in recording the information, or an error by the USMC in reporting the income. But none of these appear to have been seriously explored. Yet another example of the documentary series's "poverty of imagination."

Horne briefly considered that it might have been a mistake by the USMC or the SSA but was persuaded to reject that possibility:

> **Douglas Horne**: Because we asked to see his Marine Corps earning records that the Marine Corps deposited with the Social Security Administration. They did not pay him any money. That has serious implications to me because of all the speculation that he was a fake defector. So if he was in training for that, somebody else was paying his salary. But I can tell you the Marine Corps wasn't. I asked the lady at the Social Security Administration who was dealing with me and our staff attorneys ... She was a tough customer and I said, is there any possibility that the Marine Corps could have made a mistake and not reported this, or your records could be wrong. She said: Listen honey, and took a drag on a cigarette, blew the smoke in my face, and said: We don't make mistakes like that.

James DiEugenio has made a big deal out of Oswald's earnings:

James DiEugenio Posted January 6 (edited)

Members

9.3k
Gender:Male

Its now over one million views in one day! LOL!

BTW, that info about LeMay came from Doug Horne and its not in the two hour version. Only the four hour version.

The stuff Horne gave us about LeMay's maneuvers that day was just gold.

And there is also something about Oswald in the long version that Horne never revealed before. Oliver had to pull it out of him because Doug was worried about getting arrested. But he did finally say it.

Edited January 6 by James DiEugenio

It is true that when he saw the raw SSA data (after learning that CD 353a was public) he was "severely cautioned" that disclosure of information not found elsewhere "would be a felony."

> **-September 18, 1997:** ARRB staffers Ron Haron and Doug Horne visit the Social Security Administration in Baltimore, Maryland, in order to examine all earnings information that SSA has assembled at the Review Board's request. The primary focus is on Lee Harvey Oswald, although there was much Ruby material also. We were allowed *access* to all of the SSA earnings records on Lee Harvey Oswald, and were allowed to take notes, *but were severely cautioned that the IRS considered the SSA's earnings records to be tax information, and accordingly were warned against releasing any information we obtained solely from SSA, vice an outside source.* To release information obtained *only* from SSA, and not independently from some other source, we were reminded, would constitute a violation of Section 6103 of the IRS Code, and would be a felony. The

But the only information he reveals in the film was also in CD 353a, as he knew in 1997.

I don't think that Douglas Horne or the producers and writers of *JFK: Destiny Betrayed* will be arrested.

After all, getting things wrong is not a felony.

CHAPTER 39
WAS THERE A PLOT AGAINST JFK IN CHICAGO?

(EPISODE 4, 22:03)

JFK: Destiny Betrayed alleges that a supposed plot in Chicago in November 1963 against JFK was in the works and that a patsy was ready to be arrested. There is no evidence for any of this.

Here is an excerpt from a transcript:

Narrator (Whoopi Goldberg): Few people knew there had been at least two prior plots to kill President Kennedy in 1963. One was in Chicago on November 2nd, the second was in Tampa on November 18th.

Oliver Stone: Kennedy ended up not going to Chicago. Tell us about that plot.

Paul Bleau: An informant on October 31st, an informant named Lee, who could have been Lee Harvey Oswald, gave a warning to the FBI stating that four Cubans were headed to Chicago to shoot Kennedy. The following day, a landlady reported to the Chicago police that she had rented a room to four people that had rifles with telescopic sights, and a sketch of the motorcade. The FBI passed that on to the Secret Service. And the Secret Service botched the surveillance of these four individuals. Two of them escaped, but they actually picked up two of the snipers, and they detained them. They were stonewalled by the snipers. They didn't get any information out of them. While this was

> going on, there was another threat coming in from another alternate 'patsy,' named Thomas Arthur Vallee, who was making open and loud threats that he would assassinate Kennedy. They only picked him up when Kennedy canceled his trip on November 2nd at 10 in the morning. One day before the trip, the Diem brothers had been assassinated. And that was the stated reason for the cancellation of the trip to Chicago. What you found in Vallee, and the whole Chicago plot, is so many similarities to what eventually happened in Dallas, that it can't be considered coincidental. Vallee, if we compare him to Oswald, is an ex-Marine. He had been posted like Oswald in the far east on a station that was linked to the CIA because there were U-2 surveillance planes on it. It was easy to portray him as disgruntled, anti-Kennedy, a loner, armed. He had another intelligence link that he shared with Oswald in that he trained Cuban exiles for combat, which was a CIA responsibility. And Oswald we know, at least offered to do that. He most likely did train Cuban exiles, but we know he tried to. Oswald, as we know, was moved from New Orleans to Dallas in October to be there just at the right time for the motorcade. And he's placed in a tall building where he gets a job, he's adjacent to the perfect kill zone. Now, if we look at what happened to Vallee, he's moved like a pawn in August from Long Island to Chicago to be in there in time for the motorcade. And where does he get a job? In a tall building adjacent to the motorcade with a perfect view of a kill zone. It would have forced Kennedy's motorcade to do a sharp turn, slow down and be in a point where you could have had perfect triangulation of fire.

There's an awful lot to unpack, but let's start with the supposed plot. The source for this allegation comes from an article by Edwin Black in 1975.

> A few hours after that meeting adjourned, the phone rang in the Chicago office of the Secret Service. Agent Jay Lawrence Stocks was for a few hours the ranking agent, so he took the call. It was the Federal Bureau of Investigation calling from Washington. The FBI man warned Stocks of a serious and dangerous four-man conspiracy to assassinate Kennedy at the Army-Air Force game. The suspects were rightwing para-military fanatics armed with rifles and telescopic sights. The assassination itself would probably be attempted at one of the North-

> west Expressway overpasses. This information came from an informant named 'Lee.'

Where did Black's information come from? Well, he tells us:

> Our main supply of information was one of the Secret Service agents on duty at the time of the conspiracy. In cooperating with us, he broke the "old boy system" of the Secret Service and regulations forbidding press contacts among individual agents. His terms: total anonymity. His motive: a desire to set the record straight. We agreed.

So, there was one major source for Black's story. Here is how he pieced it all together:

> By playing one man's information off against another's, by comparing reactions to accusations, by the use of voice stress analysis and the polygraph (not as foolproof evidence, but merely a good gauge within limitations), by document analysis and other means, we were able to piece together the scenario. A scenario which has not been contradicted or even criticized by either the authorities or the principal players alleged to have taken part. "No comments," memory lapses, yes, But specific denials or contradictions—not a one.
>
> In fact, the more pieces we put together, the more reluctant the Secret Service or FBI people were. If that was any barometer of the reliability of our sources, then the scenario we recounted is accurate.
>
> And so, without using the word proof, we repeat: there are strong indications there were four men in Chicago to assassinate John F. Kennedy, November 2, 1963, twenty days before Dallas.

Of course, Black cannot use the word "proof." The only source for the allegations was former Secret Service agent Abraham Bolden. We know this from Bolden's interview with the HSCA:

> Bolden related to the interviewers that he was the informant who supplied the information for Edwin Black's article in the Chicago Independent Nov., 1975.

To verify his information, Edwin Black had Bolden take a lie detector test:

> And in our man's case, the lie detector didn't come close to the deceit range, but did fall just short of the total truthfulness range …

The HSCA could find no corroborating evidence for Bolden's allegations. For instance, they interviewed former Secret Service agent Gary McLeod:

> He remembers reading the Edwin Black story in the Chicago Independent, several years ago, and couldn't imagine where he got the information pertaining to the four subjects suspected of being involved in a threat against the President and of Jack Stocks' surveillance. Agent McLeod stated that he felt sure that if this incident had occurred, he as part of the Chicago Field Office would have been aware or informed of what had taken place.

The HSCA conclusion:

> The committee was unable to document the existence of the alleged assassination team. Specifically, no agent who had been assigned to Chicago confirmed any aspect of Bolden's version. One agent did state there had been a threat in Chicago during that period, but he was unable to recall details. Bolden did not link Vallee to the supposed four-man assassination team, although he claimed to remember Vallee's name in connection with a 1963 Chicago case. He did not recognize Vallee's photograph when shown it by the committee.

Abraham Bolden's story about the Chicago plot has changed over the years:

1967 Mark Lane Press Conference

Mark Lane held a press conference in December 1967 along with Richard Burnes from Jim Garrison's office. They had spent several hours with Bolden, and he told them that he was given the names of the people involved in the Chicago plot. At least one of the men was followed through the streets of Chicago. Lane told the press that "The identities of those who planned the assassination (in Chicago) of President Kennedy are known to the United States Secret Service. One of these men has been sought by District Attorney Jim Garrison for some time."

1968 Interview by Bud Fensterwald

Bolden said that the Special Agent in Charge of the Chicago office, Maurice Martineau, received a personal phone call from James Rowley, head of the Secret Service. He supposedly told Agent Martineau that the Secret Service "had word of an assassination plot" which was supposed to take place during JFK's visit to Chicago. The agents were told to keep it all hush-hush and were shown pictures of the four men who were allegedly in the plot. The agents investigated and found that the four men were staying with a landlady.

1975 Article by Edwin Black

A phone call came in from the FBI in Washington which was taken by agent Jay Stocks. He was warned about a "serious and dangerous four-man conspiracy to assassinate Kennedy at the Army-Air Force game." The assassination would take place at an expressway overpass. A telex then came in from Rowley about the plot. A tip came in from a landlady who said four men were renting rooms and she had seen four rifles with telescopic scopes. She told the police that "perhaps there was some threat there." Two of the men were followed and then brought in for questioning.

1978 Interview by the HSCA

Bolden claimed a telex came in from the FBI, and then a phone call came in from the FBI. Bolden was not sure if the call was from the local office or Washington. Two of the four suspects were put under surveillance and were apprehended and brought into the Chicago office. Bolden saw one of the men and he picked out the picture of ex-mobster Jim Braden as being similar. He did not recognize a picture of Vallee.

2008 Bolden Book, *The Echo from Dealey Plaza*

This time the phone call came in for Martineau from the Chicago office of the FBI who had information about JFK's upcoming trip:

"A woman who owned a rooming house on the city's North Side had gone into one of the rooms to do some housekeeping and had discovered two rifles equipped with telescopic sights. She had rented the room to two men she believed to be Hispanic, and had also seen two white men going in and out of the room. Knowing that the president was due to visit Chicago, she grew concerned and called the authorities."

Notice that there is no threat to JFK. Bolden writes "Martineau professed to believe that this was not yet a Secret Service matter, in that there had been no direct threat to the President in connection with the rifles."

Now, of course, memories fade over time. But what makes this even more suspicious is that when Bolden talked to Lane in 1967 and Fensterwald in 1968, he tied the Chicago plot to the Garrison investigation. Here is an excerpt from his interview with Bud Fensterwald:

'All S.S. agents in Chicago (including Bolden) were shown four photos of the men allegedly involved in the plot. (of the four, Bolden remembers two names: Bradley and Gonzalez).

(He recalls "Bradley" by some prior association; he believes his first name was Edward or Edgar but he is far from sure as to first name at all. He remembers "Gonzalez" by the fact that agent Robert J. Motto asked him how to spell Gonzalez")

In December 1967, Jim Garrison indicted Edgar Eugene Bradley for conspiring to kill JFK, a charge that had absolutely no foundation. Garrison also believed that Manuel Garcia Gonzalez was one of the gunmen on the grassy knoll.

Here is what really happened in Chicago.

In late October 1963, a landlady found a collage of newspaper clippings about Kennedy and local politicians on the wall of Vallee's room. She called the Chicago police, who then called the Secret Service. They noticed threatening comments on the wall. They discovered that he had several weapons and had asked for the day off when Kennedy was visiting on November 2, 1963. They had Vallee watched and arrested him when he made an illegal left turn. They then found an M1 rifle, a handgun, and three thousand rounds of ammunition in the trunk of his car. Vallee was released from custody on November 2, 1963.

JFK: Destiny Betrayed also includes some buff factoids. Vallee was indeed stationed at Camp Otsu in Japan, but it was not a U-2 base when he was there. Not that that matters at all. The allegation that Vallee "trained Cuban exiles for combat" comes directly from Vallee himself. Here is an excerpt from Black's article:

> He also gave specifics about this CIA assignment to train exiles to assassinate Castro.

But Black never mentions any specifics, except for this:

> Vallee was recruited about the same time to train members of a fiercely anti-Castro guerilla group. Objective: the assassination of Fidel Castro. Training locale: in and around Levittown, Long Island.

Levittown, Long Island? I have seen no documents to confirm this. But we do know that Vallee suffered from mental problems. Does he seem like a likely candidate to be hired by the CIA to train Cuban exiles?

Here is a document that goes over Vallee's mental health issues:

FD-302 (Rev. 1-25-60) **FEDERAL BUREAU OF INVESTIGATION** CD 117

Date December 4, 1963

1

A review of the records on file at Military Personnel Records Center, St. Louis, for THOMAS AUTHER VALLEE, Serial Number 111 44 55, indicated he enlisted in the United States Marine Corps on August 12, 1949, and entered on active duty the same date at Greenbay, Wisconsin. He was honorably discharged on November 28, 1952, as a Corporal at Campe Lejeune, North Carolina, by reason of expiration of enlistment.

He re-enlisted in the United States Marine Corps Reserve, same serial number, on February 9, 1955, and entered on active duty on November 28, 1955, at Chicago, Illinois. He was honorably discharged on September 14, 1956, as a Corporal at Great Lakes, Illinois, by reason of physical disability without severance pay.

Records contain letter dated August 31, 1956, Subject: Discharge by Reason of Physical Disability, and stated that on August 24, 1956, the Secretary of the Navy approved the proceedings and recommended findings of the Physical Evaluation Board in the case of the subject - named Marine, and directed he be discharged from service by reason of physical disability with disability shown as "Schizophrenic reaction, paranoid type, #3003, moderate, chronic (manifested by preoccupations with homosexuality and femineity and an overcompensatory magalomanic euphoric attitude)".

His record contained a Naval Speed Letter, dated August 6, 1956, to the Chief, Bureau of Medicine and Surgery, Department of the Navy, Washington, D.C., which requested a bed be designated in a Veterans Administration Hospital in the case of Caucasian male THOMAS ARTHUR VALLEE, Corporal, United States Marine Corps, Serial Number 111 44 55, diagnosis Schizophrenic reaction, paranoid type, #3003, moderate, chronic (manifested by preoccupations with homosexuality and femineity and an overcompensatory magalomanic euphoric attitude), home address - Chicago, Illinois, man's choice is Hines Memorial Veterans Administration Hospital, Hines, Illinois, man appeared before Physical Evaluation Board third August, 1956, latter patient class 1-A, length of future hospitalization is indefinite, there is no previous request for a Veterans Administration bed pending.

Records contained letter dated December 23, 1955, requesting correction be made to show VALLEE's middle name as AUTHER, instead of ARTHUR, evidenced by birth certificate. Record contained letter

- 4 -

On 12/4/63 at St. Louis, Missouri File # SL 105-3665

by IC LEONARD LEWIS/mwf Date dictated 12/4/63

This document contains neither recommendations nor conclusions of the FBI. It is the property of the FBI and is loaned to your agency; it and its contents are not to be distributed outside your agency.

2
SL 105-3665
LL/mwf

dated June 12, 1951, changing date of birth from November 15, 1931, to November 15, 1933, as evidenced by birth certificate.

Marine Corps medical records on file, Military Personnel Records Center, St. Louis, for VALLEE contained a letter dated February 23, 1956, Subject: Psychiatric evaluation of VALLEE, THOMAS ARTHUR, Corporal, 111 44 55, United States Marine Corps, report of and reflected the following:

"1. VALLEE was referred to the Neuropsychiatric Department of the post dispensary for psychiatric evaluation because of extremely abnormal nervousness and periods of excitement in which he cannot talk to anyone. He is also said to be very hyper-active and does not get along well in the barracks..."

"4. VALLEE has had two episodes of passible concussion, once when a mortar shell exploded near him in Korea and a second time in an auto accident which required hospitalization for two months. His father died as the result of the automobile accident..."

"7. VALLEE was referred for psychological testing. The conclusion reached following the testing period is as follows:

"'He is functioning well within the average range of intellectual evaluation. VALLEE shows indications of paranoid-thinking. We see then, a rather weak male person (i.e. a weak ego structure) who experiences difficulty in his interpersonal relationships with males, but compensating by building up a somewhat pseudo-concept of his own virility. There are in addition indications from psychological tests of some type of organic difficulty'....."

Record reflected that on June 19, 1956, the patient appeared before clinical board which concurred with the findings and diagnosis of "Schizophrenic reaction, paranoid type, #3003, moderate, chronic (manifested by preoccupations with homosexuality and femineity and an overcompensatory magalomanic euphoric attitude)". This clinical board also reflected that on May 21, 1953, "the patient was discharged against medical advice at the request of himself and his family, and into their custody", with a diagnosis

SL 105-3665
LL/mwf

"Schizophrenic reaction, acute undifferentiated, manifested by confused thinking, turmoil of emotion, homicidal threats, poor judgment, flattened effect, and schizoid thinking", and "chronic brain syndrome associated with brain trauma, mild, manifested by minimal impairment of mental function, very mild aphasia."

Record reflected disability claim filed with the Veterans Administration Regional Office, under Claim number 17460-615, 20[illegible] West Taylor Storee, Chicago, Illinois, with alleged disease or injury shown as "N.P. condition, head wounds".

Relatives shown as MARY CATHERINE VALLEE, sister, 6030 Sheriden Road, Chic[illegible] Illinois. Parents shown as THOMAS ARCHABALD and MARY C[illegible]RINE VALLEE (deceased). VALLEE's address at time of discharge from the United States Marine Corps was that shown for sister. Prior address shown as 3711 North Pine Grove Street, Chicago, Cook County, Illinois, 1955.

Photograph available upon request.

Educ[illegible]ion two years college. Date of birth November 1[illegible], 1933, Chicago, Illinois.

Vallee was discharged before Castro came to power, so if he trained exiles, it would have been after his stint in the Marines. But would the CIA hire him given his psychiatric record or after his arrest in Chicago in November 1963?

In any event, there is no evidence that Vallee had any links to any supposed conspiracy against JFK. It's not even clear how much of a threat Vallee actually presented. Here is his Secret Service Protective Research file:

1/U

INDIVIDUALS LISTED BY PROTECTIVE RESEARCH

Name of individual: VALLEE, THOMAS ARTHUR

Reason for PRS interest: 10-30-63 subj was reported by confidential source to have made critical remarks re JFK adm. Subj alleges to be member of JBS and previously hospitalized in VA hosp as schizo. NOt considered dangerous. Owns rifle and member of gun club. Interviewed'63 and '66. In '68 interview, spoke irrationally.

Degree of threat: 1 2 (by computer 3 info)

Organizations to which individual belongs:
John Birch Society

Nationalistic group: none

Date called to Secret Service attention: 10-30-63

Refered by other agency? NO YES

Action taken:
According to print out: SA interviewed him 10-30-63. No mention of danger. Does show that he was arrested 11/2/63 for traffic and CCW. Apparently from reports, Vallee was not dangerous. In 11/26/68 interview, SA did not considered him to be of further protective interest. No interest in protectees was shown. QI's '63 to '68/ Attempt to locate him in re to Brezhnev's visit proved negative.

Last location: Houston '71

Field office: Houston

Last UPD: 3/5/76

Bolden only started talking about a plot in 1967 despite the claims of James DiEugenio:

> But in Washington, in May of 1964, he tried to contact the Warren Commission. He wanted to tell them about the Chicago plot and the lax standards of the Secret Service White House detail, which he had seen up close.

Bolden did want to testify but not about the supposed Chicago plot:

Warren Panel Willing to Hear Accused Guard

Charged Secret Service Lax in Guarding Kennedy

Abraham Bolden, who has accused the Secret Service of "laxity" in guarding President Kennedy, is welcome to tell the Warren Commission what he knows, a commission member said Friday.

Chicago Daily News, *May 22, 1964*

The article notes that "Bolden said he was being 'framed' by the government because they knew he intended to tell of drinking and partying among agents assigned to the presidential detail." I can't find any reference in articles from 1964 about a supposed Chicago plot. The Warren Commission asked the FBI to interview Abraham Bolden. However, his lawyer decided that it was not in his best interest to be interviewed.

So, where did this all come from? Perhaps from some rumors right after the assassination:

UNITED STATES DEPARTMENT OF JUSTICE
FEDERAL BUREAU OF INVESTIGATION

Copy to:

Report of:	SA DENNIS W. SHANAHAN	Office:	Chicago
Date:	2/5/64		
Field Office File #:	62-6115	Bureau File #:	62-109060
Title:	LEE HARVEY OSWALD		
Character:	INTERNAL SECURITY - RUSSIA		

Synopsis: LARRY FANNING, Executive Editor "Chicago Daily News", advises there is no truth to story that four men were arrested in Chicago on 11/2/63 carrying concealed weapons, one of which men was reported to be OSWALD. On 1/14/64, THOMAS VALLE appeared before Branch 46, Municipal Court, Chicago, Illinois, on charge of "Unlawful Use of Weapon". Subject found guilty on above charge and in addition was imposed a $5.00 suspended fine on a traffic violation. 1/28/64 set as date of sentencing for subject who was released on $100.00 bond.

- P -

DETAILS: AT CHICAGO, ILLINOIS

LARRY FANNING, Executive Editor "Chicago Daily News", had previously advised that on November 2, 1963, four men were reportedly arrested in Chicago, Illinois, and charged with carrying a concealed weapon. One of these individuals, according to FANNING's source, was believed to be the subject OSWALD.

SAC MARLIN W. JOHNSON has periodically maintained contact with Mr. FANNING in an effort to determine FANNING's source for this story. On January 22, 1964, Mr. FANNING advised SAC JOHNSON that he had looked into the matter thoroughly and there was absolutely no truth whatsoever in the story. He stated he could not tell Mr. JOHNSON exactly how the story originated.

This page reads:

Larry Fanning, Executive Editor, "Chicago Daily News", had previously advised that on November 2, 1963, four men were reportedly arrested in Chicago, Illinois, and charged with carrying a concealed

> weapon. One of these individuals, according to Fanning's source, was believed to be the subject Oswald.
>
> SAC Marlin W. Johnson has periodically maintained contact with Mr. Fanning in an effort to determine Fanning's sources for this story. On January 21, 1964, Mr. Fanning advised SAC Johnson that he had looked into the matter thoroughly and there was absolutely no truth whatsoever in the story. He stated he could not tell Mr. Johnson exactly how the story originated.

Fanning might have gotten it from his assistant city editor, William Mooney:

> NEWMAN said he never knew JACK RUBY and has never interviewed him. He advised he learned from LARRY FAINING, editor, "Chicago Daily News", that WILLIAM MOONEY, Assistant City Editor of that newspaper, mentioned that four men were arrested in Chicago, Illinois, on November 2, 1963, for carrying a concealed weapon and he (MOONEY) believed one was named OSWALD. NEWMAN knew nothing further concerning this matter.

Was this the genesis of the story about the Chicago plot? I also find it interesting that the story of Thomas Vallee and the four-man assassination team both feature landladies who either call the police or the Secret Service. Might Bolden have been conflating the Vallee story with the rumor above?

There is no evidence to support the allegations of a plot in Chicago in November of 1963. There might well have been one, but *JFK: Destiny Betrayed* just repeats stories that have been told before, and no evidence has materialized to support the claims.

CHAPTER 40
WAS LEE HARVEY OSWALD PLACED IN DALLAS?

(EPISODE 4, 24:22)

JFK: Destiny Betrayed alleges that Lee Harvey Oswald was "moved" to Dallas and then "placed" in the Texas School Book Depository.

Here is an excerpt from a transcript:

> **Paul Bleau**: Oswald, as we know, was moved from New Orleans to Dallas in October to be there, just at the right time, for the motorcade. And he's placed in a tall building where he gets a job. He's adjacent to the perfect kill zone.

James DiEugenio's book of the annotated film transcript, *JFK Revisited,* does not give a citation for this allegation.

Oswald is supposedly void of agency; someone moved him and placed him. But who did this? And how do we know? *JFK: Destiny Betrayed* makes it seem like this is common knowledge.

While a JFK trip to Texas was first broached within the White House in June 1963, it was only announced in the *Dallas Morning News* on September 26, 1963:

DALLAS INCLUDED

Kennedy to Visit Texas Nov. 21-22

By ROBERT E. BASKIN
News Staff Writer

JACKSON HOLE, Wyo.—White House sources told The Dallas News exclusively Wednesday night that President Kennedy will visit Texas Nov. 21 and 22.

Texas Democratic leaders have urged Kennedy to come to the state to repair what they regard as a deteriorating party situation.

The presidential decision may have been prompted by what he has seen on his current tour: a

But Ruth Paine drove Marina Oswald and her daughter to Irving, Texas, on September 23. So, the decision to move the family to Texas was made before the White House had announced JFK's trip. Oswald probably left New Orleans for Mexico City on September 25.

Oswald started work at the Texas School Book Depository on October 16, which was well before plans were announced for the motorcade. When Oswald showed up for work, Roy Truly could have easily sent him to work at the other warehouse at 1917 Houston Street.

Here is an excerpt from Roy Truly's testimony before the Warren Commission:

> **Mr. Dulles**: Do you recall, Mr. Truly, whether you hired any personnel for work in this particular building, in the School Depository, after the 15th of October and before the 22nd of November?
>
> **Mr. Truly**: No, sir; I don't recall hiring anyone else other than Oswald for that building the same day I hired Oswald. I believe, if I am not mistaken, I hired another boy for a temporary job, and put him in the other warehouse at 1917 North Houston.

Secret Service agents Forrest Sorrels and Winton Lawson, who were in charge of advance preparations for Kennedy's trip to Dallas, were only informed of the trip on November 4. Lawson received a tentative schedule from Roy Kellerman on November 8, 1963.

The HSCA added this:

* An interesting subsidiary issue regarding itinerary planning and motorcade route selection is whether Oswald, when he took the job at the Depository on Oct. 15, 1963, knew President Kennedy planned to visit Dallas and that his motorcade would pass through Dealey Plaza. (*99*) It is, of course, possible that Oswald could have anticipated well before Oct. 16 that Dallas would be included in the Texas itinerary. The Sept. 26 issue of the Dallas Morning News printed an article stating that the President would visit major cities of the state on Nov. 21 and 22. (*100*) And it could be inferred that the Presidential motorcade would pass through Dealey Plaza. This is because Dealey Plaza was part of the traditional parade route through Dallas. (*101*) However, knowledge of an eastward versus westward direction would not have been possible before Oct. 16, since the route was not finalized until Nov. 15. (*102*)

Mr. Bleau makes an extraordinary statement without providing extraordinary evidence. *JFK: Destiny Betrayed* likes the former but is not so much interested in the latter.

CHAPTER 41

WAS THERE A PLOT TO ASSASSINATE JFK IN TAMPA?

Gilberto Policarpo Lopez

(EPISODE 4, 25:06)

JFK: Destiny Betrayed alleges that there was also a plot in Tampa in November of 1963 and that another patsy was ready to be arrested. Once again, there is no evidence to back up the allegation.

Here is an excerpt from a transcript:

Oliver Stone: And what about the trip to Florida?

Paul Bleau: On November 18th, Kennedy was scheduled to do a 27-mile-long motorcade in Tampa. The Secret Service was very nervous about the Floridian Hotel [sic, should be the Floridan Hotel] where the motorcade would have gone by. It would have forced a sharp turn.

Nobody fired away at him. But in this case, the alternate patsy would have been a Gilbert Policarpo Lopez. He was a Cuban exile. He attended Fair Play for Cuba Committee meetings. One day after the assassination, on November 23rd, he makes his way to Mexico City. The Fair Play for Cuba Committee loaned him money for his travel, and he ends up being the lone passenger on an airplane to Cuba. The CIA, they found out about the Fair Play for Cuba Committee, the weird trip to Mexico City, the fact that he was a lone passenger on a plane to Cuba. And they didn't pass on the information to the Warren Commission. So, when the HSCA found out about this lead that wasn't pursued, even they called it egregious.

Oliver Stone: And what do you think was the relevance of it?

Paul Bleau: Well, if he had been assassinated in Tampa, Lopez, he would have been the potential patsy. If they had to admit to a front shot, because Oswald was behind, there were rumors that he had assisted Oswald in the assassination in Dallas.

Bleau's source for the supposed plot in Tampa and Gilberto Lopez is Lamar Waldron's 2005 book, *Ultimate Sacrifice: John and Robert Kennedy, the Plan for a Coup in Cuba, and the Murder of JFK*. The only difference is that Waldron believes the Mafia was behind the JFK assassination conspiracy, while the producers of *JFK: Destiny Betrayed* believe it was the CIA and the military-industrial complex. There is no evidence to support either theory.

Let's start with the supposed threat against JFK in Tampa. Waldron referenced two articles that appeared in local newspapers:

Threats On Kennedy Made Here

Tampa police and Secret Service agents scanned crowds for a man who had vowed to assassinate the President here last Monday, Chief of Police J. P. Mullins said yesterday.

Tampa Tribune, *November 23, 1963*

Man Held In Threats To JFK

TAMPA — (UPI) — The Secret Service Saturday confirmed that a 53-year-old Washington man arrested here Oct. 19 for attempted extortion of a Tampa banker also was being held for sending threatening letters to the late President Kennedy.

Miami Herald, *November 24, 1963*

There is additional information about these threats in Gerald Blaine's 2011 book, *The Kennedy Detail: JFK's Secret Service Agents Break Their Silence*. Blaine was a special agent of the Secret Service on the White House detail who worked security in Tampa. He had called the Protective

Research Section (PRS) in New York and asked for a list of potential threats. One file that came back was for a Mr. Wayne Gainey, and here is the "flash card" provided to Blaine:

Threat suspect Wayne Gainey, as posted on the front of the agents "flash cards" provided by PRS. (OFFICIAL SECRET SERVICE PHOTO)

Blaine flipped over the card to read the profile:

> Subject made a statement of a plan to assassinate the President in October 1963.
>
> Subject stated he will use a gun, and if he can't get close he will find another way.
>
> White Male—Age 20—5'9"—155 Lbs.—Hazel Eyes—Brown Hair
>
> Light complexion—slender build

GAINEY, WAYNE L. CO-2-33,815
Route 2, Box 101 Nov. 8, 1963
Westville, Fla.

Subject made a statement of a plan to assassinate the President in October,1963; subject stated he will use a gun, and if he couldn't get closer, he would find another way. Subject is described as: white, male, 20, 155, 5'9", hazel eyes, brown hair, light complexion, slender build.

Description of threat suspect Wayne Gainey on the back of the flash card. (OFFICIAL SECRET SERVICE PHOTO)

A local agent, Arnie Peppers, visited Gainey's parents and his psychiatrist. His parents were cooperative, and they made sure that Gainey was with them during JFK's visit to Tampa. An agent was also sent out to keep surveillance on their home.

The other threat was from John William Warrington. He was fifty-three years old and had written a series of threatening letters to Kennedy in October 1963. He was arrested in Tampa on October 18, 1963, for sending an extortion letter to a bank president. Warrington had been in and out of mental hospitals for years and had been diagnosed as schizophrenic. He was still in jail when Kennedy visited Tampa.

Those were the main threats on Kennedy's life.

Kennedy visited Tampa on November 18, 1963. Here is a picture from his arrival at the airport:

Courtesy of Tony Zappone

Here is a picture from his almost thirty-mile-long motorcade:

Courtesy of Tony Zappone

It doesn't appear that the Secret Service was all that concerned, and JFK was standing during a large part of the motorcade.

Paul Bleau mentioned some concern about the Floridan Hotel. Lamar Waldron interviewed Tampa Police Chief Mullins in 1996, who said it "was a special problem" because it was the tallest building at the time.

However, one of his comments is revealing. Waldron says Mullins "said he depended on hotel staff to keep him abreast of any suspicious or strange people." Really? You're worried about the hotel, but you rely on hotel staff?

There is no mention of Mullins's concern about the Floridan Hotel in Blaine's book.

There was no assassination attempt in Tampa despite Waldron's claim that the Floridan Hotel was a better vantage point than the Texas School Book Depository:

> Ninety-nine windows of the hotel had an unobstructed view overlooking the intersection where JFK's limo would have to slow to a crawl to make a hard left turn. The angle to JFK's limo was even better than that of the Texas School Book Depository, meaning a shooter would not have to extend their rifle out of the window to get a good shot.

Perhaps there was no attempt on JFK's life because there was no assassination plot.

But what does any of this have to do with Gilberto Policarpo Lopez?

Absolutely nothing.

The CIA compiled a biographical sketch of Lopez. Here is a summary:

> **January 26, 1940**: Born in Havana, Cuba. His mother Esperanza Rodriguez y Castellamos was born in Key West, Florida and was an American citizen.
>
> **June 2, 1960**: Received an American passport in Havana which was valid until January 25, 1963. Lopez told them he planned to move to the United States.
>
> **February 23, 1962**: Lopez was classified as 4-F by the Draft Board because of "a language barrier." The Board also received a letter from Dr. James Malgrat noting that Lopez had been treated for Grand Mal Epilepsy for the last six months. He took daily medication for convulsions.
>
> **August 11, 1962**: Lopez married Blanche Andrea Leon in Key West, Florida. In June 1963, they moved to Tampa. He had had recurrent

attacks of epilepsy and in early 1963 was hospitalized at Jackson Memorial Hospital in Miami.

August 1963: Lopez's wife returned to Key West because of marital difficulties.

November 17, 1963: Lopez attended a meeting of the Fair Play for Cuba Committee in Tampa at the home of Mary Quist. Someone was showing color slides taken in Cuba. While at the Quist home, Lopez awaited a telephone call from Cuba on whether he could visit.

November 20, 1963: Lopez obtained a Mexican tourist card in Tampa, and on November 23rd, he arrived in Mexico on his way to Havana. Lopez entered Mexico at Nuevo Laredo. He registered at the Roosevelt Hotel and on November 27th boarded a Cubana flight to Havana. He was the only passenger. The photograph of Lopez at the beginning of this chapter was taken at the International Airport in Mexico City on November 27th. To get to Cuba, Lopez borrowed $150 from people in the Fair Play for Cuba Committee of which he only paid back $25.

July 14, 1964: Lopez's wife received a letter from her husband and was surprised he was in Cuba although he had told her he wanted to return before their marriage broke up. She believed that he returned to Cuba "because of his close relationship with his parents."

CIA interest in Gilberto Policarpo Lopez started in December 1963 when Mexican security asked the Mexico City CIA station for information:

178. Gilberto POLICARPO-Lopez.
First came to attention of Mexico City Station, 93 December 1963 when Mexican security asked Station for information on POLICARPO, reportedly arrived in Mexico on 23 November 1963 enroute to Havanna.

In March 1964, a source told the CIA that Lopes [sic] was involved in the Kennedy assassination.

On March 19, 1964, the Monterrey Station sent a classified message to headquarters that Enrique Ruiz Montalvo, an agent of the Mexican Federal Judicial Police, had informed the CIA that one of Ruiz's contacts reported in late February 1964, that an American citizen named Gilberto Lopes was involved in the Kennedy assassination. The message said Ruiz's contact reported that Lopes had entered Mexico on foot from Laredo, Texas about 1200 hours on November 13 carrying U.S. passport #319962, which was issued July 13, 1960. According to the dispatch, the contact related also that Lopes proceeded by bus to Mexico City "where he entered the Cuban embassy"; it said that he left the Cuban Embassy on November 27 and was the only passenger for Cuba on flight #465. It said the contact reported that Lopes was issued Mexican travel form B, #24553, at Nuevo Laredo. According to the dispatch, Ruiz reported that he could not verify the contact's information, but thought it might be of interest to the United States government.

Here is that message:

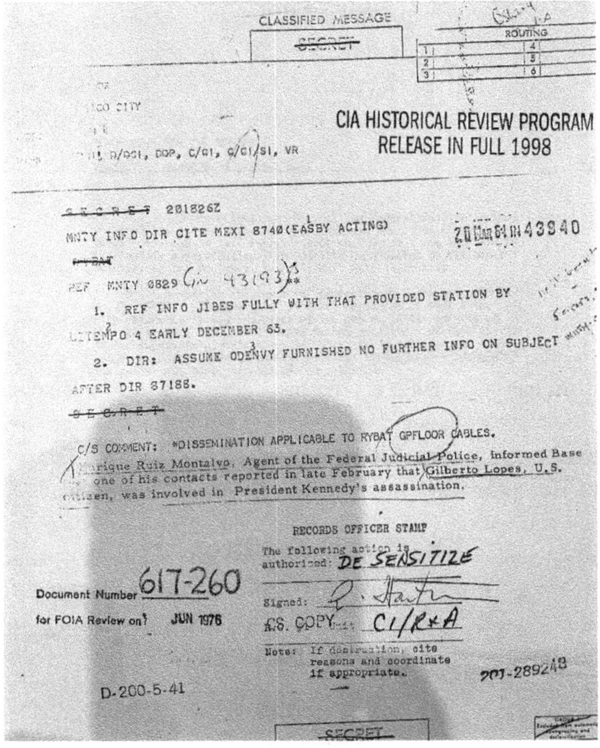

CLASSIFIED MESSAGE

~~SECRET~~

ROUTING

CIA HISTORICAL REVIEW PROGRAM
RELEASE IN FULL 1998

D/DCI, DDP, C/CI, C/CI/SI, VR

~~SECRET~~ 201826Z

MNTY INFO DIR CITE MEXI 8740(EASBY ACTING) 20 MAR 64 IN 43940

~~RYBAT~~

REF MNTY 0829 (IN 43193)**

1. REF INFO JIBES FULLY WITH THAT PROVIDED STATION BY LITEMPO 4 EARLY DECEMBER 63.

2. DIR: ASSUME ODENVY FURNISHED NO FURTHER INFO ON SUBJECT AFTER DIR 87188.

~~SECRET~~

C/S COMMENT: *DISSEMINATION APPLICABLE TO RYBAT GPFLOOR CABLES.

Enrique Ruiz Montalvo, Agent of the Federal Judicial Police, informed Base one of his contacts reported in late February that Gilberto Lopes, U.S. citizen, was involved in President Kennedy's assassination.

RECORDS OFFICER STAMP

The following action is authorized: DE SENSITIZE

Signed:

R.S. COPY: CI/R&A

Note: If destruction, cite reasons and coordinate if appropriate.

Document Number 617-260

for FOIA Review on JUN 1976

201-289248

D-200-5-41

~~SECRET~~

The Church Committee discussed this lead and criticized the FBI and the CIA for not giving enough information to the Warren Commission to evaluate the lead for themselves. The FBI had not told the Warren Commission about Lopez's attendance at a Fair Play for Cuba Committee (FPCC) meeting and that it might have relevance since V. T. Lee, national director of the FPCC, "wrote Oswald on May 29, 1963, suggesting Oswald get in touch with the Tampa chapter, which Lee had personally organized."

But the Church Committee was wrong. Lee had never made that suggestion. Here is what he did tell Oswald:

> We feel that the south-east is a very difficult area to work because of our lack of contacts. Our only southeastern Chapter right now is that in Tampa, Florida which I originally organized before coming up to work in the National Office.

In 1977, the CIA inspector general, in response to the Church Committee report on Lopez's travel, followed up on the lead. HSCA staff noted that the IG found numerous errors in that initial report about Lopez:

> The report stated additionally that the March 19, 1964 cable from the Monterey base which recounted the information on Lopez from the contact of the Mexican police and claimed Lopez was involved in the assassination was incorrect on several pornts: Lopez's name was misspelled "Lopes"; it stated that Lopez entered Mexico on foot when the C.I.A. repeated the F.B.I.'s conclusion that he had traveled by auto; it gave incorrect digits in Lopez's passport number; it stated that the Mexican tourist visa was issued in Nuevo Laredo and not Tampa; and it reported that he stayed at the Cuban Embassy. Based on these inaccuracies, the Inspector General concluded that "the source patently was extensively misinformed." Based on that observation, the Inspector General completely discounted the cable by the Deputy Chief of Station in Mexico City on March 20, 1964 that the Mexican police source information "jibed" with what had earlier been reported by the CIA's sources.

The HSCA felt that the failure of the CIA to tell the Warren Commission about the Gilberto Lopez lead was "egregious."

The CIA disagreed with that conclusion:

> The confusion in this particular case arises out of a report some months after the man's departure from Mexico. It was filled with erroneous detail on facts already reported accurately, and clearly was a report that could not be accorded any validity. The report was not disseminated because of this, although a CIA cable addressed to the reporting source in the field, made the mistaken comment that the information jibed with that already available. Quite frankly, the cable was in error. There was no reason to do anything further. The decision against its dissemination at that time remains valid today.

An HSCA memo also came up with a reason why the lead was withheld from the Warren Commission:

> The Committee has documented instances where the CIA decided to forego passing information to the Warren Commission out of a desire to not lay bare extremely sensitive sources and methods of intelligence. The LIFIRE operation certainly falls within that category and as soon as the CIA began receiving information about Lopez's travel, the cables and messages reflected the desire to not reveal that method. It also seems plausible that the FBI likewise chose not to divulge what it had learned about Lopez because in doing so, it would have had to reveal the sensitive CIA operation which generated the initial information on Lopez's travel to Cuba on November 27.

The LIFIRE operation referred to cooperation between the CIA and Mexican federal officials in a plan to photograph passengers on flights departing for Havana from Mexico City.

In any event, the HSCA concluded:

> From the information gathered by the FBI, there appeared to be plausible reasons for both Lopez' desire to return to Cuba and for his solici-

> tation of financial aid from the Tampa FPCC chapter. Lopez' contacts in Florida appeared to have been innocent and not connected with the assassination, and while there was a suggestion in the Senate committee's report that Lee Harvey Oswald also was in contact with the Tampa FPCC chapter, the committee could find no evidence of it. Nor could the committee find any evidence that Oswald was in contact with Lopez.

By the way, the FBI submitted two reports to the Warren Commission that mentioned Gilberto Lopez. One mentioned his trip to Cuba, and the other was about his passport.

It can't be denied that the HSCA and the Church Committee said the FBI and the CIA were delinquent in their obligation to inform the Warren Commission. But there is no evidence that Gilberto Policarpo Lopez had any connection to the JFK assassination. And as I have shown, there was no plot against JFK in Tampa.

Was there anything suspicious about Lopez?

- **Policarpo was in Texas on November 22nd**. Well, yes, he was on his way to Mexico from Tampa. There is no evidence he was in Dallas, and he most likely went through Houston, which leads directly to Laredo.
- **He went to a Fair Play for Cuba Committee meeting**. Not that surprising. He was anxious to go back to Cuba.
- **The mysterious flight to Havana**. Of course, the fact that Lopez was the only passenger on a Cubana flight to Havana seemed suspicious. However, it turns out that he traveled on a cargo flight.
- **The photograph of Lopez wearing sunglasses**. James Johnston, author of *Murder, Inc.: The CIA under John F. Kennedy*, writes that Lopez was wearing sunglasses "presumably to hinder identification." Perhaps he was wearing sunglasses to help with his epilepsy.
- **Policarpo was pro-Castro**. I am not sure why this makes him suspicious.

I have no reason to doubt that Gilberto Policarpo Lopez was who he appeared to be: a young man who came to the United States, got married, and then had his marriage fall apart. He couldn't speak English and could only get menial jobs. He had significant health problems, and he missed his family in Cuba. He then decided to go back to Cuba, where they could help take care of him.

So why on earth do people believe that Gilberto Lopez was going to be a patsy?

Well, Lamar Waldron notes that there are "eighteen parallels" between Oswald and Lopez that "demonstrate" that they were both "being manipulated by the same people." But consider some of the so-called parallels:

- They each had a job within the vicinity of JFK's motorcade. Not surprising that Lopez might have been near the Tampa motorcade. It was almost thirty miles long.
- Both men were in a Texas city the week of November 22, 1963.
- Neither man was a good driver, and neither owned a car.
- Both were white males and twenty-three years of age during "most" of 1963.
- Both spent part of 1963 "in a southern city that was headquarters for one of the two mob bosses that the HSCA says were most likely behind the JFK assassination."
- Both are "said" to be informants for "some US agency."
- Both were living apart from their wives.

This is the kind of propinquity that perhaps Jim Garrison would appreciate.

How does Waldron tie this all to the Mafia? He quotes a 2003 article from the *Key West Citizen* that notes that Lopez "worked in the construction industry in Tampa—which has had a long-established organized crime connection with Key West—before traveling to Texas at the time of the assassination."

That's a pretty loose connection.

While Paul Bleau dismisses the Mafia theory, he does believe there are "parallels" between not just Oswald and Lopez but several other "alternative patsies." Bleau even put this all into a handy chart.

> Case comparison analysis of the potential patsies and prior plots to assassinate JFK would bring investigators to study common traits, behavior patterns, entity links, chronological sequences in order to develop a profile of the offenders.

This is indeed cutting-edge JFK assassination research, no?

The last part of Bleau's segment on Gilberto Lopez is just plain ridiculous:

> Well, if he [JFK] had been assassinated in Tampa, Lopez, he would have been the potential patsy. If they had to admit to a front shot, because Oswald was behind, there were rumors that he had assisted Oswald in the assassination in Dallas.

Bleau elevates old rumors into spurious allegations. Two patsies in Dallas?

The segments in *JFK: Destiny Betrayed* on the supposed plots against JFK in Chicago and Tampa are outright embarrassing. There is no evidence of any plot in either city, and the notion that there were "patsies-in-waiting" cannot be taken seriously.

NEW ORLEANS

JFK: Destiny Betrayed tries to ignore Jim Garrison but also tries to present as fact some of the fictions he heralded throughout his fraudulent investigation. In addition, facts are mangled and misrepresented to add suspicion to the activities of Lee Harvey Oswald in the summer of 1963.

WHAT EVER HAPPENED TO JIM GARRISON?

Like the child star gone bad in the film *What Ever Happened to Baby Jane?*, Jim Garrison was the reformist district attorney gone kooky, and Oliver Stone is the famous director who went down the rabbit hole. Modern-day Baby Janes, they are irredeemably linked, although it does look like Oliver Stone is trying to break free.

JFK: Destiny Betrayed includes three scenes from the film *JFK.* All of them showcase actor Kevin Costner without telling the audience that he's playing Jim Garrison.

Stone assumes that the audience knows it's fiction or (even worse) doesn't care if they think it is real.

JFK: Destiny Betrayed is the film that dares not speak Garrison's name.

It's all the more remarkable since Oliver Stone's two-hour documentary film is titled *JFK Revisited: Through the Looking Glass*. Revisited, you say?

But how can you revisit *JFK* without even mentioning Jim Garrison?

JFK: Destiny Betrayed only mentions Jim Garrison once, and that is in Episode 4: (12:35)

Narrator (Whoopi Goldberg): One of the places Oswald leafletted in front of was Clay Shaw's International Trade Mart. Shaw, who was arrested by New Orleans D.A. Jim Garrison on charges that he was part of the conspiracy to kill President Kennedy, always denied he was associated with the CIA.

Nowhere in the film does it even say that Clay Shaw was tried and was acquitted of conspiracy. This is an astounding error of omission because Stone makes a big deal out of the fact that Lee Harvey Oswald never had his day in court.

And like thousands of other businessmen, Clay Shaw was just a domestic contact of the CIA who provided information about his overseas trips. See Chapter 46 for more details.

With a substantial part of his savings spent on his defense, Clay Shaw had to come out of retirement and go back to work. He then sued Garrison for $5 million in damages, but he unfortunately died of cancer before the case could be heard. The best years of Clay Shaw's life were stolen—he had retired to write plays and restore properties in the French Quarter of New Orleans—and for what?

In the early part of his investigation, Garrison told journalists Hugh Aynesworth, James Phelan, Jack Anderson, Jerrold Footlick, Merriman Smith, Art Kevin, Lawrence Schiller, and Max Lerner that a homosexual conspiracy killed JFK. Ultimately, JFK conspiracy theorists got him to move away from that theory and view the CIA as the culprit.

Even so, Clay Shaw's name was raked through the mud. Here is a short excerpt from the infamous Sciambra memorandum, written right after Andrew Sciambra first interviewed Perry Russo:

He remembers seeing him [Clay Shaw] again at the Nashville Street Wharf when he went to see J.F.K. speak. He said he particularly remembers this guy because he was apparently a queer. It seems that instead of looking at J.F.K. speak, SHAW kept turning around and looking at all the young boys in the crowd. He said that SHAW eventually struck up a conversation with a young kid not too far from him. It was perfectly obvious to him that SHAW stared at his penis several times. He said that SHAW eventually left with a friend. He said that SHAW had on dark pants which fit very tightly and was the kind of pants that a lot of queers in the French Quarter wear.

That memo was read out loud in court during the Shaw trial. What a homophobic slur!

Stone believed that Jim Garrison was a crusading prosecutor who was trying to take on the CIA, the military-industrial complex, and the national security infrastructure. He claimed it was "worth the sacrifice of one man," and so Stone kept Clay Shaw as the evil mastermind along with his band of conspiring homosexuals.

So, for Oliver Stone to use a homophobic prosecution as the basis for *JFK* was not just vicious; it victimized Clay Shaw a second time, and this time in front of a worldwide audience.

Nor does *JFK: Destiny Betrayed* mention what Judge Herbert Christenberry said in 1971 after three days of hearings regarding Garrison's perjury charges against Shaw. He found that Garrison "undertook his baseless investigation with the specific intent to deprive Shaw of his rights under the First, Fifth, and Fourteenth amendments ... The only conclusion that can be drawn from Garrison's actions is that he intentionally used the arrest for his own purposes, with complete disregard for the rights of Clay Shaw."

Perhaps the firestorm over *JFK* tempered Stone's enthusiasm for Garrison. Back in late 1991, gay rights groups were horrified at reports of what was in the script.

LOS ANGELES TIMES

Gay Rights Activists Protest 'JFK'

■ **Movies:** One organizaton dubbed the Oliver Stone film 'as homophobic as films get.'

By ANDY MARX
SPECIAL TO THE TIMES

Los Angeles Times, *December 6, 1991*

Stone told them to watch the film and then decide. They did, and they weren't impressed.

SATURDAY LETTERS

Gay and Lesbian Alliance Looks at 'JFK'

The Dec. 6 Calendar article on the Gay and Lesbian Alliance Against Defamation's concerns regarding the script of Oliver Stone's "JFK" bore the inaccurate headline, "Gay Rights Activists Protest 'JFK.'" Contrary to that headline, GLAAD told the story's writer that we would not reach a decision on whether to protest the film until GLAAD representatives had actually screened it.

GLAAD representatives have since met with Stone and attended an advance screening.

In our view, the film's negative portrayal of three gay characters and disproportionate focus on the sexual aspects of their lives can only reinforce inaccurate impressions held by moviegoers who derive their primary information about gays and lesbians from consistently negative screen portrayals.

We are particularly concerned about an unlikely and gratuitous scene depicting gay characters dressed in elaborate costumes and involved in some kind of sadomasochistic activity. We also question the inherent imbalance in the portrayal of the gay characters as kinky, bizarre and pathetic, while Jim Garrison, played by Kevin Costner, is a classic Hollywood hero—whitewashed, according to most critics, of real historical blemishes.

One of Stone's next projects is "The Mayor of Castro Street," based on Randy Shilts' biography of slain San Francisco Supervisor Harvey Milk. Having met with Stone and others involved in this next project, we are hopeful that he has been sufficiently sensitized to gay and lesbian concerns to produce in this film, about a real-life gay hero, the kind of powerful and enlightening screen images needed to counteract overused Hollywood stereotypes.

RICHARD JENNINGS
Executive Director
GLAAD/LA

Bellamy at Equity's Helm

In your obituary of Ralph Bellamy ("Ralph Bellamy Dies; Veteran Actor Won Fame for F.D.R. Role," Metro, Nov. 30), there was no mention of a very important part of Bellamy's life. He served as president of Actors' Equity Assn. from 1952 until 1964. In those 12 years his accomplishments were many. Bellamy did not consider his position as president to be that of a figurehead but rather made his position one of great leadership through very difficult years for theater actors.

Bellamy brought Equity through the McCarthy era of political

Please see LETTERS, F9

The Advocate, one of the major gay magazines, ran a huge feature on the film and Jim Garrison.

From the front cover of The Advocate. *One small quibble: they weren't 'pinkos.'*

A few months later, Oliver Stone sat down for an interview with *The Advocate* and said this:

Q: In pushing your point that all of these guys knew each other, aren't you verging on a stereotypical assumption—and a homophobic one—that all gay people know each other?

> **Stone**: It's not about their being gay, it's about the connections that being gay makes. Jack Ruby may have been gay. I didn't get into that in the film, but several people in Texas told me he was. He lived with a roommate for several years, George Senator, whom I met. Senator says he himself is straight but still leads "a bachelor existence." I believe Garrison. I believe all these guys were peripherally involved. Ferrie had something to do with this thing. He knew Oswald, Shaw, and Guy Banister—who was running Oswald. I have second and third sources on all of this.

Back in 1991, it was primarily gays who objected to *JFK*'s homophobic content. Times have changed, and referring to Clay Shaw's homosexuality today would upset most decent people.

But the biggest fuss about *JFK* came not from the gay community but from people who knew what the Garrison investigation was really like. Rosemary Jones was a reporter in New Orleans who wrote a book about the case:

> Stone, in fact, exemplifies the entire coterie of self-aggrandizing acolytes who have hung onto the former district attorney's coattails since Garrison announced he had 'solved' all the mysteries surrounding the presidential assassination.
>
> That was back in 1967 and 1968 when Garrison was fabricating a new phony 'conspiracy' to kill the president, almost daily, including the one that ruined an innocent man's life. I know for a fact that Garrison deliberately proceeded with a fraudulent case against Clay Shaw.
>
> He knew he had nothing, his key assistants—Jim Alcock, Al Oser and John Volz—knew he had nothing and yet proceeded in the most Machiavellian fashion to abuse the power entrusted to them.
>
> In the style of the Dreyfuss case of the last century, they deliberately selected a scapegoat for purposes totally political, totally petty, and then set about destroying one of the most creative business and cultural leaders this city has ever produced.

Does Oliver Stone now realize that Jim Garrison is toxic? Perhaps he finally understands that most people believe that his investigation into the JFK assassination was not just a sham but, as the *Washington Post* noted, that his case was based on "fantasy, imagination and absurdity." Most likely, he is probably tired of defending Jim Garrison and wants to move the debate to more fertile ground.

Ray Osrin / The Plain Dealer / *January 9, 1992. © 1992* The Plain Dealer. *All rights reserved. REPRINTED/USED with permission.*

Reporter Jed Horne from the New Orleans *Times-Picayune* told *The Advocate:*

> You want to know what people in New Orleans think of this *JFK* thing? They think Oliver Stone is a sucker. Garrison is considered a kook, a local joke. That Stone would come in and seek to beautify this guy is just one more instance of the gullibility of the national media and their complete inability to fathom a place like New Orleans.

It looks like Oliver Stone has abandoned *JFK* to the weeds.

CHAPTER 42
WAS DAVID FERRIE A TRAINER AND A PILOT FOR THE CIA?

(EPISODE 4, 10:14)

JFK: Destiny Betrayed erroneously claims that David Ferrie flew missions for the CIA.

Here is an excerpt from a transcript:

Narrator (Whoopi Goldberg): In the spring of 1963, Oswald moved from Dallas back to his hometown of New Orleans, where he began associating with men who, it would be revealed, had clear connections with these government efforts. One of these men, David Ferrie, had been with Oswald in the Civil Air Patrol back in 1955, and was known as an extreme anti-communist. He was also a trainer and a pilot for the CIA in its secret war against Cuba. Oswald was involved with these Cuban exile training activities with Ferrie.

While it is true that Oswald, for a very brief period, was in the Civil Air Patrol (CAP) at the same time as David Ferrie, there is little evidence that they knew each other.

And David Ferrie was not a trainer for the CIA, nor was he a pilot for them.

James DiEugenio inferred that Ferrie was involved in Operation

Mongoose from a December 1967 statement of Mr. Herbert Wagner, a man who had helped David Ferrie with his finances and to whom he bragged about some of his activities:

> One day at my company DAVE called me one afternoon and asked me if he could meet me at my office after working hours as he had something very important to talk to me about. When ARCACHA and FERRIE came in, we sat down and we talked for a while and he told me, "HERB, you can be real valuable to us." FERRIE looked at me and said, "Did you ever hear of "Operation ..." And he stopped and looked at ARCACHA and ARCACHA shook his head in an affirmative manner and then FERRIE said, "Operation Mosquito?" I made some funny little remark about so many mosquitos in the area and he said, "No, HERB, with your knowledge of motors, you could be helpful to us." Of course, he then went on to explain to me that they were planning a sabotage campaign to Cuba to sabotage machinery and transportation and so forth.

The Wagner memo above references Operation Mosquito, which DiEugenio believes is Operation Mongoose:

> When Operation Mongoose began, Ferrie let it slip that he was part of "Operation Mosquito." Clearly a miscommunication, Ferrie meant Mongoose.

But Operation Mongoose took place in 1962, which was after David Ferrie left his Cuban activities to focus on his dismissal from Eastern Airlines and his legal problems regarding a morals charge. In addition, Ferrie was ostracized by the Cubans after his August 1961 arrest.

Another source for the allegations about David Ferrie was Eladio del Valle. Here is what DiEugenio wrote in his book *Destiny Betrayed*:

> Ferrie developed an obsession for the regime of Fidel Castro. This led him to become more intertwined with the Agency and its underground

Cuban exile community in New Orleans. He bombed targets inside of Cuba at the request of former Cuban Congressman Eladio del Valle. Del Valle was linked to the CIA, Santo Trafficante, and Senator George Smathers.

The source for the del Valle claim? None other than the *National Enquirer,* which claimed that David Ferrie flew "scores of missions" with del Valle to drop bombs on Cuba.

The author, Diego Gonzalez Tendedera, claimed to have inside information about Eladio del Valle:

> He set up a grocery store as a front for his operations. And after I fled to Miami in May, 1960, I became a frequent visitor at the "store."
>
> It was there that I met Ferrie. As a free-lance pilot, he was flying scores of missions with del Valle to drop bombs on Cuba.
>
> For six months, I saw Ferrie and del Valle together almost every day.
>
> They'd take off two or three times a week in del Valle's twin-engine Apache to drop incendiaries on strategic targets and rescue anti-Communist Cubans who wanted to escape.
>
> Del Valle told me he gave Ferrie $1,000 to $1,500 per flight, depending on whether they would just drop bombs or would have to land on some highway to pick up refugees, a far more dangerous mission.
>
> I never really trusted Ferrie. And del Valle didn't either.
>
> He once told me: "Ferrie has guts. We've saved dozens of our friends. But I don't fully trust him. He'd sell us out if he could."

There is no evidence to support any of this.

It is doubtful that he flew to Cuba. Ferrie was asked about flying to Cuba in his first interview with the DA's office on December 15, 1966:

Volz: Did you do any charter work?

Ferrie: It is prohibited. Martin had me going to Cuba. It was in the newspapers ... in a 110 mile an hour airplane with four hours of gas.

Here is what Stephen Roy (aka Blackburst), an expert on the life of David Ferrie, wrote on an internet forum about Ferrie flying to Cuba:

I have spent many years examining the life of David Ferrie and his role in the New Orleans milieu. I have conducted numerous interviews with primary sources and obtained or read many thousands of pages of documents relating to these matters.

Ferrie's period of activity with the Cubans was very brief, beginning in late 1960 and abruptly ending in the fall of 1961 after his morals arrests. Throughout most of this period, his whereabouts are established by his employment and other records. He had very little opportunity to fly any missions.

Roy also added:

1) Prior to September 1961, Ferrie was flying for Eastern Air Lines three times a week from New Orleans to Houston and other Texas cities, including two overnighters. There would not have been a great deal of opportunity for him to have made such flights from Florida. (And the flight log on his Stinson contains no indication of any such flights.)

2) Prior to April 1961, Ferrie was not fully accepted as an active participant by the anti-Castro Cubans.

3) After his August 1961 morals arrests, Ferrie was soon ostracized by the Cubans. Further, his Stinson soon entered a long period of inactivity.

Ferrie denied ever going to Cuba. However, he did tell a friend about one sojourn into Cuba in August 1960, which he said was for the CIA. He said he was wounded in the process, but his friends doubted this.

So, the assertion that Ferrie made "flights" or extensive flights into Cuba is not strongly supported by the evidence.

The friend that Stephen Roy refers to is Al Cheramie, who was also a member of CAP. *Ramparts* writer Bill Turner told Stephen Burton that Al Cheramie could provide more information about Ferrie's "Cuban adventures." Here is an excerpt from a memo that Stephen Burton sent to Jim Garrison:

I began by reading Cheramie the lead TURNER gave me. He said that the reference to FERRIE'S gunshot wound was correct only in that Ferrie said it was a gunshot wound. He saw FERRIE when he returned from Miami when FERRIE said he had been shot while flying for Castro in Cuba. However, CHERAMIE said that the scar looked more like a burn. It was in the chest on the extreme right side but had no exit wound. He added that FERRIE was prone to making such false statements.

Another friend of David Ferrie's, Al Landry, told a similar story:

LANDRY said that approximately one year later [1961] while FERRIE was living at 331 Atherton Drive, FERRIE told him about the incident that occurred to him when he had disappeared for about seven to nine weeks. FERRIE mentioned this after he had a lively discussion with LANDRY with regard to his views concerning the Cuban situation that he and ARCACHA SMITH and some other Cuban friends would liberate Cuba from CASTRO. LANDRY told him that he had no idea that FERRIE could liberate Cuba and that he questioned his ability to do so. FERRIE at this time told him of the incident which had occurred when he was away from the city for about seven to nine weeks. FERRIE said that a couple of weeks prior to the time when LANDRY had seen him in the car with CHERAMIE at the airport removing his equipment, he and several other Cubans had been to Cuba in an effort to help Cubans escape from CASTRO's prison. FERRIE told him that during one of these visits to Cuba he ran into some trouble and was attacked by a CASTRO soldier and was stabbed in the stomach. He showed LANDRY a scar across his stomach approximately ten to fifteen inches long which he said resulted from the stab wound.

FERRIE at this time told him that he was working for the C.I.A. recruiting Cubans out of CASTRO's prison in Cuba. He said that he was called down to Miami and stayed there approximately one week in a hotel before he was contacted by C.I.A. men in Miami. He said that he attributed the delay in being contacted to the fact that the C.I.A. wanted to test him to see if he was the type of person who told his business to anybody on the street. He said that a woman from the C.I.A. was sent to his apartment and tried to get information from him about his activi-

> ties with the C.I.A. but that he did not tell her anything and it was after this test that he was actually contacted by the C.I.A. people in Miami. He said that shortly thereafter he and about nine Cubans flew down to a point close to Cuba and rescued some prisoners out of the prison camps. He said it was during this incident that he was stabbed. The soldier who stabbed him was killed by some of the people in his party and they carried him to safety with them.

Landry was a fifteen-year-old kid when this supposedly happened. David Ferrie wanted a relationship with Landry and, as Al Cheramie remarked, liked to make up stories. There is no evidence in the autopsy report of such a wound, nor do pictures of Ferrie on his death bed show such a scar.

Another CAP cadet, John Irion, was interviewed by Garrison's investigators in January 1967:

> **Irion**: Somewhere in the beginning of this training period, Dave Ferrie was mysteriously absent for a week's time which he explained was a small invasion by a group which tried to reach these hostages. He claimed that he had been wounded in the attempt which had failed, and he supported his claim by showing bandages which he claimed were wounds.
>
> **Q**: At this time of the alleged incident, you saw no actual wounds?
>
> **Irion**: Yes, that is correct. I didn't actually see any wounds and I didn't believe that he had any.

Stephen Roy writes in his unpublished manuscript *Perfect Villain: David Ferrie and the JFK Mystery*:

> While the sources on Ferrie's anti-Castro activities from, at the earliest, summer 1959 to about October 1961 are many, detailed, mutually corroborative and reliable, there are no reliable sources for significant anti-Castro activities on his part after October 1961. This is an important point missed in most studies of Ferrie's life and career. The single thread of Al Landry's runaway, pulled by New Orleans area police, led to the virtual collapse of Ferrie's life: his job, his Falcon [CAP] group,

his position in the anti-Castro group and his standing in the community. While he would have loved to have continued on in the fight against Castro, nobody would have him. What scattered reports there are of anti-Castro activities by Ferrie in 1962 and 1963, such as running training camps, all come from sources of questionable reliability and are impossible to corroborate. Ferrie had other battles to fight.

There is no evidence that David Ferrie worked for the CIA and no evidence that he flew missions for them. There is also no evidence that he was involved with any anti-Castro Cuban training activities with Lee Harvey Oswald.

Here is an excerpt of a CIA memo about Ferrie:

~~SECRET/SENSITIVE~~

P. 4

544 Camp Street: Is there a CIA connection with Guy Banister? With David Ferrie? With other associates of Banister?

Answer:

According to CIA records, during 1960 Guy Banister operated a private detective agency in New Orleans called Banister and Associates. CIA considered contacting him for use as a foreign intelligence source and for possible use of his firm for cover purposes. However, security investigation revealed derogatory information about his professional conduct, and he was not contacted. With regard to Mr. Ferrie, Agency files indicate that CIA never considered contacting him for any purpose at any time. Our record search to date has not revealed any contacts with other associates of Guy Banister.

Stephen Roy summed up the evidence about Ferrie and the CIA:

Ferrie did imply a CIA connection to a few people. He claimed in late 1960 to have been injured in a raid on Cuba. He told Al Landry a vivid story about it. He implied to Herb Wagner a connection with something called Operation Mosquito (by the way, this was too early to have been a misunderstanding of Mongoose, as Davy postulates). When he ran a training camp for his "Falcon Squadron" in early 1961, he claimed to have the backing of either the CIA or the State Department. And he claimed to Bob Boylston that, in the event of an attack on the US, he would pass along "secret orders" from the government. How much, if any, of this is true and how much might be Walter Mitty-type fantasy is unclear. But it all seems to have ended by late 1961.

The notion of Ferrie flying raids into Cuba is doubtful. The Eladio del Valle story of spending 3 days each week in Miami on such raids is inconsistent with Ferrie's work schedule. And other accounts, such as Robert Morrow and Ron Lewis, are inconsistent with Ferrie's documented activities.

Jane Roman checked in 1967 and reported that Ferrie was "not of operational interest" to the CIA. I consider this credible, since such a document would not be expected to reach the public in 1967, and because it and other documents were very candid about Shaw and others. Roman does not deny ANY connection (see the FRD connection above), but no "operational interest" suggests that Ferrie's FRD connection may have been at the local level, and very short term.

As I have noted here, there is no credible evidence of a later Ferrie-CIA connection, and Ferrie's pathetic financial situation from 1962 to his death suggests that he was not paid for any such activities.

CHAPTER 43
WHY DOES JFK: DESTINY BETRAYED SHOW FAKE OSWALD HANDBILLS?

(EPISODE 4, 10:55)

JFK: Destiny Betrayed misleads viewers into believing that Oswald gave out handbills on the streets of New Orleans stamped with the 544 Camp Street address. The use of the address would tie Oswald to Guy Banister, an extreme right-winger whose office was in the same building but with an entrance around the corner.

In fact, Oswald used his real address or his PO box on those handbills, and the 544 Camp Street address was only used on Fair Play for Cuba Committee (FPCC) pamphlets by Corliss Lamont.

Here is an excerpt from a transcript:

> **Narrator (Whoopi Goldberg)**: Another person Oswald was seen with in New Orleans in 1963 was Guy Banister. Banister was an extreme right-winger who was close to the FBI, the CIA, and the American Nazi Party. Banister gave Oswald his own office at 544 Camp Street. Oswald now began to use his office to print up and stamp pro-Castro literature, much of it associated with the Fair Play for Cuba Committee centered in New York.

Screenshot from JFK: Destiny Betrayed

There is no evidence to support the allegation that Oswald had an office at 544 Camp Street.

In *JFK Revisited: Through the Looking Glass,* Jefferson Morley makes a similar point about the pamphlets:

Jefferson Morley: In the spring of 1963, Oswald started handing out pamphlets for the Fair Play for Cuba Committee, a pro-Castro, pro-Cuban Revolution group that was popular on college campuses and some of them he stamped 544 Camp Street which was an office in downtown New Orleans near where the CIA's offices were, right across the street, in fact. It was also the home of the Cuban Revolutionary Council which was the leading anti-Castro group. Why would a pro-Castro activist put his headquarters in the same headquarters as the leading anti-Castro group in the country? Because he was a provocateur.

According to the HSCA, the Cuban Revolutionary Council (CRC) only had offices at 544 Camp Street for about six months from 1961–1962. Sam Newman, the owner of the building, told Jim Garrison that the CRC was only in the building for the last three months of 1961. This was well before Oswald had moved back to New Orleans in the spring of 1963. He also had no recollection of ever seeing Oswald in or around the building.

Oswald ordered a thousand handbills from Jones Printing in New Orleans, and on these flyers, he stamped either his home address or his post office box. The Corliss Lamont pamphlets that he stamped with 544

Camp Street were from a limited stock that he received from the Fair Play for Cuba Committee in New York. *JFK: Destiny Betrayed* moves the 544 Camp Street stamp to the "Hands Off Cuba" handbills to increase the importance of the address stamp.

To reiterate: the handbills that Oswald gave out three times in New Orleans did ***not*** have 544 Camp Street stamped on them. He only stamped 544 Camp Street on pamphlets by Corliss Lamont.

When Oswald was arrested in August 1963, the handbill that was confiscated by the police did not have the 544 Camp Street address:

The propaganda appearing on this circular reads as follows: "HANDS OFF CUBA!" "Join the Fair Play for Cuba Committee" "New Orleans Charter Member Branch" "Free Literature, Lectures Location: A. J. Hidell P. O. Box 30016 New Orleans, La." "EVERYONE WELCOME!"

Here are two real Oswald handbills:

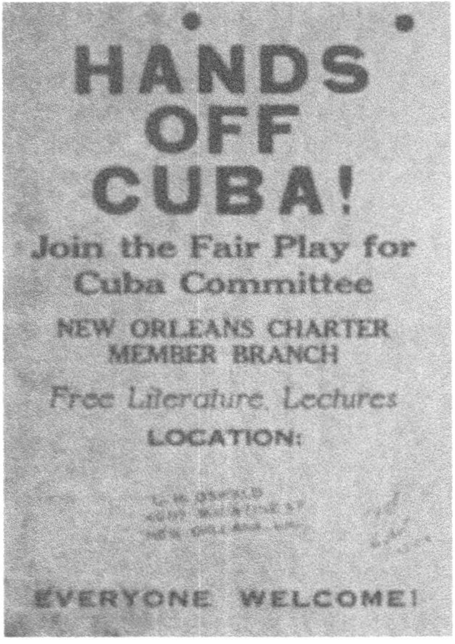

Warren Commission Exhibit 2966-A

Warren Commission Exhibit 2966-B

Here is one of the Corlisss Lamont pamphlets with the 544 Camp Street address:

SUGGESTED REFERENCES

In this pamphlet I have not endeavored to describe in any detail the immense progress that Cuba has made under the Castro regime. For information about this aspect of the Cuban Revolution I refer the reader to the following:

Books and pamphlets

Leo Huberman and Paul M. Sweezy, *Cuba, Anatomy of a Revolution*, Monthly Review Press, New York, 1960. Cloth, $3.50, paperback, $1.75.

C. Wright Mills, *Listen, Yankee: The Revolution in Cuba*, Ballantine Books, New York, 1960. 50¢.

Paul A. Baran, *Reflections on the Cuban Revolution*, Monthly Review Press, New York, 1961. 35¢.

Sources for both internal developments in Cuba and the invasion of April 1961

Fair Play, bulletin of the Fair Play for Cuba Committee, 799 Broadway, New York 3, N. Y.

The Independent, 225 Lafayette Street, New York 12, N. Y.

Monthly Review, 66 Barrow Street, New York 14, N. Y.

38

National Guardian, 197 East 4th Street, New York 9, N. Y. (especially see dispatches from *Guardian* Editor-in-Exile, Cedric Belfrage, Havana).

New York Times, Times Square, New York, N. Y.

I. F. Stone's Weekly, 5018 Nebraska Avenue, N.W., Washington 15, D.C.

Petition to the President of the United States and the Attorney General, by American Lawyers, and supporting Memorandum of Law concerning the Policy of the American Government relating to Cuba under the Neutrality Laws, Treaties with Cuba, and International Law, New York, 1961. (Copies may be obtained from Mr. Jesse Gordon, 333 Sixth Avenue, New York 14, N. Y. Price $1.00 to cover cost of printing and mailing.)

544 CAMP ST.
NEW ORLEANS,

39

COMMISSION EXHIBIT No. 3120—Continued

Note that only the flyer (aka handbill) tried to lure the recipient to a destination:

"Join ... Free Literature ... Lectures ... Location"

If Oswald was intending to be a provocateur, he would have tried to lure people to 544 Camp Street, no? Instead, he lured them to his home or his post office box.

What about the handbills that allegedly contain the address 544 Camp Street?

The handbill shown in *JFK: Destiny Betrayed* is fake, and its precursor in Oliver Stone's feature film, *JFK,* was also a fake. Let's start with those.

There is a fake flyer in Robert Groden's 1993 book, *The Killing of a President*:

Gus Russo published a similar handbill in his 1998 book, *Live by the Sword*:

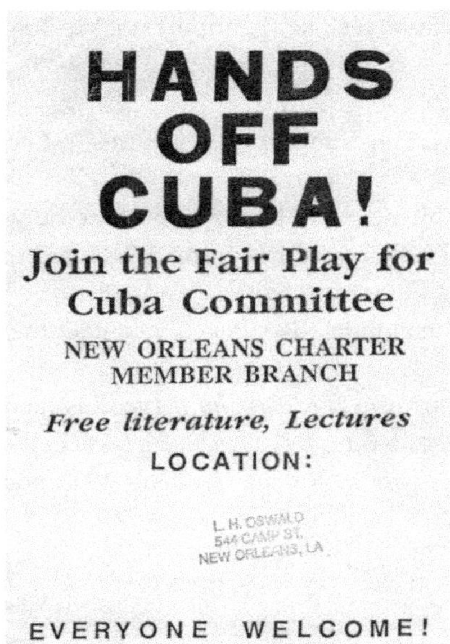

There are several errors in these fakes, which are obvious once you see them.

Note that the Groden and Russo handbills have a lower-case l in "Literature," while the real pamphlet has an upper-case L. In addition, the word "LOCATION" in the real handbill starts under the i in "Literature," while in the fake handbills, "LOCATION" starts under the t. There is also a different spacing of OC in "LOCATION"—the fake flyers have more space.

These fake handbills were made for Oliver Stone's film *JFK*. Now, one can make a reasonable case that using such a fake handbill in a fictional film is OK. Keep in mind that Oliver Stone combined four real people into his composite character Willie O'Keefe. So, dramatic license does give some leeway to stretch the truth. I have argued, and I would still argue, that turning Jim Garrison into a heroic prosecutor was a bridge too far.

Here is a screenshot from *JFK* that shows a fake handbill:

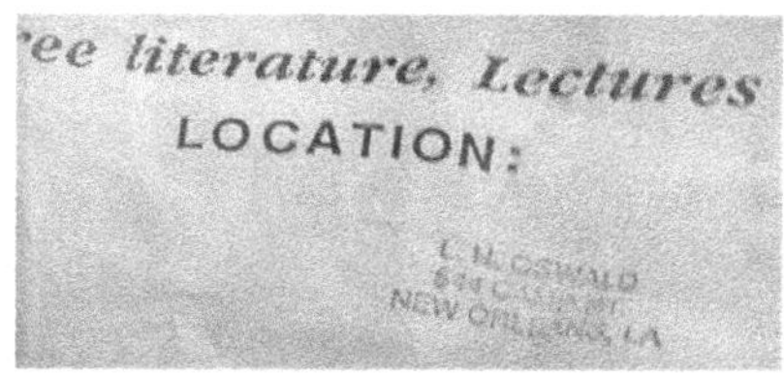

Note the small l in "literature" and that the word "LOCATION" starts under the t in "literature." This is clearly a fake handbill.

As for the handbill used in *JFK: Destiny Betrayed,* DiEugenio also used it in a PowerPoint presentation:

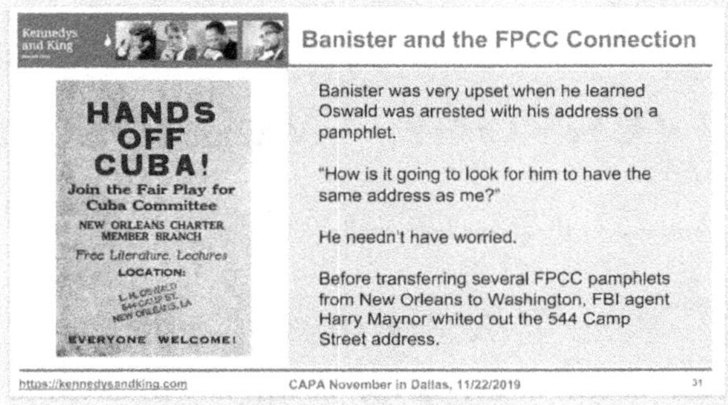

FBI agent Harry Maynor did not "white out" the 544 Camp Street address. It was probably done at the Government Printing Office, and it was not done for nefarious reasons.

In addition, DiEugenio's quotation is just a plain fiction derived from *JFK*:

DiEugenio: Banister was very upset when he learned Oswald was arrested with his address on a pamphlet. "How is it going to look for him to have the same address as me?"

***JFK* (1991)**: Guy Banister intercepts him on the sidewalk, holding a leaflet and pointing to "544 Camp Street" stamped on it. Guy seems miffed at Oswald, tells him something quickly, and then moves on. Banister: "See this? What the hell is this doing on this piece of paper? … (he moves away) Asshole."

The quotation attributed to Banister comes from an HSCA interview with his secretary, Delphine Roberts. However, the HSCA concluded that much of her testimony "lacked credibility."

While the the flyer is more carefully done, there is one unambiguous proof of fakery. The size of the L. H. Oswald stamp in relation to the handbill. Here is the real thing:

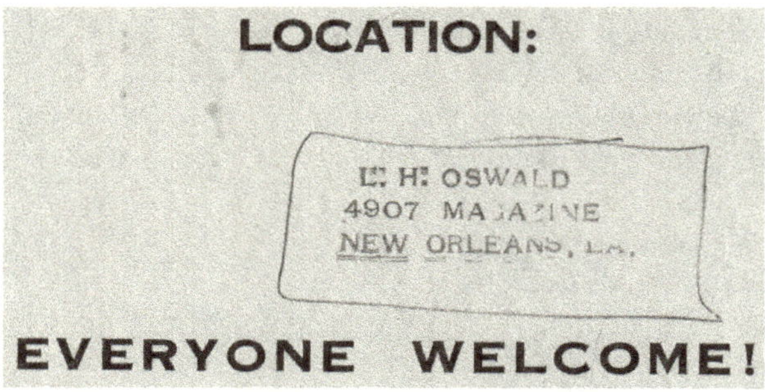

And here is the DiEugenio handbill:

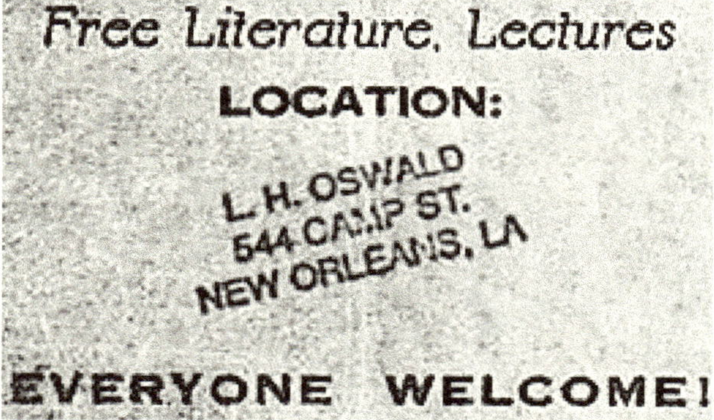

The size is all wrong. On the fake flyer, the stamp takes up most of the space between "LOCATION" and "EVERYONE WELCOME." On the real flyer, the stamp is much smaller. Compare the size of "L. H. OSWALD" and "LOCATION" in each of the two flyers.

You can easily see in the illustration below the size differences between the real handbill (on the top) and the fake handbill (on the bottom):

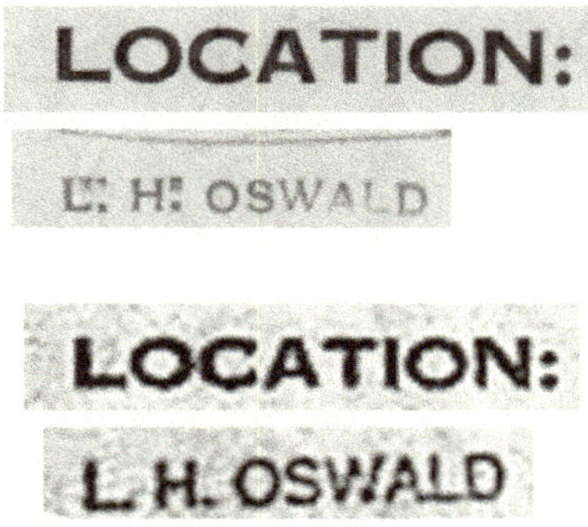

In addition, Lee Harvey Oswald put a period after "LA" on his handbills and pamphlets. The fake flyers do not have a period after the "LA." Oswald might have changed his punctuation just as he changed the content of his stamp, but he could not have changed the type size.

It's one thing for Oliver Stone to use a fake flyer in *JFK*. It's quite another for James DiEugenio and Oliver Stone to use a fake flyer in a documentary film. It's nothing short of the transubstantiation of fiction into fact.

James DiEugenio and Oliver Stone owe us an explanation.

So, where does the fake flyer come from?

Well, perhaps from self-declared Oswald girlfriend Judyth Vary Baker. Steve Roe noticed that on page 435 of her generally unreliable 2010 book, *Me & Lee*, she presents a handbill:

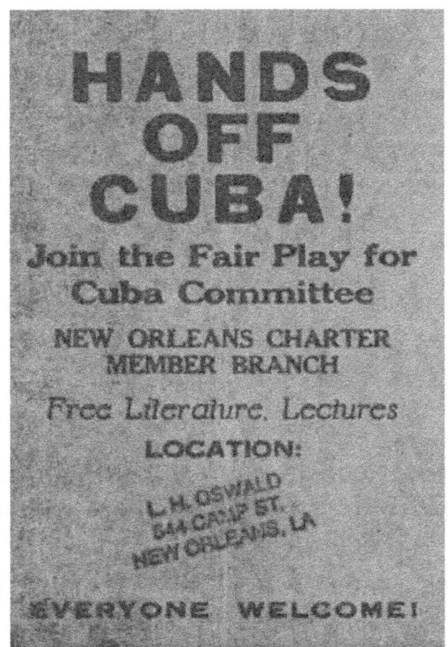

Compare the bottom part of an original flyer (above) with that of the flyer found in Baker's book (below):

Original flyer

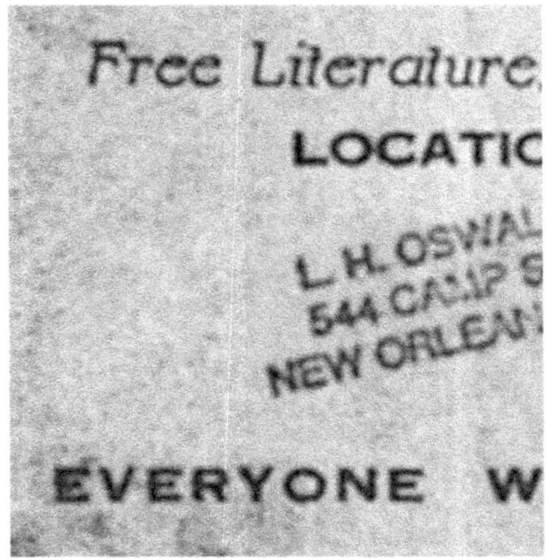

The flyer found in Baker's book

You can see the exact same fold and paper marks running vertically through the stamp and the angled fold from the large "L." These fold and paper marks are from a real flyer.

In addition, the Oswald stamp on the fake flyer is identical to the stamp on the Oliver Stone fake from *JFK*. So, someone took the stamp from the Stone flyer and applied it to a real flyer.

When I blogged about the fake flyers, James DiEugenio had this to say on the Education Forum:

James DiEugenio Posted September 25 (edited) Author

Members

10.5k
Gender:Male

The New Orleans Historical Society had the same flyer, not pamphlet, under glass with 544 Camp Street.

Is that a fake also ?

That is where our editors got it.

BTW, that collection, which I have been at more than once, is a valuable place. John Volz told me that he questioned Bundy for Garrison. So he decided to test him. He asked what color were the flyers he saw exchanged that night. Bundy said they were yellow. This surprised Volz. But if you go to that collection you will see that one of the flyers LHO handed out that summer was yellow.

But hey, if Litwin and Roe say so, that much be fake also, right?

DiEugenio is just plain wrong about the New Orleans Historical Society. The Historic New Orleans Collections does have a flyer, but it is a real handbill acquired from Jesse Core, the former public relations officer at the International Trade Mart, where Oswald handed them out. Here is the flyer in their collection:

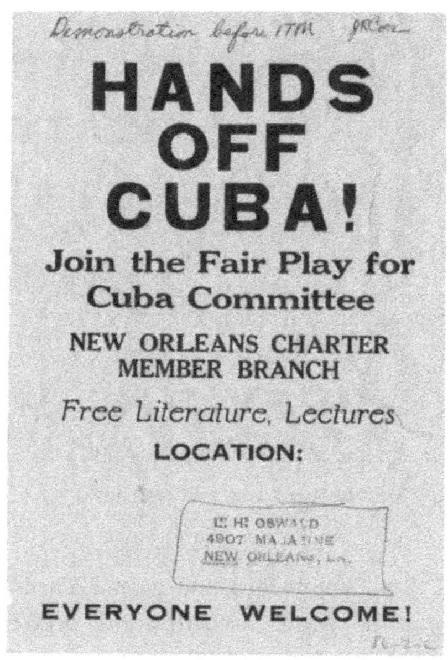

New Orleans Historical Society, a web platform that shares stories about New Orleans, did have a story on its website about the Newman building that relied on the fake flyer. I emailed one of the managers and asked about the provenance of its flyer, and they have since removed the article.

So, there is no evidence that Oswald handed out handbills with the 544 Camp Street address.

Researcher John Newman suggested an explanation for the absence of handbills with the 544 Camp Street address from the official record in Episode 4 of *JFK: Destiny Betrayed*:

John Newman: At some point, the FBI, I think probably after the assassination, decided they wanted to disconnect Oswald from the FBI. And of course, Banister, who's associated with the FBI would have to be disconnected as well. The problem with that, many of those handbills had the 544 Camp Street address on them. There was a message from New Orleans to the bureau written by a special agent Maynor, who actually mentioned pamphlets that had the 544 Camp Street address on it. And before that message was sent, it was scratched out.

Here is one page from that document:

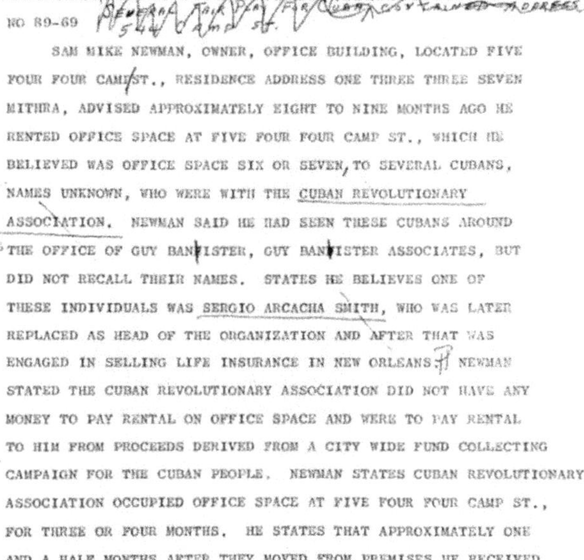

NO 89-69

SAM MIKE NEWMAN, OWNER, OFFICE BUILDING, LOCATED FIVE FOUR FOUR CAMP ST., RESIDENCE ADDRESS ONE THREE THREE SEVEN MITHRA, ADVISED APPROXIMATELY EIGHT TO NINE MONTHS AGO HE RENTED OFFICE SPACE AT FIVE FOUR FOUR CAMP ST., WHICH HE BELIEVED WAS OFFICE SPACE SIX OR SEVEN, TO SEVERAL CUBANS, NAMES UNKNOWN, WHO WERE WITH THE CUBAN REVOLUTIONARY ASSOCIATION. NEWMAN SAID HE HAD SEEN THESE CUBANS AROUND THE OFFICE OF GUY BANISTER, GUY BANISTER ASSOCIATES, BUT DID NOT RECALL THEIR NAMES. STATES HE BELIEVES ONE OF THESE INDIVIDUALS WAS SERGIO ARCACHA SMITH, WHO WAS LATER REPLACED AS HEAD OF THE ORGANIZATION AND AFTER THAT WAS ENGAGED IN SELLING LIFE INSURANCE IN NEW ORLEANS. NEWMAN STATED THE CUBAN REVOLUTIONARY ASSOCIATION DID NOT HAVE ANY MONEY TO PAY RENTAL ON OFFICE SPACE AND WERE TO PAY RENTAL TO HIM FROM PROCEEDS DERIVED FROM A CITY WIDE FUND COLLECTING CAMPAIGN FOR THE CUBAN PEOPLE. NEWMAN STATES CUBAN REVOLUTIONARY ASSOCIATION OCCUPIED OFFICE SPACE AT FIVE FOUR FOUR CAMP ST., FOR THREE OR FOUR MONTHS. HE STATES THAT APPROXIMATELY ONE AND A HALF MONTHS AFTER THEY MOVED FROM PREMISES HE RECEIVED

The crossed-out notation at the top reads as follows: "Several Fair Play for Cuba pamphlets contained address 544 Camp St."

There is no evidence that the note was written by Special Agent Maynor. And the note might have been added after the message was sent.

There is a sentence in the above document about Sam Newman, owner of the Newman building on the corner of Camp and Lafayette, who "does not have any recollection of any individual by that name [Oswald]."

Paul Hoch found this message as it was actually sent:

NOV 26 1963

TELETYPE

CONFIDENTIAL

TO DIRECTOR, FBI AND SAC, DALLAS

FROM SAC, NEW ORLEANS /89-69/

ASSASSINATION OF PRESIDENT JOHN F. KENNEDY, NOVEMBER TWENTYTWO, SIXTYTHREE, DALLAS, TEXAS.

RE NEW ORLEANS TEL TO BUREAU AND DALLAS, NOVEMBER TWENTYFOUR INSTANT.

RE FAIR PLAY FOR CUBA COMMITTEE.

ON AUGUST EIGHT SIXTYTHREE, OSWALD FURNISHED A PAMPLET ENTITLED CRIME AGAINST CUBA BY CORLISS LAMONT. PAGE THIRTYNINE OF PAMPLET BORE STAMPED IMPRESSION QUOTE F P C C FIVE FOUR FOUR CAMP ST., NEW ORLEANS, LOUISIANA. UNQUOTE.

SAM MIKE NEWMAN, OWNER, OFFICE BUILDING, LOCATED FIVE FOUR FOUR CAMP ST., RESIDENCE ADDRESS ONE THREE THREE SEVEN MITHRA, ADVISED APPROXIMATELY EIGHT TO NINE MONTHS AGO HE RENTED OFFICE SPACE AT FIVE FOUR FOUR CAMP ST., WHICH HE BELIEVED WAS OFFICE SPACE SIX OR SEVEN, TO SEVERAL CUBANS,

A more precise version of the scratched-out sentence was added:

> ON AUGUST EIGHT SIXTYTHREE, OSWALD FURNISHED A PAMPLET ENTITLED CRIME AGAINST CUBA BY CORLISS LAMONT. PAGE THIRTYNINE OF PAMPLET BORE STAMPED IMPRESSION QUOTE F P C C FIVE FOUR FOUR CAMP ST. NEW ORLEANS, LOUISIANA. UNQUOTE.

The document cited by John Newman was a draft; various edits marked there were implemented when the text was sent to FBI HQ.

There is no evidence that 544 Camp Street was stamped on any of the handbills that Oswald handed out on the streets of New Orleans. But it was important to the producers of *JFK: Destiny Betrayed* to have a strong Oswald link to that address. Thus, they used fake handbills to bolster their incredibly weak case.

CHAPTER 44
DID GUY BANISTER GIVE OSWALD AN OFFICE AT 544 CAMP STREET?

(EPISODE 4, 10:55)

The last chapter examined Oswald's handbills and the 544 Camp Street address. *JFK: Destiny Betrayed* also claims that Guy Banister gave Lee Harvey Oswald an office at 544 Camp Street in New Orleans.

While the documentary mentions the 544 Camp Street address, it doesn't mention that Guy Banister's actual address was 531 Lafayette Street, which was right around the corner.

Joseph Newbrough was a detective who worked for Guy Banister from 1958 to 1964. He was interviewed for the *PBS Frontline* documentary "Who Was Lee Harvey Oswald?"

Q: Oswald handed out his leaflets as you well know, they were addressed 544 Camp Street [sic; the last chapter showed that these leaflets did not have that address stamped on them]. Did he have an office there?

Newbrough: To my best knowledge and belief he did not have an office at 544 Camp Street, but if he did it would have not necessarily have connected him with Guy Banister who used the address 531 Lafayette Street which was around the corner.

Q: If you go through 544 Camp Street can you reach Banister's office?

Newbrough: You absolutely could not reach Banister's office unless you exited ... If you entered 544 Camp Street the only way you could have gotten to Banister's office was to go out a window. There was no staircase, though much has been said of a staircase, it didn't exist.

Q: So, they had separate entrances?

Newbrough: Totally separate entrances and probably 60 steps apart.

So, was there any relationship between Guy Banister and Lee Harvey Oswald? Did Oswald operate out of Banister's office? Did Oswald use the office to print his literature?

There is little firm evidence to place Lee Harvey Oswald in Banister's office. Yes, there are some witnesses, but they all lack credibility. Jim Garrison talked to most, if not all, of the people who worked at Guy Banister's office, and none of them remembered seeing Oswald.

Delphine Roberts was Banister's secretary, she was interviewed by Garrison's office in January of 1967, and she didn't say one word about seeing Oswald in the office.

The allegation that Oswald was using a room in Banister's office probably came from an August 27, 1978, HSCA interview with Delphine Roberts:

Delphine Roberts believes that LEE OSWALD came into the office to be interviewed for a job but doesn't remember anything specific because so many people came in for interviews. At a later date Banister introduced MARINA AND LEE to her in his office but they walked right out, and she did not talk to them. She could not recall hearing Marina speak or how they were dressed. On several occasions LEE OSWALD would come in and go to Banister's office and she could not hear any conversation from that room. She believed that OSWALD was either working or attempting to work for BANISTER. She does remember hearing BANISTER holler at SAM NEWMAN AND JAMES ARTHUS about letting OSWALD use the second-floor room and keeping the FPCC literature from his office.

Does this story make any sense? Oswald was either "working or attempting to work for Banister"? Roberts doesn't know? Oswald came to visit with Marina? Why would Banister yell at Sam Newman, the owner of the building, for letting Oswald use a room if he was part of Banister's operation?

By the way, in an earlier HSCA interview on July 6, 1978, Delphine Roberts "stated that she never saw Oswald in person. She states that she did see Fidel Castro and his top aide Che Guevara walking on Canal St. when she had the flag booth."

Over the years, Sam Newman was interviewed many times by the FBI, Jim Garrison, and the HSCA, and he always denied ever meeting Lee Harvey Oswald.

The HSCA noted Roberts's testimony and wrote:

> The committee did not credit the Roberts' testimony standing alone. It came late in the investigation and without corroboration or independent substantiation, and much of Roberts' other testimony lacked credibility.

Another witness who supposedly saw Oswald in Banister's office was Jack Martin. But he was a crackpot who never had any credibility. He did not convince the HSCA:

> Martin has also told the committee he saw Lee Harvey Oswald with Ferrie in Guy Banister's office in 1963. Nevertheless, in light of Martin's previous contradictory statements to authorities shortly after the assassination in which Martin made no such allegation about having seen Oswald, it may be argued that credence should not be placed in Martin's statements to the committee.

No witnesses came forward in 1964 to claim that Oswald was hanging out in Banister's office. If Oswald really had operated out of Banister's office, surely someone would have talked, and word would have gotten out. The whole office would have been talking about it. The only person coming forward with such a story when Jim Garrison was investigating was the crackpot Jack Martin.

The preponderance of the evidence leads me to conclude that there was no connection between Oswald and Banister. It's hard to prove a negative, but until someone comes out with some hard and credible information, I'll leave it at that.

The HSCA also agreed:

> Thus, the committee could find no documentary proof that Banister had a file on Lee Harvey Oswald, nor could the committee find credible witnesses who ever saw Lee Harvey Oswald and Guy Banister together.

The claim that Guy Banister gave Lee Harvey Oswald an office at 544 Camp Street is not sustained by the evidence.

CHAPTER 45
WAS CLAY SHAW A "CONTRACT AGENT" FOR THE CIA?

(EPISODE 4, 13:22)

JFK: Destiny Betrayed claims that Clay Shaw was a "highly valued contract agent" of the CIA.

Here is an excerpt from the transcript:

Narrator (Whoopi Goldberg): One of the places Oswald leafletted in front of was Clay Shaw's International Trade Mart. Shaw, who was arrested by New Orleans DA Jim Garrison on charges he was part of the conspiracy to kill President Kennedy, always denied he was associated with the CIA.

[Archive clip] **Canadian Broadcasting Corporation (CBC) Interviewer**: You have never yourself had any CIA connection?

[Archive clip] **Clay Shaw**: None whatsoever.

[Archive clip] **CBC Interviewer**: Any association with the organization?

[Archive clip] **Clay Shaw**: No, none.

Narrator (Whoopi Goldberg): The [Assassination Records] Review Board has shown these denials to be false. Shaw was both a highly valued contract agent and had a covert security clearance for a project codenamed QKENCHANT.

Where did these incredible claims come from?

I will start with the first claim about Shaw being a contract agent.

Joan Mellen, in her book *A Farewell to Justice*, claimed that she found a smoking gun that proved Clay Shaw worked for the CIA:

> Incontrovertible proof has come to hand from the bowels of the CIA itself convicting Shaw of perjury. Notwithstanding CIA's insistence that "we have never remunerated him," Shaw had indeed worked as an employee for CIA, a job for which he was paid handsomely, according to the Agency. CIA's History Staff surveyed CIA records that had been made available to the House Select Committee on Assassinations between 1977 and 1979. There were sixty-four sequestered boxes of documents and the one outing Clay Shaw as an Agency employee was among them.
>
> In 1992, the PROJFILES "CIA Matters," a component of CIA addressed by its History Staff, released a document that entirely vindicates Jim Garrison in his conviction that Shaw was acting not for himself in his relationship with Oswald, but for the Central Intelligence Agency. CIA prefaces its revelation about Shaw with a predictable disclaimer. The Agency declares that nothing was found in the records "that indicates any CIA role in the Kennedy assassination or assassination conspiracy (if there was one) or any CIA involvement with Oswald." Then CIA's History Staff Chief, J. Kenneth McDonald, adds:
>
> *"These records do reveal, however, that Clay Shaw was a highly paid CIA contract source until 1956."*

Here is an excerpt of that document:

> 7. CIA Complicity? Our survey found nothing in these records that indicates any CIA role in the Kennedy assassination or assassination conspiracy (if there was one), or any CIA involvement with Oswald. These records do reveal, however, that Clay Shaw was a highly paid CIA contract source until 1956. While nothing surfaced on Carlos Marcello in the collection, we found substantial documentation on other members of the mob, including Santos Trafficante.

CIA Document RIF #104-10428-10104, dated February 10, 1992, page 3.

To Garrisonites, this document was akin to the Rosetta Stone. Note that the document says, "contract source" and not "contract agent."

But there are problems.

Shaw was a domestic *contact* source until 1956; like thousands of other businessmen, he provided the CIA with information about trade and conditions behind the iron curtain. Might the word "contract" be a simple typo?

Or perhaps a 1955 document that refers to Shaw as a "valued source" of the CIA's Domestic Contact Service was misunderstood by the unknown person who compiled this information in 1992.

2. We have also discussed subject case, and particularly your memo of 26 July 1955, with Clay Shaw, Managing Director of International Trade Mart, New Orleans, who has represented the Mart at quite a number of international fairs including the Milan Fair, the Brussels Fair, the Swiss Fair at Basle, the Paris Fair, and the British Industries Federation Fairs at London and Birmingham, all in 1952, and the Milan Fair, the Hannover Fair, the Brussels Fair, and the British Industries Fair at London, all in 1954.

A 33412

3. Messrs. Duffy and Shaw are both valued sources of this office, and we deem it sufficiently important to compromise a "Y" number to refer you to the reports submitted by Clay Shaw as Y 145.1, and particularly 00-B-547[illegible], Subject: "Observations on International Fairs at Milan, Brussels, Basle, Paris and London/Comments on Western European Economics and Desire to Trade with the Soviet Bloc." Mr. Duffy's most recent reports are 00-B-04026 and 00-B-04210 on the Inter-American Investment Conference.

This 1955 document is indeed in the segregated collection. You can find it in reel 17. "This set of CIA documents is a microfilmed collection of documents to which the House Select Committee on Assassinations had access, split into 72 reels. See also a related and overlapping set of documents which were not recorded on microfilm."

It is important to note the McDonald summary document in question (which is factually unreliable for reasons apart from its description of Shaw) was not prepared contemporaneously during Shaw's years of service to the Agency but decades later. It was compiled for the purpose of describing a collection of assassination-related documents the Agency was preparing to release on the order of then CIA Director Robert Gates, months before the Assassination Records Collection Act became law. All of this material was given to the HSCA.

As for the document's reliability, researcher Paul Hoch has found another example of where this document was wrong. It refers to "records relating to Gilberto Alvarado, who maintained that he witnessed Cubans passing Oswald cash at a party on the night before the assassination." This description is obviously a confused mashup of two allegations that were separately made: one by Gilberto Alvarado in 1963 (which he ultimately retracted), and another, made later, by Elena Garro de Paz.

A different page in the 1992 document correctly describes Alvarado as "the Nicaraguan who claimed he saw Lee Harvey Oswald receive cash in [a] meeting inside Mexico City Cuban embassy."

Elena Garro de Paz claimed to have seen Oswald and two companions at a "twist party" in Mexico City.

The date given for this twist party (November 21) matches neither allegation and is an error, thus establishing that the 1992 document is not a reliable accounting of what is in the CIA's archive.

On the night before the assassination, Oswald was in Dallas with Marina at Ruth Paine's house (thus he could not have received cash in Alvarado's presence or have been at a party in Mexico City). Oswald was only in Mexico City from September 26 to October 3. If he attended a party, which is a big if, it could only have happened during this time period.

The 1992 memo was written by J. Kenneth McDonald, a CIA historian. Max Holland spoke with McDonald, who told him:

> His recollection was that the memo was assembled from a couple of summaries that were prepared for him by the History Staff.

In an email, Holland noted that "Unless someone can produce a document contemporaneous with Shaw's service as a domestic contact source that states he was well-remunerated or compensated, then I think whatever extant documents we have from his actual service trump a description in a summary that was prepared hastily."

It seems clear that the History Staff made an error. The actual documents sequestered by the CIA are available, and none of them mentions "contract source." If that term had actually appeared in any document that the HSCA examined, we would have known this well before 1992. In addition, the term "contract source" is not in the standard CIA lexicon. Searching for "contract source" on the Mary Ferrell website only returns the 1992 document.

Jerry Shinley has also raised the possibility of a scribal error. He noticed that there are typist's initials on the document:

```
SUBJECT: Survey of CIA's Records from House Select Committee
         on Assassinations Investigation

DA/OTE/CSI/HS  JKMcD:nkl (10 Feb 92) 30147
```

Is it possible that something like "highly-rated CIA contact source" was rendered as "highly-paid CIA contract source"? Could the typist have been working from a handwritten draft or an audio recording?

Other documents in the CIA file on Shaw contradict the notion that Shaw was paid. These were prepared in 1967, during the height of the CIA's concern that Garrison might actually know about the Agency's innocuous relationship with Shaw and purposely misrepresent it in public utterances. A document dated 16 October 1967 flatly stated that Shaw was never remunerated for his services.

2. SHAW HAS A SECURITY STATUS OF "NO INFO" DATED 23 MAR 49; BANISTER, ONE OF NI(R) DATED 12 NOV 63. AS WE HAVE ALREADY REPORTED, WE MAINTAINED PROFESSIONAL CONTACT WITH SHAW FROM 1949 THROUGH 1956 AS MANAGER OF INTERNATIONAL TRADE MART. THIS RESULTED IN EIGHT REPORTS OF WHICH SIX WERE EVALUATED "OF VALUE" AND TWO "OF SLIGHT VALUE." WE HAVE NEVER REMUNERATED HIM; HIS NOFO CONTACT WAS HUNTER C. LEAKE AND THE RELATIONSHIP WAS DISCONTINUED AS THE "SHOTGUN APPROACH" TO COLLECTION EFFORTS WANED AND IT BECAME OBVIOUS THAT SHAW WAS BECOMING MORE AND MORE INTERESTED IN HIS PRIVATE VENTURES AND LESS AND LESS IN THE ACTIVITIES OF INTERNATIONAL TRADE MART. HE RESIGNED AS MANAGER OF INTERNATIONAL TRADE MART ON 1 OCT 65.

Conspiracy theorists who jumped on the 1992 document have to face the fact that there are no underlying CIA documents that support the allegation that Shaw was paid by the CIA. No doubt, they will fall back on the old standby that the documents must have been destroyed. That doesn't quite work in this case because the documents were sequestered by the CIA, seen by the HSCA, and examined again in 1992.

Now on to Project QKENCHANT.

A CIA document on Clay Shaw had this mysterious paragraph:

11. A memorandum marked only for file, 16 March 1967, signed M.D. Stevens, says that J. Monroe SULLIVAN, #280207, was granted a covert security approval on 10 December 1962 so that he could be used in Project QKENCHANT. SHAW has #402897-A.

A staffer from the HSCA also made notes on Clay Shaw from the CIA segregated collection:

- 18 Sept 68 Memo re: Monroe J. Sullivan
or (J. Monroe)
~~00024500~~: poss. CIA connection – granted Covert
Security Approval for use under Project
QKENCHANT on an unwitting basis
10 Dec. 62
Executive Director of San Francisco World
Trade Center, claimed to have seen w/ Shaw
22 NOV. 63.
~~SECRET~~

J. Monroe Sullivan was the executive director of the San Francisco World Trade Center, and he was with Clay Shaw on November 22, 1963. He certainly had approval under QKENCHANT, but it was on an "unwitting" basis. The "covert" in "covert security approval" appears to mean that the approval itself was covert, not that Sullivan was approved for covert operations.

The number after Clay Shaw's name, #402897-A, was not related to QKENCHANT. It's just a CIA identifying number for Clay Shaw that you find on many documents.

What was Project QKENCHANT? Here is an excerpt from another CIA document:

b. (S) QKENCHANT was a project for obtaining clearances, that is, Provisional Covert Security Approvals (PCSA) and Covert Security Approvals (CSA), with the Office of Security in connection with the acquisition of Corporate Cover for Action (CCA). In connection with the acquisition of CCA, Directorate of Operations guidelines require that a PCSA/CSA be obtained in most instances before a corporate entity can be used as a Cover for Action (CFA) sponsor.

Here is a better description in plain English:

1. QKENCHANT was the name of an Agency project used to provide security approvals on non-Agency personnel and facilities. Such approvals were required so that Agency personnel could meet individuals to discuss proposed projects, activities, and possible relationships.

There is no evidence that Clay Shaw had clearance under this program:

c. (U) With regard to Clay Shaw and his association with the QKENCHANT project: A review of Shaw's security file indicates that he received a "five Agency" clearance on 23 March 1949. Our records indicate the QKENCHANT project did not begin until sometime in 1952, therefore, Shaw in all probability was not cleared by the QKENCHANT program.

That is certainly not definitive. But QKENCHANT was not an operational project. And so, there is no evidence that Clay Shaw was an operational agent of the CIA.

JFK: Destiny Betrayed is very selective in the information it provides to viewers. The film omits paragraph b above, and its highlights of paragraph c do not include the 1949 date, well before Project QKENCHANT even started.

c. (U) With regard to Clay Shaw and his association with the QKENCHANT project: A review of Shaw's security file indicates that he received a "five Agency" clearance on 23 March 1949. Our records indicate the QKENCHANT project did not begin until sometime in 1952, therefore, Shaw in all probability was not cleared by the QKENCHANT program.

Screen shot from JFK: Destiny Betrayed

Clay Shaw was just a source for the Domestic Contact Service from 1948 to 1956. But why would Clay Shaw lie when talking to the CBC?

Here is a CIA document that offers an explanation:

~~SECRET~~ 291945Z CITE NEW ORLEANS 005
HEADQUARTERS
ATTN: OFFICE OF GENERAL COUNSEL

IN REPLY TO HEADQUARTERS 137, THE CONTACTS WHICH THIS OFFICE HAS HAD WITH CLAY SHAW AND HIS SECURITY STATUS ARE AS SET FORTH IN NEW ORLEANS MEMORANDUM NO-84-67, TO DIRECTOR, DCS, IN DCS CASE 49364 - GARRISON INVESTIGATION, DATED 3 MARCH 1967, THE MOST RECENT OFFICIAL CALL ON HIM HAVING BEEN MADE ON 25 MAY 1956. WE HAVE NO RECORD AND NO RECOLLECTION OF HIS EVER HAVING SIGNED A SECRECY AGREEMENT. HOWEVER, IN OUR EARLY OFFICIAL CONTACTS WITH HIM WE ARE QUITE SURE, IN OUR FIRST GENERAL BRIEFINGS, WE STRESSED THE CLASSIFIED NATURE OF THE CONTACTS AND ENJOINED HIM TO SECRECY REGARDING THEM. NONETHELESS, IN THE NORMAL LAWYER-CLIENT RELATIONSHIP, BECAUSE OF CIA INVOLVEMENT IN THE GARRISON INVESTIGATION, AND IN VIEW OF OUR PERSONAL AND SOCIAL CONTACTS WITH IRVING DYMOND, WE FIND IT HARD TO BELIEVE THAT THE SHAW/NOFO CONTACTS HAVE NOT BEEN MENTIONED TO DYMOND BY SHAW. IT IS CONCEIVABLE SUCH CONTACTS MAY NOT HAVE BEEN MENTIONED INITIALLY BUT AFTER THE PRESS PUBLICITY ON THE ROLE OF CIA, IN OUR OPINION THESE CONTACTS MUST SURELY HAVE BEEN DISCUSSED.

~~SECRET~~

So, the CIA "enjoined him to secrecy" regarding their relationship.

Clay Shaw was a patriotic American who provided information to the CIA. He honored the requirement to keep that secret. Had he broken his oath of secrecy, he understood that Garrison could have—no, would have—taken it all out of context.

Clay Shaw wrote about the CIA at the beginning of his attempt to write a book:

> While he [Jim Garrison] was quite impartial in scattering vituperative abuse on all of these agencies and persons, his special target was to be the CIA. This, too, was quite understandable. The CIA is a mysterious group, engaged on the carrying out of tasks that seem to have been invented by the more sensational fiction writers. It is an agency operating in complete secrecy. Even its budget is not made public, being scattered under innocuous titles throughout the budgets of various other departments.
>
> It is, in short, the most un-American of activities, and the average American has a most ambivalent attitude toward it. Of course, everyone knows and admits, that as long as the other great powers, particularly Russia, maintain intelligence systems, we must do the same. And yet, most of us consider the CIA with abhorence [sic], and a man who works for it is considered not a patriot serving his country but as a kind of E. Phillips Oppenheim villain … a somewhat sinister James Bond.

American attitudes toward the CIA in 1967 were much different than attitudes in the late 1940s and 1950s. Clay Shaw understood this perfectly.

And so, Clay Shaw respected his commitment to secrecy about his connection to the CIA and at the same time understood that that information, in the hands of Jim Garrison, would put him in serious jeopardy.

He made a wise choice.

CHAPTER 46
WAS CLAY SHAW THE ELUSIVE CLAY BERTRAND?

(EPISODE 4, 14:03)

JFK: Destiny Betrayed claims that Clay Shaw was the elusive Clay Bertrand. Here is an excerpt from a transcript:

> **Goldberg**: New Orleans attorney Dean Andrews had worked with Oswald in May of '63 in an attempt to upgrade his military discharge from its undesirable status. After the assassination, a man calling himself Clay Bertrand, phoned Andrews and asked him to consider going to Dallas to defend Oswald. Under oath, Clay Shaw denied that he was Clay Bertrand and Andrews claimed that because of the medication he was on, he had only imagined the phone call. But today, because of the work of the Assassination Records Review Board, we now have evidence and 12 people who confirm that Shaw used this name as an alias. Andrews later admitted that Shaw was Bertrand to author Harold Weisberg but made him promise not to reveal this until after Andrews' death.

Was Clay Shaw really Clay Bertrand?

Let's start with Harold Weisberg. He spent a lot of time in New Orleans assisting Jim Garrison and interviewing witnesses. He also spent some time with Dean Andrews, the jive-talking hip lawyer who told the Warren Commission that a Mr. Bertrand called him looking for a lawyer to represent Lee Harvey Oswald.

In one of their conversations, Weisberg believed that Andrews admitted that Shaw was Bertrand. Here is what Harold Weisberg wrote in his unpublished book:

> I have no way of knowing what Dean Andrews told the FBI. Andrews and I had a friendly relationship. He did tell me that Shaw and Bertrand were one.

Ok, but what specifically did Dean Andrews say? Well, researcher Joan Mellen was wondering the same thing, and she wrote Weisberg a letter:

I recall last summer when I visited: one of the things you told me, quickly, was the Dean Andrews had told you - in your talk with him - that Clay Bertrand was Clay Shaw....

Do you remember any details of that moment? Do you remember your question, and his exact answer, and his demeanor, i. e. did he seem frightened (You write about his fears in **Oswald In New Orleans**). Did he ask you not to tell anyone.

Of course by now it's TELL ALL.

Courtesy of The Weisberg Collection. Hood College, Frederick, MD, USA. URL: http://jfk.hood.edu/

And here was his reply:

Dear Joan, 6/20/01

Many apologies! This and some other mail had something laid over them and were promptly forgotten. I am sorry.

Andrews told me that Shaw was Bertrand without putting it that way. We were in his office discussing some of the evidence, what I now do not recall, when Andrew said, approximately these words, "If the Green Giant gets past that, he is home clear."

Courtesy of The Weisberg Collection. Hood College, Frederick, MD, USA. URL: http://jfk.hood.edu/

So, Andrews never really came out and said that Shaw was Bertrand. He said, "If the Green Giant gets past that, he is home clear." I think that Weisberg read just a little too much into Andrews's words.

How about the "12 people who confirm that Shaw used this name as an alias"? Over the past year, I have systematically debunked every witness that James DiEugenio uses for the allegation that Shaw was Bertrand. He went for quantity rather than quality. The sources section contains links to posts that debunk all of these witnesses.

More importantly, Garrison couldn't find Clay Bertrand back in 1967:

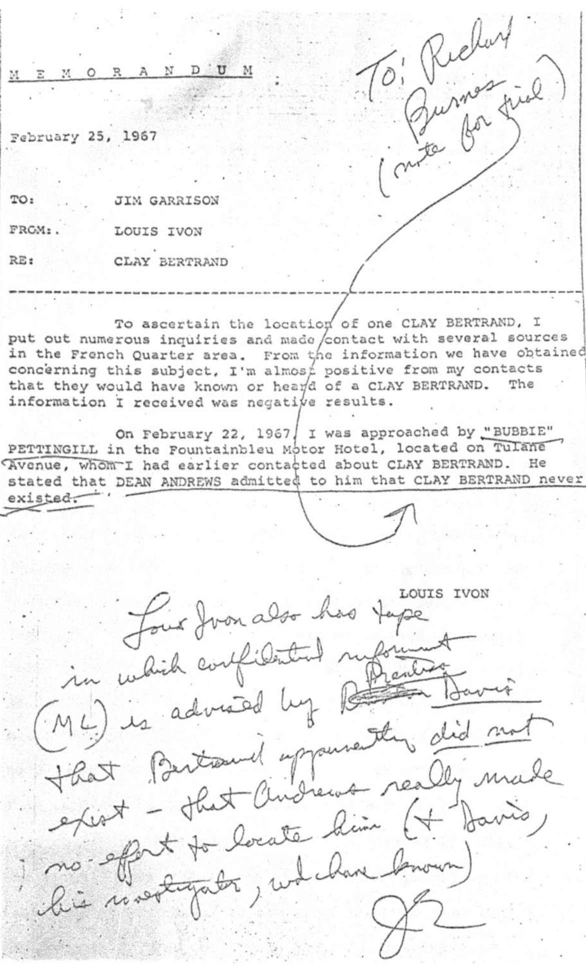

M E M O R A N D U M

To: Richard Burnes (note for trial)

February 25, 1967

TO: JIM GARRISON

FROM: LOUIS IVON

RE: CLAY BERTRAND

To ascertain the location of one CLAY BERTRAND, I put out numerous inquiries and made contact with several sources in the French Quarter area. From the information we have obtained concerning this subject, I'm almost positive from my contacts that they would have known or heard of a CLAY BERTRAND. The information I received was negative results.

On February 22, 1967, I was approached by "BUBBIE" PETTINGILL in the Fountainbleu Motor Hotel, located on Tulane Avenue, whom I had earlier contacted about CLAY BERTRAND. He stated that DEAN ANDREWS admitted to him that CLAY BERTRAND never existed.

LOUIS IVON

Lou Ivon also has tape in which confidential informant (ML) is advised by Prentiss Davis that Bertrand apparently did not exist – that Andrews really made no effort to locate him (+ Davis, his investigator, wd have known)

JG

Garrison's note at the bottom reads, "Lou Ivon [one of his chief investigators] also has tape which confidential informant (ML) is advised by Prentiss Davis [Dean Andrews' investigator] that Bertrand apparently did not exist—that Andrews really made no effort to locate him (+ Davis, his investigator, wd have known)"

Of course, the FBI and the Secret Service put in a lot of work in late 1963 trying to find Clay Bertrand, without any success.

That search for Bertrand reached right into Garrison's office:

v. 1-25-60) FEDERAL BUREAU OF INVESTIGATION

Date 11/27/63

1

RAYMOND COMSTOCK, Investigator, District Attorney's Office, advised that DEAN ANDREWS, attorney-at-law, had contacted him, attempting to identify CLAY BERTRAND. COMSTOCK advised he was familiar with a number of homosexuals in the New Orleans French Quarter but has been unable to identify this individual.

If there was a Clay Bertrand, Jim Garrison never found him. And he never came up with any credible evidence that Clay Shaw was Clay Bertrand.

THE POLITICS OF JFK: DESTINY BETRAYED

The crux of *JFK: Destiny Betrayed* is a jejune political theory that JFK was going to withdraw from Vietnam and usher in an era of peace and detente. The CIA and the military-industrial establishment had to stop this, and the only way was to have JFK killed.

Emerging from this erroneous reading of history is a nihilist prescription, that unless we unravel the JFK conspiracy, the United States can never fully realize the promise of democracy.

Here is author David Talbot: (54:11 in Episode 4)

> I think there's a direct thread between the events of 1963, and the kind of horror show that America is having to endure right now. And I think once you kill a president in broad daylight on the streets of an American city, and everyone knows that powerful forces did it, and it can never be solved, that crime, that sends a signal, not only to the American people, but to the American media, to American future leaders. And if American really wants a democratic society, then we should get to the bottom of this traumatic crime that continues to reverberate throughout American history.

What kind of message is this? Telling people that their actions are useless unless the supposed JFK conspiracy and cover-up are revealed? Is this not a nihilist recipe for inaction?

A minute later (55:30) the narrator asks this question:

> Can a democracy survive if it does not know its deepest secrets about the darkest days of its past?

None of this is new. Stone is just recycling the discredited theories of Fletcher Prouty, the model for Mr. X in his film *JFK*. Here is what Prouty wrote in his article "The Shadow of Dallas" in the January 1974 issue of *Genesis* magazine:

> Until our government moves positively against this continuing cover-up of the three assassinations, and the many related crimes, we shall not have a free and unfettered country. The "offer they cannot refuse" hangs over the head of every man in office and over his every decision.
>
> Watergate has helped us considerably. It has shown us what the will of the people can do. But until the people of this country rise up and demand that the stains of Dallas be removed, we shall continue in an uncertain manner and with an unknown shadow over us all.

This message of hopelessness is courtesy of a man who believes that Russian dictator Vladimir Putin is rational, calm, and thoughtful.

This naive theory rests on the belief that JFK wanted to completely withdraw from Vietnam, an assertion that is not backed up by the evidence.

JFK certainly understood the problems of being embroiled in a colonial war in Southeast Asia. At the same time, he was also a confirmed cold warrior, and he did not want to lose South Vietnam to the communists. He knew that the Vietnamese people would see the Americans as colonialists, and thus he thought it important to find proper Vietnamese nationalists who could defend the country.

To that end, JFK increased the number of military advisors in South Vietnam from 800 when he took office to 16,700 in November 1963. In addition, under Kennedy, the United States assisted the South Vietnamese in covert raids against North Vietnam and helped launch the strategic hamlet program, and some military advisors even participated in combat.

Let's go back and briefly look at what Kennedy was facing in Vietnam.

By the fall of 1961, the situation in Vietnam was dire. Attacks by the National Liberation Front (NLF) had greatly increased, and their control of the countryside also expanded. Kennedy sent General Maxwell Taylor and Walter Rostow to Vietnam to investigate South Vietnamese President Ngo Dinh Diem's request for American combat troops. This started an internal debate about how to move forward. Many people in the administration favored combat troops, but Kennedy decided against that option in early November. Interestingly, he was supported in that view by the CIA.

To stem the tide, Kennedy increased economic aid and sent more advisors. He also sent air reconnaissance, air transport, and helicopter units to Vietnam. American advisors were then sent to the Army of the Republic of South Vietnam (ARVN) field battalions, which then allowed them to help plan and direct operations. They were now able to fly helicopters and planes and move alongside ARVN troops in the field.

In 1962, Robert McNamara was in the midst of a major review of the Pentagon's spending. As part of his systematic approach to planning, he began to think about a long-term program to train and fund the South Vietnamese army and to phase out American combat and support activities. This partly reflected the initial optimism in the Kennedy White House that the war was going well. McNamara was also wary of an open-ended commitment like the one in South Korea.

By the end of 1962, Kennedy had sent 11,000 advisors, 300 military aircraft, 120 helicopters, and heavy weapons to Vietnam. Kennedy also allowed an experimental program of crop destruction using defoliants and herbicides such as Agent Orange.

However, by the spring of 1963, only about 20 percent of strategic hamlets were viable, and the NLF was collecting taxes in most of South Vietnam. Despite the aid, the advisors, and the military equipment, Kennedy's counterinsurgency strategy was failing.

On May 7, 1963, Robert McNamara had a meeting with President Kennedy to discuss Vietnam. He had just returned from high-level meetings in Honolulu.

Here is an excerpt from a transcript:

McNamara: I think that, as I've mentioned before, that both for domestic political purposes and also because of the psychological effect

> it would have in South Vietnam, we ought to think about the possibility of bringing a thousand men home by the end of the year. Now I've asked them to lay out that plan, without at the present time making any decision to—
>
> **Kennedy**: That's right. Because in the case that—if it isn't in very good shape you don't want to make—
>
> **McNamara**: Absolutely.
>
> **Kennedy**: Yeah. Yeah.
>
> **McNamara**: It would be … have a negative influence. But on the other hand if we had two or three victories, this would be just exactly the shot in the arm we ought to have. So they're going to do that.

As you can see, McNamara was interested in a token withdrawal for "domestic political purposes" and to pressure Diem and get the South Vietnamese moving to defend their country.

On August 29, 1963, President de Gaulle of France issued a statement:

> The serious events in Vietnam are being followed in Paris with attention and emotion. The work which France accomplished in the past … the ties which she retains in the whole country, and the interest she has in its development, lead her to understand particularly well, and share sincerely, the hardships of the Vietnamese people …

President de Gaulle also said that Vietnam would be better off free "from foreign influence." Journalist Patrick McNulty noted that "there was speculation that Gen. de Gaulle had in mind a neutral status for Vietnam, similar to that of Laos, and was casting a straw to get U.S. and Communist reaction to a troop withdrawal by both sides."

This was all dismissed by Kennedy in an interview with Walter Cronkite on September 2, 1963, in which he replied to a question about de Gaulle. "It doesn't do us any good to say, 'Well why don't we all just go home and leave the world to those who are our enemies.'" He added that "I don't agree with those who say we should withdraw. That would be a great mistake. That would be a great mistake."

And it wasn't only de Gaulle who was calling for negotiations and the possibility of neutralization. *Newsweek* and *The New Republic* both supported de Gaulle, and columnist Walter Lippman wrote that "If there is no settlement such as de Gaulle proposes, then a protracted and indecisive war of attrition is all that is left."

Walter Lippmann:

Why De Gaulle May Be Right About Viet-Nam

Seattle Daily Times, *September 5, 1963*

Logevall commented on this in his book *Choosing War*:

> What is most striking here is not the Kennedy team's rejection of de Gaulle's vaguely worded neutralization proposal; rather, it is that they refused to even consider resolving the conflict at the conference table and indeed worked to thwart any and all efforts in that direction. The vagueness of de Gaulle's plan might have been imaginatively utilized by an administration genuinely interested in negotiations; it would certainly have been utilized by a president determined to withdraw from South Vietnam.

Kennedy then told David Brinkley and Chet Huntley that "What I am concerned about is that Americans will get impatient and say because they don't like events in Southeast Asia or they don't like the government in Saigon, that we should withdraw. That only makes it easy for the communists. I think we should stay."

On September 12, JFK held a press conference:

> **QUESTION**: Mr. President, in view of the prevailing confusion, is it possible to state today just what this Government's policy is toward the current government of South Vietnam?
>
> **THE PRESIDENT**: I think I have stated what my view is and we are for those things and those policies which help win the war there. That is why some 25,000 Americans have traveled 10,000 miles to participate in that struggle. What helps to win the war we support. What interferes with the war effort we oppose. I have already made it clear that any action by either government which may handicap the winning of the war is inconsistent with our policy or our objectives. This is the test which I think every agency and official of the United

> States Government must apply to all of our actions, and we shall be applying that test in various ways in the coming months, although I do not think it desirable to state all of our views at this time. I think they will be made more clear as time goes on.
>
> But we have a very simple policy in that area. I think in some ways, I think the Vietnamese people and ourselves agree: We want the war to be won, the Communists to be contained and the Americans to go home. That is our policy. I am sure it is the policy of the people of Vietnam. But we are not there to see a war lost, and we will follow the policy which I have indicated today of advancing those causes and issues which help win the war.

On October 2, 1963, the White House issued a statement claiming that "the military program in South Viet-Nam has made progress." It also said that "the major part of the U.S. military task can be completed by the end of 1965" and that "by the end of this year, the U.S. program for training Vietnamese should have progressed to the point where 1,000 U.S. military personnel assigned to Viet-Nam can be withdrawn."

However, during the meeting with Robert McNamara, General Maxwell Taylor, and other senior advisors on October 2, 1963, Kennedy indicated that the 1965 date was not firm at all.

> **Taylor**: I will just say this: that we talked to 174 officers, Vietnamese and U.S., and in the case of the U.S., I always asked the question, "When can you finish this job in the sense that you will reduce this insurgency to little more than sporadic incidents?" Inevitably, except for the Delta, they would say, " '64 would be ample time." I realize that's not necessarily … I assume there's no major new factors entering. I realize that—
>
> **Kennedy**: Well, let's say it anyway. Then '65, if it doesn't work out, we'll get a new date.
>
> **Taylor**: '65, we'll get another.

Marc Selverstone, associate professor in presidential studies at the Miller Center, says that this conversation indicates that JFK would only withdraw from Vietnam "under propitious military circumstances."

On October 5, 1963, a cable was sent to Henry Cabot Lodge that noted:

> Actions are designed to indicate to Diem Government our displeasure at its political policies and activities and to create significant uncertainty in that government and in key Vietnamese groups as to future intentions of United States. At same time, actions are designed to have at most slight impact on military or counterinsurgency effort against Viet Cong, at least in short term.

This was codified in NSAM 263, which was issued on October 11, 1963. The purpose of this plan was to put pressure on Diem. To that end, Kennedy also canceled some future aid shipments, threatened to cut off aid for Special Forces, and recalled the CIA station chief.

Meeting with the press on October 31, Kennedy was cautious: (Emphasis added.)

> **QUESTION:** Mr. President, back to the question of troop reductions, are any intended in the Far East at the present time, particularly in Korea, and is there any speed-up in the withdrawal from Viet Nam intended?
>
> **THE PRESIDENT:** When Secretary McNamara and General Taylor came back, they announced we would expect to withdraw a thousand men from South Viet Nam before the end of the year, and there has been some reference to that by General Harkins. *If we are able to do that,* that would be our schedule. I think the first unit or first contingent would be 250 men who are not involved in what might be called front-line operations. It would be our hope to lessen the number of Americans there by 1,000, as the training intensifies, and is carried on in South Viet Nam.

On November 1, 1963, President Diem was removed in a coup and then killed. One week later, the *New York Times* call for a negotiated settlement was rejected by the Kennedy administration. Dean Rusk sent out the following memo:

DEPARTMENT OF STATE TO AMEBASSY SAIGON 781

NOV 13, 1963 6:17 PM

INFO: CINCPAC POLAD

AMEBASSY LONDON 3066

AMEBASSY PARIS 2470

AMEBASSY BANGKOK 773

AMEBASSY OTTAWA (POUCH)

AMEBASSY NEW DELHI (POUCH)

AMEBASSY VIENTIANE (POUCH)

AMEBASSY PHNOM PENH (POUCH)

At your discretion you may wish to reassure GVN that New York Times Nov 10 editorial and Reston column few days earlier suggesting new negotiated settlement of Vietnam problem do not rpt not represent US Government policy.

Our policy remains as outlined by President Kennedy in December 1961:

"The United States, like the Republic of Vietnam, remains devoted to the cause of peace and our primary purpose is to help South Vietnam's people maintain their independence. If the Communist authorities in North Vietnam will stop their campaign to destroy the Republic of Vietnam, the measures we are taking to assist South Vietnam's defense efforts will no longer be necessary." This policy reaffirmed by Secretary at Nov. 8 press conference.

Our goal is thus to return to cease-fire established by 1954 Geneva Accords. If Hanoi will cease and desist in subversive aggression against RVN, and GVN is thereby enabled to extend its authority throughout South Vietnam, US will withdraw its forces from South Vietnam because reason for their presence and support of GVN will have ceased to exist.

We see no necessity for international negotiations as suggested by Times to return to a peaceful SVN free of attempted subversion from outside. Within concept US policy as outlined by President we cannot envisage any points that would be negotiable. Good faith of our withdrawal intentions has already been established by announcement we shall withdraw 1,000 US military personnel by end 1963.

Rusk

This cable underscores the complete lack of interest of the Kennedy administration in using diplomacy to settle the Vietnam conflict. The ARVN generals were not an improvement over Diem, and the situation in Vietnam continued to deteriorate.

At his news conference on November 14, 1963, Kennedy indicated that the number of troops to be withdrawn was not set in stone:

> QUESTION: Mr. President, in view of the changed situation in South Viet Nam, do you still expect to bring back 1,000 troops before the end of the year, or has that figure been raised or lowered?
>
> Kennedy: No, we are going to bring back several hundred before the end of the year, but I think on the question of the exact number I thought we would wait until the meeting of November 20th.

On November 20, 1963, many of Kennedy's top advisors met in Honolulu to discuss the situation in Vietnam. Their briefing book had the following chart indicating a large increase in Viet Cong attacks:

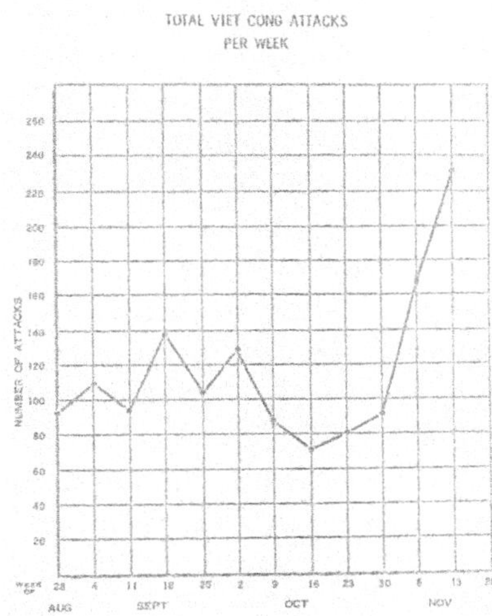

A summary of their discussion included this paragraph:

> Secretary McNamara summarized the present situation as follows. South Vietnam is under tremendous pressure from the VC. The VC are as numerous today as they were a year or two years ago. The surrounding area is weaker. The Cambodian situation is potentially very serious to the RVN. The input of arms from Cambodia before the recent developments was very worrisome in the Delta. The Generals head a very fragile government. The United States should not try to cut the comers too fine. We must be prepared to devote enough resources to this job of winning the war to be certain of accomplishing it instead of just hoping to accomplish it.

This was the message that was supposed to have been delivered to JFK.

Unfortunately, Lee Harvey Oswald got in the way.

The speech that JFK was going to deliver in Dallas mentioned the possibility that American combat troops might be needed in Vietnam:

> But American military might should not and need not stand alone against the ambitions of international communism. Our security and strength, in the last analysis, directly depend on the security and strength of others, and that is why our military and economic assistance plays such a key role in enabling those who live on the periphery of the Communist world to maintain their independence of choice. Our assistance to these nations can be painful, risky and costly, as is true in Southeast Asia today. But we dare not weary of the task.
>
> For our assistance makes possible the stationing of 3-5 million allied troops along the Communist frontier at one-tenth the cost of maintaining a comparable number of American soldiers. A successful Communist breakthrough in these areas, necessitating direct United States intervention, would cost us several times as much as our entire foreign aid program, and might cost us heavily in American lives as well.
>
> About 70 percent of our military assistance goes to nine key countries located on or near the borders of the Communist bloc—nine countries confronted directly or indirectly with the threat of Communist aggression—Viet-Nam, Free China, Korea, India, Pakistan, Thailand, Greece, Turkey, and Iran. No one of these countries possesses on its

> own the resources to maintain the forces which our own Chiefs of Staff think needed in the common interest. Reducing our efforts to train, equip, and assist their armies can only encourage Communist penetration and require in time the increased overseas deployment of American combat forces.

JFK: Destiny Betrayed makes the claim that NSAM 273, drafted two days before Kennedy was killed but released after the assassination, made a big change in American foreign policy. However, it was virtually identical to NSAM 263 and had the same commitment to the one-thousand-troop withdrawal. The only change was in article 7 pertaining to military action against North Vietnam. Fredrick Logevall called the differences "insignificant" as the United States was already directing covert military action against the North. Stanley Karnow, one of the foremost historians of the Vietnam war, said that NSAM 273 "perpetuated the Kennedy policy."

Even Robert McNamara agreed and wrote in his book *In Retrospect: The Tragedy and Lessons of Vietnam* that NSAM 273 "made clear that Johnson's policy remained the same as Kennedy's: 'To assist the people and Government of South Vietnam to win their contest against the externally directed and supported Communist conspiracy' through training support and without the application of overt U.S. military force."

Marc Selverstone noted that "operations against North Vietnam had never generated much discomfort for JFK. In fact, Kennedy's interest in supporting covert action against Hanoi actually increased during his time in office, from his initial eagerness in January 1961, to his repeated inquiries about their impact in 1962, to his support for improving their effectiveness in 1963."

JFK: Destiny Betrayed mentions OPLAN 34A, a set of covert operations against Hanoi that was adopted in December 1963 by Lyndon Johnson, as proof that NSAM 273 changed policy. However, planning for this operation began during the Kennedy administration and was discussed at the November conference in Honolulu. Selverstone writes that the plan "stemmed from a belief that actions against the North needed to be larger, more frequent, and more systematic, even in the face of CIA doubts about their value."

While McNamara was planning for a withdrawal, other Kennedy aides were unaware of what Kennedy really wanted. Dean Rusk wrote in his book *As I Saw It* that he "talked with John Kennedy on hundreds of occasions about Southeast Asia, and not once did he ever suggest or even hint at withdrawal."

He added:

> Kennedy liked to bat the breeze and toss ideas around and it is entirely possible that he left the impression with some that he planned on getting out of Vietnam in 1965. But that does not mean that he made a decision in 1963 to withdraw in 1965. Had he done so, I think I would have known about it.

And Robert Kennedy said much the same thing in an oral history interview with John Bartlow Martin in 1964:

> **Kennedy**: The President felt that he had a strong, overwhelming reason for being in Vietnam and that we should win the war in Vietnam.
>
> **Martin**: What was the overwhelming reason?
>
> **Kennedy**: The loss of all of Southeast Asia if you lost Vietnam. I think everybody was quite clear that the rest of Southeast Asia would fall.
>
> **Martin**: What if it did?
>
> **Kennedy**: It would just have profound effects on our position throughout the world, and our position in a rather vital part of the world. It would affect what happened in India, of course, which in turn has an effect on the Middle East. It would have, everybody felt, a very adverse effect. It would have an effect on Indonesia, with a hundred million population. All of these countries would be affected by the fall of Vietnam to the Communists, particularly as we had made such a fuss in the United States both under President Eisenhower and President Kennedy about the preservation of the integrity of Vietnam.
>
> **Martin**: There was never any consideration given to pulling out?
>
> **Kennedy**: No.
>
> **Martin**: But the same time, no disposition to go in—
>
> **Kennedy**: No.
>
> **Martin**: —in an all-out way as we went into Korea. We were trying to avoid a Korea—is that correct?
>
> **Kennedy**: Yes, because everybody, including General MacArthur felt that land conflict between our troops—white troops and Asian—

> would only end in disaster. So we went in as advisers to try to get the Vietnamese to fight, themselves, because we couldn't win the war for them. They had to win the war for themselves.
>
> **Martin**: That's generally true all over the world, whether it's in a shooting war or a different kind of a war. But the President was convinced that we had to stay in there?
>
> **Kennedy**: Yes.
>
> **Martin**: And we couldn't lose it.
>
> **Kennedy**: Yes.
>
> **Martin**: And if Vietnamese were about to lose it, would he propose to go in on land if he had to?
>
> **Kennedy**: Well, we'd face that when we came to it.

JFK never had to face it. Logevall notes that "the Vietnam problem that he left behind that day was much larger than the one he inherited."

Professors Lawrence Bassett and Stephen Pelz elaborate on the problems awaiting Lyndon Johnson:

> In any case, by late 1963 Kennedy had radically expanded the American commitment to Vietnam. By putting advisors in harm's way and allowing the press to chronicle their tribulations and casualties, he helped to engage American patriotism in a war against the Vietnamese people. By arguing that Vietnam was a test of American credibility in the Cold War, he raised the costs of withdrawal for his successor. By launching a strategic hamlet program, he further disrupted peasant society. By allowing Harkins and the ARVN to bomb, shell, search, and destroy, he made so many recruits for the NLF that he encouraged North Vietnam and the NLF to move the war into its final military phase. By participating in Diem's removal, he brought warlords politics to Saigon. By downplaying publicly the American role in Vietnam, he discouraged a constitutional debate about the commitment of American advisors to battle. By publicly and privately committing the United States to the survival of an anti-Communist state in South Vietnam, he made it much more difficult for his successors to blame the South Vietnamese government for its own failures and to withdraw. And by insisting that military victory was the only acceptable outcome, he ignored the possibility that negotiations might lead to an acceptable process of retreat. Kennedy bequeathed to Lyndon B. Johnson a failing

> counterinsurgency program and a deepened commitment to the war in South Vietnam.

JFK was facing quite the mess in Vietnam when he was assassinated. The truth is that we don't know what he would have done had he not been killed. Unfortunately, *JFK: Destiny Betrayed* has a certainty that is belied by the official record.

DID THE ARRB PROVE A CONSPIRACY IN THE JFK ASSASSINATION?

Oliver Stone claims in *JFK Revisited: Through the Looking Glass* that the Assassination Records Review Board (ARRB) turned conspiracy theories into conspiracy facts.

Here is an excerpt from a transcript:

> With all the documents declassified by the Review Board, we can see this scene [Dealey Plaza] in a new light. In regard to the JFK assassination, conspiracy theories are now conspiracy facts. The forensics show evidence of multiple shooters, with Oswald not even at the sixth-floor window at the time of the assassination. And his fingerprints not found on the supposed murder weapon. Still, there was no trial for Lee Harvey Oswald.

James DiEugenio, the screenplay writer of *JFK Revisited,* also said this on Twitter:

James DiEugenio
@jimmydie1963

Oliver Stone and JFK Revisited are trending on Twitter due to Glenn Greenwald. Oliver will discuss his new documentary on Joe Rogan tomorrow. It is not conspiracy theory. It is conspiracy fact.

9:42 AM · Dec 15, 2021 · Twitter Web App

30 Retweets 4 Quote Tweets 146 Likes

The idea that the ARRB has proved conspiracy in the JFK assassination has been repeated many times by James DiEugenio. For instance:

> By creating a smoke and mirrors distraction, [film reviewer James] Kirchick can sidestep what does exist in the film [JFK Revisited]. That is the revelations of the Assassination Records Review Board (ARRB) which completely overturn the verdict of the Warren Commission.

Here he claims the ARRB passed judgment on the Warren Commission:

> What the film does is it exposes the Commission as an utterly corrupt body. And that view was made possible only by the ARRB.

And here:

> Oliver could make much more money doing features. He took a very big pay cut in doing this film. He did it because no one else would tell the public about the ARRB discoveries. Patrick Collins sure as heck is not going to, because they destroy the W[arren] R[eport].

DiEugenio says the ARRB even proved Jim Garrison was right:

> It turned out the ARRB proved he was right about almost everything he said.

And he makes ridiculous claims about the ARRB:

> *We know today that CE 399 was worse than a joke: it was a smoke and mirrors illusion. The work of the ARRB—which Litwin avoids like CV-19—has made it superfluous.*

DiEugenio makes unwarranted conclusions about the ARRB:

> All one needs to know about what happened to the HSCA is that it took the ARRB to show us the depth of the fraud the Magic Bullet was mired in.

The ARRB did some amazing work in seeing that millions of pages of documents were released. But did those documents prove conspiracy? Let's quickly look at a few examples from Oliver Stone's pseudo-documentary.

The story of John Stringer, the photographer of JFK's autopsy, is extremely illustrative (see Chapter 16). Anybody who reads through his deposition before the ARRB quickly realizes that his memory was not very good.

For instance, he could not remember if he had used Kodachrome or Ektachrome film. And yet *JFK: Destiny Betrayed* makes a big deal of the fact that he did not remember using ANSCO film for the photographs of JFK's brain. Stringer was momentarily confused when he was shown these photographs because there were no identification tags, although he did not remember if he even used them.

But to Oliver Stone and James DiEugenio, that is more than enough for them to believe that Stringer photographed a different brain. Now, which is more likely? A different brain, or forgetting minor details after thirty-two years?

There are many other examples of how *JFK: Destiny Betrayed* misrepresents ARRB interviews and depositions to make unwarranted conclusions. For instance, forensic pathologist Robert Kirschner told the ARRB that there was a perfectly reasonable explanation for the greyish appearance of JFK's brain in the autopsy photographs. *JFK: Destiny Betrayed* ignored his explanation and made it appear that he also agreed that there was something amiss with the photographs.

The family of White House photographer Robert Knudsen told the ARRB suspicious stories about the autopsy photographs that were hard to believe. *JFK: Destiny Betrayed* ignored Knudsen's testimony before the HSCA that the autopsy photographs were not inconsistent with the ones he saw. And Saundra Spencer told the ARRB that she developed autopsy photographs that were different from the current inventory. But the pictures she supposedly saw could hardly have been taken at the autopsy.

It is one thing for Stone and DiEugenio to use ARRB documents to reach their own conclusions. It is quite another thing to mislead people into believing that the ARRB uncovered proof that there was a conspiracy.

This overreach obscured the real mission of the organization. The final report of the ARRB notes:

> The JFK Act, however, necessitates that the Review Board's report be different from reports of other assassination-related commissions and committees. Previous assassination-related commissions and committees were established for the purpose of issuing final reports that would draw conclusions about the assassination. Congress did not, however, direct the Review Board to draw conclusions about the assassination, but to release assassination records so that the public could draw its own conclusions. Thus, the Final Report does not offer conclusions about what the assassination records released did or did not prove.

In 1998, Tom Samoluk, deputy director of the ARRB, had to reiterate this in a letter to James DiEugenio:

> First, the statutory mission of the Board under the JFK Act is to release records related to the assassination of President John F. Kennedy (as opposed to reaching any substantive conclusions about who killed the President) and that is the sole measure by which it should be judged. By this measure, the Board has done an outstanding job. Publication of this Probe issue comes at a time when the Board has once again demonstrated its effectiveness by processing 5,000 additional records in January for public release, more than any other month. The Board has taken a firm stance against the CIA, the

> FBI, and other federal agencies in dealing with important issues related to the release of records. Similarly, the Board and the staff have been aggressive in locating additional records both within and outside of government.
>
> Second, in all of the closed meetings, no Board member has ever argued that something should not be released because it did or did not support any theory of the assassination. The Board has scrupulously opened all information without regard to any particular belief about the assassination. For the Board's work of declassifying records, theories are not relevant. Hence the Board members have put aside their own personal opinions and have done a professional and objective job. Moreover, in hiring the staff, the Board never once imposed a litmus test or even asked what staff member opinions are relative to the assassination.

Judge Tunheim and Tom Samoluk both appear in *JFK: Destiny Betrayed* to talk about the work of the ARRB. But their segments are sandwiched between allegations that the ARRB proved conspiracy.

For instance, in Episode 1 of *JFK: Destiny Betrayed*, Tunheim and Samoluk discuss the processing of documents for release and the process of purchasing the Zapruder film for the National Archives. Tunheim calls it "the most important piece of evidence." (47:55) The next scene shows the "back and to the left" motion of JFK's head. Do viewers think, at least subliminally, that Tunheim and Samoluk are back-and-to-the leftists?

In Episode 4, Tunheim and Samoluk discuss the Secret Service's destruction of two boxes of domestic survey reports. Here is an excerpt from a transcript: (19:25)

> **Judge Tunheim**: They destroyed a group of records which involved threats to President Kennedy in the fall of 1963. They have what they're called threat sheets and there were many threats made to President Kennedy's life during the year 1963. They fought us on the release of those records. They even enlisted Vice President Gore's wife to help them because she had a very legitimate concern for mental health records. And the idea was that this might disclose the names of people who had mental health problems.

No doubt Tunheim and Samoluk were right to be upset about the destruction of two boxes of records. But right after their appearance in *JFK: Destiny Betrayed,* the documentary moves to supposed plots against JFK in Chicago and Miami. The juxtaposition is not by accident. Since there is no documentary evidence that there was a threat in Chicago, *JFK: Destiny Betrayed* uses Tunheim and Samoluk to imply that the destroyed records contained valuable information related to the supposed plot.

But the HSCA had already looked at Secret Service documents during that period:

> The committee discovered that the 1963 Protective Research Section files had since been summarized and computerized, (*36*) and the original files then destroyed. The committee thus reviewed the computerized summaries of PRS case files for the period March to December 1963. (*37*) The summaries indicated that during this period, the PRS received information on over 400 possible threats to the President, approximately 20 percent of which could have been attributed to political motivation. The committee then reviewed the trip files for 1963 to determine which threats the Secret Service had recognized as significant. (*38*) Although there are other concepts of significance, the committee decided to limit its review to those that actually caused cancellation of a trip, an alteration of the President's planned itinerary, or an intensive preliminary investigative effort by the Secret Service. By limiting the definition in this way, the committee believed it could reach a clear determination of the manner in which the Secret Service responded to significant threats.

No evidence has ever materialized to corroborate the supposed Chicago plot.

The Secret Service wrote a letter to the ARRB noting that "the folder concerning the canceled trip to Chicago would only have contained a preliminary survey report, if any document at all, since final reports are not conducted when a trip is canceled." Preliminary survey reports are just the basic plans for a trip. And Secret Service Agent Gerald Blaine found copies of the survey reports at his house and has since donated them to the National Archives.

As indicated earlier, DiEugenio and Stone's "poverty of imagination" means they aren't capable of considering non-conspiratorial explanations. For instance, they claim that the refusal of the family of Dr. George Burkley to allow ARRB investigators to go through the papers of his lawyer was sinister. But he was conferring with his lawyer on tax issues, and there was no reason to believe he would have any relevant documents.

Indeed, Judge Tunheim has never claimed that the ARRB proved conspiracy in the JFK assassination. Here is what he had to say in 2017:

Reporter: Based on everything that you've read, which is the whole file that has been a secret, do you believe that President Kennedy's assassination was a conspiracy or done by a lone gunman?

Judge Tunheim: I think, first of all, the only hard evidence supports Oswald. It was his rifle, his prints were all over it, he worked in the building. He was in the building during the assassination. The bullets in the vehicle that hit Kennedy were tied to that gun. This is all evidence that would have convicted Oswald beyond a shadow of a doubt. I think he was the sole shooter that day ....

Judge Tunheim: That's probably the best evidence of a conspiracy is Ruby ....

Judge Tunheim: [Kennedy] had a lot of enemies, yeah. But when you actually look at the massive evidence through the years, there's no evidence of a conspiracy ... I think everyone should keep an open mind in case there are further disclosures in the future, but up until this point, there's no real hard evidence of a conspiracy that could convict anyone of a conspiracy ....

Anna Nelson, one of the historians on the ARRB, concurred with Judge Tunheim that they did not find evidence of conspiracy:

The Review Board found no conspiracy. The Review Board looked for conspiracy. Very clearly looked for conspiracy. It felt that was something we, we had to do. We found no conspiracy inside the government. Whether anyone can ever go through all those records and find conspiracy outside the government, we didn't see it. Maybe somebody can. I think that we did not help the conspiracy theories but there are many people who are still using our records to prove their own theories. As will always happen. But I have a great trust that in the long run, once you release documents and you have a number of people looking at them, the truth ultimately will come to the fore, my optimism as a historian.

Henry Graff, former chairman of Columbia University's history department, concurred:

> I have found nothing to suggest there was anything but a single gunman. What put him up to it and whether this was just one of those random acts of history, I don't think we'll ever know.

The millions of pages of documents that the ARRB released gave James DiEugenio and Oliver Stone a larger playpen. Their documentary proves that it takes adults to actually understand the documents.

AFTERWORD—THE DEMAGOGUE OF DEALEY PLAZA

As I was finishing up this book, I started reading Jonathan Rauch's book *The Constitution of Knowledge: A Defense of Truth.* He claims that the United States is facing an "epistemic crisis: a multifront challenge to America's ability to distinguish fact from fiction and elevate truth above falsehood."

JFK: Destiny Betrayed is part of that challenge. It is certainly a direct assault on truth.

The issue of 544 Camp Street (see Chapter 43) is a good example of the transubstantiation of fiction into fact. *JFK: Destiny Betrayed* used a fake flyer to imply that Lee Harvey Oswald worked out of Guy Banister's office at 544 Camp Street. Viewers are never informed that Banister's office was actually around the corner at 531 Lafayette. Anybody using the entrance on Camp Street in 1963 would find the offices of the Hotel, Motel and Restaurant Workers' Union and the Amalgamated Association of Street Electric Railway and Motor Coach Employees of America. They would not find Guy Banister.

Statement upon statement in *JFK: Destiny Betrayed* is just not true. For instance, in Episode 4, it is stated that David Ferrie was "a trainer and a pilot for the CIA." There is absolutely no evidence to back up this statement, and the sources presented in the book of the film transcript just point to other conspiracy books. I count at least thirty conspiracy books among the citations for *JFK: Destiny Betrayed.*

And *JFK: Destiny Betrayed* gets outright kooky when it claims that "few people knew that there had been at least two prior plots to kill Kennedy in

1963." As I have shown earlier, there was no prior plot to kill JFK in Chicago (see Chapter 39), nor was there a plot in Tampa (see Chapter 41). But at least two? The book of the annotated film transcript contains an interview with conspiracy theorist Paul Bleau:

Oliver Stone: Describe please the prior plots around John F. Kennedy before Dallas and explain for us their importance.

Paul Bleau: Well, the complete failure by the Warren Commission to look into at least seven plots that failed during the last six months—

Stone: Seven?

Bleau: At least seven, seven that failed in the last six months of Kennedy's life, is a glaring example of how the Warren Commission investigation was inept. Because had they done so, they would have recognized the template, they would have been able to build an offender profile, and even round up suspects.

Because Bleau believes there is a connection between these plots, the Warren Commission should have "been able to build an offender profile, and even round [ed] up suspects." Unfortunately, Bleau's allegations of other plots are equally as tendentious as his allegations about plots in Chicago and Tampa.

When I downloaded my copy of the Kindle edition of James DiEugenio's annotated screenplay for *JFK: Destiny Betrayed,* I was astonished by the fact he did not provide hot links to articles and documents. For my last book, *On the Trail of Delusion—Jim Garrison: The Great Accuser,* I spent weeks adding hundreds of links to my "Notes and Sources" section. This book provides links to relevant documents that should have been included by DiEugenio.

For instance, here is DiEugenio's note on the segment regarding the Katzenbach memo: (55:30 in Episode 2; page 177; See Chapter 2)

Hoover's memo to LBJ is written about by reporter Alex Johnson in an NBC news report of October 26, 2017. The tape and transcript of Hoover saying the case against Oswald is not that strong is at history-matters.com titled "LBJ-Hoover 11-22-63." The memorandum by Katzenbach is at the Mary Ferrell Foundation website, labeled simply "Katzenbach Memo."

The link to history-matters.com just goes to the web site and not to the actual document. He could have easily put in a link to the Katzenbach memo, as I did in my post on this section of the documentary (see Chapter 2 for the actual memo).

Worse, most of the citations for *JFK: Destiny Betrayed* are from other conspiracy books. For instance, in Episode 4, *JFK: Destiny Betrayed* presented a segment on David Ferrie: (10:14)

> **Narrator (Whoopi Goldberg)**: In the spring of 1963, Oswald moved from Dallas back to his home town of New Orleans, where he began associating with men who, it would be revealed, had clear connections with these government efforts. One of these men, David Ferrie, had been with Oswald in the Civil Air Patrol back in 1955, and was known as an extreme anti-communist. He was also a trainer and a pilot for the CIA in its secret war against Cuba. Oswald was involved with these Cuban exile training activities with Ferrie.

The footnote regarding this segment caught my eye:

> The relationship of David Ferrie in the CAP with Oswald, and Ferrie's anti-Castro activities are dealt with in William Davy's Let Justice Be Done, pp 3–10, 25–33; information about Oswald being at the training camp is on p. 30; that information is also noted in Dick Russell's book The Man Who Knew Too Much (p. 329). Ferrie's activities are sketched in Deadly Secrets by Warren Hinckle and William Turner (pp. 232–33). Ferrie's life and career is also written about in HSCA, vol. 10 (pp. 105–114).

Once again, no link to the HSCA volume and not even Amazon links to the conspiracy books that he cites. Besides the HSCA, primary sources are not cited.

The Turner and Davy books are standard conspiracy books that accept that Jim Garrison really did have a case against Clay Shaw. The Dick Russell book required some investigation, and it provides a good case study of why you should not rely upon secondary sources.

Page 329 of *The Man Who Knew Too Much* had the following quote from a Colonel William C. Bishop:

> In many instances, what I picked up was after the fact. I did look into Oswald's background. I'd never met him, but I'd seen him in a training film in New Orleans the past summer. He just happened to be in the group out there at the Pontchartrain camp.

But Colonel William C. Bishop was a contact of Robert D. Morrow, an author of two books claiming that he had inside knowledge of the JFK assassination. His first book, *Betrayal,* claimed that Jack Ruby, Eladio del Valle, Guy Banister, David Ferrie, and Clay Shaw organized a plot to kill John F. Kennedy. Morrow claimed that he was the man who bought the Mannlicher-Carcano rifle that killed JFK.

According to Dick Russell, Morrow met a man in the early 1960s who had the "war name" of Oscar del Valle Garcia. His true name was Bill Bishop, and he called Morrow up in 1983 because he was dying of terminal cancer and "wanted to set the record straight." Supposedly Morrow flew to Cleburne, Texas, and interviewed Bishop.

Bishop's terminal cancer wasn't that terminal, and in 1990 Russell received Morrow's file on Bishop and then went to researcher Gary Shaw's house to actually meet him. Bishop told Russell a variety of ridiculous claims, including that he was assigned by the CIA to assassinate Dominican Republic dictator Rafael Trujillo.

In 1992, researcher Gary Shaw played Russell a portion of a tape on which Bishop claimed he participated in the CIA's MK-ULTRA program:

> "That was how, after the Korean War, I got involved with the CIA," Bishop said. "I have been subjected to every known type of drug. The medical doctors connected with the agency found that certain drugs work quite well in conjunction with hypnosis—hypnotic power of suggestion—with some subjects. It did with me. I speak with absolute certainty and knowledge and experience that this is not only possible, but did and is taking place today."

The talkative Bishop had more to say.

In 1983, Robert Morrow submitted a script for a one-hour documentary on the JFK assassination, in which Colonel Bishop played a major role. Morrow alleged Bishop was the "CIA man selected to personally report to President Kennedy on all matters pertaining to Cuba," that he gave Kennedy proof of missiles in Cuba in March 1962, that he personally met with Jack Ruby several times and that Ruby was a gun runner for Alpha 66, that he met Clay Shaw in 1967 as Clay Bertram, that he flew with David Ferrie into Cuba at the Bay of Pigs, that he had killed Jimmy Hoffa in Canada, and that he was at Parkland Hospital when JFK was brought in after the assassination.

Concluding the script, Morrow wrote that "Bishop seems to be the most likely candidate to have engineered the President's death."

Could this get any sillier?

And yet Colonel William Bishop is a key source, cited indirectly by James DiEugenio, regarding Lee Harvey Oswald being at an anti-Castro Cuban training camp across Lake Pontchartrain in the summer of 1963.

Total fantasy is presented as fact.

The commentary track on the Blu-Ray disc of *JFK Revisited: Through the Looking Glass* offers even more fiction. For instance, Oliver Stone views the sixth floor of the Texas School Book Depository as a stage, complete with props:

Oliver Stone: The Sixth Floor seems to me to be a staging ground for your theater. This is your, this is your stage, the props are put here.

James DiEugenio: Yes.

Oliver Stone: The bullets, the rifle, but no one's up there.

Despite the fact that several witnesses saw a gunman fire from the sixth-floor window, to Oliver Stone and James DiEugenio, no one was there. The rifle and bullet cartridges, to them, are just part of a spectacle perpetrated by the conspirators.

Going even further, Oliver Stone wonders about the coffin on the plane going to Washington:

Oliver Stone: Amazing shots. I wish there had been more coverage of the sixth floor, because people would understand that it was a setup,

> and here's Johnson going back to Washington, very famous, very famous scene and the famous coffin coming off the plane, which of course was questioned by David Lifton and people like that. Now who's in the coffin is a very good question.

Who's in the coffin? Really?

As shown in Chapter 12, *JFK: Destiny Betrayed* maligns Dr. George Burkley with several falsehoods. But Stone goes even further:

> **Oliver Stone**: Burkley is like [Dr.] Malcolm Perry but he's even more scared. You have to understand the human factor, your fear, always fear, so many of the witnesses died. So many people were mysteriously killed in the aftermath of that murder. And, it's obvious that something was going wrong. Cooperation with the authorities had a price.

Burkley was scared because "so many people were mysteriously killed"?

And then Oliver Stone moves on to his ultimate fantasy:

> **Oliver Stone**: I'm firmly convinced that Oswald knew something was gonna go down against Kennedy. And he was thinking that I'm protecting the president. I'm helping to protect him. This is what I'm worried—I'm working with people who were supposed to be protecting the president. Yet, in the in the months that ensue, which are closing in now, at the end of '63, he starts to realize that there's not ... they're not being straight with him, that there are people who want to hurt Kennedy.

Oswald thought he was protecting JFK?

Jonathan Rauch believes that "the purpose of the [Russian] disinformation campaign [to convince people that the Kremlin not poison former Russian military intelligence officer Sergei Skripal in 2018] is to drown Western intelligence in a cacophony of wild claims, rather than a coherent counter-narrative."

This could equally apply to Oliver Stone and James DiEugenio. They can string together a whole bunch of wild claims, but they will never provide a "coherent counter-narrative" about the JFK assassination. In a rare attempt to provide some sort of explanation, James DiEugenio said this on *Black Op Radio* in September 2022:

> In the film, we cast aspersions upon Allen Dulles, and I believe that Allen Dulles, and Jim Garrison thought so also, that he was part of the conspiracy. And I believe that what Allen Dulles was, he was the connection point between the upper level of the plot, which I believe was the Eastern establishment, power elite, whatever you want to call it, and the actual working out of the plot, okay, which I believe was done by people like Jim Angleton and David Phillips, at the management level, and then you had the people on the ground, who were actually doing the handiwork.

He believes many things, but is there any actual evidence?

Jonathan Rauch writes that "reverence for facts is the true north of the reality-based community." He quotes Aleksandr Solzhenitsyn:

> You can resolve to live your life with integrity. Let your credo be this: Let the lie come into the world, let it even triumph. But not through me. The simple step of a courageous individual is not to take part in the lie. One word of truth outweighs the world.

In my opinion, *JFK: Destiny Betrayed* belongs on the ash heap of history.

After the release of *JFK: Destiny Betrayed*, another documentary, *The Assassination and Mrs. Paine,* went after innocent people. This time it's Ruth and Michael Paine—honest people who went out of their way to help the Oswalds. Aspersions are now being cast on their good deeds, and accusations of their being involved with the CIA abound. Not surprisingly, James DiEugenio plays a prominent role in this documentary.

When will the JFK conspiracy crowd realize that they are hurting innocent people? And when will decency finally return?

A VIEWER'S GUIDE TO JFK: DESTINY BETRAYED

Here is a listing of all the essays and posts from my blog at https://www.onthetrailofdelusion.com/blog related to *JFK: Destiny Betrayed*. In many cases, these blog posts contain more documents and pictures than appear in this book. Please note that some of these posts were written before the release of the four-hour *JFK: Destiny Betrayed* and thus refer to the two-hour *JFK Revisited*.

This Viewer's Guide is available on my web site:

https://www.onthetrailofdelusion.com/post/a-viewer-s-guide-to-jfk-destiny-betrayed-and-jfk-revisited

Essays

Oliver Stone's Poverty of Imagination

https://www.onthetrailofdelusion.com/post/oliver-stone-s-poverty-of-imagination

He cannot imagine any sort of non-conspiratorial explanations for any of the suspicious pieces of evidence in his film.

What Ever Happened to Jim Garrison?

https://www.onthetrailofdelusion.com/post/what-ever-happened-to-jim-garrison

Jim Garrison is AWOL in Oliver Stone's so-called documentary *JFK: Destiny Betrayed*.

The Enabling of Oliver Stone

https://www.onthetrailofdelusion.com/post/the-enabling-of-oliver-stone

An essay on the intellectual monstrosity of *JFK: Destiny Betrayed*.

Max Boot on Oliver Stone's Lies

https://www.onthetrailofdelusion.com/post/max-boot-on-oliver-stone-s-lies

A good review of *JFK Revisited* by historian Max Boot in the *Washington Post*.

Oliver Stone with *JFK Revisited* Crucifies Clay Shaw Once Again

https://www.onthetrailofdelusion.com/post/oliver-stone-with-jfk-revisited-crucifies-clay-shaw-once-again

There is something really obscene about Oliver Stone once again going after Clay Shaw.

JFK Revisited Lays an Egg

https://www.onthetrailofdelusion.com/post/jfk-revisited-lays-an-egg

Oliver Stone took to Twitter last weekend to bemoan the fact that the mainstream press is ignoring his so-called documentary, *JFK Revisited: Through the Looking Glass.*

JFK Revisited Star Believes in a Massive COVID Conspiracy

https://www.onthetrailofdelusion.com/post/jfk-revisited-star-believes-in-a-massive-covid-conspiracy

Robert Kennedy, Jr. believes in a massive conspiracy regarding COVID-19 and the intelligence agencies.

Is the JFK Assassination Linked to 9/11 and COVID-19?

https://www.onthetrailofdelusion.com/post/is-the-jfk-assassination-linked-to-9-11-and-covid-19

Just when I thought conspiracy theorists couldn't get any crazier.

"Guilt by Orientation"—The CIA Strikes Again!

https://www.onthetrailofdelusion.com/post/guilt-by-orientation-the-cia-strikes-again

James Kirchick's terrific article on Oliver Stone and homosexuality.

Oliver Stone's *JFK Revisited* Screenwriter Reprimanded by ARRB in 1998 https://steveroeconsulting.wixsite.com/website/post/oliver-stone-s-jfk-revisited-screenwriter-reprimanded-by-arrb-in-1998

An exchange of letters between James DiEugenio and Jeremy Gunn of the ARRB.

Did the ARRB Prove a Conspiracy in the JFK Assassination?

https://www.onthetrailofdelusion.com/post/did-the-arrb-prove-a-conspiracy-in-the-jfk-assassination

Oliver Stone makes the claim in his so-called documentary *JFK Revisited: Through the Looking Glass* that the Assassination Records Review Board (ARRB) turned conspiracy theories into conspiracy facts. But is this really true?

A Letter from Bill Baxley about Oliver Stone

https://www.onthetrailofdelusion.com/post/a-letter-from-bill-baxley-about-oliver-stone

A former attorney general of Alabama, Bill Baxley, writes a letter about Oliver Stone.

Oliver Stone Admits *JFK Revisited* is a Flop

https://www.onthetrailofdelusion.com/post/oliver-stone-admits-jfk-revisited-is-a-flop

Oliver Stone admits that the mainstream media is ignoring his cartoon.

Grovelling at the Feet of *Le Grand Complotiste*

https://www.onthetrailofdelusion.com/post/grovelling-at-the-feet-of-le-grand-complotiste

A look at Oliver Stone's visit to Quebec City.

JFK: Destiny Betrayed, Episode 1

(11:49)

JFK: Destiny Betrayed Misleads on Allen Dulles and the Warren Commission

https://www.onthetrailofdelusion.com/post/jfk-destiny-betrayed-misleads-on-allen-dulles-and-the-warren-commission

The evidence is clear: Robert Kennedy wanted Allen Dulles on the Warren Commission.

(23:05)

JFK Revisited Misleads by Putting Words in Kennedy's Mouth, Part Two

https://www.onthetrailofdelusion.com/post/jfk-revisited-puts-words-in-kennedy-s-mouth-part-two

Did President Kennedy actually say that he was going to shatter the CIA into a thousand pieces and scatter it to the wind?

(23:05)

JFK Revisited Misleads on Supposed CIA Support of the 1961 Coup Attempt in France

https://www.onthetrailofdelusion.com/post/jfk-revisited-misleads-on-supposed-cia-support-of-the-1961-coup-attempt-in-france

JFK Revisited claims that the CIA supported the 1961 coup attempt against French President Charles de Gaulle in 1961. The only thing missing is evidence.

(24:59)

JFK Revisited Misleads by Putting Words in Kennedy's Mouth

https://www.onthetrailofdelusion.com/post/jfk-revisited-misleads-by-putting-words-in-kennedy-s-mouth

David Talbot claims that JFK told the French ambassador that he was not in full control of his entire government. There is no evidence he ever said that.

(25:24)

JFK: Destiny Betrayed Misleads on CIA Involvement in Plot against de Gaulle

https://www.onthetrailofdelusion.com/post/jfk-destiny-betrayed-misleads-on-cia-involvement-in-plot-against-de-gaulle

JFK: Destiny Betrayed alleges that the CIA was involved in an assassination plot against French President Charles de Gaulle. Scenes from a fictional film are used to buttress the allegation. The truth is that the CIA had nothing to do with the supposed plot.

(28:10)

JFK Revisited Doesn't Tell the Whole Truth about John Connally

https://www.onthetrailofdelusion.com/post/jfk-revisited-doesn-t-tell-the-whole-truth-about-john-connally

You won't learn everything you need to know about Connally's position on the shots from Oliver Stone's so-called documentary.

(47:57)

Oliver Stone Disses the Sixth Floor Museum

https://www.onthetrailofdelusion.com/post/oliver-stone-disses-the-sixth-floor-museum

JFK: Destiny Betrayed needlessly, and unfairly, criticizes the Sixth Floor Museum.

(49:32)

Tripping on the Stairs

https://steveroeconsulting.wixsite.com/website/post/jfk-revisited-tripping-on-the-stairs

JFK: Destiny Betrayed alleges that the testimony of Vickie Adams and Sandra Styles proves that Oswald was not on the sixth floor of the Texas School Book Depository. But there was a shooter on the sixth floor, and they didn't see anyone going down the stairs. TSBD expert Jerry Dealey provides a simple explanation.

JFK Destiny Betrayed, Episode 2

(4:01)

JFK Revisited Misleads on JFK's Throat Wound

https://www.onthetrailofdelusion.com/post/jfk-revisited-misleads-on-jfk-s-throat-wound

The preponderance of evidence indicates that JFK's throat wound was one of exit.

(8:38)

Was James Gochenaur a Credible Witness in *JFK Revisited*?

https://www.onthetrailofdelusion.com/post/was-james-gochenaur-a-credible-witness-in-jfk-revisited

Gochenaur's writings don't back up his allegations in *JFK Revisited.*

(9:59)

JFK: Destiny Betrayed Misleads on Dr. Charles Crenshaw

https://www.onthetrailofdelusion.com/post/jfk-destiny-betrayed-misleads-on-dr-charles-crenshaw

JFK: Destiny Betrayed features Dr. Charles Crenshaw to bolster its claim that President Kennedy was shot from the front. Viewers are not informed about Dr. Crenshaw's credibility problems.

(11:48)

JFK: Destiny Betrayed Misleads on JFK's Head Wound, Part Three

https://www.onthetrailofdelusion.com/post/jfk-destiny-betrayed-misleads-on-jfk-s-head-wound-part-three

JFK: Destiny Betrayed misleads viewers on the opinions of Parkland Hospital doctors and Bethesda witnesses regarding JFK's head wound.

(14:48)

JFK: Destiny Betrayed Misleads on the Harper Fragment

https://www.onthetrailofdelusion.com/post/jfk-destiny-betrayed-misleads-on-the-harper-fragment

JFK: Destiny Betrayed misleads viewers into thinking the Harper fragment was occipital bone that came from the back of Kennedy's head.

(38:40)

JFK Revisited Uses Marina Porter to Mislead Viewers

https://www.onthetrailofdelusion.com/post/jfk-revisited-uses-marina-porter-to-mislead-viewers

Oliver Stone tries to make it seem like Marina Porter denied taking the backyard photographs of Lee Harvey Oswald.

(39:16)

JFK Revisited Again Caught Creating False Mysteries

https://steveroeconsulting.wixsite.com/website/post/jfk-revisited-again-caught-creating-false-mysteries

Stone and DiEugenio hatch another bogus mystery with sinister strap/sling mounts on Oswald's rifle.

(40:41)

JFK Revisited: Were the Oswald Backyard Photographs Faked?

https://www.onthetrailofdelusion.com/post/jfk-revisited-were-the-oswald-backyard-photographs-faked

Oliver Stone once again raises the issue of the legitimacy of the backyard photographs of Lee Harvey Oswald.

(42:06)

A Look at the *JFK Revisited: Through The Looking Glass* by Oliver Stone

https://steveroeconsulting.wixsite.com/website/post/a-look-at-the-jfk-revisited-through-the-looking-glass-film-by-oliver-stone

Oliver Stone distorts the testimony about Oswald's palm print on the Mannlicher-Carcano rifle.

(47:55)

JFK: Destiny Betrayed Misleads on CE 399

https://www.onthetrailofdelusion.com/post/jfk-destiny-betrayed-misleads-on-ce399

JFK: Destiny Betrayed misleads viewers on the bullet found at Parkland Hospital, CE 399. They imply that Darrell Tomlinson, the maintenance employee who found the bullet, said that the bullet he found didn't look like CE 399. The truth is somewhat different.

(47:56)

A Single Photograph Disproves Oliver Stone's Conspiracy Claim

https://www.washingtondecoded.com/site/2022/06/roe3.html

JFK: Destiny Betrayed claims that the initials of Elmer Lee Todd are missing from CE 399. Steve Roe proves them wrong.

(52:43)

JFK: Destiny Betrayed Misleads by Claiming Jack Ruby was Signaled

https://www.onthetrailofdelusion.com/post/jfk-destiny-betrayed-misleads-by-claiming-jack-ruby-was-signaled

JFK: Destiny Betrayed alleges that Jack Ruby was signaled by car horns in the basement of the Dallas Police Department. The evidence clearly shows that many horns could be heard in the basement.

(53:30)

JFK: Destiny Betrayed Misleads on the Katzenbach Memorandum

https://www.onthetrailofdelusion.com/post/jfk-destiny-betrayed-misleads-on-the-katzenbach-memorandum

JFK: Destiny Betrayed misleads viewers on a memo written by Nicholas Katzenbach about investigating JFK's assassination.

(55:07)

JFK: Destiny Betrayed Misleads on Jack Ruby

https://www.onthetrailofdelusion.com/post/jfk-destiny-betrayed-misleads-on-jack-ruby

JFK: Destiny Betrayed misleads viewers on the motivations of Jack Ruby.

JFK Destiny Betrayed, Episode 3

(1:33)

JFK: Destiny Betrayed Misleads on Admiral George Burkley

https://www.onthetrailofdelusion.com/post/jfk-destiny-betrayed-misleads-on-admiral-george-burkley

JFK: Destiny Betrayed makes several outrageous allegations about Admiral George Burkley, JFK's personal physician, as well as a slanderous accusation.

(1:33)

JFK Revisited Misleads on Dr. Burkley's Suspicions of a Conspiracy

https://www.onthetrailofdelusion.com/post/jfk-revisited-misleads-on-dr-burkley-s-suspicions-of-a-conspiracy

JFK Revisited: Through the Looking Glass misleads viewers into believing that JFK's doctor, Admiral George Burkley, said there were multiple gunmen.

(1:33)

JFK Revisited Misleads on the ARRB's Quest for Dr. Burkley's Lawyer's Papers

https://www.onthetrailofdelusion.com/post/jfk-revisited-misleads-on-the-arrb-s-quest-for-dr-burkley-s-lawyer-s-papers

JFK Revisited: Through the Looking Glass misleads viewers on the context of discussions between Burkley's family and the ARRB regarding supposed papers in the possession of his lawyer.

(1:33)

JFK Revisited Recklessly Accuses George Burkley of Being Involved in a Cover-Up

https://www.onthetrailofdelusion.com/post/jfk-revisited-recklessly-accuses-george-burkley-of-being-involved-in-a-cover-up

Reckless charges are made against George Burkley with no evidence.

(1:33)

JFK Revisited Misleads on Admiral Burkley and the HSCA

https://www.onthetrailofdelusion.com/post/jfk-revisited-misleads-on-admiral-burkley-and-the-hsca

JFK Revisited: Through the Looking Glass greatly misleads viewers on Admiral George Burkley and his interactions with the HSCA.

(1:33)

JFK Revisited Misleads on Admiral George Burkley and Conspiracy Theorists

https: / / www.onthetrailofdelusion.com / post / jfk-revisited-misleads-on-admiral-george-burkley-and-conspiracy-theorists

JFK Revisited puts words in Burkley's mouth.

(6:22)

JFK: Destiny Betrayed Misleads on JFK's Head Wound, Part One

https: / / www.onthetrailofdelusion.com / post / jfk-destiny-betrayed-misleads-on-jfk-s-head-wound-part-one

JFK: Destiny Betrayed uses a variety of supposed witnesses to allege that the wound in the back of Kennedy's head was one of exit. Audrey Bell is one such witness, and she doesn't have much credibility.

(6:52)

JFK: Destiny Betrayed Misleads on JFK's Head Wound, Part Two

https: / / www.onthetrailofdelusion.com / post / jfk-destiny-betrayed-misleads-on-jfk-s-head-wound-part-two

JFK: Destiny Betrayed tries to make the case that the cerebellum extruding from Kennedy's head wound that Parkland Hospital doctors saw indicated an exit wound.

(10:08)

JFK Revisited Misleads on the Weight of JFK's Brain

https: / / www.onthetrailofdelusion.com / post / jfk-revisited-misleads-on-the-weight-of-jfk-s-brain

JFK Revisited makes a big deal about the weight of JFK's brain and ignores a non-conspiratorial explanation.

(12:16)

JFK Revisited Misleads on JFK's Brain, Again

https: / / www.onthetrailofdelusion.com / post / jfk-revisited-misleads-on-jfk-s-brain-again

Dr. Robert Kirschner's consultation with the ARRB explains a mystery in the documentary.

(15:09)

JFK Revisited Distorts John Stringer's Testimony

https://www.onthetrailofdelusion.com/post/jfk-revisited-distorts-john-stringer-s-testimony

JFK Revisited makes it sound like the autopsy photographer said he did not take the photos of JFK's brain that are in the current inventory.

(17:08)

JFK Revisited Misleads on Autopsy Photographs of JFK

https://www.onthetrailofdelusion.com/post/jfk-revisited-misleads-on-autopsy-photographs-of-jfk

JFK Revisited tries to make the case that a White House photographer took photos at the autopsy. The only problem is that there is no evidence he was actually there.

(19:30)

JFK Revisited Misleads on the Autopsy Photographs of JFK, Part Two

https://www.onthetrailofdelusion.com/post/jfk-revisited-misleads-on-the-autopsy-photographs-of-jfk-part-two

Did Saundra Spencer really develop a completely different set of autopsy photographs?

(20:59)

JFK: Destiny Betrayed Misleads on JFK's Autopsy Photographs, Part Three

https://www.onthetrailofdelusion.com/post/jfk-destiny-betrayed-misleads-on-jfk-s-autopsy-photographs-part-three

JFK: Destiny Betrayed misleads viewers into believing there are missing autopsy photographs. In the process, the autopsy photographer is quoted egregiously out of context.

(26:05)

JFK: Destiny Betrayed Misleads on Supposed Extra Bullet

https://www.onthetrailofdelusion.com/post/jfk-destiny-betrayed-misleads-on-supposed-extra-bullet

JFK: Destiny Betrayed alleges that an extra bullet was found in JFK's limousine the evening of the assassination. This is just not true.

(27:49)

JFK: Destiny Betrayed Misleads on Supposed Extra Bullet, Part Two

https://www.onthetrailofdelusion.com/post/jfk-destiny-betrayed-misleads-on-supposed-extra-bullet-part-two

JFK: Destiny Betrayed misleads viewers by intimating that that there was a through-and-through hole in the windshield. This is simply not true.

(34:22)

JFK Revisited Misleads on Kennedy's Back Wound

https://www.onthetrailofdelusion.com/post/jfk-revisited-misleads-on-kennedy-s-back-wound

While Gerald Ford edited some language in the Warren Report, he did not change the location of the back wound. Autopsy photographs show exactly the location of the back wound.

(34:45)

JFK Revisited Misleads on Valery Giscard D'Estaing

https://www.onthetrailofdelusion.com/post/jfk-revisited-misleads-on-valery-giscard-d-estaing

Did Gerald Ford really disclose to French President Valery Giscard D'Estaing that the JFK assassination was a conspiracy? Perhaps not.

(54:07)

JFK: Destiny Betrayed Misleads on General Curtis LeMay, Part One

https://www.onthetrailofdelusion.com/post/jfk-destiny-betrayed-misleads-on-general-curtis-lemay-part-one

JFK: Destiny Betrayed claims that General Curtis LeMay was ordered by General Zuckert to land at Andrews Air Force Base from his holiday in Canada and that LeMay then decided to go to National Airport. That is not what happened.

(56:27)

JFK: Destiny Betrayed Misleads on General Curtis LeMay, Part Two

https://www.onthetrailofdelusion.com/post/jfk-destiny-betrayed-misleads-on-general-curtis-lemay-part-two

JFK: Destiny Betrayed alleges that General Curtis LeMay was at JFK's autopsy.

(56:51)

JFK: Destiny Betrayed Misleads on JFK's Autopsy

https://www.onthetrailofdelusion.com/post/jfk-destiny-betrayed-misleads-on-jfk-s-autopsy

JFK: Destiny Betrayed alleges that autopsy pathologists were told to fit the wounds to a presupposed conclusion.

JFK Destiny Betrayed, Episode 4

(1:37)

JFK: Destiny Betrayed Misleads on Otto Otepka

https://www.onthetrailofdelusion.com/post/jfk-destiny-betrayed-misleads-on-otto-otepka

JFK: Destiny Betrayed misleads viewers into believing that Otto Otepka uncovered evidence that Oswald was a fake defector.

(7:51)

JFK: Destiny Betrayed Misleads on Oswald's Income

https://www.onthetrailofdelusion.com/post/jfk-destiny-betrayed-misleads-on-oswald-s-income

JFK: Destiny Betrayed makes the erroneous claim that Lee Harvey Oswald was not paid for his last quarter of service in the U.S. Marines.

(10:14)

JFK: Destiny Betrayed Misleads on David Ferrie and the CIA

https://www.onthetrailofdelusion.com/post/jfk-destiny-betrayed-misleads-on-david-ferrie-and-the-cia

JFK: Destiny Betrayed erroneously claims that David Ferrie was an asset of the CIA and that he also flew missions for the CIA. This is simply not true.

(10:55)

JFK Revisited Misleads on Guy Banister

https://www.onthetrailofdelusion.com/post/jfk-revisited-misleads-on-guy-banister

JFK Revisited claims that Guy Banister gave Oswald a room at 544 Camp Street. The evidence does not support the allegation.

(13:22)

Was Clay Shaw a "Contract Agent" for the CIA?

https://www.onthetrailofdelusion.com/post/was-clay-shaw-a-contract-agent-for-the-cia

No, Clay Shaw was not a "contract agent."

(14:03)

JFK Revisited: Was Clay Shaw the elusive Clay Bertrand?

https://www.onthetrailofdelusion.com/post/jfk-revisited-was-clay-shaw-the-elusive-clay-bertrand

This post debunks every witness that has ever claimed Shaw was Bertrand

(22:03)

JFK Revisited Misleads on the Supposed Chicago Plot

https://www.onthetrailofdelusion.com/post/jfk-revisited-misleads-on-the-supposed-chicago-plot

There is no evidence that there was actually a plot against JFK in Chicago.

(24:22)

JFK Revisited Alleges Oswald was "Placed"

https://www.onthetrailofdelusion.com/post/jfk-revisited-alleges-oswald-was-placed

JFK Revisited alleges that Oswald was "moved" to Dallas and "placed" in the Texas School Book Depository. This is ridiculous.

(25:06)

JFK: Destiny Betrayed Misleads on Supposed Tampa "Patsy"

https://www.onthetrailofdelusion.com/post/jfk-destiny-betrayed-misleads-on-supposed-tampa-patsy

JFK: Destiny Betrayed alleges that there were plots to assassinate JFK in Chicago and Tampa in November of 1963. In addition, the documentary alleges that Thomas Vallee and Gilberto Policarpo Lopez were patsies in waiting in Chicago and Tampa respectively who would have been arrested had the supposed plots succeeded. The only problem with this thesis is that there is no evidence that there was a plot in Chicago. And there is no evidence of a plot in Tampa either.

(25:06)

Was Gilberto Policarpo Lopez an Assassin or a Patsy?

https://www.onthetrailofdelusion.com/post/was-gilberto-policarpo-lopez-an-assassin-or-a-patsy

Researcher Paul Hoch has uncovered evidence that significantly adds to our understanding of this story. It turns out that the Church Committee got an important fact wrong.

(41:19)

JFK: Destiny Betrayed Misleads on Israel and Nuclear Weapons

https://www.onthetrailofdelusion.com/post/jfk-destiny-betrayed-misleads-on-israel-and-nuclear-weapons

JFK: Destiny Betrayed makes it appear that Israel was about to use nuclear weapons in the 1973 Yom Kippur War. A key important fact was left out.

JFK Revisited: The Book of the Film

Doubling Down on Phony Theories

https://steveroeconsulting.wixsite.com/website/post/doubling-down-on-phony-theories

Steve Roe made a rude discovery when perusing the book of the film transcript. James DiEugenio included a debunked allegation that Oswald's money order for his rifle could not have reached Chicago in time.

Anatomy of a James DiEugenio Citation

https://www.onthetrailofdelusion.com/post/anatomy-of-a-james-dieugenio-citation

A citation about the segment on David Ferrie in the book leads to a Colonel William Bishop, who was quite the fabulist.

Anatomy of a James DiEugenio Citation, Part Two

https://www.onthetrailofdelusion.com/post/anatomy-of-a-james-dieugenio-citation-part-two

An analysis of the footnotes related to the anti-Castro training camp north of Lake Pontchartrain in New Orleans in the summer of 1963.

Paul Bleau's Plots

https://www.onthetrailofdelusion.com/post/paul-bleau-s-plots

Paul Bleau is a so-called expert on plots against JFK, and his interview in the book *JFK Revisited* is revealing.

JFK Revisited: **Commentary Track on the Blu-Ray Disc**

Highlights of Oliver Stone's and James DiEugenio's Commentary Track on *JFK Revisited*

https://www.onthetrailofdelusion.com/post/highlights-of-oliver-stone-and-james-dieugenio-s-commentary-track-on-jfk-revisited

SOURCES

A document with all of these sources is available at https://www.onthetrailofdelusion.com/documents. This will allow purchasers of a hard-copy of this book easy access to all of the links contained below.

Introduction

Oliver Stone told the press: https://variety.com/2019/tv/global/agc-television-picks-up-worldwide-oliver-stones-jfk-destiny-betrayed-1203368818/

Alecia Long's book: Cruising for Conspirators: How a New Orleans DA Prosecuted the Kennedy Assassination as a Sex Crime (University of North Carolina Press, 2021)

James DiEugenio quote on the timing of our books: https://educationforum.ipbhost.com/topic/27450-alecia-long-lays-an-egg/#comment-448917

Paris Match on JFK Revisited: https://www.parismatch.com/Actu/International/Oliver-Stone-C-est-la-CIA-qui-a-tire-sur-Kennedy-1751061

Oliver Stone interview with Spike Lee: https://variety.com/2021/film/news/spike-lee-oliver-stone-da-5-bloods-1234903611/

Tim Weiner in Rolling Stone: https://www.rollingstone.com/politics/politics-features/jfk-oliver-stone-conspiracy-theory-russian-disinformation-1260223/

Max Boot in the Washington Post: https://www.washingtonpost.com/opinions/2021/12/21/oliver-stone-just-cant-stop-spreading-lies-about-jfks-assassination/

James DiEugenio on Izvestia: https://educationforum.ipbhost.com/topic/27466-jfk-revisited-through-the-looking-glass/page/18/#comment-450838

Oliver Stone's Interview with Abby Martin: https://www.youtube.com/watch?app=desktop&v=cJd3Y94etd4

James Kirchick on Abby Martin: https://www.tabletmag.com/sections/news/articles/rt-anchors-riff-not-as-rogue-as-it-seems

Oliver Stone interview with Trey Elling: https://www.youtube.com/watch?v=U74Le16c2CE

Article in Gallery Magazine on umbrella flechette: http://jfk.hood.edu/Collection/Weisberg%20Subject%20Index%20Files/G%20Disk/Gallery/Item%2001.pdf

James DiEugenio tweet about Stone learning his lines: https://twitter.com/jimmydie1963/status/1506864287158980611

James DiEugenio on Stone turning to alternative media: https://educationforum.ipbhost.com/topic/27466-jfk-revisited-through-the-looking-glass/page/52/#comment-456996

James Kirchick on Oliver Stone's documentary on Ukraine: https://www.thedailybeast.com/oliver-stones-latest-dictator-suckup

Oliver Stone interview with Matt Taibbi and Katie Halper: https://www.youtube.com/watch?v=V6ZeJ2FsCJs

Oliver Stone interview with Robert Scheer: https://scheerpost.com/2022/02/11/oliver-stone-american-exceptionalism-is-on-deadly-display-in-ukraine/

Oliver Stone interview with Lex Fridman: https://www.youtube.com/watch?v=ygAqYC8JOQI

Oliver Stone at the Barcelona Film Festival: https://www.eldiario.es/cultura/cine/oliver-stone-eeuu-doberman-asesino-metodico-dinero_1_8942044.html

Sandy Larsen comment: https://educationforum.ipbhost.com/topic/27666-destiny-betrayed-2022/page/8/#comment-458196

Article in Le Soleil: https://www.lesoleil.com/2022/06/19/a-propos-doliver-stone-a-quebec-c66d6bb3d4f6e2d98a6fcbb1628ee131

My article on Oliver Stone for Terry Glavin's substack: "Grovelling at the feet of Le Grand Complotiste: A guest post, by Fred Litwin," June 13, 2022; https://therealstory.substack.com/p/grovelling-at-the-feet-of-le-grand?s=r

La Presse article on Oliver Stone: https://www.lapresse.ca/actualites/chroniques/2022-06-15/tapis-rouge-pour-un-apologiste-de-poutine.php

Sirhan Sirhan was firing blanks at Robert Kennedy: "CIA may have used contractor who inspired 'Mission: Impossible' to kill RFK, new book alleges," Tom Jackman, *Washington Post*, February 9, 2019; https://www.washingtonpost.com/history/2019/02/09/cia-may-have-used-contractor-who-inspired-mission-impossible-kill-rfk-new-book-alleges/

Lisa Pease tweet on Uvalde: https://twitter.com/lisapease/status/1529299700955742210

Robert Kennedy quote that his father's assassination had not been investigated: Episode 4 of *JFK: Destiny Betrayed*, page 255.

Robert F. Kennedy Jr. and the connection between vaccines and autism: "The truth about vaccines, autism and Robert F. Kennedy Jr.'s conspiracy theory," Sarah Kaplan, *Washington Post*, January 10, 2017; https://www.washingtonpost.com/news/speaking-of-science/wp/2017/01/10/the-facts-about-vaccines-autism-and-robert-f-kennedy-jr-s-conspiracy-theory/; see also: "The Anti-Vaccine Propaganda of Robert F. Kennedy, Jr.," Jonathan Jarry, McGill Office for Science and Security, April 16, 2021; https://www.mcgill.ca/oss/article/covid-19-health-pseudoscience/anti-vaccine-propaganda-robert-f-kennedy-jr

Robert F. Kennedy Jr.'s book: *The Real Anthony Fauci: Bill Gates, Big Pharma, and the Global War on Democracy and Public Health* (Skyhorse, 2021)

RFK Jr. quote on "pervasive CIA involvement": *The Real Anthony Fauci*, op. cit., page 810 in Kindle version.

Quote from RFK Jr. on the "ultimate coup d'etat": *The Real Anthony Fauci*, op. cit., page 893 of the Kindle version.

RFK Jr. comparison of anti-vaxxers to victims of the holocaust: https://www.huffpost.com/entry/rfk-jr-anti-vaxx-rally-5g-bill-gates_n_61edd1cee4b023957946b2de

RFK tweet about Bill Gates: https://twitter.com/RobertKennedyJr/status/1357436042475941888

Dr. Donald Miller chart on JFK conspirators: https://www.lewrockwell.com/2019/07/donald-w-miller-jr-md/if-not-oswald-who-killed-president-kennedy-and-why/

Dr. Donald Miller on the dangers of fluoride: https://www.lewrockwell.com/1970/01/donald-w-miller-jr-md/fluoride-is-poison/

Dr. Donald Miller on danger of vaccines: https://www.lewrockwell.com/1970/01/donald-w-miller-jr-md/vaccines-are-dangerous/

Dr. Donald Miller on HIV: https://www.lewrockwell.com/2008/03/donald-w-miller-jr-md/questioning-hivaids/

Dr. Donald Miller on flu shots: https://www.lewrockwell.com/2008/10/donald-w-miller-jr-md/dont-get-a-flu-shot-2/

Dr. Donald Miller on death of JFK Jr.: https://www.lewrockwell.com/1970/01/donald-w-miller-jr-md/pursuing-truth-on-the-kennedy-assassinations/

Douglas Horne on the alteration of the Zapruder film: https://youtu.be/J_QIuu6hsAc

Douglas Horne on Greer shooting JFK: Douglas Horne, *Inside the Assassination Records Review Board*, Volume IV, page 1150; Volume V, page 1416, 2009

The Enabling of Oliver Stone

New York Times quote on the prosecution of Clay Shaw: "Justice in New Orleans," The *New York Times*, March 2, 1969, page 12E; https://www.onthetrailofdelusion.com/post/the-new-york-times-on-clay-shaw-s-acquittal

Rosemary James quote on Garrison book: "She does have something," *New Orleans Times-Picayune*, July 11, 1999; https://www.onthetrailofdelusion.com/post/rosemary-james-reviews-patricia-lambert-s-false-witness

Oliver Stone quotes on Garrison book: "Film; Oliver Stone Under Fire Over the Killing of J.F.K."

New York Times, July 28, 1991; https://www.nytimes.com/1991/07/28/movies/film-oliver-stone-under-fire-over-the-killing-of-jfk.html

Oliver Stone quote on Garrison as Jimmy Stewart: "The Shooting of JFK," Robert Sam Anson, *Esquire*, November 1991; https://classic.esquire.com/article/1991/11/1/the-shooting-of-jfk; https://www.onthetrailofdelusion.com/post/i-ve-been-blocked-by-oliver-stone

Ehrenstein quote on the film JFK: The Advocate, January 14 1992, "JFK is more offensive than Basic Instinct could dare to be," David Ehrenstein; https://www.onthetrailofdelusion.com/post/is-oliver-stone-s-film-jfk-homophobic

Warren Report quote on a "posthumous trial": page xiv; https://www.maryferrell.org/showDoc.html?docId=946#relPageId=14

Richard Mosk quote: http://www.kenrahn.com/JFK/History/WC_Period/Legal_views_of_WC/Mosk/Mosk--WC_and_legal_process.html

Quote on Warren Commission and rumors: Ibid.

Alfredda Scobey quotes on admissibility of evidence: "A Lawyer's Notes on the Warren Commission Report," https://www.assassinationresearch.com/v1n1/v1n1scobey.pdf

James DiEugenio quote on Scobey: https://educationforum.ipbhost.com/topic/25715-beyond-theory/page/3/#comment-399665

Warren Commission Exhibit 399: https://www.maryferrell.org/showDoc.html?docId=1134#relPageId=75

Kenneth Rahn quote on the planting of evidence: "Why The Fragments Weren't Planted," http://www.kenrahn.com/JFK/Scientific_topics/NAA/Frags_not_planted.html

Links for DiEugenio and Stone beliefs:

https://www.onthetrailofdelusion.com/post/jfk-revisited-distorts-john-stringer-s-testimony

https://steveroeconsulting.wixsite.com/website/post/jfk-revisited-again-caught-creating-false-mysteries

https://www.onthetrailofdelusion.com/post/jfk-revisited-misleads-on-the-autopsy-photographs-of-jfk-part-two

https://www.onthetrailofdelusion.com/post/jfk-revisited-were-the-oswald-backyard-photographs-faked

https://www.onthetrailofdelusion.com/post/jfk-destiny-betrayed-misleads-on-supposed-extra-bullet

https://www.onthetrailofdelusion.com/post/jfk-destiny-betrayed-misleads-on-supposed-extra-bullet-part-two

https://www.onthetrailofdelusion.com/post/jfk-revisited-recklessly-accuses-george-burkley-of-being-involved-in-a-cover-up

James DiEugenio quote on not advancing a theory of the case: https://educationforum.ipbhost.com/topic/27576-noam-chomsky-vs-oliver-stone/page/2/#comment-452861

James DiEugenio quote on General Curtis LeMay: https://educationforum.ipbhost.com/topic/27466-jfk-revisited-through-the-looking-glass/page/40/#comment-455341

The Warren Commission

1. Did the CIA Lobby to Have Allen Dulles Put on the Warren Commission? (Episode 1, 11:49)

Excerpt of transcript of Eric Sevareid interview with Allen Dulles: "CBS Reports: The Hot and Cold Wars of Allen Dulles." https://www.cia.gov/readingroom/document/cia-rdp70-00058r000100150009-5

Talbot quote that Helms "personally persuaded" Johnson: Michael Kurtz, *The JFK Assassination Debates*, (University Press of Kansas), page 173

Pat Speer quote about Kurtz: https://www.patspeer.com/chapter-19d-lost-in-the-jungle-with-kurtz

Talbot elaboration on Corson: David Talbot, *The Devil's Chessboard: Allen Dulles, the CIA, and the Rise of America's Secret Government*, (Harper Perennial, 2016), page 174

Corson from Trento's book: Joseph Trento, *The Secret History of the CIA*, (MJF, 2007), page 269

A CIA review of Trento's book (...the worst book yet purporting to provide an account of the Agency's past): https://web.archive.org/web/20080312053504/https://www.cia.gov/library/center-for-the-study-of-intelligence/csi-publications/csi-studies/studies/vol46no2/article09.html

John Prados, senior fellow at the National Security Archive, reviewed Trento's book, "Trento employs circumstantial and marginally suggestive evidence throughout the book, which makes his conspiracy charges seem far-fetched and unbelievable." https://journals.sagepub.com/doi/pdf/10.2968/058002018

For a full elaboration on the Marchetti story: https://www.muckrock.com/news/archives/2018/may/29/huntdallas-cia-memo-hoax/

Marchetti's 1978 story in Spotlight: https://www.maryferrell.org/showDoc.html?docId=60186#relPageId=3#relPageId=1

Talbot quote about people urging Johnson to appoint Dulles: *The Devil's Chessboard*, op. cit., page 574.

Quote from Peter Grose's book: Peter Grose, *Gentleman Spy: The Life of Allen Dulles*, (Houghton Mifflin Harcourt, 1994), page 541; https://archive.org/details/gentlemanspylife00gros/page/n1/mode/2up

Lyndon Johnson phone call to Dean Rusk: https://youtu.be/DPL878jaJNw

Johnson quote from his memoirs about appointing Dulles and McCloy: Lyndon B. Johnson, *The Vantage Point*, (Weidenfeld & Nicolson, 1972), page 27; https://archive.org/details/vantagepointpers0000john/mode/2up

Walter Jenkins memo: https://www.jfk-assassination.net/pdf/WalterJenkins11-29-63.pdf

The HSCA mentioned this memo: https://www.maryferrell.org/showDoc.html?docId=83#relPageId=12

Robert Caro's discussion of the formation of the Warren Commission: Robert Caro, *The Passage of Power*, (Vintage, 2013), page 442

Caro's source: Oral history transcript, Lyndon B. Johnson, 8/19/1969; https://www.discoverlbj.org/item/oh-lbj-19690819-66-1-rem

Johnson/Fortas transcript from Dec. 17, 1966: Max Holland, *The Kennedy Assassination Tapes: The White House conversations of Lyndon B. Johnson regarding the assassination, the Warren Commission and the aftermath, (Alfred A. Knopf, 2004)*, pages 339 – 340; https://www.discoverlbj.org/item/tel-11150

Johnson/Bobby Kennedy discussion on Dulles: *The Kennedy Assassination Tapes*, op. cit., page 242.

2. Were the Conclusions of the Warren Commission Preordained? (Episode 2, 53:30)

Telephone conversation between J. Edgar Hoover and Lyndon Johnson: https://www.maryferrell.org/showDoc.html?docId=807#relPageId=2

Howard Willens quote: Howard Willens, *History Will Prove Us Right: Inside the Warren Commission Report on the Assassination of John F. Kennedy*, (Abrams Press, 2013), page 18

Hoover phone call with Walter Jenkins: https://www.maryferrell.org/showDoc.html?docId=147408#relPageId=1

Quote from Vincent Bugliosi on Hoover statement: Vincent Bugliosi, *Reclaiming History*, (W. W. Norton & Co., 2007), page 321

Katzenbach memo: https://www.maryferrell.org/showDoc.html?docId=62268#relPageId=29

Katzenbach testimony before the HSCA: https://www.maryferrell.org/showDoc.html?docId=954#relPageId=730

Memo to Alan Belmont: https://www.maryferrell.org/showDoc.html?docId=62268#relPageId=31

McAdams comment on Katzenbach memo: John McAdams, *JFK Assassination Logic: How to Think about Claims of Conspiracy*, (Potomac Books, 2014), page 81

Katzenbach testimony on FBI: https://www.maryferrell.org/showDoc.html?docId=954#relPageId=702

Executive Order 1130: https://www.maryferrell.org/showDoc.html?docId=946#relPageId=495

Howard Willens quote on the executive order: *History Will Prove Us Right*, op. cit., page 25.

The CIA

3. Did JFK Threaten to Shatter the CIA into a Thousand Pieces? (Episode 1, 23:05)

New York Times article on the CIA: https://ratical.org/ratville/JFK/Unspeakable/JFK-scatterCIAtoWinds.pdf

History of supposed Kennedy quote: https://gizmodo.com/the-story-behind-that-jfk-quote-about-destroying-the-ci-1793151211/amp

Fakesy Kennedy: https://www.snopes.com/fact-check/linkin-kennedy/; Lincoln did not have a secretary named Kennedy.

Arthur Schlesinger quote: Arthur Schlesinger, *A Thousand Days: John F. Kennedy in the White House*, (Random House, 1988), page 492; https://archive.org/details/thousanddays00arth

Kennedys chewing out Bissell: https://www.maryferrell.org/showDoc.html?docId=1156#relPageId=155

Talbot quote about Ralph McGehee: *The Devil's Chessboard*, op. cit., page 411.

McGehee quote about the CIA: Ralph McGehee, *Deadly Deceits: My 25 Years in the CIA*, (Sheridan Square Publications, 1983), page 54; https://archive.org/details/deadlydeceitsmy20000mcge/mode/

Origins of the 701 program: "The Support Services Historical Series, The Office of Personnel: Special Activities Staff, 1957 – 70"; https://www.cia.gov/readingroom/docs/CIA-RDP90-00708R000200150001-1.pdf

Study on the 701 program: https://archive.org/details/SpecialActivitiesStaff1957-1970/page/n17/mode/2up

Designation of surplus personnel: "John McCone As Director of Central Intelligence 1961 – 1965" by David Robarge; https://documents.theblackvault.com/documents/cia/DOC_0001262720.pdf

Tim Weiner quote on firings: Tim Weiner, *Legacy of Ashes: The History of the CIA, (Anchor, 2008)*, page 188

Schlesinger quote about 20% budget cut: A Thousand Days, op. cit., page 492.

CIA budget for 1963: https://sgp.fas.org/foia/1947/cia050405att.pdf

CIA budget early years of Johnson administration: Ibid.

National Security Action Memoranda, NSAM 57: https://www.jfklibrary.org/asset-viewer/archives/JFKNSF/330/JFKNSF-330-007

Kennedy Memorandum on the CIA: https://www.maryferrell.org/showDoc.html?docId=1169#relPageId=143

Tim Weiner on the Kennedys and covert action: *Legacy of Ashes*, op. cit., page 180.

Kennedy revamping covert action: Ibid., page 181.

Kennedys starting Operation Mongoose: Ibid., page 185.

Memo from October, 1962: https://nsarchive2.gwu.edu/nsa/cuba_mis_cri/621004%20Minutes%20of%20Meeting%20of%20Special.pdf

4. Did the CIA Support a 1961 Coup Attempt in France? (Episode 1, 24:07)

President de Gaulle on French television: https://youtu.be/Nn3_5m5vALg

James Reston article in The New York Times: https://www.nytimes.com/1961/04/29/archives/pentagon-to-get-some-cia-duties-plan-reflects-kennedy-aim-to.html

Talbot quote on de Gaulle concluding that Challe was acting with support from the U.S. intelligence: *Devil's Chessboard*, op. cit., page 413.

Vincent Jauvert's book: Vincent Jauvert, *L'Amérique Contre De Gaulle: Histoire secrète 1961 – 1969*, (Editions Du Seuil, 2000); https://archive.org/details/lameriquecontred0000jauv

Excerpt from Jauvert book on what de Gaulle really thought: Jauvert, op. cit., pages 198 – 199.

Talbot quote on French foreign ministry being source of charges: *Devil's Chessboard*, op. cit., page 414

Jauvert's quote, "Rumors, unconfirmed information, but no proof.": Jauvert, op. cit., page 193.

Quote from Jauvert's book on Agency A: Jauvert, op. cit., page 199.

Quote from Christopher Andrew's and Vasili Mitrokhin's book: Christopher Andrew & Vasili Mitrokhin, *The KGB and the World*: The Mitrokhin Archive II (Penguin, 2018), page 432

Richard Helms' Testimony on Communist forgeries: https://www.google.ca/books/edition/Communist_Forgeries/gZ4KeT5i_nkC?hl=en&gbpv=1&dq=communist+forgeries&printsec=frontcover, see pages 2 -5.

DiEugenio's sources on allegations in this section: James DiEugenio, *JFK Revisited: Through the Looking Glass*, (Skyhorse, 2022), page 88 of Kindle version; see also, https://www.kennedysandking.com/john-f-kennedy-articles/why-tim-weiner-never-called-me?\

Quote from Andrew Tully's book: Andrew Tully, *CIA: The Inside Story*, (William Morrow and Company, 1962), page 48; https://archive.org/details/ciainsidestory00tull/page/n7/mode/2up?q=Ghali

Salinger and Baraduc: Tully, op. cit., page 50.

Dialog between Pierre Salinger and Maurice Couve de Murville about evidence: Tully, op. cit., page 45.

Couve de Murville testifying before the Foreign Affairs Committee: Tully, op. cit., page 52.

The Nation, May 20, 1961: https://archive.org/details/sim_nation_1961-05-20_192_20_0/page/434/mode/2up

Jauvert on meeting in Madrid: Jauvert, op. cit., page 196 – 197.

Quote from Irwin Wall: Irwin Wall, *Challe*: *France, the United States, and the Algerian War*, (University of California Press, 2001), page 239; https://archive.org/details/franceunitedstat0000wall/page/n6/mode/2up?q=France%2C+the+United+States%2C+and+Algerian+War+irwin+wall

Quote from Thomas Powers' book: Thomas Powers, *The Man Who Kept the Secrets: Richard Helms and the CIA*, (Alfred A. Knopf, 1979), page 337; https://archive.org/details/manwhokeptsecret0000powe/mode/2up?q=%22The+man+who+kept+the+secrets%22+thomas+powers

Quote from Peter Geismer: *Fanon: A biography*, (The Dial Press, 1971), page 182; https://archive.org/details/fanon00pete/page/182/mode/2up?q=%22negotiated+fanon%27s+transportation%22

Quote from Thomas Meaney: "Frantz Fanon and the CIA Man," *American Historical Review*, June 2019; https://academic.oup.com/ahr/article/124/3/983/5509740?guestAccessKey=482804d3-9218-4a7e-962e-155f7c542ecc

Joseph Alsop on Fanon: "The Strange Saga of Frantz Fanon," September 24, 1969, in his syndicated column.

Irwin Wall agrees with Thomas Powers: Wall, op. cit., page 240.

U.S. News & World Report: Quoted in *The CIA and American Democracy*, Rhodri Jeffreys-Jones, Yale University Press, 1989, page 125; https://archive.org/details/ciaamericandemoc0000jeff_s3n3/page/124/mode/2up?q=%22were+to+blame+for+supporting+the+conspirators.%22

Quote about Kennedy being irritated: Wall, op. cit., page 242.

5. Did JFK Say that He was Not in Control of the CIA? (Episode 1, 24:59)

Quote from Talbot's book: Talbot, op. cit., page 418.

Jauvert quoting Dean Rusk: Jauvert, op. cit., page 197.

Quote on differentiating JFK and the CIA: Talbot, op. cit., page 419.

Talk hitting the New York Times: "Paris Rumors on C.I.A." May 1, 1963; https://www.cia.gov/readingroom/docs/CIA-RDP80M01009A000100040006-9.pdf

6. Was the CIA Involved in a 1967 Plot against de Gaulle? (Episode 1, 25:24)

Text of the Chicago Tribune article: https://www.onthetrailofdelusion.com/post/jfk-destiny-betrayed-misleads-on-cia-involvement-in-plot-against-de-gaulle

Colby's submission to the Rockefeller Commission: https://www.maryferrell.org/showDoc.html?docId=148995#relPageId=4#relPageId=1

A Note on Human Memory

Loftus on human memory: Elizabeth Loftus, *Eyewitness Testimony,* (Harvard University Press, 1996), page viii; https://archive.org/details/eyewitnesstestim0000loft_v0q1/page/n3/mode/2up?q=%22eyewitness+testimony%22+loftus

Internal ARRB report on medical records: https://www.maryferrell.org/showDoc.html?docId=204683%23relPageId=1#relPageId=1

ARRB Final Report on Memory: Chapter 6, "Clarifying the Federal Record on the Zapruder Film and the Medical and Ballistic Evidence," page 123; https://www.archives.gov/files/research/jfk/review-board/report/chapter-06-part2.pdf

Jeremy Gunn's speech at Stanford, May 18, 1998: https://www.maryferrell.org/showDoc.html?docId=217859%23relPageId=48#relPageId=38

The Medical Evidence

7. Was JFK's Throat Wound One of Entrance? (Episode 2, 4:01)

Transcript of Press conference at Parkland Hospital on November 22, 1963: https://www.jfk-assassination.net/press.htm

Hoover letter about shirt fibers: https://www.maryferrell.org/showDoc.html?docId=62313#relPageId=56

Dr. Cyril Wecht diagram of neck wound: "The Medical Evidence in the Assassination of President John F. Kennedy," Cyril H. Wecht and Robert P. Smith, Forensic Science, 3, 1974; http://jfk.hood.edu/Collection/Weisberg%20Subject%20Index%20Files/A%20Disk/Autopsy%20JFK%20Cyril%20Wecht%20Dr/Item%2018.pdf

Dr. Cyril Wecht on the throat wound from 2021: The JFK Assassination Dissected: An Analysis by Forensic Pathologist Cyril Wecht, Exposit, 2022, page 447 in Kindle edition; https://www.onthetrailofdelusion.com/post/dr-cyril-wecht-on-the-bullet-wound-to-kennedy-s-back-throat

Dr. Perry interview with the HSCA: https://aarclibrary.org/publib/jfk/arrb/master_med_set/pdf/md58.pdf

The HSCA Forensic Pathology Panel report on the throat wound: https://www.maryferrell.org/showDoc.html?docId=82#relPageId=185

Dr. Perry and Dr. Jones meet with the ARRB: https://aarclibrary.org/publib/jfk/arrb/medical_testimony/pdf/Parkland_8-27-98.pdf

Study on why we have autopsies: "Clinicians' Forensic Interpretations of Fatal Gunshot Wounds Often Miss the Mark," *JAMA*, April 1993; https://jamanetwork.com/journals/jama/article-abstract/405624

8. Was Dr. Perry Pressured to Change His Opinion? (Episode 2, 8:38)

Gochenaur phone interview with the HSCA: https://www.maryferrell.org/showDoc.html?docId=49383%23relPageId=24#relPageId=24

Gochenaur letter to Harold Weisberg: http://jfk.hood.edu/Collection/Weisberg%20Subject%20Index%20Files/G%20Disk/Gochenauer%20James/Item%2012.pdf

9. Is Dr. Charles Crenshaw a Credible Witness? (Episode 2, 9:59)

Crenshaw's book: Charles A. Crenshaw, M.D. with Jens Hansen and J. Gary Shaw, *JFK: Conspiracy of Silence*, (Signet, 1992); https://archive.org/details/jfkconspiracyofs00cren/mode/2up

Crenshaw feared the Secret Service: Crenshaw, op. cit., page 8

Crenshaw quote on 'conspiracy of silence': Crenshaw, op. cit., page 153 – 154.

John McAdams on Crenshaw: https://www.jfk-assassination.net/crenshaw.htm

Crenshaw belief that cover-up efforts included "even death": Crenshaw, op. cit., page 9.
Crenshaw even got basic details wrong: Crenshaw, op. cit., page 33.
The 'Wanted for Treason' handbill: https://slate.com/human-interest/2013/11/jfk-assassination-flyer-distributed-in-dallas-by-edwin-walker-s-group-before-his-visit.html
Ad in the Dallas Morning News: https://www.maryferrell.org/showDoc.html?docId=1138#relPageId=746
Crenshaw buys into the Rose Cherami story: Crenshaw, op. cit., page 43.
The Rose Cherami story was nonsense: https://www.onthetrailofdelusion.com/blog/tags/rose-cherami
Crenshaw also believes the Julia Mercer story: Crenshaw, op. cit., pages 55 – 56.
Mercer's story is demonstrably false: https://www.onthetrailofdelusion.com/post/why-do-conspiracy-theorists-still-believe-julia-ann-mercer
Crenshaw claimed that 75% of witnesses said the shots came from the grassy knoll: Crenshaw, op. cit., pages 66 – 67.
HSCA on the number and source of the shots: https://www.maryferrell.org/showDoc.html?docId=81%23relPageId=126#relPageId=126
HSCA on four witnesses who mentioned "dual locations" for the shots: https://www.maryferrell.org/showDoc.html?docId=81%23relPageId=129#relPageId=129
Crenshaw's bizarre statement: Crenshaw, op. cit., page 114.
Dr. Crenshaw had this to say about Kennedy's head wound in his book: Crenshaw, op. cit., pages 78 – 79.
Crenshaw on ABC's 20/20: https://youtu.be/pPcH1RNMC6M
Dr. Marion Jenkins told Dennis Breo that he doubted Crenshaw got a great look at the head wound: "JFK's Death: Part Two - Dallas MDs Recall Their Memories"; https://www.maryferrell.org/showDoc.html?docId=748#relPageId=38
Dr. Perry had this to say about Crenshaw: Ibid.
Dr. Crenshaw wrote that he entered Trauma Room 1 with Dr. Robert McClelland and he saw Kennedy's throat wound: Crenshaw, op. cit., page 79.
Only problem Dr. Perry had already made tracheotomy incision: https://www.maryferrell.org/showDoc.html?docId=748#relPageId=38
Crenshaw on picture of Kennedy's throat wound: Crenshaw, op. cit., page 11.
The Dallas doctors took great exception: "JFK's Death: Part Two - Dallas MDs Recall Their Memories"; https://www.maryferrell.org/showDoc.html?docId=748#relPageId=38
Crenshaw's interview by the ARRB: https://www.maryferrell.org/showDoc.html?docId=714#relPageId=1&search=%22MD_183%22
Researcher Pat Speer on Crenshaw: https://www.patspeer.com/chapter-18c-reason-to-doubt
David Perry on the timing of Crenshaw's belief in conspiracy: http://jfk.hood.edu/Collection/Weisberg%20Subject%20Index%20Files/C%20Disk/Crenshaw%20Charles%20A%20Dr/Item%2014.pdf; See also *Tales of Deception and Imagination: Investigating Kennedy Assassination Stories*, David Perry, 2021, pages 163 – 173
One of the bigger stories to come out of Crenshaw's book: Crenshaw, op. cit., pages 184 – 186.
Phone logs and Johnson's calendar of events: http://jfk.hood.edu/Collection/Weisberg%20Subject%20Index%20Files/C%20Disk/Crenshaw%20Charles%20A%20Dr/Item%2005.pdf
Crenshaw's claim he told Dr. Thomas Shires about the LBJ phone call: Crenshaw, op. cit., page 188.
David Perry's interview of Jack Price: Perry, op. cit., pages 165 – 166.
Harrison Livingstone on Johnson ordering Oswald be murdered: *Killing the Truth: Deceit and Deception in the JFK Case*, Carroll & Graf, 1993, page 506; https://archive.org/details/killingtruthdece00livi
Gus Russo's email to John McAdams: https://www.jfk-assassination.net/crenshaw.htm

10. Was There a Big Defect in the Back of JFK's Head? (Episode 2, 11:48)
Quote on thirty-year-old memories: McAdams, op. cit., page 28

Dr. Aguilar's quote about Clint Hill: DiEugenio, op. cit., page 147 of Kindle version.

Clint Hill's statement from November 30, 1963: https://www.maryferrell.org/showDoc.html?docId=1135#relPageId=756

Clint Hill also told National Geographic: McAdams, op. cit., page 29.

Sibert's drawing for the ARRB: https://www.maryferrell.org/showDoc.html?docId=719

Sibert's sketch for the HSCA: https://www.maryferrell.org/showDoc.html?docId=347#relPageId=9&search=%22MD_85%22

Sibert told the HSCA: https://www.maryferrell.org/showDoc.html?docId=627#relPageId=3&search=%22MD_46%22

O'Neill's chart for the HSCA: https://www.maryferrell.org/showDoc.html?docId=348#relPageId=10&search=%22pointed_towards%20the%20right%20side%22

Dr. Peters' testimony before the ARRB: https://www.maryferrell.org/showDoc.html?docId=793#relPageId=16&search=%22it_was%20difficult%20to%20see%20down%22

Dr. Gary Aguilar on the Parkland and Bethesda witnesses: "John F. Kennedy's Fatal Wounds: The Witnesses and the Interpretations from 1963 to the Present"; http://www.assassinationweb.com/ag6.htm

John McAdams on Dr. Gary Aguilar: McAdams, op. cit., page 28.

Custer's drawing of the head wound: https://www.maryferrell.org/showDoc.html?docId=738#relPageId=1&search=%22MD_207%22

Lipsey's interview with the HSCA and his drawing: https://www.maryferrell.org/showDoc.html?docId=349#relPageId=11&search=%22MD_87%22

Boyers interview with the HSCA: Aguilar, op. cit.; see also, https://www.maryferrell.org/showDoc.html?docId=326#relPageId=3&search=boyers; "Mr. Boyers stated that there was a large wound to the right side and towards the rear of the head."

John Stringer interview with the ARRB: https://www.maryferrell.org/showDoc.html?docId=749#relPageId=3&search=%22MD_227%22

Edward Reed ARRB testimony: https://www.maryferrell.org/showDoc.html?docId=794#relPageId=7&search=%22was_the%20scalp%20intact%22

General Philip Wehle on Kennedy's wounds: Dr. Gary Aguilar, op. cit.

Pat Speer on memory: https://www.patspeer.com/chapter-18d-reason-to-believe

11. Did the Harper Fragment Come from the Back of JFK's Head? (Episode 2, 14:48)

The Harper fragment, CD 1269: https://www.maryferrell.org/showDoc.html?docId=11664#relPageId=9

FBI report on William Harper: https://www.maryferrell.org/showDoc.html?docId=95615#relPageId=25&search=%22William_allen%20harper%22

Dr. Cairns analysis of the fragment: https://www.maryferrell.org/showDoc.html?docId=59625#relPageId=57&search=%22Cairns_advised%22

Discussion by members of the HSCA forensic pathology panel: https://www.maryferrell.org/showDoc.html?docId=82#relPageId=257&search=%22clearly_parietal%20bone%22

Dr. Angel's report: https://www.maryferrell.org/showDoc.html?docId=82#relPageId=239&search=%22upper_middle%20third%22

Dr. Angel's diagram of the Harper fragment: https://www.maryferrell.org/showDoc.html?docId=82#relPageId=240&search=%22upper_middle%20third%22

HSCA conclusion on the Harper fragment: https://www.maryferrell.org/showDoc.html?docId=82#relPageId=134&search=%22paper_cutouts%22

William Harper's letter to Howard Roffman: http://jfk.hood.edu/Collection/Weisberg%20Subject%20Index%20Files/H%20Disk/Harper%20Jack%20C%20Dr/Item%2001.pdf

Louis Girdler's diagram: "Your Lying Eyes" – Josiah Thompson's Lonely Labyrinth; https://www.jfk-assassination.net/pdf/LABYRINTH.pdf

Itek Corporation analysis of the Zapruder Film: https://www.maryferrell.org/showDoc.html?docId=60448#relPageId=60&search=%22radiates_matter%20in%20all%20directions%22

James DiEugenio changing the words of Dr. Gary Aguilar: DiEugenio, op. cit., page 150 in the Kindle edition.

It was parietal bone: "Anatomy of the 'Harper Fragment'" by Joseph N. Riley, Ph.D.; http://www.kenrahn.com/Marsh/Jfk-conspiracy/harperfrag.html

12. Did Dr. Burkley Cover Up the Medical Evidence? (Episode 3, 1:33)

Henry Hurt on Dr. Burkley: *Reasonable Doubt*, Holt, Rinehart and Winston, 1985, page 49; https://archive.org/details/reasonabledoubti00hurt/mode/2up?q=%22reasonable+doubt%22+henry+hurt

ARRB on Dr. Burkley: https://sgp.fas.org/advisory/arrb98/part09.htm

Richard Sprague's memo: https://www.history-matters.com/archive/jfk/hsca/numbered_files/box_23/180-10086-10295/html/180-10086-10295_0002a.htm

Pat Speer on Michael Kurtz: https://www.patspeer.com/chapter-19d-lost-in-the-jungle-with-kurtz

Paul Hoch's speech from 1993: "Winnowing the Wheat and the Chaff"; https://www.jfk-assassination.net/hoch.htm

Paul Hoch's newsletter, Echoes of Conspiracy, May 31, 1987, Volume 9, #1: https://archive.org/details/nsia-HochPaulCorrespondence/nsia-HochPaulCorrespondence/Hoch%20Paul%200941/page/n1/mode/1up?view=theater

Best Evidence picture of Dr. Burkley: *Best Evidence: Disguise and Deception in the Assassination of John F. Kennedy*, David S. Lifton, Carroll & Graf, 1988, photograph is in section just before page 587; https://archive.org/details/bestevidencedisg0000lift/page/n635/mode/2up

Lifton quote on Burkley: Lifton, op. cit., page 401.

Paul Hoch on evaluating evidence: https://www.jfk-assassination.net/hoch.htm

Warren Commission Exhibit 1126: https://www.maryferrell.org/showDoc.html?docId=1317#relPageId=123

Burkley's interview with the HSCA: https://www.maryferrell.org/showDoc.html?docId=600#relPageId=4&search=%22ARRB_MD%2019%22

Dr. George Burkley's oral history interview for the JFK Library: https://www.jfklibrary.org/sites/default/files/archives/JFKOH/Burkley%2C%20George%20G/JFKOH-GGB-01/JFKOH-GGB-01-TR.pdf

Dr. George Burkley's specialty: https://www.washingtonpost.com/archive/local/1991/01/04/george-g-burkley-88-dies/9473823e-44d2-4e1f-bf01-9547ecf3fd17/

Dr. George Burkley's affidavit for the HSCA: https://www.maryferrell.org/showDoc.html?docId=145280#relPageId=434

Dr. Donald Miller's article mentioning friendship with one of Dr. Burkley's sons: https://www.lewrockwell.com/1970/01/donald-w-miller-jr-md/pursuing-truth-on-the-kennedy-assassinations/

JFK's death certificate: https://www.history-matters.com/archive/jfk/arrb/master_med_set/md6/html/Image1.htm

Dr. Miller on Boswell diagram: https://www.lewrockwell.com/2013/11/donald-w-miller-jr-md/jfk-thought-control-and-thought-crimes/

JFK Autopsy Face-Sheet: https://www.maryferrell.org/showDoc.html?docId=82#relPageId=98&search=%22autopsy_descriptive%20sheet%22

JFK autopsy report: https://www.maryferrell.org/showDoc.html?docId=62463#relPageId=90&search=%22situated_on%20the%20upper%20right%20posterior%22

Quote from Dr Donald Miller on Burkley's observations: "Pursuing Truth on the Kennedy Assassinations"; https://www.lewrockwell.com/1970/01/donald-w-miller-jr-md/pursuing-truth-on-the-kennedy-assassinations/

Dr. Donald Miller's accusation against the Warren Commission: Ibid.

"Miller went off the deep end": "If Not Oswald, Who Killed President Kennedy and Why," July 24,

2019; https://www.lewrockwell.com/2019/07/donald-w-miller-jr-md/if-not-oswald-who-killed-president-kennedy-and-why/

"Where does all this come from?": Ibid.

Miller goes even further: "Reflections on the Assassination of President John F. Kennedy, 50 Years Later," November 16, 2013; https://www.lewrockwell.com/2013/11/donald-w-miller-jr-md/jfk-thought-control-and-thought-crimes/

One of the books Miller recommends: *Harvey and Lee: How the CIA framed Oswald*, Quasar, 2003 ; https://archive.org/details/HarveyAndLeeByJohnArmstrong2003/mode/2up?q=%22harvey+and+Lee%22+armstrong; Dr. Donald Miller's quote on Armstrong - https://www.lewrockwell.com/2019/07/donald-w-miller-jr-md/if-not-oswald-who-killed-president-kennedy-and-why/

Miller buys into the two-Oswalds theory: "Reflections on the Assassination of President John F. Kennedy, 50 Years Later," November 16, 2013; https://www.lewrockwell.com/2013/11/donald-w-miller-jr-md/jfk-thought-control-and-thought-crimes/

Miller even believes that saying Oswald is innocent is considered a thought-crime: https://www.lewrockwell.com/2013/11/donald-w-miller-jr-md/jfk-thought-control-and-thought-crimes/

Miller's belief that JFK Jr. was killed by a conspiracy: https://www.lewrockwell.com/1970/01/donald-w-miller-jr-md/pursuing-truth-on-the-kennedy-assassinations/

Dr. Donald Miller's writings for LewRockwell.com: https://www.lewrockwell.com/author/donald-w-miller-jr-md/

Some of his articles speak for themselves: Vaccines are dangerous: https://www.lewrockwell.com/1970/01/donald-w-miller-jr-md/vaccines-are-dangerous/; Fluoride is poison: https://www.lewrockwell.com/1970/01/donald-w-miller-jr-md/fluoride-is-poison/; Questioning HIV/AIDs: https://www.lewrockwell.com/2008/03/donald-w-miller-jr-md/questioning-hivaids/; Flu shots: https://www.lewrockwell.com/2008/10/donald-w-miller-jr-md/dont-get-a-flu-shot-2/; HIV is harmless: https://www.lewrockwell.com/2014/05/donald-w-miller-jr-md/hiv-is-harmless/; RFK Jr. and the Covid coup: https://www.lewrockwell.com/2022/01/donald-w-miller-jr-md/robert-f-kennedy-jr-tackles-the-covid-coup/

Baseless charges of conspiracy theorists:

Clay Shaw's life was ruined by Jim Garrison: see *On the Trail of Delusion*, Fred Litwin, NorthernBlues Books, 2020. www.onthetrailofdelusion.com

Larry Crafard's marriage: https://www.onthetrailofdelusion.com/post/jim-garrison-names-the-grassy-knoll-gunman

Kerry Thornley went off the deep end: Litwin, op. cit., page 192.

Insinuations about Ruth Paine: https://wtracyparnell.blogspot.com/search/label/The%20Assassination%20and%20Mrs.%20Paine

Carlos Bringuier: Dr. Carlos J. Bringuier, *Crime Without Punishment: How Castro Assassinated President Kennedy and Got Away with It*, (2014), pages 301 – 302

Roger Craig: https://www.jfk-assassination.net/craig.htm

Article by John Titus: "Dr. Burkley and The Bullet": https://www.covertbookreport.com/dr-burkley-and-the-bullet/

DiEugenio posting about Burkley's family: https://educationforum.ipbhost.com/topic/27466-jfk-revisited-through-the-looking-glass/page/34/#comment-453604

James DiEugenio reference to Titus article at his website: https://www.kennedysandking.com/john-f-kennedy-articles/bending-the-story-on-a-bent-bullet

DiEugenio posting about Burkley and 'extra bullet': https://educationforum.ipbhost.com/topic/27105-the-extra-bullet-at-bethesda/#comment-440779

DiEugenio posting about Burkley being a central character: https://educationforum.ipbhost.com/topic/27105-the-extra-bullet-at-bethesda/#comment-440821

Bill Baxley's famous reply: https://flashbak.com/kiss-my-ass-bill-baxleys-1976-letter-to-the-kkk-384536/

13. Was the Wound in the Back of JFK's Head One of Exit? (Episode 3, 6:22)

Audrey Bell's interview with the ARRB: https://www.maryferrell.org/showDoc.html?docId=715#relPageId=2&search=%22MD_184%22

Excerpt from a transcript from Bell's interview: I made transcripts from the tapes that are here - https://history-matters.com/archive/jfk/arrb/medical_interviews/audio/ARRB_Bell.htm

Audrey Bell's diagram for the ARRB: https://www.maryferrell.org/showDoc.html?docId=715#relPageId=6&search=%22MD_184%22

Bell's other diagram: https://www.maryferrell.org/showDoc.html?docId=715#relPageId=7&search=%22MD_184%22

Pat Speer on Audrey Bell: https://www.patspeer.com/chapter-18d-reason-to-believe

Dr. Jones oral history: *We Were There: Revelations from the Dallas Doctors Who Attended JFK on November 22, 1963*, Allen Childs, MD, Skyhorse, 2013, pages 30-31

Dr. Jenkins told Dennis Breo: Breo, op. cit., page 2805; https://www.maryferrell.org/showDoc.html?docId=748%23relPageId=38#relPageId=39

14. Was Cerebellum Extruding from JFK's Head Wound? (Episode 3, 6:52)

Drawing of the photograph of JFK's brain: https://www.maryferrell.org/showDoc.html?docId=82#relPageId=140; https://www.maryferrell.org/archive/photos/HSCA-EXHIBITS/Photo_hsca_ex_302.jpg

Testimony of Dr. Carrico before the Warren Commission: https://www.maryferrell.org/showDoc.html?docId=35#relPageId=16

Bugliosi asking Carrico about cerebellum: *Reclaiming History: The Assassination of President John F. Kennedy*, W. W. Norton & Company, 2007, page 405.

Dr. Jenkins seeing cerebellum: https://www.maryferrell.org/showDoc.html?docId=1134#relPageId=41&search=cerebellum

Dr. Jenkins going to the National Archives: https://www.jfk-assassination.net/cerebellum.htm

Gerald Posner talked to Dr. Jenkins: *Cased Closed: Lee Harvey Oswald and the Assassination of JFK*, Random House, 1993, page 311

Dr. Perry quote about cerebellum: https://www.maryferrell.org/showDoc.html?docId=82#relPageId=312

Gerald Posner also talked to Dr. Perry: Posner, op. cit., page 312.

Dr. Michael Baden explained to Gerald Posner: Posner, op. cit., page 309.

Dr. Paul Peters and the autopsy X-rays and photographs: https://www.jfk-assassination.net/cerebellum.htm

Dr. Jenkins on Dr. McClelland: Posner, op. cit., page 313.

Quote from Pat Speer: https://www.patspeer.com/chapter17newerviewsonthesamescene

Speer quotes Larry Sturdivan: Ibid; *The JFK Myths: A Scientific Investigation of the Kennedy Assassination*, Larry Sturdivan, Paragon House, 2005, page 209

Here is how Larry Sturdivan sees the trajectory: Sturdivan, op. cit., page 210.

15. Is There a Problem with the Weight of JFK's Brain? (Episode 3, 10:08)

Excerpt from Bugliosi's book: Bugliosi, op. cit., Endnote 441.

Baden on the weight of JFK's brain: Ibid.

Supplementary Report of the autopsy: https://www.maryferrell.org/showDoc.html?docId=62463#relPageId=94

Table on brain weights: *Current Methods of Autopsy Practice*, Jurgen Ludwig, M. D., W. B. Saunders Company, 1979, page 666.

Another source on the weights of brains: *The Human Brain in Figures and Tables: A Quantitative Handbook*, S. M. Blinkov and I. I. Glezer, Basic Books, 1968, page 3; https://archive.org/details/humanbraininfigu0000blin?q=

Humes used a formalin concentration of 10%: https://www.maryferrell.org/showDoc.html?docId=208753#relPageId=111

Guy Banister's autopsy: https://archive.org/details/GarrisonPapers/Garrison%20and%20Alcock/page/n20/mode/1up

16. Did the Conspirators Substitute JFK's Brain? (Episode 3, 12:16)

Kirschner's interview with the ARRB: https://www.maryferrell.org/showDoc.html?docId=145280#relPageId=229

17. Did John Stringer Take Photographs of JFK's Brain? (Episode 3, 15:09)

Stringer interview with the ARRB: https://www.maryferrell.org/showDoc.html?docId=749#relPageId=4

Stringer deposition before the ARRB: https://www.maryferrell.org/showDoc.html?docId=798#relPageId=1

Excerpt from the document "Search for missing autopsy materials,": https://www.maryferrell.org/showDoc.html?docId=600#relPageId=14

Letter that Stringer sent to Purdy: https://www.maryferrell.org/showDoc.html?docId=343#relPageId=1

18. Did a White House Photographer Take Autopsy Photographs? (Episode 3, 17:08)

Robert Knudsen testimony before the HSCA: https://www.maryferrell.org/showDoc.html?docId=666#relPageId=1

ARRB interviews with Knudsen's family: https://www.maryferrell.org/showDoc.html?docId=752#relPageId=1

Tape of the Knudsen family's interview with the ARRB: https://history-matters.com/archive/jfk/arrb/medical_interviews/audio/ARRB_KnudsenFamily_R1S1.mp3

List of attendees at JFK's autopsy: https://www.maryferrell.org/showDoc.html?docId=625#relPageId=3

HSCA authentication of JFK's autopsy X-rays and photographs: https://www.maryferrell.org/showDoc.html?docId=958#relPageId=231

Knudsen's family on his appearance at an inquiry in 1988: https://www.maryferrell.org/showDoc.html?docId=752#relPageId=5

Dr. Randy Robertson called Douglas Horne: https://www.maryferrell.org/showDoc.html?docId=752#relPageId=6

ARRB interview with Joe O'Donnell: https://www.maryferrell.org/showDoc.html?docId=753#relPageId=5

Mrs. Knudsen calling associates of her husband: https://www.maryferrell.org/showDoc.html?docId=752#relPageId=7

Quote from John Stringer on Knudsen: John Thomas Stringer, Jr., *MEDPHOTO: Snapshots of Life in Peace & War with the U. S. Navy*, (Wishbone Creative Product Services, 2008), page 84; https://www.lulu.com/shop/john-stringer/medphoto-snapshots-of-life-in-peace-war-with-the-us-navy/paperback/product-1pmmdw7.html?page=1&pageSize=4

JFK: Destiny Betrayed once again ignored issues of memory: https://www.onthetrailofdelusion.com/post/oliver-stone-pulls-the-wool-over-joe-rogan-s-eyes-part-two

19. Did Saundra Spencer Develop a Completely Different Set of Autopsy Photographs? (Episode 3, 19:30)

Saundra Spencer interview with the ARRB: https://www.maryferrell.org/showDoc.html?docId=755#relPageId=2

Saundra Spencer deposition before the ARRB: https://www.maryferrell.org/showDoc.html?docId=200943#relPageId=1

Autopsy film developed on November 27, 1963: https://www.maryferrell.org/showDoc.html?docId=653#relPageId=1

ARRB interview of Vince Madonia: https://www.maryferrell.org/showDoc.html?docId=754#relPageId=2

James Fox contact report with the HSCA: https://www.maryferrell.org/showDoc.html?docId=655#relPageId=1

Vincent Bugliosi raised the possibility: Bugliosi, op. cit., Endnote 428.

20. Are There Any Missing Autopsy Photographs? (Episode 3, 20:59)

Stringer talking about offering suggestions: https://www.maryferrell.org/showDoc.html?docId=208758#relPageId=165

Last page from inventory of autopsy materials: https://www.maryferrell.org/showDoc.html?docId=594#relPageId=11

Stringer asked about missing views: https://www.maryferrell.org/showDoc.html?docId=208758#relPageId=143

Stringer asked about missing photographs: https://www.maryferrell.org/showDoc.html?docId=208758#relPageId=153

Dr. Humes remembers two photographs: https://www.maryferrell.org/showDoc.html?docId=208753#relPageId=100

Dr. Humes asked about missing photographs: https://www.maryferrell.org/showDoc.html?docId=208753#relPageId=198

Dr. Boswell was also asked about missing photographs: https://www.maryferrell.org/showDoc.html?docId=204574#relPageId=156

"Even the orientation of the current photographs confused Dr. Humes": https://www.maryferrell.org/showDoc.html?docId=788#relPageId=200

Bugliosi on chest photograph: Bugliosi, op. cit., Endnote 428.

Bugliosi noting that a missing photograph wouldn't change anything: Ibid.

21. Did Gerald Ford Change the Location of JFK's Back Wound? (Episode 3, 34:22)

JFK autopsy face-sheet: https://www.maryferrell.org/showDoc.html?docId=95#relPageId=232

Introductory section of the Warren Report: https://www.maryferrell.org/showDoc.html?docId=946#relPageId=27

ARRB Press Release on Gerald Ford edits: http://jfk.hood.edu/Collection/Weisberg%20Subject%20Index%20Files/F%20Disk/Ford%20Gerald%20R%20Warren%20Report%20Sugested%20Changes/Item%2001.pdf

Neck wounds discussed in a later section: https://www.maryferrell.org/showDoc.html?docId=946#relPageId=111

Author Jean Davison asked a good question: "Gerald Ford and the Single-Bullet Theory,"; http://jfk-archives.blogspot.com/2010/06/gerald-ford-and-sbt.html

Warren Commission Exhibit 903: https://www.maryferrell.org/showDoc.html?docId=1135#relPageId=110

Robert Croft photo #3: https://www.maryferrell.org/archive/photos/HSCA-EXHIBITS/Photo_hsca_ex_135.jpg; https://www.maryferrell.org/showDoc.html?docId=81#relPageId=178&search=%22f-135%22

22. Did the Autopsy Pathologists have a Presupposed Conclusion? (Episode 3, 56:51)

Clinical summary of JFK's autopsy report: https://www.maryferrell.org/showDoc.html?docId=1133#relPageId=1003

Teletype on the assassination: https://dygtyjqp7pi0m.cloudfront.net/i/8185/9627464_1.jpg?v=8CCE5DF3637EDA0

Dr. Gary Aguilar's article: "How Five Investigations Into JFK's Medical/Autopsy Evidence Got it Wrong"; https://www.history-matters.com/essays/jfkmed/How5Investigations/How5InvestigationsGotItWrong_1a.htm

Dr. Pierre Finck's ARRB Deposition: https://www.maryferrell.org/showDoc.html?docId=

787#relPageId=13

Quote from Dr. Humes: Breo, op. cit.; https://www.maryferrell.org/showDoc.html?docId=748#relPageId=34

Nick Nalli's review of Josiah Thompson's book, Last Second in Dallas: http://jfkfiles.blogspot.com/2021/06/the-ghost-of-grassy-knoll-gunman.html

Nick Nalli's important 2018 paper: "Gunshot Wound Dynamics model for John F. Kennedy Assassination," Heliyon, April 2018; https://www.ncbi.nlm.nih.gov/pmc/articles/PMC5934694/

Physical Evidence

23. Did Lee Harvey Oswald Have an Alibi? (Episode 1, 49:32)

Warren Commission conclusions about Victoria Adams: https://www.maryferrell.org/showDoc.html?docId=946#relPageId=178

Styles told an interviewer: https://youtu.be/pkUa3NeTZYQ

Warren Commission testimony of Victoria Adams: https://www.maryferrell.org/showDoc.html?docId=35#relPageId=402

Sandra Styles said: https://www.maryferrell.org/showDoc.html?docId=1317#relPageId=706

Vickie Adams on time from window to the top of the stairs: https://www.maryferrell.org/showDoc.html?docId=35#relPageId=402

Human memory is not like a video camera: "Memory Errors in Alibi Generation: How an Alibi Can Turn Against Us," *Behavioral Sciences & the Law*, Crozier, Strange and Loftus; https://escholarship.org/content/qt48p7n1zr/qt48p7n1zr.pdf?t=ooyl1x

Barry Ernest asked Adams: *The Girl on the Stairs: The Search for a Missing Witness to the JFK Assassination*, Pelican, 2018; page 251

Sandra Styles told researcher Sean Murphy: https://groups.google.com/g/alt.assassination.jfk/c/3Dsk9bpdySI

Quote from Jerry Dealey: "The Ups and Downs of the TSBD – Aftermath."; http://dealey.org/updown3.pdf

Victoria Adams identifying Jack Ruby: https://www.maryferrell.org/showDoc.html?docId=35#relPageId=403

Adams telling Ernest about Jack Ruby: Ernest, op. cit., page 244 – 245.

Ernest on Adams' husband: Ernest, op. cit., page 139.

Barry Ernest on a supposed assassin leaving the sixth floor: https://thegirlonthestairs.wordpress.com/2014/01/07/the-sixth-floor-escape/

Sealing of the TSBD: *JFK Assassination:* Jerry T. Dealey, *Shades from the Fence*, 2022, page 260

Jerry Dealey quote on the sealing of the TSBD: Email to Fred Litwin.

24. Did Marina Oswald Take the Backyard Photographs? (Episode 2, 38:40)

Three backyard photographs of Oswald: http://www.famouspictures.org/wp-content/uploads/2013/05/CE-133-all.jpg

Tom Brokaw interview of Marina Porter, August 1993: https://youtu.be/swHZ0DxB8n8

The HSCA showed the backyard photographs to Marina Porter: https://www.maryferrell.org/showDoc.html?docId=81#relPageId=243

The HSCA introduced another picture: https://www.maryferrell.org/showDoc.html?docId=81#relPageId=245

Marina Porter said Oswald used to practice with his rifle: https://www.maryferrell.org/showDoc.html?docId=81#relPageId=235

25. Is There an Issue with the Strap and Sling Mounts on the Mannlicher-Carcano? (Episode 2, 39:16)

Warren Commission Exhibit 139: https://www.maryferrell.org/showDoc.html?docId=1133#relPageId=536

Steve Roe has debunked this segment: https://steveroeconsulting.wixsite.com/website/post/jfk-revisited-again-caught-creating-false-mysteries

Waldman Exhibit 1: https://www.maryferrell.org/showDoc.html?docId=1138#relPageId=716

Photos of ads in the American Rifleman magazine: Courtesy of David Von Pein's blog on the JFK assassination; https://jfk-archives.blogspot.com/search?q=rifleman

26. Were the Backyard Photographs Faked? (Episode 2, 40:41)

Excerpt of testimony from Guy Rose: https://www.maryferrell.org/showDoc.html?docId=41#relPageId=241

Here is a close-up of CE 133-A: https://www.maryferrell.org/showDoc.html?docId=1134#relPageId=543; https://www.maryferrell.org/showDoc.html?docId=1133#relPageId=534

Photo of 133-C: https://www.maryferrell.org/showDoc.html?docId=81#relPageId=250

Farid's 3-D study: "A 3-D Stability Analysis of Lee Harvey Oswald in the Backyard Photo," Pittala, Whiting & Farid; https://static1.squarespace.com/static/54d8440ae4b0a80ddb2b9e1c/t/5702e6dcab48deec9808c314/1459808039173/jdfsl15.pdf

The HSCA on fakery: https://www.maryferrell.org/showDoc.html?docId=958#relPageId=221; The HSCA study on the backyard photographs was conducted by three experts from the Rochester Institute of Technology; https://scholarworks.rit.edu/cgi/viewcontent.cgi?article=1482&context=article

27. Was Oswald's Palmprint on His Mannlicher-Carcano Rifle? (Episode 2, 42:06)

Steve Roe has debunked this allegation: https://steveroeconsulting.wixsite.com/website/post/a-look-at-the-jfk-revisited-through-the-looking-glass-film-by-oliver-stone

Sebastian Latona's testimony before the Warren Commission: https://www.maryferrell.org/showDoc.html?docId=34#relPageId=31

Warren Commission Exhibit 637: https://www.maryferrell.org/showDoc.html?docId=1134#relPageId=316

28. Was there a Problem with the Chain of Custody of CE 399? (Episode 2, 44:36)

Steve Roe's article on CE 399: "A Single Photograph Disproves Oliver Stone's Conspiracy Claim, June 11 2022; https://www.washingtondecoded.com/site/2022/06/roe3.html

Tammi Long examines CE 399: https://www.maryferrell.org/showDoc.html?docId=203393#relPageId=7

Dr. David Mantik admits Todd's initials are on CE 399: https://www.onthetrailofdelusion.com/post/dr-david-mantik-admits-elmer-todd-s-initials-are-on-ce-399

James DiEugenio demurred: https://educationforum.ipbhost.com/topic/27827-new-photographic-proof-todds-initials-on-399/page/5/#comment-462064

James DiEugenio admits Todd's initials are on CE 399: https://educationforum.ipbhost.com/topic/27895-steve-roe-consulting/#comment-463931

The allegation on the timing: https://web.archive.org/web/20210425212917/http:/www.jfklancer.com/hunt/mystery.html

29. Did CE 399 Look like the Bullet Found at Parkland Hospital? (Episode 2, 47:56)

FBI Airtel: https://www.maryferrell.org/showDoc.html?docId=59607#relPageId=29

Tomlinson and Wright interviews with the FBI: https://www.maryferrell.org/showDoc.html?docId=1140#relPageId=430

Raymond Marcus spoke to Tomlinson: http://jfk-archives.blogspot.com/2011/12/marcus-tomlinson-interview-7-25-66.html

Tomlinson quoted in the Dallas Morning News: https://www.onthetrailofdelusion.com/post/jfk-destiny-betrayed-misleads-on-ce399

Conspiracy

30. Was Jack Ruby Signaled in the Dallas Police Department Basement? (Episode 2, 52:43)

Video of Jack Ruby shooting Oswald: https://youtu.be/r6PcVCqg3tg

Longer video of the Dallas police basement: https://youtu.be/m5khMFFKslw

Mark Lane testimony before the Jim Garrison grand jury: https://www.maryferrell.org/showDoc.html?docId=1193#relPageId=57

James DiEugenio's analysis of the horns: James DiEugenio, *The JFK Assassination: The Evidence Today*, (Skyhorse, 2018), page 228

Bugliosi is quite specific and mentions who was doing the honking: Bugliosi, op. cit., pages 272 – 273.

31. Why Did Jack Ruby Kill Lee Harvey Oswald? (Episode 2, 55:07)

Full transcript of that video: https://youtu.be/NiPl2DNwJJk

Video shot during a break in court: https://www.maryferrell.org/showDoc.html?docId=57094#relPageId=28

Another clip of Ruby: https://youtu.be/TxfXNzbSFcQ

Warren Commission on Jack Ruby's polygraph test: https://www.maryferrell.org/showDoc.html?docId=946#relPageId=839

Warren Commission biography of Jack Ruby: https://www.maryferrell.org/showDoc.html?docId=946#relPageId=804

"Welcome Mr. Kennedy" ad in the Dallas Morning News: https://www.maryferrell.org/showDoc.html?docId=1138#relPageId=746

Jack Ruby at his sister's apartment: https://www.maryferrell.org/showDoc.html?docId=946#relPageId=372

Jack Ruby awakened his roommate George Senator: https://www.maryferrell.org/showDoc.html?docId=1138#relPageId=459

Ruby called his friend Stanley Kaufman: https://www.maryferrell.org/showDoc.html?docId=946#relPageId=371

Ruby shooting Oswald: https://www.youtube.com/watch?v=r6PcVCqg3tg

Ruby on killing Oswald to save a lot of people trouble: https://www.maryferrell.org/showDoc.html?docId=56994#relPageId=113

Ruby told Assistant District Attorney Bill Alexander, "Well, you guys couldn't do it. Someone had to do it. That son of a bitch killed my President": Posner, op. cit., page 399.

Ruby told his Rabbi: Garry Wills and Ovid Demaris, *Jack Ruby: The Man Who Killed The Man Who Killed Kennedy*, (The New American Library, 1968), page 85; https://archive.org/details/willsdemaris0000unse/page/84/mode/2up

Ruby's claim he kills Oswald to spare Jackie returning for a trial: https://www.jfk-assassination.net/sorrow.htm

Ruby became extremely paranoid: The Trial of Jack Ruby, John Kaplan and Jon R. Waltz, The Macmillan Company, 1965, pages 344 – 345

Ruby's impassioned plea to be taken to Washington: https://www.maryferrell.org/showDoc.html?docId=40#relPageId=220

Jack Ruby's examination by Dr. Werner Tuteur: http://jfk.hood.edu/Collection/Weisberg%20Subject%20Index%20Files/R%20Disk/Ruby%20Jack%20Psychiatric/Item%2004.pdf

32. Was a Bullet Found in JFK's Limousine? (Episode 3, 26:05)

James Young wrote Gerald Ford: https://aarclibrary.org/white-house-physician-autopsy-eyewitness-questions-president-ford-about-missing-bullet/

Young sat down for an oral history project: https://whowhatwhy.org/politics/government-integrity/navy-doctor-bullet-found-jfks-limousine-never-reported/; see page 51 of his manuscript.

Warren Commission Document 80: https://www.maryferrell.org/showDoc.html?docId=10482#relPageId=1

The FBI analysis: https://www.maryferrell.org/showDoc.html?docId=57697#relPageId=176

Warren Commission Exhibit 569: https://www.maryferrell.org/showDoc.html?docId=1134#relPageId=283

Aguilar, DeSalles and Simpich report rebutting Dr. Robertson's review: https://aarclibrary.org/rebuttal-summary-of-robertsons-salient-mistakes/

Mills and Paterni identified fragments Q2 and Q3: https://www.maryferrell.org/showDoc.html?docId=11653#relPageId=5

Excerpt of Robert Frazier testimony: https://www.history-matters.com/archive/jfk/wc/wcvols/wh5/html/WC_Vol5_0039a.htm

33. Was There a Hole in the Windshield of JFK's Limousine? (Episode 3, 27:49)

Aguilar, DeSalles and Simpich on flares: https://aarclibrary.org/rebuttal-summary-of-robertsons-salient-mistakes/

As for the flare in frame 329: https://www.kennedysandking.com/john-f-kennedy-reviews/a-review-of-last-second-in-dallas-by-josiah-thompson

Josiah Thompson believes that the flare substantiates his theory: Josiah Thompson, *Last Second in Dallas*, (University Press of Kansas, 2021), page 234

Quote on the "the progressive movement of the reflected sunlight on the curve of the windshield.": "'Your Lying Eyes' – Josiah Thompson's Lonely Labyrinth" by Louis Girdler, page 78; https://www.jfk-assassination.net/pdf/LABYRINTH.pdf

Team of five FBI agents examining the limousine: https://www.maryferrell.org/showDoc.html?docId=10482

At about 10 PM, Chief Mills and Martinell: https://www.maryferrell.org/showDoc.html?docId=10482#relPageId=3

A team of FBI agents thoroughly examined the car: https://www.maryferrell.org/showDoc.html?docId=40#relPageId=81

Warren Commission Exhibit 350: https://www.maryferrell.org/showDoc.html?docId=1133#relPageId=970

Warren Commission Exhibit 349: https://www.maryferrell.org/showDoc.html?docId=1133#relPageId=969

Robert Frazier was asked about the windshield: https://www.maryferrell.org/showDoc.html?docId=40#relPageId=78

Memo written by F. Vaughn Ferguson: https://www.maryferrell.org/showDoc.html?docId=1461#relPageId=53

In March 1964, the windshield was further examined: https://www.maryferrell.org/showDoc.html?docId=11293#relPageId=312

The HSCA Firearms Panel on the windshield: https://www.maryferrell.org/showDoc.html?docId=82#relPageId=378

Six witnesses who said they saw a hole in the windshield: https://insidethearrb.livejournal.com/7512.html

Here is what Ellis told author Larry Sneed: Larry Sneed, *No More Silence: An Oral History of the Assassination of President Kennedy*, (Three Forks, 1998), page 147

Richard Dudman in The New Republic: "Commentary of an Eyewitness"; http://jfk.hood.edu/Collection/Weisberg%20Subject%20Index%20Files/M%20Disk/Minnis%20Jack%20Staughton%20Lynn/Item%2001.pdf

Quote from George Whitaker: https://insidethearrb.livejournal.com/7512.html

The only problem was that the car was still in Washington: "In Broad Daylight: The JFK Presidential Limousine SS-100-X and the Crime of the Century," Pamela Brown; http://ss100x.com/

Evalea Glanges on the windshield: https://youtu.be/3TisPzyrM-0

Report from Charles Taylor, Jr.: https://www.maryferrell.org/showDoc.html?docId=10482#relPageId=14

Church Committee on Taylor allegation: https://www.maryferrell.org/showDoc.html?docId=1464#relPageId=109

The Committee staff interviewed Taylor: https://www.maryferrell.org/showDoc.html?docId=1464#relPageId=111

Charles Taylor affidavit: https://www.onthetrailofdelusion.com/post/jfk-destiny-betrayed-misleads-on-supposed-extra-bullet-part-two

Bullet hole would have looked like this: https://www.pinterest.ca/pin/342766221639504453/

The windshield is still in existence: https://catalog.archives.gov/id/305143

Douglas Horne notes: https://insidethearrb.livejournal.com/7512.html

To Douglas Horne, this is all part and parcel of a series of altered evidence: Ibid.

Oliver Stone on the alteration of the Zapruder Film: https://www.onthetrailofdelusion.com/post/oliver-stone-claims-the-zapruder-film-was-altered

34. Did Gerald Ford Tell French President Valéry Giscard D'Estaing that There was a Conspiracy? (Episode 3, 34:45)

Giscard supposedly told the story in 2013 when he was 87 years old: https://www.leparisien.fr/week-end/vge-raconte-jfk-21-11-2013-3336729.php

Even Jefferson Morley finds it hard to believe: https://jfkfacts.org/president-ford-spoke-jfk-plot-says-former-french-president/

It wasn't the only story: https://www.washingtonpost.com/local/obituaries/valery-giscard-destaing-dead/2020/12/02/62511218-34ec-11eb-8d38-6aea1adb3839_story.html

James DiEugenio's review of my book: https://www.kennedysandking.com/john-f-kennedy-articles/litwin-and-the-warren-report

Summers' quote about Byars: Official and Confidential: The Secret Life of J. Edgar Hoover, Anthony Summers, G. P. Putnam's Sons, 1993, page 330

DiEugenio also tells a whopper of a story about Clay Shaw: https://www.kennedysandking.com/john-f-kennedy-reviews/fred-litwin-on-the-trail-of-delusion-part-two

35. Was General Curtis LeMay Ordered to Fly to Andrews Air Force Base? (Episode 3, 54:07)

Transcript of Air Force 1 Tape by Douglas P. Horne: https://www.maryferrell.org/showDoc.html?docId=146531#relPageId=20

Holmes logbook: https://educationforum.ipbhost.com/topic/4250-jfk-lancer-conference/page/5/#comment-46191

Dialog between Behn and Clifton: *The Kennedy Assassination Tapes: The White House conversations of Lyndon B. Johnson regarding the assassination, the Warren Commission and the aftermath*, Max Holland, Alfred A. Knopf, 2004, page 34.

After Action Report: http://jfk.hood.edu/Collection/Weisberg%20Subject%20Index%20Files/K%20Disk/Kennedy%20John%20F%20Funeral/Item%2001.pdf

Here is an excerpt from the Military District of Washington After Action Report: Ibid.

Oral history transcript, Curtis LeMay: https://discoverlbj.org/item/oh-lemayc-19710628-1-76-30

Curtis LeMay expense report for November 1963: https://downloads.paperlessarchives.com/p/general-curtis-lemay-personnel-files-defense-department-reports-monographs/

Larry Haapanen spoke to Air Force Colonel Aaron Burleson in 2001: E-mail to Fred Litwin from Larry Haapanen.

Quote about Aaron Burleson: *Lawton Constitution* from June 26, 1974, which discussed retirement ceremonies for Aaron Burleson, commander of the 443rd Air Force Group.

A more nuanced view of General Curtis LeMay: https://www.historyonthenet.com/dr-strangeloves-real-life-air-force-general-curtis-lemay; excerpt from Warren Kozak's *Curtis LeMay: Strategist and Tactician*

According to Carl Kaysen: Oral History Interview, 7/11/1966; https://www.jfklibrary.org/asset-viewer/archives/JFKOH/Kaysen%2C%20Carl/JFKOH-CK-01/JFKOH-CK-01

James DiEugenio quote about LeMay: https://educationforum.ipbhost.com/topic/27466-jfk-revisited-through-the-looking-glass/page/40/#comment-455341

36. Did General Curtis LeMay Attend JFK's Autopsy? (Episode 3, 56:29)

Douglas Horne on 'Deep Throat' and LeMay: *Inside the Assassination Records Review Board, Volume V*, 2009, page 1784.

Horne ultimately dismissed 'Deep Throat': Ibid, page 1778.

O'Connor's interview by William Matson Law: *In the Eye of History: Disclosures in the JFK Assassination Medical Evidence*, William Matson Law, (Trine Day, page 195)

O'Connor told a similar story to James DiEugenio in 1991: James DiEugenio, *Destiny Betrayed: JFK, Cuba, and the Garrison Case*, (Skyhorse, 2012), page 302

O'Connor's story to Douglas Horne: *Inside the Assassination Records Review Board*, Volume II, page 487.

Harrison Livingstone on his press conference: http://jfk.hood.edu/Collection/Weisberg%20Subject%20Index%20Files/A%20Disk/Assassination%20Information%20Center/Item%2008.pdf

O'Connor in the Dealey Plaza Echo: https://www.maryferrell.org/showDoc.html?docId=16255#relPageId=49

Bill Kelly's anecdote: https://educationforum.ipbhost.com/topic/10724-curtis-lemay-and-john-f-kennedy/page/5/#comment-165361

Sibert and O'Neill's FBI report listing attendees at the autopsy: https://www.maryferrell.org/showDoc.html?docId=625#relPageId=3

Law's interview of Francis O'Neill: Law, op. cit., page 302 of Kindle edition.

HSCA list of attendees at the autopsy: https://www.maryferrell.org/showDoc.html?docId=82#relPageId=18

Dr. Humes on whether LeMay was at the autopsy: https://www.maryferrell.org/showDoc.html?docId=208753#relPageId=67

Dr. Boswell on whether LeMay was at the autopsy: https://www.maryferrell.org/showDoc.html?docId=204574#relPageId=33

O'Connor's first interview with the HSCA: https://www.maryferrell.org/showDoc.html?docId=328#relPageId=1

Sibert and O'Neill FBI report says Kennedy was wrapped in a sheet: https://www.maryferrell.org/showDoc.html?docId=625#relPageId=4

Humes also took exception: https://www.maryferrell.org/showDoc.html?docId=603#relPageId=6

O'Connor also told the HSCA that Kennedy's brain was gone: https://www.maryferrell.org/showDoc.html?docId=328#relPageId=3

Bugliosi spoke to Stringer: Bugliosi, op. cit., page 1,069.

O'Connor's difficult moments: https://www.maryferrell.org/showDoc.html?docId=328#relPageId=8

Harrison Livingstone interview of O'Connor: *High Treason 2*, Harrison Livingstone, Carroll & Graf, 1992, pages 268 – 269; https://archive.org/details/hightreason2grea0000livi/page/268/mode/2up?q=%22soaked+with+blood%22

Livingstone tried to get O'Connor to recant: Livingstone, op. cit., page 272

David Lifton does not believe LeMay was at the autopsy: https://educationforum.ipbhost.com/topic/28105-why-did-jfk-make-curtis-lemay-a-joint-chief-and-keep-him/#comment-470728

Lifton warned about some interviews of O'Connor: https://educationforum.ipbhost.com/topic/7502-paul-kelly-oconnor/page/2/#comment-284551

37. Was Lee Harvey Oswald a Fake Defector? (Episode 4, 1:37)

Church Committee, Book V: https://www.maryferrell.org/showDoc.html?docId=1161#relPageId=1&tab=toc

Quote about Otepka being the leading expert on Communist subversion in the State Department: "McCarthyite in Camelot: The "Loss" of Cuba, Homophobia, and the Otto Otepka Scandal in the Kennedy State Department," Eric Paul Roorda, *Diplomatic History*, September 2007; https://academic.oup.com/dh/article-abstract/31/4/723/353786

After the 1954 election, Otepka started a comprehensive review of State Department employees: Roorda, op. cit.

Quote about SISS hearings: Ibid.

Quote about Otepka's supervisor: Ibid.

Quote that Otepka's activities had even troubled John Foster Dulles: Ibid.

Quote about Otepka's 1,750,000 words of testimony before the SISS: Ibid.

Otepka met privately with SISS staff: Ibid.

Rusk told the SISS that "Otepka worked for the wrong boss.": Ibid.

Otepka memo to Gatewood: https://www.maryferrell.org/showDoc.html?docId=98432#relPageId=2

Hugh Cumming wrote to Bissell: https://www.maryferrell.org/showDoc.html?docId=110345#relPageId=2

Bissell reply to Cumming: https://www.maryferrell.org/showDoc.html?docId=5537#relPageId=43

Bannerman "told his staff to support Counterintelligence Staff (CI)." , John Newman, *Oswald and the CIA: The Documented Truth About the Unknown Relationship Between the U.S. Government and the Alleged Killer of JFK,* (Skyhorse, 2008), page 171

The allegation that Angleton "instructed that there be no research done on Oswald": Newman, op. cit., page 172.

Excerpt from the memo that Newman references: https://www.maryferrell.org/showDoc.html?docId=40133#relPageId=2

Bissell then sent a detailed reply to Cumming: https://www.maryferrell.org/showDoc.html?docId=5537#relPageId=44

Here is what he sent on Lee Henry [sic] Oswald: https://www.maryferrell.org/showDoc.html?docId=5537#relPageId=46

Henry Hurt on Otepka: Henry Hurt, op. cit., page 245; https://archive.org/details/reasonabledoubti00hurt/page/244/mode/2up

Quote from William Gill: William Gill, *The Ordeal of Otto Otepka,* (Arlington House, 1970), page 324; https://archive.org/details/ordealofottootep00gill/page/324/mode/2up

Gill quote on what make Otepka suspicious: Ibid.

Gill elaborates on what Otepka would have studied: Gill, op. cit., page 326.

One of Hurt's other sources is Anthony Summers' book: Anthony Summers, *The Kennedy Conspiracy,* (Warner Books, 1992), page 118; https://archive.org/details/kennedyconspirac0000summ/page/230/mode/2up

Summers' source is Bernard Fensterwald's 1977 book: Bernard Fensterwald, Jr., *Assassination of JFK by Coincidence or Conspiracy?* (Zebra Books, 1977), page 231

Quote from Jim Hougan: *Spooks:* Jim Hougan, *The Haunting of America – The Private Use of Secret Agents,* (William Morrow and Company, 1978), page 371; https://archive.org/details/spookshauntingof0000houg/page/370/mode/2up

Hougan interviewed Otepka in 1977: Ibid.

1978 interview of Otepka by the HSCA: https://drive.google.com/drive/folders/18zS6bOY8lPHkEwkmPaPDjgk6GQ7SLWHT; Courtesy of the Malcolm Blunt Archives.

The best source might be Peter Dale Scott who interviewed Otepka in 1978: Peter Dale Scott, *Dallas '63: The First Deep State Revolt Against the White House,* (Open Road, 2015), page 153; https://archive.org/details/dallas-63-the-first-deep-stat-peter-dale-scott_20210214/page/n153/mode/2up

Scott elaborated in his book: Peter Dale Scott, *Oswald, Mexico, And Deep Politics,* (Skyhorse, 2013); https://books.google.ca/books?id=zS51EAAAQBAJ&pg=PT29&dq=%22Otepka+was+not+alone+in+his+suspicions.%22&hl=en&newbks=1&newbks_redir=1&sa=X&ved=2ahUKEwiy6O7D5_b6AhW2GFkFHVP1C7IQ6AF6BAgHEAI

In the early 1970s, researcher Fred Newcomb corresponded with Otepka who then sent him several documents: Courtesy of Larry Haapanen.

Otepka confirmed all of this in a letter to the reporters: Letter dated March 18, 1993 from Otto

Otepka to Joe Rosenbloom III, Staff Reporter for Frontline; Papers of Gus Russo at Baylor University; https://www.baylor.edu/library/index.php?id=974847

I should add that Mr. Otepka was pretty dismissive of conspiracy theorists: Ibid.

38. Was Lee Harvey Oswald Paid by the CIA? (Episode 4, 7:51)

Steve Roe has uncovered evidence: https://steveroeconsulting.wixsite.com/website/post/oliver-stone-s-jfk-destiny-betrayed-film-never-checked-the-facts

FBI report from December 1963: https://www.maryferrell.org/showDoc.html?docId=95676#relPageId=65

Oswald upon release from the USMC was paid in cash: https://www.maryferrell.org/showDoc.html?docId=10487#relPageId=66

This excerpt from the USMC pay records: https://www.maryferrell.org/showDoc.html?docId=1142#relPageId=746

You can see the withholding: https://www.maryferrell.org/showDoc.html?docId=1142#relPageId=761

Oswald's 1040 tax return for 1959: https://web.archive.org/web/20001208105400/http:/www.redacted.com/lhotax5_1.htm

His form was indeed filed by Marguerite Oswald: https://www.maryferrell.org/showDoc.html?docId=57755#relPageId=132

And even Douglas Horne admits: https://www.maryferrell.org/showDoc.html?docId=201077#relPageId=13

Warren Commission Document 353a: https://www.maryferrell.org/showDoc.html?docId=10754#relPageId=3

Horne knew about this when he worked at the ARRB: https://www.maryferrell.org/showDoc.html?docId=201077#relPageId=13

Quote from Douglas Horne about the possibility of a mistake: Interview with Douglas Horne in *JFK Revisited*, op. cit., page 361 in the Kindle version.

James DiEugenio has made a big deal out of Oswald's earnings: https://educationforum.ipbhost.com/topic/27466-jfk-revisited-through-the-looking-glass/page/26/#comment-452351

It is true that when he saw the raw SSA data (after learning that CD 353a was public) he was "severely cautioned" that disclosure of information not found elsewhere "would be a felony.": https://www.maryferrell.org/showDoc.html?docId=201077#relPageId=6

39. Was There a Plot Against JFK in Chicago? (Episode 4, 22:03)

The source for this allegation comes from an article by Edwin Black from 1975: http://jfk.hood.edu/Collection/Weisberg%20Subject%20Index%20Files/V%20Disk/Vallee%20Thomas%20Arthur/Item%2005.pdf

Bolden's interview with the HSCA: https://www.maryferrell.org/showDoc.html?docId=197033#relPageId=9

Interview with former Secret Service agent Gary McLeod: https://aarclibrary.org/joe-backes-arrb-summaries-page-13-2/

The HSCA conclusion on the supposed plot in Chicago: https://www.maryferrell.org/showDoc.html?docId=800#relPageId=261

1967 Mark Lane Press Conference: "Jim Garrison's Probe Moves to Springfield," Springfield News, December 6, 1967; the full text of this article is in this blog post: https://www.onthetrailofdelusion.com/post/paul-bleau-and-the-supposed-chicago-plot-against-jfk

1968 interview by Bud Fensterwald: "Memorandum of Conversation This Date with Abraham Bolden, dated March 29, 1969; Papers of Dick Russell, Baylor University; https://www.baylor.edu/doc.php/310506.pdf

1975 article by Edwin Black: Black, op. cit.

1978 interview by the HSCA: https://www.maryferrell.org/showDoc.html?docId=197033#relPageId=4

2008 Bolden book: Abraham Bolden, *The Echo from Dealey Plaza: The true story of the first African American on the White House Secret Service detail and his quest for justice after the assassination of JFK*, (Harmony Books, 2008), pages 55 – 56

Excerpt from Bolden interview with Bud Fensterwald: op. cit.

In December 1967, Jim Garrison indicted Edgar Eugene Bradley: https://www.onthetrailofdelusion.com/post/jim-garrison-finds-another-jfk-assassination-conspirator; https://www.onthetrailofdelusion.com/post/edgar-eugene-bradley-another-garrison-victim

Garrison also believed that Manuel Garcia Gonzalez was one of the gunmen on the grassy knoll: https://www.onthetrailofdelusion.com/post/was-the-quick-article-about-a-homosexual-conspiracy-written-by-jim-garrison-part-two

In late October 1963, a landlady found a collage of newspaper clippings: https://www.maryferrell.org/showDoc.html?docId=800#relPageId=261; https://drive.google.com/drive/folders/1l3dELXnpREfvb2K6sy2xfUGigJT9vaBb

Document on Vallee's mental health: https://www.maryferrell.org/showDoc.html?docId=10521#relPageId=4

Vallee's Secret Service Protective Research file: https://www.maryferrell.org/showDoc.html?docId=196747#relPageId=173

Quote from James DiEugenio on Bolden trying to contact the Warren Commission: *The JFK Assassination*, op. cit., page 275.

The Warren Commission asked the FBI to interview Abraham Bolden: https://www.maryferrell.org/showDoc.html?docId=11393#relPageId=2

Rumors right after the assassination: https://www.maryferrell.org/showDoc.html?docId=57766#relPageId=119

Fanning might have gotten it from: https://www.maryferrell.org/showDoc.html?docId=10488#relPageId=489

40. Was Lee Harvey Oswald Placed in Dallas? (Episode 4, 24:22)

A trip to Texas was first broached: https://www.maryferrell.org/showDoc.html?docId=946#relPageId=52

Excerpt from Roy Truly's testimony before the Warren Commission: https://www.maryferrell.org/showDoc.html?docId=39#relPageId=245

The HSCA added this: https://www.maryferrell.org/showDoc.html?docId=83#relPageId=520

41. Was There a Plot to Assassinate JFK in Tampa? (Episode 4, 25:06)

Gilberto Lopez in Lamar Waldron's 2005 book: Lamar Waldron with Thom Hartmann, *Ultimate Sacrifice: John and Robert Kennedy, the Plan for a Coup in Cuba, and the Murder of JFK*, (Carroll & Graf, 2005), pages 254 - 259, 500 - 504, 698 – 703; https://archive.org/details/ultimatesacrific0000wald_u6h2/mode/2up?q=%22ultimate+sacrifice%22+waldron

Gerald Blaine's book: *The Kennedy Detail: JFK's Secret Service Agents Break Their Silence*, Gerald Blaine with Lisa McCubbin, Gallery Books, 2010

Flash Card on Mr. Gainey: Blaine, op. cit., page 60 in the Kindle edition.

The other threat was from John William Warrington: Blaine, op. cit., page 61.

Lamar Waldron interviewed Tampa Police Chief Mullins: Waldron, op. cit., page 710.

Mullins said he depended on hotel staff: Ibid.

Waldron's claim that the Floridan Hotel was a better vantage point than the Texas School Book Depository: Ibid.

CIA biographical sketch of Gilberto Lopez: https://www.maryferrell.org/showDoc.html?docId=5003

CIA interest in Gilberto Policarpo Lopez: https://www.maryferrell.org/showDoc.html?docId=7516#relPageId=23

In March 1964, a source told the CIA that Lopes [sic] : https://www.archives.gov/files/research/jfk/releases/2018/180-10142-10406.pdf

Here is that message: https://www.maryferrell.org/showDoc.html?docId=49999#relPageId=2

The Church Committee discussed this lead: https://www.maryferrell.org/showDoc.html?docId=1161#relPageId=69

But the Church Committee was wrong: https://www.onthetrailofdelusion.com/post/was-gilberto-policarpo-lopez-an-assassin-or-a-patsy; *V.T. Lee's letter to Oswald*: https://www.maryferrell.org/showDoc.html?docId=1137#relPageId=534

The Church Committee on Lopez's travel: https://www.maryferrell.org/showDoc.html?docId=1161#relPageId=67

The HSCA staff noted that the IG found numerous errors: https://www.maryferrell.org/showDoc.html?docId=31936#relPageId=12

The HSCA found that the failure of the CIA to tell the Warren Commission was 'egregious': https://www.maryferrell.org/showDoc.html?docId=800#relPageId=150

The CIA disagreed with that conclusion: https://www.maryferrell.org/showDoc.html?docId=26039#relPageId=18

An HSCA memo also came up with a reason why the lead was withheld from the Warren Commission: https://www.maryferrell.org/showDoc.html?docId=108884#relPageId=9

The HSCA concluded: https://www.maryferrell.org/showDoc.html?docId=800#relPageId=151

Two FBI reports on Lopez that were forwarded to the Warren Commission: https://www.maryferrell.org/showDoc.html?docId=10672#relPageId=755; https://www.maryferrell.org/showDoc.html?docId=10552

He traveled on a cargo flight: https://www.maryferrell.org/showDoc.html?docId=5190#relPageId=42; see also https://www.archives.gov/files/research/jfk/releases/2022/104-10213-10011.pdf

Perhaps he was wearing sunglasses to deal with his epilepsy: https://eyewearinsight.com/links/How_Tinted_Lenses_Can_Help_People_With_Epilepsy_

Waldron's eighteen parallels between Lopez and Oswald: Waldron, op. cit., page 502.

This is the kind of propinquity that perhaps Jim Garrison would appreciate: https://www.onthetrailofdelusion.com/post/garrison-s-weird-investigative-technique-the-theory-of-propinquity; https://www.onthetrailofdelusion.com/post/garrison-s-weird-investigative-technique-propinquity-part-two

Bleau's several other alternative 'patsies': "The Three Failed Plots to Kill JFK," https://www.kennedysandking.com/john-f-kennedy-articles/the-three-failed-plots-to-kill-jfk-part-2

New Orleans

What Ever Happened to Jim Garrison?

Clay Shaw was only a domestic contact of the CIA: https://www.onthetrailofdelusion.com/post/was-clay-shaw-a-contract-agent-for-the-cia

Garrison told journalists about a homosexual conspiracy:

- *Hugh Aynesworth*: https://www.onthetrailofdelusion.com/post/did-a-homosexual-conspiracy-kill-jfk
- *James Phelan*: https://www.onthetrailofdelusion.com/post/did-a-homosexual-conspiracy-kill-jfk
- *Jack Anderson*: https://www.onthetrailofdelusion.com/post/james-phelan-and-mark-lane-discuss-garrison-s-homosexual-conspiracy; see page 78 of On The Trail of Delusion, op. cit.
- *Jerrold Footlick*: https://www.onthetrailofdelusion.com/post/jim-garrison-does-it-again-claims-oswald-and-ruby-were-homosexuals
- *Merriman Smith*: https://www.onthetrailofdelusion.com/post/merriman-smith-on-jim-garrison-and-the-saga-of-david-lewis-part-one
- *Art Kevin*: https://www.onthetrailofdelusion.com/post/art-kevin-looks-back-at-the-garrison-investigation
- *Lawrence Schiller*: https://www.onthetrailofdelusion.com/post/was-the-quick-article-about-a-homosexual-conspiracy-written-by-jim-garrison-part-three

- *Max Lerner*: https://www.onthetrailofdelusion.com/post/garrison-mentions-a-homosexual-plot-to-yet-another-journalist
- Don't miss my multi-part post on Quick magazine which published a first-person article in 1968, supposedly written by Jim Garrison, about the homosexual conspiracy that killed JFK; https://www.onthetrailofdelusion.com/blog/tags/quick-magazine

The infamous Sciambra memorandum being read out in court: https://www.maryferrell.org/showDoc.html?docId=1275#relPageId=109

Oliver Stone claiming it was worth the sacrifice of one man: "The Shooting of JFK," Robert Sam Anson, *Esquire,* November 1991; https://classic.esquire.com/article/1991/11/1/the-shooting-of-jfk; https://www.onthetrailofdelusion.com/post/i-ve-been-blocked-by-oliver-stone

Judge Christenberry's ruling about Jim Garrison's case: https://www.onthetrailofdelusion.com/post/the-christenberry-decision

The Advocate ran a huge feature on Oliver Stone and Jim Garrison: "JFK – A New Low for Hollywood: Oliver Stone's Film is Fueled by Jim Garrison's Homophobia," David Ehrenstein, *The Advocate,* January 14, 1992, and "JFK is more offensive than Basic Instinct could dare to be," David Ehrenstein, same issue of *The Advocate*; https://www.onthetrailofdelusion.com/post/is-oliver-stone-s-film-jfk-homophobic

Oliver Stone sat down for an interview with The Advocate: https://archive.org/details/jfkbookoffilmdoc0000ston/page/512/mode/2up

Quote from Rosemary James about Jim Garrison: "Stone's plans for Garrison movie are offensive," Rosemary James, New Orleans Times-Picayune, June 20, 1991; https://www.onthetrailofdelusion.com/post/a-new-orleans-look-at-oliver-stone-s-jfk

Washington Post on Garrison's case: "The Carnival Ought To Be Over," *Washington Post,* March 4, 1969; https://www.onthetrailofdelusion.com/post/washington-post-editorial-on-the-acquittal-of-clay-shaw

Jed Horne told The Advocate: Ehrenstein in *The Advocate,* op. cit.

42. Was David Ferrie a Trainer and a Pilot for the CIA? (Episode 4, 10:14)

Very little evidence that David Ferrie knew Lee Harvey Oswald: https://www.onthetrailofdelusion.com/post/did-david-ferrie-know-lee-harvey-oswald

James DiEugenio inferred that Ferrie was involved in Operation Mongoose: *Destiny Betrayed,* op. cit., page 115 in the Kindle edition; "When Operation Mongoose began, Ferrie let it slip that he was a part of "Operation Mosquito." Clearly a miscommunication ..."

December 1967 statement of Herbert Wagner: https://www.onthetrailofdelusion.com/post/did-herbert-wagner-see-shaw-and-ferrie-together

James DiEugenio on Eladio del Valle: *Destiny Betrayed,* op. cit., page 85.

The source for the del Valle claim: "Was Eladio del Valle David Ferrie's Paymaster?"; https://www.onthetrailofdelusion.com/post/was-eladio-del-valle-david-ferrie-s-paymaster; the complete article from *The National Enquirer* is in this post.

Ferrie was asked about flying to Cuba: "David Ferrie Talks to Garrison's Assistant District Attorney,"; https://www.onthetrailofdelusion.com/post/david-ferrie-talks-to-garrison-s-assistant-district-attorneys

Stephen Roy (aka Blackburst) on Ferrie flying to Cuba: https://www.jfk-online.com/dbdfbackfile.html

Here is an excerpt of a memo that Stephen Burton sent to Jim Garrison: "Interview of Al Cheramie," memo from Steven J. Burton to Jim Garrison, retrieved from NARA.

Al Landry's story: "Interview with Al Landry, March 23, 1967," memo from Andrew J. Sciambra to Jim Garrison, dated March 28, 1967; retrieved from NARA.

David Ferrie's autopsy report: https://www.jfk-assassination.net/ferrie_autopsy.htm

Interview of John Irion: Statement of John Irion, memo dated January 30, 1967; retrieved from the papers of Richard Billing, Georgetown University.

Quote from Stephen Roy's unpublished manuscript: *Perfect Villain: David Ferrie and the JFK Mystery*.

CIA memo about David Ferrie: https://www.maryferrell.org/showDoc.html?docId=9532#relPageId=8

Stephen Roy summed up the evidence about David Ferrie and the CIA: https://www.jfk-online.com/dbdfciaposts.html

43. Why Does *JFK: Destiny Betrayed* Show Fake Oswald Handbills? (Episode 4, 10:55)

There is no evidence that Oswald had an office at 544 Camp Street: https://www.onthetrailofdelusion.com/post/jfk-revisited-misleads-on-guy-banister

The HSCA on the Cuban Revolutionary Council: https://www.maryferrell.org/showDoc.html?docId=1212#relPageId=65

Sam Newman on the CRC at 544 Camp Street: Statement of Sam Newman, January 24, 1967; retrieved from the papers of Richard Billings, Georgetown University.

Sam Newman had no recollection of ever seeing Oswald: https://www.maryferrell.org/showDoc.html?docId=62271#relPageId=122

Oswald ordered 1,000 handbills: https://www.maryferrell.org/showDoc.html?docId=10407#relPageId=392

Limited stock of Corliss Lamont pamphlets: https://www.maryferrell.org/showDoc.html?docId=1137#relPageId=531

When Oswald was arrested in August 1963, the handbill that was confiscated by the police did not have the 544 Camp Street address: https://www.maryferrell.org/showDoc.html?docId=10490#relPageId=602

Here are two real Oswald handbills: https://www.maryferrell.org/showDoc.html?docId=1142#relPageId=484

A Corliss Lamont pamphlet with the 544 Camp Street stamp: https://www.maryferrell.org/showDoc.html?docId=1142#relPageId=819

Robert Groden's book: Robert Groden, *The Killing of a President*, (Bloomsbury, 1993), page 141

Gus Russo published a similar handbill: Gus Russo, *Live by the Sword: The Secret War Against Castro and the Death of JFK*, (Bancroft Press, 1998). There is a picture of the handbill in the photograph section. Gus Russo also sent me via email a photograph of the handbill; https://archive.org/details/livebyswordsecre00russ/page/n339/mode/1up

Oliver Stone combined four real people into his composite character Willie O'Keefe: https://www.jfk-online.com/jfk100okeefe.html

Screenshot from JFK with a fake handbill: https://getyarn.io/yarn-clip/42b93325-b9ed-4820-ac92-f635df815029

DiEugenio also used a fake handbill in a PowerPoint presentation: https://www.kennedysandking.com/images/pdf/FBI-JFK-Garrison-2019.pdf

Quote from the film JFK regarding Banister and Oswald: *JFK: The Documented Screenplay*, Oliver Stone & Zachary Sklar, Applause Books, 1992, pages 33 – 34.

Judyth Vary Baker's book: *Me & Lee: How I came to know, love and lose Lee Harvey Oswald*, Judyth Vary Baker, (Trine Day, 2010), page 435; https://archive.org/details/meleehowicametok0000bake/page/434/mode/1up

James DiEugenio on the fake handbills: https://educationforum.ipbhost.com/topic/28163-exposing-the-fpcc-part-3/page/5/#comment-472722

The Historic New Orleans Collections does have a flyer: https://www.hnoc.org/sites/default/files/quarterly/Quarterly_1986_15_Spring.pdf

New Orleans Historical, a web platform that shares stories about New Orleans, did have a story on its website about the Newman building which relied on the fake flyer: https://neworleanshistorical.org/items/show/1470 (the article no longer exists), you can still see the article here*: https://web.archive.org/web/20210301122934/https://neworleanshistorical.org/items/show/1470*

John Newman suggested an explanation for the absence of handbills with the 544 Camp Street address from the official record in JFK: Destiny Betrayed: (12:28 in episode 4); *JFK Revisited*, op. cit., page 228 in the Kindle edition.

Here is one page from that document: Courtesy of the Malcolm Blunt Archive - https://drive.google.com/file/d/1ug6Xa5ZHWXJgmEMsyiKATc2c-h6We8h5/view

Paul Hoch found this message as it was actually sent: https://www.maryferrell.org/showDoc.html?docId=62271#relPageId=121

44. Did Guy Banister Give Oswald an Office at 544 Camp Street? (Episode 4, 10:55)

Joseph Newbrough was interviewed for PBS Frontline: https://www.pbs.org/wgbh/pages/frontline/shows/oswald/etc/script.html; *for more on Newbrough*: https://www.onthetrailofdelusion.com/post/did-david-ferrie-speak-to-clay-shaw-on-the-telephone-from-guy-banister-s-office; *Sam Newman interview with the HSCA on the Newman building*: https://www.maryferrell.org/showDoc.html?docId=49346#relPageId=233

Delphine Roberts interview with Garrison's office: "Did Delphine Roberts see Oswald in Banister's Office?"; https://www.onthetrailofdelusion.com/post/did-delphine-roberts-see-oswald-in-banister-s-office

HSCA interview with Delphine Roberts on August 27, 1978: Courtesy of the Malcolm Blunt Archives - https://drive.google.com/file/d/1RRdo1nyiRIN61r1Aaitogy9E3tMdhjXA/view?usp=sharing

HSCA interview with Delphine Roberts on July 6, 1978: https://digitalcollections-baylor.quartexcollections.com/Documents/Detail/new-orleans-witnesses-delphine-roberts/707611?item=707612

Sam Newman interview with the FBI: https://www.maryferrell.org/showDoc.html?docId=47745#relPageId=57

Sam Newman interview with the HSCA: https://www.maryferrell.org/showDoc.html?docId=1212#relPageId=128

The HSCA noted Roberts' testimony and wrote: https://www.maryferrell.org/showDoc.html?docId=800#relPageId=176

Jack Martin was a crackpot who had no credibility: https://www.onthetrailofdelusion.com/post/did-david-ferrie-introduce-jack-martin-to-lee-harvey-oswald-in-banister-s-office; other examples:

- *Jack Martin told the HSCA that Jim Garrison was framed by John Dean, of Watergate fame*: https://www.onthetrailofdelusion.com/post/did-john-dean-frame-jim-garrison;
- *Jim Garrison interviewed Jack Martin on December 14, 1966*: https://www.onthetrailofdelusion.com/post/exclusive-jim-garrison-talks-to-jack-martin;
- *Here is the YouTube link to that conversation*: https://youtu.be/aAjR3e2iilc

Jack Martin did not convince the HSCA: https://www.maryferrell.org/showDoc.html?docId=1212#relPageId=134

The HSCA also agreed: https://www.maryferrell.org/showDoc.html?docId=1212#relPageId=135

45. Was Clay Shaw a "Contract Agent" for the CIA? (Episode 4, 13:22)

Quote from Joan Mellen: A Farewell to Justice: Jim Garrison, JFK's Assassination, and the Case That Should Have Changed History, (Skyhorse, 2013), page 388

Here is an excerpt of that document: https://www.maryferrell.org/showDoc.html?docId=7302#relPageId=3

1955 document that refers to Shaw as a 'valued source': https://www.maryferrell.org/showDoc.html?docId=67724#relPageId=2

This 1955 document is indeed in the segregated collection: https://www.maryferrell.org/php/showlist.php?docset=1093

An overlapping set of documents: https://www.maryferrell.org/php/showlist.php?docset=1092

Records relating to Gilberto Alvarado: https://www.maryferrell.org/showDoc.html?docId=7302#relPageId=9

A different page in the 1992 document: https://www.maryferrell.org/showDoc.html?docId=7302#relPageId=12

Elena Garro de Paz claimed to have seen Oswald: https://www.maryferrell.org/showDoc.html?docId=800#relPageId=153

On the night before the assassination: https://www.maryferrell.org/showDoc.html?docId=946#relPageId=764

Oswald was only in Mexico City from September 26, 1963 to October 3, 1963: https://www.maryferrell.org/showDoc.html?docId=946#relPageId=323

Max Holland spoke with McDonald who told him: https://jfkfacts.org/how-does-new-orleans-figure-in-the-jfk-story/

A document dated 16 October 1967 flatly stated that Shaw was never remunerated for his services: https://www.maryferrell.org/showDoc.html?docId=55187#relPageId=9

A CIA document on Clay Shaw had this mysterious paragraph: https://www.maryferrell.org/showDoc.html?docId=42764#relPageId=5

A staffer from the HSCA also made notes: https://www.maryferrell.org/showDoc.html?docId=31932#relPageId=3

What was Project QKENCHANT: https://www.maryferrell.org/showDoc.html?docId=162783#relPageId=8

Here is a better description in plain English: https://www.maryferrell.org/showDoc.html?docId=162783#relPageId=10

There is no evidence that Clay Shaw had clearance under this program: https://www.maryferrell.org/showDoc.html?docId=162783#relPageId=8

Here is a CIA document that offers an explanation: https://www.maryferrell.org/showDoc.html?docId=101726#relPageId=2

Clay Shaw wrote about the CIA: "Two Reasons why Clay Shaw Never Admitted to being a Domestic Contact of the CIA"; https://www.onthetrailofdelusion.com/post/two-reasons-why-clay-shaw-never-admitted-to-being-a-domestic-contact-of-the-cia

46. Was Clay Shaw the Elusive Clay Bertrand? (Episode 4, 14:03)

Here is what Harold Weisberg wrote in his unpublished book: http://jfk.hood.edu/Collection/Weisberg%20Subject%20Index%20Files/HW%20Manuscripts/MAILER05.DOC

Joan Mellen wrote Weisberg a letter and his reply: Letters from May and June 2001; http://jfk.hood.edu/Collection/Weisberg%20Subject%20Index%20Files/M%20Disk/Mellen%20Joan/Item%2010.pdf

The sources section contains links to posts that debunk all of these witnesses:

- *Dr. Jacob Kety*: "Did Carlos Marcello's Doctor Friend Know about Clay Bertrand?"; https://www.onthetrailofdelusion.com/post/did-carlos-marcello-s-doctor-know-about-clay-bertrand
- *William Morris*: "Did William Morris Know Clay Shaw as Clay Bertrand?"; https://www.onthetrailofdelusion.com/post/did-william-morris-know-clay-shaw-as-clay-bertrand
- *Dean Andrews*: "Did Dean Andrews admit that Clay Shaw was Clay Bertrand?"; https://www.onthetrailofdelusion.com/post/did-dean-andrews-admit-that-clay-shaw-was-clay-bertrand

- *Virginia Johnson*: "Did Clay Shaw's Maid Know He was Clay Bertrand?"; https://www.onthetrailofdelusion.com/post/did-clay-shaw-s-maid-know-he-was-clay-bertrand
- *Jessie Parker*: "Did Clay Shaw Sign the VIP Room Guestbook as Clay Bertrand?"; https://www.onthetrailofdelusion.com/post/did-clay-shaw-sign-the-guestbook-as-clay-bertrand-at-the-vip-room
- *Aloysius Habighorst*: "Did Clay Shaw Admit to Aloysius Habighorst that he was Clay Bertrand?"; https://www.onthetrailofdelusion.com/post/did-clay-shaw-admit-to-aloysius-habighorst-that-he-was-clay-bertrand
- *Thomas Breitner*: "Did Thomas Breitner Meet Clay Bertrand?"; https://www.onthetrailofdelusion.com/post/did-thomas-breitner-meet-clay-bertrand
- *Ed Guthman*: "David Chandler Talks to Shaw's Investigators"; https://www.onthetrailofdelusion.com/post/david-chandler-talks-to-shaw-s-investigators
- *Aaron Kohn and Joseph Oster*: "Did the FBI Know that Shaw was Bertrand?"; https://www.onthetrailofdelusion.com/post/did-the-fbi-know-that-shaw-was-bertrand
- *Valentine Ashworth*: "Did Valentine Ashworth Meet the Second Oswald?"; https://www.onthetrailofdelusion.com/post/did-valentine-ashworth-meet-the-second-oswald
- *Fred Leemans*: "Did Clay Shaw Take Lee Harvey Oswald to the Gay Baths? The Fred Leemans Story, Part One."; https://www.onthetrailofdelusion.com/post/did-clay-shaw-take-lee-harvey-oswald-to-the-gay-baths-the-fred-leemans-story-part-one;
- *Perry Russo*: Perry Russo was administered sodium Pentothal, hypnotized three times, and then had a recovered memory that Clay Shaw was Clem Bertrand. However, he said nothing of the sort in his initial interviews in Baton Rouge. See "Perry Russo Talks – in Baton Rouge, Part One"; https://www.onthetrailofdelusion.com/post/perry-russo-talks-in-baton-rouge-part-one; Part two: https://www.onthetrailofdelusion.com/post/perry-russo-talks-in-baton-rouge-part-two; Part Three: https://www.onthetrailofdelusion.com/post/perry-russo-talks-in-baton-rouge-part-three
- There are two other witnesses mentioned in Joan Mellen's book, *And Justice For All*, Rickey Planche and Barbara Bennett. But neither of these witnesses came forward during Garrison's investigation and there are no formal statements from either of them.

More importantly, Garrison couldn't find Clay Bertrand back in 1967: "Was Jim Garrison Searching for Clay Bertrand in 1963?"; https://www.onthetrailofdelusion.com/post/was-jim-garrison-searching-for-clay-bertrand-in-1963

Of course, the FBI and the Secret Service put in a lot of work in late 1963 trying to find Clay Bertrand, without any success: "The Search for Clay Bertrand."; https://www.onthetrailofdelusion.com/post/the-search-for-clay-bertrand

That search for Bertrand reached right into Garrison's office: see "Was Jim Garrison Searching for Clay Bertrand in 1963," op. cit.

The Politics of *JFK: Destiny Betrayed*

Here is what Prouty wrote in his article: Fletcher Prouty, "The Shadow of Dallas," January 1974; http://jfk.hood.edu/Collection/Weisberg%20Subject%20Index%20Files/P%20Disk/Prouty%20L%20Fletcher/Item%2045.pdf

Oliver Stone on Putin: "Oliver Stone: Putin is a rational, calm, thoughtful man: The United States is a Doberman ..."; https://www.onthetrailofdelusion.com/post/oliver-stone-putin-is-a-rational-calm-thoughtful-man-the-united-states-is-a-doberman

Transcript of meeting between McNamara and John Kennedy: https://millercenter.org/the-presidency/secret-white-house-tapes/meetings-tape-85-vietnam-defense-budget-nomination-new

On August 29, 1963, President de Gaulle of France issued a statement: "France's Bid to Regain an Empire," Waverley Root, *San Francisco Chronicle*, September 1, 1963, page 12.

President de Gaulle also said that Vietnam would be better off free "from foreign influence.": "De Gaulle Slaps U.S. in Play for Position in Viet Nam," Patrick McNulty, *The Atlanta Journal*, August 30, 1963.

Patrick McNulty on speculation that de Gaulle had in mind a neutral status: "De Gaulle Slaps at U.S. Role in Vietnam," *Akron Beacon Journal*, August 30, 1963, page 16.

Kennedy's interview with Walter Cronkite: https://www.jfklibrary.org/asset-viewer/archives/JFKPOF/046/JFKPOF-046-025

Newsweek and The New Republic both supported de Gaulle: Fredrick Logevall, *Choosing War: The Lost Chance for Peace and the Escalation of War in Vietnam*, (University of California Press, 2001), Page 55

Logevall commented on this in his book Choosing War: Logevall, op. cit., page 72.

Kennedy then told David Brinkley and Chet Huntley: https://www.presidency.ucsb.edu/documents/transcript-broadcast-nbcs-huntley-brinkley-report

On September 12th, JFK held a press conference: https://www.jfklibrary.org/archives/other-resources/john-f-kennedy-press-conferences/news-conference-61

On October 2, 1963, the White House issued a statement: https://2001-2009.state.gov/r/pa/ho/frus/kennedyjf/iv/12651.htm

It also said that "the major part of the U.S. military task can be completed by the end of 1965,": Ibid.

" ... and that "by the end of this year, the U.S. program for training Vietnamese ..."; https://www.maryferrell.org/showDoc.html?docId=152#relPageId=46

However, during the meeting with Robert McNamara: https://millercenter.org/the-presidency/educational-resources/the-kennedy-withdrawal-combined

Marc Selverstone, associate professor in Presidential Studies at the Miller Center, says that this conversation indicates that JFK would only withdraw from Vietnam "under propitious military circumstances.": https://youtu.be/HYbdyt3Gdog

On October 5, 1963, a cable was sent to Henry Cabot Lodge: https://www.maryferrell.org/showDoc.html?docId=152#relPageId=49

NSAM 263: https://www.jfklibrary.org/asset-viewer/archives/JFKNSF/342/JFKNSF-342-007

Meeting with the press on October 31st: https://www.jfklibrary.org/archives/other-resources/john-f-kennedy-press-conferences/news-conference-63

Dean Rusk sent out the following memo: https://www.jfk-assassination.net/viet12.htm

News conference on November 14, 1963: https://www.jfklibrary.org/archives/other-resources/john-f-kennedy-press-conferences/news-conference-64

On November 20, 1963, many of Kennedy's top advisors met in Honolulu to discuss the situation in Vietnam: https://www.maryferrell.org/showDoc.html?docId=146534#relPageId=28

A summary of their discussion included this paragraph: https://history.state.gov/historicaldocuments/frus1961-63v04/d321

The speech that JFK was going to deliver in Dallas: https://www.jfklibrary.org/archives/other-resources/john-f-kennedy-speeches/dallas-tx-trade-mart-undelivered-19631122

NAM 273: https://history.state.gov/historicaldocuments/frus1961-63v04/d331

Fredrick Logevall called the differences "insignificant": Logevall, op. cit., page 71.

Stanley Karnow, one of the foremost historians of the Vietnam war, said that NSAM 273 "perpetuated the Kennedy policy": https://www.jfk-assassination.net/karnow.htm

Robert McNamara wrote in his book: Robert S. McNamara with Brian VanDeMark, *In Retrospect: The Tragedy and Lessons of Vietnam*, (Vintage Books, 1995), page 102;

https://archive.org/details/inretrospecttra00mcna/page/102/mode/2up?q=%22remained+the+same%22

Quote from Marc Selverstone on JFK and covert action in Vietnam: The Kennedy Withdrawal:

Camelot and the American Commitment to Vietnam, Mark Selverstone (Harvard University Press, 2022), page 207.

Selverstone on OPLAN 34A: op. cit., page 208.

Dean Rusk wrote in his book: Dean Rusk as told to Richard Rusk, *As I Saw It*, (W. W. Norton & Company, 1990), page 441; https://archive.org/details/asisawit00rusk/page/440/mode/2up

He added: Rusk, op. cit., page 442.

And Robert Kennedy said much the same thing in an oral history interview with John Bartlow Martin from 1964: *Robert Kennedy In His Own Words: The Unpublished Recollections of the Kennedy Years*, Edited by Edwin O. Guthman and Jeffrey Shulman, (Bantam Books, 1988); https://archive.org/details/robertkennedyinh00kenn/page/394/mode/2up

Professors Lawrence Bassett and Stephen Pelz elaborate on the problems left for Lyndon Johnson: "The Failed Search for Victory," contained in the book, *Major Problems in the History of the Vietnam War: Documents and Essays Edited by Robert J. McMahon*, D. C. Heath and Company, 1995, pages 194 – 195; https://archive.org/details/majorproblemsinh0000unse_u2e8/page/194

Did the ARRB Prove a Conspiracy in the JFK Assassination?

James DiEugenio, the screenplay writer of JFK Revisited, has also said this on Twitter: https://twitter.com/jimmydie1963/status/1471128493287088128

James DiEugenio quote about James Kirchick: "James Kirchick and his JFK Assassination Gurus," February 19, 2022; https://www.kennedysandking.com/john-f-kennedy-reviews/james-kirchick-and-his-jfk-assassination-gurus

James DiEugenio on exposing the [Warren] Commission by the ARRB: https://educationforum.ipbhost.com/topic/27576-noam-chomsky-vs-oliver-stone/page/2/#comment-452918

James DiEugenio on the ARRB destroying the Warren Report: https://www.facebook.com/groups/387164721481044/posts/1922559831274851/?comment_id=1924525994411568&reply_comment_id=1925183941012440

The ARRB even proved Jim Garrison was right: https://www.facebook.com/groups/387164721481044/posts/2002440109953489/?comment_id=2002520076612159

And here about CE 399: "Litwin and the Warren Report,"; https://www.kennedysandking.com/john-f-kennedy-articles/litwin-and-the-warren-report

And here: Ibid.

Deposition of John Stringer before the ARRB: https://www.maryferrell.org/showDoc.html?docId=798#relPageId=1

This overreach obscured the real mission of the organization. The final report of the ARRB notes: https://www.archives.gov/files/research/jfk/review-board/report/preface.pdf

In 1998, Tom Samoluk, Deputy Director of the ARRB, had to reiterate this in a letter to James DiEugenio: https://www.maryferrell.org/showDoc.html?docId=215637#relPageId=1

But the HSCA had already looked at Secret Service documents during that period: https://www.maryferrell.org/showDoc.html?docId=800#relPageId=260

No evidence has ever materialized to corroborate the supposed Chicago plot: See Chapter 39; https://www.onthetrailofdelusion.com/post/jfk-revisited-misleads-on-the-supposed-chicago-plot

The Secret Service wrote a letter to the ARRB: Courtesy of the Malcolm Blunt Archives -https://drive.google.com/file/d/1TJavaPdTc-JiqbTA17ijCRZ8zmo5ENSA/view

DiEugenio and Stone's poverty of imagination: https://www.onthetrailofdelusion.com/post/oliver-stone-s-poverty-of-imagination

Burkley was conferring with his lawyer on tax issues: See Chapter 12; https://www.onthetrailofdelusion.com/post/jfk-revisited-misleads-on-the-arrb-s-quest-for-dr-burkley-s-lawyer-s-papers

Judge Tunheim never said the ARRB proved a conspiracy: https://www.kare11.com/article/news/judge-john-tunheim-on-the-jfk-files/89-488588095

Anna Nelson, one of the historians on the ARRB, concurred with Judge Tunheim that they did not find

evidence of conspiracy: Interview for Patricia Lambert's documentary on The History Channel, August 29, 2000, Papers of Patricia Lambert, Sixth Floor Museum.

Henry Graff, former chairman of Columbia University's history department, concurred: "Chickens Coming Home to Roost," *Penthouse Magazine*, January 1997.

Afterword—The Demagogue of Dealey Plaza

Jonathan Rauch's book: The Constitution of Knowledge: A Defense of Truth, Brookings Institution Press, 2021

In the book of the film, conspiracy theorist Paul Bleau elaborated: *JFK Revisited*, op. cit., page 436 of the Kindle edition.

DiEugenio's note on the segment regarding the Katzenbach memo: *JFK Revisited*, op. cit., page 177 of the Kindle edition.

The footnote regarding this segment caught my eye: *JFK Revisited*, op. cit., pages 225 – 226.

The Dick Russell book required some investigation: Dick Russell, *The Man Who Knew Too Much*, (Carroll & Graf, 2003)

Robert Morrow's first book: *Betrayal: Who Really Murdered JFK?*, Robert Morrow, Warner Books, 1976

According to Dick Russell, Morrow met a man in the early 1960s who had the 'war name' of Oscar del Valle Garcia: Russell, op. cit., page 327.

Russell went to Gary Shaw's house to meet Bishop: Russell, op. cit., pages 328 – 329.

In 1992, researcher Gary Shaw played Russell a portion of a tape in which Bishop claimed he participated in the CIA's MK-ULTRA program: page 681 in the first edition of *The Man Who Knew Too Much* (Carroll & Graf, 1992); https://archive.org/details/manwhoknewtoomuc00russ/page/681/mode/1up?q=ULTRA

In 1983, Robert Morrow submitted a script for a one-hour documentary: http://jfk.hood.edu/Collection/Weisberg%20Subject%20Index%20Files/M%20Disk/Morrow%20Robert%20D/Item%2010.pdf

Excerpts from the commentary tracks on the Blu-Ray edition of JFK Revisited: https://www.onthetrailofdelusion.com/post/highlights-of-oliver-stone-and-james-dieugenio-s-commentary-track-on-jfk-revisited

Jonathan Rauch believes that "the purpose of the disinformation campaign ...": Rauch, op. cit., page 165.

James DiEugenio said this on Black Op Radio in September 2022: Show from September 1, 2022; http://www.blackopradio.com/pod/black1110.mp3

Jonathan Rauch writes that "reverence for facts is the true north of the reality-based community.": Rauch, op. cit., page 262.

Rauch quoting Aleksandr Solzhenitsyn: Rauch, op. cit., Ibid.

ACKNOWLEDGMENTS

I want to thank my dear partner, Andrew Yip, who has now heard way too many stories about Oliver Stone and James DiEugenio. I'd say that was above and beyond the call of duty.

This is the fourth time that Michael Totten has been my editor, and it's a joy to work with him. Thanks, Michael. The fifth book won't be far off.

I am not sure there is a way to adequately thank Paul Hoch, who has been part of the JFK assassination research community since 1965. Paul contributed editorial suggestions and links for my blog posts both before and after publication. He provided most of the research in the chapter on Dr. George Burkley as well as the chapter on 544 Camp Street. Our collaboration has been a delight, and his contribution to this book cannot be overstated. Thank you very much, Paul.

Steve Roe has also provided some important research on the Oliver Stone documentary. His work on the chain of custody of CE 399 is an important contribution to our knowledge of the case. His expertise on firearms came in handy when debunking allegations about Oswald's Mannlicher-Carcano rifle. If you have a chance, please visit Steve's website: https://steveroeconsulting.wixsite.com/website

Max Holland provided some important research on the supposed CIA involvement in the 1961 coup attempt against French President Charles de Gaulle. He also helped debunk the allegation that Clay Shaw was a CIA contract agent, and he published Steve Roe's research on CE 399 at his terrific website: https://www.washingtondecoded.com/. He is a superb historian, and I greatly appreciate his help.

Larry Haapanen provided some important research on General Curtis LeMay and Otto Otepka. I really appreciate his help and his prodigious knowledge of the case.

I want to thank Richard Burkley, who took my phone calls and answered every question I had. He is a gracious man, and he should be proud of his father. I am greatly appreciative that he put me in touch with Bill Baxley, a true American hero.

Tracy Parnell is another researcher whose important work on the intelligence aspects of the case deserves a wider audience. He has bravely linked to many of my blog posts on conspiracy bulletin boards. His website, http://wtracyparnell.blogspot.com/, has many articles debunking both *JFK: Destiny Betrayed* and the documentary on Ruth Paine.

I have lost count of the number of times I have asked Gus Russo a question about a variety of witnesses. Not surprisingly, Gus typically has an answer somewhere.

Jerry Dealey provided an excellent chart of movements in the Texas School Book Depository after the assassination. Few people know as much as he does about the TSBD, and he was always there when I needed an answer.

At the Quora website, I met two people who have done their fair share of debunking conspiracy theories: Christopher Strimbu and Andrew Jackson. They are the next generation of real JFK assassination researchers.

Megan Bryant of the Sixth Floor Museum in Dallas was also helpful in the licensing of the Zapruder Film Frames. The Sixth Floor is not only an important resource for researchers, but it also does its best to be helpful.

It's been a delight to get to know Alecia Long, whose important book on the Garrison case broke new ground in 2021. She is always helpful and provides excellent advice when needed.

Don Carpenter is the expert on the life of Clay Shaw. No one has interviewed more witnesses in the Garrison investigation than Don, and he also has helped me at every opportunity.

Robert Reynolds is an expert on the JFK files, and he was very helpful in the chapter on Clay Shaw and the CIA.

Nick Nalli and Louis Girdler both wrote excellent critiques of Josiah Thompson's book *Last Second in Dallas*. Nick is a scientist whose important work deserves to be in any documentary about the JFK assassination. Louis's commentary on the Harper fragment was a handy corrective to *JFK: Destiny Betrayed*.

James Kirchick brought the important story of Clay Shaw's persecution to a wider audience with his important history of Gay Washington, *Secret City*. Please, do yourself a favor and buy a copy of his tremendous book.

Kathleen Lynch has once again designed an amazing cover for this book. She is definitely one of the best book designers in the country.

The Mary Ferrell Foundation has once again proved to be an indispensable resource. I couldn't have written this book without their massive repository of documents. I urge everybody to become members.

A special thanks to Gerald Posner, whose book *Case Closed* played an important role in my understanding of the JFK assassination.

There are several other JFK assassination experts who deserve thanks: Tim Nickerson, Frank Badalson, Bill Brown, Mark Zaid, Patrick Collins, Todd Vaughan, Martin J. Kelly, Todd Ehrman, Jimmy Orr, Paul Matthews, Matthew Kordelski, Ed Murray, Dave Ledbetter, Freda Dillard, and David Von Pein.

I want to acknowledge some personal friends—Terry Glavin, David Roytenberg & Dora Benbaruk, Roy Eappen, Tamara & Anthony Fulmes, Mark & Denise Collins, and Shelley & Brian Lee Crowley. You all bring joy in my life, and I am blessed with your friendship. And thank you for letting me kvetch.

Lastly, my sister Sandi Levy and her husband Ron are important parts of my life. I cherish every time we manage to get together.

www.ingramcontent.com/pod-product-compliance
Lightning Source LLC
Chambersburg PA
CBHW021613270326
41931CB00008B/670